Eyewitness to War

Prints and Daguerreotypes of the Mexican War, 1846-1848

Eyewitness to War
Prints and Daguerreotypes of the Mexican War, 1846-1848

Martha A. Sandweiss

Rick Stewart

Ben W. Huseman

Amon Carter Museum   Fort Worth, Texas

Smithsonian Institution Press   Washington, D.C.

Published on the occasion of the exhibition
November 18, 1989 — January 14, 1990
Amon Carter Museum, Fort Worth, Texas

Printed in Hong Kong by South China Printing Co.

Library of Congress Cataloging-in-Publication Data

Amon Carter Museum of Western Art.
    Eyewitness to war : prints and daguerreotypes of the Mexican War 1846-1848 / Martha A.
Sandweiss, Rick Stewart, Ben W. Huseman.
      p. cm.
    Includes index.
    ISBN 0-87474-862-3
    1. United States — History — War with Mexico, 1845-1848 — Art and the war — Catalogs.
2. Lithography, American — Catalogs. 3. Lithography — 19th century — United States — Catalogs.
4. Daguerreotype — United States — Catalogs. 5. Lithography — Texas — Fort Worth — Catalogs.
6. Daguerreotype — Texas — Fort Worth — Catalogs. 7. Amon Carter Museum of Western Art —
Catalogs. I. Sandweiss, Martha A. II. Stewart, Rick, 1944-   . III. Huseman, Ben W. IV. Title.
E415.2.A78A47   1989
760′ .044997362 — dc19   89-6450
                                                   CIP

Frontispiece:

American Volunteer Infantry in Saltillo
Cat. No. 71
Amon Carter Museum

Contents

Foreword

The visual record of the Mexican War presented in this volume had its genesis at the Amon Carter Museum a number of years ago. The Museum's director at that time, the late Mitchell Wilder, was keenly interested in building a collection of historical prints. He encouraged the Museum's curator, Ron Tyler, whose background was in Latin American studies, to research and acquire visual materials relating to Mexico. As the collection grew, Tyler became more interested in the Mexican War as depicted in American and Mexican prints, and the Museum acquired many additional examples. In the meantime, Marni Sandweiss joined the staff and expanded the Museum's photography collection, which today includes more than a quarter of a million images.

When the Amon Carter Museum acquired a significant group of daguerreotypes taken in Mexico during the war, the Museum staff began to think about the visual depictions of the war in a different light. Where they had previously viewed the prints as part of a historical narrative, they began to compare prints and daguerreotypes from the same time and place for insights into the meaning of eyewitness reportage. Such an investigation combined several areas of interest among the Museum's curatorial staff, not the least of these being the congruent development of two forms of visual expression that were directed to a popular audience. It should be emphasized that this project was never intended to be a graphic history of the war; rather, it was to illuminate a significant moment in the history of American graphics.

The authors of this volume, Marni Sandweiss, Rick Stewart, and Ben Huseman, are to be congratulated for bringing together such an impressive amount of research and organizing it in this volume. Many of the works illustrated here will be shown in a special exhibition at the Amon Carter Museum beginning in November 1989, but it is the book itself which best demonstrates the magnitude of their collective effort. I join with them in expressing appreciation and heartfelt thanks to all those individuals and organizations listed in the acknowledgments who helped bring this project to its successful conclusion.

Jan Keene Muhlert
Director

Acknowledgments

*T*his book, culminating a lengthy study of Mexican War-era prints and photographs, would not have been possible without the patient and generous support of the Amon Carter Museum and its director, Jan Keene Muhlert. A large share of credit for this book should go to Ron Tyler, now director of the Texas State Historical Association, who helped build the Amon Carter Museum's collection of historical prints during his seventeen years here. His pioneering study of Mexican War lithographs inspired and encouraged this project at every step, and even after he left the Museum he advised on the project and critiqued the manuscript.

We are greatly indebted to Thomas Kailbourn of Wellsville, New York, who has generously shared with us his encyclopedic knowledge of the American occupation of Mexico, providing incisive leads for some of the more puzzling daguerreotypes. Special thanks also go to William Reese for his role in steering the Mexican War daguerreotypes to the Amon Carter Museum; to Grace Hamilton Kellogg and her family for their prior stewardship of the Museum's daguerreotype collection and their generosity to the Museum, and to the late Robert Hallowell Gardiner and his family, who graciously made available to us the resources and archives at Oaklands, their family home in Gardiner, Maine. The authors are also grateful to the heirs of George Wilkins Kendall, who allowed use of family papers that had not been examined by scholars for over forty years. The exhibition has been supported by a grant from the Union Pacific Foundation on behalf of the Union Pacific Corporation and its operating companies — Union Pacific Railroad Company, Union Pacific Resources Company, and Union Pacific Realty Company.

We are also indebted to a number of individuals and institutions who have allowed us to reproduce materials from their collections or have lent their own expertise to this project: Georgia Barnhill, Curator of Graphic Arts, American Antiquarian Society; Archibald Hanna, Jr., and George Miles of the Beinecke Rare Book and Manuscript Library, Yale University; Henrietta M. Frye of the Bowdoin College Museum of Art; David H. Woodward, Librarian of the Huntington Library; Joel Silver of the Lilly Library, Indiana University; Bernard Reilly, Curator of Prints in the Prints and Photographs Division, Patrick Dempsey of the Geography and Map Division, and Eveline Nave of Photoduplication Services, Library of Congress; Bryan Stephen Thomas of the Missouri Historical Society; James Cheevers, Sigrid Trumpy, and Leah Hubicsak of the U.S. Naval Academy Museum, Annapolis; Wendy J. Shadwell, Curator of Prints at the New-York Historical Society; Ronna Hurd, Curator of Exhibits at the San Jacinto Museum of History Association; Michael Vinson, DeGolyer Library, Southern Methodist University, Dallas; Jane Garner, Archivist of the Nettie Lee Benson Latin American Collection, University of Texas Libraries, Austin; Gerald Saxon, Director, and Kit Goodwin, Marcelle Hull, Shirley Rodnitzky, Sally Gross, and Lupita Martinez at the Division of Special Collections, University of Texas at Arlington; and Malcolm Maclean, University of Texas at Arlington.

David Miller of Cameron University deserves a special note of thanks for reading the manuscript and offering his critical comments. Others who have assisted us in this project include Mary Lou Gjernes, Army Art Collection, Alexandria, Virginia; Ralph Elder, William Richter, and Larry Landis at the Barker Texas History Center, Austin; Peter C. Merrill, Department of Languages and Linguistics, Florida Atlantic University; David Dunnett, Fort Worth Public Library; Grant Romer of the George Eastman House, Rochester, New York; Jeanette Dixon, Kimbell Art Museum Library; Michael McAfee of the U.S. Military Academy, West Point; Richard Rudisill of the Museum of New Mexico; Andrew Birrell of the National Archives of Canada, Ottawa; Donald Kloster, Harold Langley, and Helena Wright of the National Museum of American History; Will Stapp, Curator of Photographs, and Wendy Wick Reaves, Curator of Graphic Arts, National Portrait Gallery, Washington, D.C.; Barbara Wolanin, Curator of the Office of the Architect of the U.S. Capitol; and Elizabeth Jarvis, Curator of the Pennsylvania Historical Society.

Thanks also go to Ken Apollo of Portland, Oregon; Rosa Casanova of Mexico City; Ann Fabian of Yale University; Robert H. Ferrell of Indiana University, Bloomington; David Margolis of Santa Fe; John A. Neff of Greenville, Ohio; Peter Palmquist of Arcata, California; David Reynolds of Cambridge University; Carol Roark of Fort Worth; William J. Schultz of Olmsted Township, Ohio; and Bill Turner of Fort Worth.

A project of this magnitude has required assistance from most of the Amon Carter Museum staff, but a few should be recognized individually. Milan Hughston, Associate Librarian, processed a multitude of bibliographic requests with his customary speed and efficiency. Linda Lorenz, the Museum's photographer, posesses skills nearly unequalled in her field. She carefully photographed the great majority of objects illustrated in this study from the originals. Her capable assistants, Rynda Lemke, Steve Watson, Gayle Herr, and Dan Bartow were often called upon to produce copy prints on short notice, but they always came through. Kathie Bennewitz and Paula Stewart, curatorial assistants, furnished curatorial data on some of the material in the catalogue and doublechecked existing information with painstaking skill. The Museum's editor, Matthew Abbate, took on the unenviable task of reading many draft versions of the essays and catalogue entries, and managed to greatly strengthen and unite the work of three very disparate authors. Even after Mr. Abbate left Texas, he continued to perform valuable editorial service from afar. Meanwhile the Museum's new editor, Nancy Stevens, found herself thrust into the middle of the project but managed to add her editorial expertise and assume the mantle of project director to bring the book to completion. Jim Ledbetter has taken numerous revisions in his stride, renumbering and reworking materials to accommodate each set of changes. Many others on the Museum staff who have aided in this project, as well as friends and family members who have lived through the war with us in recent years, also deserve our deep appreciation.

Martha A. Sandweiss, Adjunct Curator
Rick Stewart, Curator of Western Painting and Sculpture
Ben Huseman, Curatorial Assistant

Introduction

*T*he Mexican War, declared in May 1846 and concluded by treaty in February 1848, was a significant event in American history from many standpoints.* The first major American war fought primarily on foreign soil, it ended with American acquisition of new territories south to the Rio Grande and west to the Pacific Ocean. The outcome of the Mexican War thus hastened the conquest and settlement of the trans-Mississippi West. While historians have analyzed the war in terms of American expansionism and the politics of Mexican-American relations, the conflict also marked a pivotal point in graphic history, becoming the first event to be documented by both printmakers and practitioners of the fledgling art of photography. This study approaches the war through its graphic record, examining the eyewitness prints and daguerreotypes of the war both for their content and their popular reception.

The Mexican War produced the first identifiable war correspondents, whose reports fueled public interest in the conflict and precipitated the rise of popular lithographic prints based on current events. Graphic renderings of battles and military heroes could convey information to a popular audience more effectively and vividly than written accounts, and technological innovations in printmaking made it possible to produce better prints, sometimes printed in color or hand-colored, to meet the public's demand for news.

While sketch artists had long since proved their value as chroniclers of war, the Mexican War was the first in history to be documented also by the astonishing new medium of photography, announced to the world in 1839. The daguerreotype, the earliest type of photograph, could claim greater immediacy and contain greater detail than the most meticulously drawn sketch. Its very name entered the language as a word connoting absolute accuracy.

* The very name of the conflict suggests the interpretive problems it presents. Historians in the United States refer to it as the Mexican War; their counterparts in Mexico variously call it the War of 1846, the War Between the United States and Mexico, the War of North American Intervention, or the North American Invasion.

Editors coined an admiring phrase, "daguerreotype reports," to describe either literary or journalistic accounts that conveyed news with the immediacy and clarity of a photographic view.

Eyewitness accounts of the war took many forms, ranging from on-the-spot reactions to more carefully considered responses recorded days or even weeks following the event. Though based on actual events, both literary and visual reports could stray from accuracy for a number of reasons, some well beyond the control of the reporter. The sketches of field artists, for example, were usually translated to the lithographic stone by other hands. The "eyewitness prints" in this study thus are prints *based on* materials (verbal or visual) provided by eyewitnesses.

The development of photography gave new meaning to the idea of an eyewitness view. While lithographic stones were drawn and printed in studios far from the battle sites, daguerreotypes were made on the spot, without the mediation or intervention of a sketch artist or printmaker. The image on the sensitized daguerrian plate was made by light reflecting off the subject itself. No negative was involved in the daguerrian process; each image was exposed in the camera and developed as a unique positive. Thus every daguerreotype plate, while in the camera, was in close proximity to the subject recorded on its surface. When we hold a daguerreotype of Mexican War troops in our hand, we hold a piece of silver-plated copper that was actually on the same street as those soldiers 140 years ago. The inanimate daguerreotype, a "mirror with a memory," survives as the closest thing we have to a true "eyewitness" to people and events of long ago.

Prints produced during the Mexican War were first studied a number of years ago by Ron Tyler, then curator of the Amon Carter Museum's collection of American historical prints. His groundbreaking work, *The Mexican War: A Lithographic Record*, published by the Texas State Historical Association in 1973, examined the importance of these prints to the historical record. The present undertaking expands that earlier effort not only by including daguerreotypes, but by examining many more lithographs both for their historical accuracy and for the stylistic elements that establish their key position in the development of this powerful graphic medium.

Since its inception, the Amon Carter Museum has collected and encouraged the study of American historical prints. Though only a part of its extensive collection of Mexican War lithographs is examined in the present study, the most important eyewitness prints have been included. Because American prints of the war greatly outnumber those by Mexican printmakers, the point of view documented in this study reflects the bias of North American artists. The history of lithography in Mexico needs further study, and the Museum's own collection of nineteenth-century Mexican prints merits a future exhibition.

If the Museum assembled its collection of Mexican War prints in slow, methodical fashion, it acquired its collection of thirty-eight Mexican War daguerreotypes, the largest such group known, in a more serendipitous way. Until 1981, only nine daguerreotypes made in Mexico during the war were known to survive, and for twenty years they had been in the care of the Beinecke Rare Book and Manuscript Library at Yale University. Then, in 1981, the Museum received a call from a bookseller who reported that a much larger group of images had surfaced and had been offered to a military museum that was about to turn down their acquisition. Within the next few hours they might again be available for sale. The Museum's long-standing interest in prints of the Mexican War and its large collection of American photographs, combined with the great scarcity of Mexican War daguerreotypes, made the rumor tantalizing. By late afternoon, the dealer handling the daguerreotypes had been traced, and a week later a brown paper grocery bag containing the photographs was handed over to a museum curator in the waiting room at Dulles Airport in suburban Washington, D.C. The bag was filled with wads of rough paper towels, each wad concealing a naked daguerreotype, unprotected by the customary presentation case that kept its fragile surface free from dust, abrasions, and fingerprints. Every time the paper bag moved, the towels rubbed a bit more information off the surface of the world's first photographs of war. A quick examination of the plates revealed that they included not only portraits of identified military figures, but scenes of towns and troops in Mexico and, most surprising of all, variations of some of the known Yale views of American soldiers in and around the Mexican city of Saltillo. Soon after, the collection of daguerreotypes was acquired for the Museum.

The Mexican War was the most extensively recorded event in history up to that time — a fact subsequently overshadowed by the greater coverage of the Civil War. If the Mexican War can be said to have been the baptism by fire for many great military figures of the war between the states, then it was also a preview of a revolutionary age in visual communication. But though daguerreotypists joined printmakers for the first time in chronicling an event, the Mexican War did not mark the emergence of photography as an important recording medium. Printmakers were more knowledgeable about marketing than their photographic counterparts, and current technology permitted the wide distribution of lithographic prints while photographers could produce only one-of-a-kind images. But it was the content of the prints, as much as their distribution, that won the interest of the American people. With their superior ability to record the drama and color of the war and their capacity to show simplified versions of complex activities, prints earned and kept the interest of a news-hungry public that had not yet learned to appreciate the exquisite detail or symbolic resonance of the photographic image.

M.A.S.

R.S.

Artists and Printmakers of the Mexican War

Rick Stewart

*T*he United States war with Mexico, which occurred from May 1846 to February 1848, was a major event in the growth of the nation. At the war's end, vast stretches of northern Mexico, including most of modern-day New Mexico, Arizona, Nevada, Utah, and California, were ceded to the United States, climaxing a period of great territorial expansion in which the United States had annexed Texas and added the Oregon Country. Although many studies have been written about the conflict with Mexico, few have addressed its effects on the history of visual communication. As it happened, the events of the war coincided with two very important developments in American cultural history: the rise of lithography and the advent of popular journalism. The Mexican War became the first event of its kind to be photographed, the first to be reported by war correspondents for mass circulation newspapers, and the first to be extensively recorded in lithographs intended for a broad audience.

The outbreak of the war coincided with a series of technological innovations that greatly increased printmaking activity. Lithography had become commercially viable in America in the late 1820s and was clearly suited to the growing mechanization of visual communication. Lithography was much more adaptable and accessible than the older methods of engraving and etching; artists and printers were able to implement it quickly and produce a result, however imperfect in its refinement, in very little time. Many of the prints of Mexican War scenes, especially those produced by lesser artists and smaller printing establishments, would not have existed except for the lithographic medium. Moreover, lithographs were relatively inexpensive to produce and the process much more durable than other mediums of illustration, yielding a greater number of prints at cheaper prices for a substantially larger audience. Once an image was printed, the stone could be reground to accept another. Mistakes were easy to correct, and changes were easy to make; the latter was important if lithographs were to illustrate current events. Likewise, the speed of producing a lithograph was a decided advantage for publishers; many of the Mexican War prints were brought out in a highly competitive atmosphere where being first was most important and the difference between success or failure was a matter of days.

News of the Mexican War traveled faster than any event before it, and lithography was the only visual medium that had the potential to keep pace with the battle reports. Unfortunately, the technology of mass printing, which was revolutionizing the newspaper industry, would not be able to utilize lithography directly until early the following decade. The first illustrated newspaper, *Frank Leslie's Illustrated Weekly,* would not be established until 1855, followed by *Harper's Weekly* (1857) and the *New York Illustrated News* (1859).[1] However, lithographers in the 1840s were already printing a wide range of commercial jobs, from invoices to sheet music covers, and prints of the war with Mexico became one more commercial product for their shops.[1]

Because lithography could imitate the style of other mediums, lithographers also began to create larger, more carefully produced images that sought a narrower audience. As technological improvements in the medium itself led to greater pictorial effect, printing processes grew increasingly complex, and some artisans and firms in the larger cities attained new status as fine-art printers. Michael Twyman, in his indispensable history of lithography in England and France in the first half of the nineteenth century, has chronicled this rapid adaptation of new ideas; American lithographic firms quickly adopted the newest techniques from Europe.[2] During the Mexican War, lithography reached a climax with the development of chromolithography, a method of printing colors mechanically, with a series of stones, to duplicate the color effects of painting. One of the earliest and finest chromolithographs, published in New York in 1848, depicted a Mexican War subject, and one of the earliest books illustrated with chromolithographs was a popular history of the Mexican War published in Philadelphia the following year.

If improvements in lithographic technology made possible a boom in popular printmaking, developments in the field of journalism opened up new markets at the same time. The words and images recording the Mexican War were propelled by the rise of the "penny press" newspaper, which was more progressive, opportunistic, competitive, and technology-minded than its predecessors. As soon as the initial battles on the Rio Grande occurred, these newspapers began printing eyewitness accounts, by professional and amateur correspondents, that arrived far in advance of the official government reports. Most of the penny press newspapers were avid participants in the new "magnetic age" of communication, a phrase referring to the recently invented telegraph that instantly carried news wherever its wires could reach. As the Mexican War progressed, additional miles of telegraph wire linked an ever-widening network of American cities and towns. The war was also the first major event to take place in the dawning era of ocean steam navigation. As a result, verbal and visual accounts of the war were part of a new age of competitive journalism, which dramatically enlarged the audience for news of current events.[3]

"The spirit of the age is irresistible," trumpeted the New York *Herald* in 1845. "It is the spirit of progress, of commerce, of trade, of business enterprise, of liberal and enlightened principles." As this spirit widened "like a fire over the prairies of Texas," the newspapers recognized the value of eyewitness correspondents to report important events as soon as they happened.[4] These reports often consisted of information synthesized from several eyewitness accounts by the correspondent in the field. Solitary accounts were filed as well, usually for the sake of speed, as editors back home realized that whoever reached the streets first with the latest news reaped the benefits of increased circulation and advertising revenues. Every aspect of the war's initial campaigns was widely reported; even military and government officials routinely wrote to their hometown newspapers before filing their official dispatches. These "occasional" correspondents sometimes wrote under pseudonyms for fear of reprisal by their superiors. "The papers from the United States are now arriving, freighted with various reports of sieges, and marches, and battles on the frontiers of Mexico," wrote one disgusted officer in General Zachary Taylor's army; "it would appear that almost every camp follower, whatever his capacity or means of information, has believed that his own circumstantial report of transactions here, was a sacred debt he owed his country and the world."[5]

But this officer held a minority view. There seemed to be no end to the public's demand for news of the war, and the greatest interest focused on testimony from observers at the front. The largest and most competitive newspapers found that receiving dispatches from occasional correspondents was not enough. Several editors arranged for full-time reporters to be in the field with the advancing American forces—the first professional war correspondents. New Orleans became the communications and supply hub for the nation's war effort, and the city's two leading penny press newspapers, the *Picayune* and the *Delta,* sent the three most important eyewitness reporters to the front. George Wilkins Kendall and Christopher M. Haile dispatched their reports to the *Picayune,* while James L. Freaner sent his to the *Delta,* under the byline "Mustang"; other newspapers across the nation copied their reports from the New Orleans papers. Of the three men, Kendall proved to be the most productive, innovative, and significant; he clearly deserves the distinction as history's first professional war correspondent. He also played a pivotal role in the history of Mexican War printmaking, for he initiated, authored the accompanying text for, and published the most lavish and authoritative set of lithographs to record the conflict in that period.

Taken together, correspondents to the nation's newspapers generated a wealth of information that was viewed at the time as unique—the result of a free press in a rapidly expanding democracy. "The persons who were actors as well as those who observed, were far better qualified to furnish correct accounts of what transpired," declared the editor of *Niles' National Register* in 1847, "and the faculties for diffusing their statements have never been equalled."[6]

None of the artists examined in this study were regular sketch artists for any newspaper; that development awaited the Civil War a decade and a half later. All, however, were dealing in some sense with firsthand observations. In his groundbreaking study *The Mexican War: The Lithographic Record,* Ron Tyler divided the eyewitness prints into two groups: prints made by eyewitnesses themselves, and those made with the assistance of eyewitnesses. This division may still apply, but only in a general sense. Among the prints "made" by eyewitness artists, the artist may have actually executed the design on stone or merely furnished a design for the print. In the latter case especially, accuracy in the final product was more apt to be compromised by a host of factors, as Ben Huseman's thorough catalogue entries demonstrate. Prints made with the "assistance" of an eyewitness could be drawn from either verbal or visual resources, and these were not always furnished directly. For instance, many printers and publishers copied existing eyewitness prints or attempted to translate an unusually precise verbal description lifted from one of the newspapers. Copyright laws were only in force at the county level, and there are numerous instances of cross-fertilization of images, as well as outright plagiarism by some editors and publishers. On the other hand, George Wilkins Kendall was an astute eyewitness observer whose synthesis of others' views and reports in his own work permitted him to offer a more comprehensive version of the story with greater historical and artistic accuracy.[7]

Prints of the Mexican War can be divided into four categories of relative accuracy, based on their levels of topographical and figural verisimilitude. In the most accurate eyewitness prints, both topography and figural elements are somewhat exact. If the prints depict military actions, both the orientation of the units and the vantage point of the locality are accurately presented. Such prints usually resulted from direct and methodical observation by the artist himself, who was frequently a member of one of the military units engaged in the action.

A second category of prints displays accurate topography but is less reliable on the figural side. For instance, one print showing the victorious American troops entering Mexico City depicts the architecture knowledgeably but places figures in the scene in ways that do not conform to the eyewitness accounts. Prints of this sort generally relied heavily on views of Mexico that had been published before the war and were predominantly topographical in nature. Printmakers copied these earlier versions but added figures to depict the event itself, sometimes incorporating fragments from other print sources, such as military subjects or portraits, or transcribing details from written eyewitness accounts. Among the earlier sources most often copied was an imposing volume of fifty lithographic plates by the German-born artist Carl Nebel, titled *Voyage pittoresque et archéologique dans la partie la plus intéressante du Mexique* (Paris, 1836). Other sources that provided topographical information were Daniel Thomas Edgerton's *Views of Mexico* (New York, 1840), H.G. Ward's *Travels in Mexico* (London, 1829), and a number of individual views published by Pedro Gualdi in Mexico City during the war itself; all featured lithographs by artists who had visited the site. Another topographical source of varying accuracy was *Mexico Illustrated in Twenty-six Views* (London, 1848), which must have been completed either just before the war or during its initial stages by an English artist named John Phillips. Some of the Phillips views are included in the catalogue section because they record the topographical settings of important wartime events.

A number of prints of the Mexican War are accurate as to figural details but inaccurate or confused as to topography. In hindsight this is understandable; an eyewitness reporter was more apt to focus on the event itself than on the place where it occurred, and many observers assembled their recollections after the fact. A daguerreotype recorded scenes with uncompromising objectivity, but human eyewitnesses sorted and combined many elements of a scene into a far less objective whole. Apart from this, many eyewitness observers were apt to use maps of an area, rather than sketches, to transcribe topographic details.

Finally, a number of Mexican War prints are simply inaccurate all around. Some of these prints exhibit traces of eyewitness influence; others were not concerned with topography or figural objectivity at all but were designed to appeal to widely held social, racial, or nationalist feelings. Such prints can merit study for other reasons, including what they tell us about the publishing practices of the time. Moreover, as the war progressed, even the most sensationalist prints began to reflect the pervasive influence of eyewitness reportage.

Ron Tyler's earlier account of Mexican War prints introduced the work of approximately ten eyewitness artists; the present study expands that number more than threefold. No attempt has been made to chronicle every print made of the United States' war with Mexico during this period; the list could certainly be much longer. The prints in the catalogue have been selected for their close relationship to eyewitness observation. Out of the thirty or so artists examined, two-thirds served in some capacity with American military units in Mexico. Fourteen were members of the regular armed forces, while seven joined the volunteer ranks. Ten were officers; four had attended West Point, and two of them were known to have studied art under its noted instructor, Robert W. Weir. At least five of the artists who had enlisted into the armed forces gave their previous occupation as house painter, sometimes adding sign and ornamental painting to their list of skills as well. The artist ranks also included a lawyer, a grocer, a schoolteacher, a printer, and a carpenter-joiner. All of these individuals possessed drawing skills, for their efforts survive, at least through lithographs, to the present day. Five of the eyewitness artists who were military men had received formal art training; one was the son of the painter Thomas Sully, and another claimed to have studied with Samuel F.B. Morse. Outside the military ranks, there were eight practicing artists, most with formal training, who traveled to the scene of the war in order to portray its leading figures and events.

Some of the most important eyewitness views were by an English-born artist, James Walker, who had spent time in Mexico before the war and was familiar with the country and the language. Having eluded the authorities in Mexico City, Walker became an interpreter for American forces as they moved inland after Veracruz. He painted a number of vivid sketches of the battles that he witnessed; after the capital fell, he set up a studio and began work immediately on larger versions of his field sketches. Some of the smaller paintings that survive include two views of the march from Puebla, two of the battle of Contreras, a sketch of the action at Molino del Rey, two views taken from the American side of the fighting at Mexico City's Belen Gate, and several different sketches of the battle of Chapultepec. Every one of these sketches is filled with details that ring of truth, and all were intended to be incorporated, in some way, into larger finished works.[8]

Walker completed several important paintings of the battle of Chapultepec, two of which were eventually copied into lithographs. The story of their execution reveals a great deal about the fortunes of an eyewitness artist among many other eyewitnesses. Walker was at work on the first of his paintings of Chapultepec within days after American troops reached the capital. He soon became embroiled in a controversy that pitted General Gideon J. Pillow against the adherents of General John A. Quitman. At stake was which general's forces would go in the foreground of Walker's painting; on this choice would hinge the interpretation of who had contributed the most to the victory of Chapultepec. All of the controversialists had, of course, been present at the battle; they offered the artist their detailed recollections of the event, as well as at least one map of the battle prepared by the Corps of Engineers, in support of their respective interpretations.[9]

Historical truth, at least in this case, was in the eye of the beholder. The supporters of General Quitman carried the day, but the enterprising Walker also painted a version of the battle from General Pillow's point of view. Moreover, a young captain named Benjamin S. Roberts commissioned another copy of the first version and noted in his diary that Walker had completed the work but had conspicuously added, at the captain's request, the "5 gun battery taken by my storming party" in the lower right portion of the canvas. Roberts thus added his own perspective to the eyewitness record. As it turns out, the Roberts version is best known today, for it was copied into a magnificent chromolithograph the following year.[10]

Walker was not the only artist of this period to feel the pressure of "truth" upon his efforts. General William Jenkins Worth, headquartered in the Mexican capital in the early part of 1848, desired a painting of the battle of Molino del Rey and summoned Lieutenant Albert Tracy, who described himself as "an artist of some practice, and originally a student of Professor Morse." As Tracy later recollected, the general had become enveloped in "a bitter war of words, touching the merits and general conduct of the action" with partisans of General Winfield Scott. "To settle fixedly points in dispute, as regarded the battle proper, General Worth determined to have depicted in as clear and perfect a manner as possible, both the ground upon which the engagement took place, and the relative positions of the several bodies of troops participating, as taken at a given stage." Worth then ordered Lieutenant C.S. Hamilton of the Fifth Infantry to survey the battlefield with his instruments and a Captain Bomford of the Eighth Infantry to make careful sketches of the site with pencil and watercolor. "The Captain used to say that he sketched with his pistol in one hand and his brush in the other," Tracy recalled.[11] After the two officers had finished their work, Tracy was called in to give "the whole a final finish in oil." It was the intention to have the completed picture "engraved or lithographed in colors for general distribution."

From the beginning General Worth hovered over the artist:

> Every morning, after the disposal of the more official matters at his office, it was the wont of the General to seat himself beside the artist, pointing out any incorrectness as to the positions of troops, and indicating detail necessary to have included, that the picture might be as complete and perfect as in his power to suggest, or that of the painter to execute. More than once considerable groups and bodies of men were required to be obliterated, and a more correct rendering given, so that in reality, there are as good as two or three pictures at different points of the canvas, one above the other. Of course, the task was at times exhausting, but the General had set his heart upon accuracy, and nothing short could be allowed to take the place of it.[12]

As if this were not enough, Tracy was visited by many other officers under Worth's command, as well as from nearby divisions, all of whom offered their comments and corrections to the painting. Not without some justification, Tracy pronounced the finished work "the only really historic or exact presentation" of that controversial battle. Although the promise to have the painting lithographed was never kept, Tracy's painting of this battle, as well as two others that he made for the general, survive to the present day.[13]

Other officers in the armed forces were in positions to produce eyewitness depictions of the war that did find their way into print; all are described in detail in the catalogue section. Major Joseph Horace Eaton, an aide-de-camp to General Zachary Taylor, provided a number of sketches for various printmaking enterprises, including one of the better field portraits of "Old Rough and Ready," complete with signatures from high military personnel to attest to its accuracy (cat. no. 42). Eaton had no direct hand in executing the final prints, but his sketches were responsible for one of the most complex lithographs published during the period, a depiction of the climactic battle at Buena Vista (cat. no. 36). When it appeared

Puente Purisima, Monterey.

Figure 1
After Lieutenant Alfred Sully
Puente Purisima, Monterey
Wood engraving
From William Seaton Henry, *Campaign Sketches of the War with Mexico* (New York: Harper and Brothers, 1847), p. 199
Courtesy of Special Collections Division, The University of Texas at Arlington Libraries, Arlington, Texas

in September 1847, the *Daily National Intelligencer* praised it not only as a superb example of "scenic art" but also as a painstakingly accurate record of the historical event. Indeed, the print was accompanied by the testimony of several officers who had been present at the battle, together with a separate sheet that served as a meticulous descriptive key. Eaton's overview doubtless drew on information from a number of eyewitness sources, and the print also reveals the army artist's training as a topographer and instructor of tactics. While its scale is panoramic and inclusive, it conveys a wealth of detail. Indeed, examination of Eaton's print reveals a carefully ordered set piece, a grand tableau of tactics. It is as if, at some point during that chaotic two-day battle, all the participants were instructed to get up, dust themselves off, and assume their ideal tactical positions. Much is accurate in Major Eaton's print, but there is also plenty of fancy. Despite its purported perfection of detail, the battle has been transposed into "an attractive theme for the poet and painter," as the *Literary World* correctly termed it.[14]

Major Eaton, along with Lieutenant Alfred Sully, also supplied sketches for one of the more important illustrated books authored by eyewitness participants. Captain William Seaton Henry, who had written a series of vivid eyewitness accounts under the pseudonym "G. de L." for the *Spirit of the Times,* published his *Campaign Sketches of the War with Mexico* following the battle of Buena Vista and dedicated the book to General Taylor. Henry, like other eyewitness chroniclers, sought to include information about every aspect of the army's surroundings, from the nature of the landscape to the customs of the people, and his book is valuable for its wealth of detail. It is illustrated with a number of interesting

VIEW OF MATAMOROS, FROM FORT BROWN.

Figure 2
After Thomas Bangs Thorpe
View of Matamoros from Fort Brown
Engraving
From Thomas Bangs Thorpe, *"Our Army" on the Rio Grande* (Philadelphia: Carey and Hart, 1846), p. 128
Courtesy of Special Collections Division, The University of Texas at Arlington Libraries, Arlington, Texas

engravings and useful maps. The latter were apparently supplied by Major Eaton, while Lieutenant Sully, son of the famed portrait painter of Philadelphia, is credited with the "spirited embellishments"— mostly picturesque vignettes illustrating the landscape and people of northern Mexico (fig. 1; see also cat. no. 3).[15]

Two other significant books that appeared during the first phase of the Mexican War were written and illustrated by Thomas Bangs Thorpe, who had originally joined General Taylor's army as a correspondent for the New Orleans *Tropic*. Thorpe had studied painting with John Quidor and was a noted writer of western humor prior to the war. Arriving in Matamoros after the battles of the Rio Grande, he busied himself making sketches and collecting eyewitness accounts of the battles, then rushed back to New Orleans to cast the materials in book form and began sending sketches to his publisher in Philadelphia for engraving. He was certain that the expense would be justified by the demand for a well-illustrated volume brought out quickly enough to appeal to public curiosity about the first victories of the war. "I believe I shall give you one of the most readable books of the season," he confidently wrote his publisher, "containing more stirring incidents, serious and comic, together with the war's particulars than is often in a volume." Thorpe continually pestered his editors to make sure the book was "handsomely got up" with the best engravings, though he worried about the delays that this occasioned and chafed at the thought of being "scooped" by a rival author.[16] *"Our Army" on the Rio Grande* finally appeared in August 1846, with twenty-six illustrations "from Nature" (fig. 2; see also cat. no. 2) and a text written in Thorpe's florid, romantic prose. The book received good reviews, and spurred

by his initial success, Thorpe persuaded his publishers to bring out another volume, *Our Army at Monterey.* Then a combination of factors, including poor sales, derailed any future books in the series; a completed manuscript for a volume on Buena Vista apparently survives, but Thorpe's stated intention to write one on Veracruz never came to fruition.[17]

Another eyewitness artist who published his own illustrated account was George C. Furber, whose narrative was titled *The Twelve Months Volunteer; or, Journal of a Private in the Tennessee Regiment of Cavalry, in the Campaign in Mexico, 1846-7.* It is filled with everyday observations and minute descriptions, together with twenty-three wood engravings crudely transferred from "drawings by the author." In the preface to the book, Furber asserted that there was no chance "for the flight of the imagination, or any departure from the truth" in his account. Thus, when an engraver dared to take artistic license with one of the book's drawings (fig. 3), Furber voiced his frustrations in a note in the text opposite the offending illustration:

This plate, showing most accurately the appearance of the plants and trees, was drawn upon the ground by the author. A single cavalry soldier was placed in the foreground, to show, by comparison, the height of the trees; and the engraver was directed to copy these in every line, and moreover, to place a small scouting party in the background. To the author's surprise, when the picture was completed, he found that the engraver had put in the scouting party, but had set them all to cooking; and the volumes of smoke inserted, would convey the idea that the scouts were more anxious for their dinner, than to catch the enemy, that, at this place, were hanging so thickly around us. This is wrong; and the reader will therefore, in imagination, put out the engraver's fire, and place the party in a position of vigilance.— The soldier in front, also, though dressed correctly, and having all right about him, has, by the engraver's command, taken off his sword and cartridge box, and set them up against that sun palm, together with his gun, which, too, the engraver has cut, not a carbine, but rather a fowling piece. This is incorrect; for no scout was caught in this fix.— His holsters are right, but his sword should be upon his side, and his carbine slung to his shoulder, or in his hand, ready to act in an instant.— Owing to these mistakes, the author would not have inserted this picture, but for the remarkable correctness of the trees and plants which it represents, and the excellent workmanship of the whole cut.[18]

In his descriptions, Furber attempted to lead the reader step by step through his illustrations. His keen eye for detail and propensity to describe the minutiae of his surroundings establish his effort as one of the more valuable eyewitness chronicles of the war.

Yet the artist who produced the most important series of eyewitness views of the war was, ironically, himself a witness to none of them. Carl Nebel was a native of Germany who had spent nearly five years in Mexico producing the sketches and paintings that would become the basis for his monumental *Voyage pittoresque,* published in Paris in 1836. In Mexico City again shortly after American forces occupied the area, Nebel met George Wilkins Kendall. The two men agreed to collaborate on an ambitious project: a portfolio-sized edition of twelve hand-colored lithographs that would depict the principal battles of the war with Mexico. Nebel was to remain in Mexico until he had produced sufficient sketches or paintings of the various battle sites; Kendall journeyed on to Paris, where he began to assemble his notes for the text that would accompany the finished plates and made arrangements for production of the whole. The result was *The War Between the United States and Mexico Illustrated,* discussed at length at the end of this essay.

Printed views of the Mexican War can be divided into three broad groups: single prints, series or sets of prints in portfolio editions, and prints found in contemporary illustrated books. The prints by Carl Nebel in George Wilkins Kendall's *War Between the United States and Mexico Illustrated* were actually distributed in all three formats: singly, as a set suitable for framing; in an elegant portfolio with text; and bound as a folio-sized book, in which the text was interspersed with the plates.

Two other portfolio editions, one by an army captain and another by a naval lieutenant, also deserve special mention. Captain Daniel Powers Whiting, an officer with the Seventh Infantry, provided the drawings or watercolors for five beautifully executed lithographs brought together as the *Army Portfolio* (cat. nos. 1, 11-14) and offered to the public in the summer of 1847. One print depicts the army encampment at Corpus Christi Bay at the beginning of the war; the other four are of scenes in and around Monterrey, an area whose dramatic and picturesque landscape dominated most eyewitness accounts of the battle.[19] Whiting's portfolio was accompanied by testimony from fellow officers as to its fidelity of representation. The editors of the *Knickerbocker* declared the prints "unmistakably faithful to the scene...a *complete* illustration of the military operations of our army in this portion of Mexico." The New Orleans *Picayune,* which informed its readers that the portfolio was available for viewing and purchase, praised its "strict adherence to nature" and declared that "a half hour's study of Captain Whiting's sketches will elucidate better than a volume of written description." *The Daily National Intelligencer* reported that the prints were "entitled to the name of pictures"—meaning that they should be considered as Art—because they were "authentic and accurate representations of the scenes they portray" that "for the sake of their beauty, were worthy of a place on the most fashionable centre-table."[20]

Whiting's prints are indeed gorgeous to behold, and they were successful in part because they avoided what they might have been expected to portray, the "terrible carnage among our men who penetrated the streets" of Monterrey.[21] Instead, they present picturesque views of the city and its environs set against the romantically tinted backdrop of magnificent scenery, of the type that would confound the senses of the overland emigrants to California in the following decade. Whiting occasionally portrayed troop movements, but for the most part he chose to let the viewer imagine, as one reviewer of the portfolio observed, the reality of the battle's darker moments. Much of the same attitude prevailed with Corporal Samuel Reid, author of a memorable illustrated eyewitness account titled *Scouting Expeditions of McCulloch's Texas Rangers,* published in Philadelphia in 1847. When he returned to the hilltop surrounding the Bishop's Palace in Monterrey a few days after American troops carried it in a bloody struggle, Reid preferred to turn quickly away from "the dreadful scene" of shrieking wounded, to look out across the valley, where he found solace in "the beauty and grandeur" of nature. He felt comforted as he dwelled upon "the green vales softened by the rich crimson light," where "all seemed as calm as if nature's repose had never been disturbed by the unhallowed strife of war." In this respect, while Whiting's prints could be justifiably praised for their "most truthful representation of nature," they were selective in their vision, reflecting the admonition of Henry Tuckerman, a contemporary writer on art, that the romantic artist sought "to elicit the ideal from the real, to look beyond the immediate and material, without distorting the perspective."[22] Captain Whiting chose to look beyond the realities of war to contemplate the higher order of things.

Another superb and historically valuable set of prints was the *Naval Portfolio,* produced from the watercolors of Lieutenant Henry Walke of the United States Navy. The eight lithographs, chronicling the exploits of Commodore Matthew C. Perry's squadron following the capture of the port city of Veracruz, were advertised to the public in April 1848. The technique of these prints, like that of Whiting's, is unusually fine as well as innovative. Walke's original watercolors for several of the prints survive, enabling a rare glimpse into the relationship between an artist's eyewitness drawings and the finished lithographs. Moreover, Walke himself is credited as lithographer of several of the prints, one of the very few instances in which the artist was directly involved in transferring his designs to stone. Curiously enough, Walke himself apparently compromised the accuracy of the originals by altering both topography and figural arrangements in the lithographic versions, for the sake of artistic composition. Further, Walke merged multiple studies to bring a climactic narrative focus to his prints. Thus the watercolors, for all their lack of refinement, bear a greater degree of accuracy and immediacy than the prints of the *Naval Portfolio,* which order the confusion of events into an aesthetic and dramatic whole.[23]

Beyond the ambitious illustrated books and portfolio-sized prints, the pictorial record includes more modest attempts by common soldiers to preserve their personal experiences on stone. These prints are often interesting and significant in their own right, not the least because they illuminate a smaller part of the Mexican War through a more individualized perspective. Sergeant Angelo Paldi's views of the battles of Palo Alto and Resaca de la Palma were taken from a point at a distance from the front lines, where he doubtless witnessed them, and do not focus on any particular heroes or key moments in the battles; instead, they are generalized records of what he saw. His prints were published in Cincinnati after his return, as were the prints of Private Stephen G. Hill of the Ohio Volunteers.[24]

Hill's unit saw brutal action at Monterrey, but his prints, like those of Captain Whiting, emphasize topography or logistics rather than the chaos of military action. Hill produced prints that mirror his own experiences—and those of many common soldiers—at Monterrey. One print shows a distant view of the city and its redoubts from the eastern side, where Hill's regiment participated in an assault that sacrificed many lives. Instead of the action, however, the artist has chosen the moment when the soldiers were ordered to form their lines for the impending attack. Another print shows the central plaza itself following the capture of the city. It was a memorable sight to all who saw it, after the bitter street-by-street struggle to conquer the city.

Private Hill was like many other eyewitness artists in ignoring the trauma of battle and the deaths of fellow soldiers in his visual images.[25] Another was Sergeant Fabian Brydolf, a Swedish immigrant trained as a landscape painter, who returned home to the Midwest and arranged the printing of a small scenic lithograph of the castle of Chapultepec, which he had assaulted as a member of the Fifteenth Infantry. Brydolf chose to portray a picturesque site, quiet and secure, rather than the hellish arena where he remembered the bodies so thick that one could "walk on them without touching the ground."[26]

Private John Allison of the New York Volunteers has left no record of his life that historians have been able to trace, but he listed himself as a painter before the war. He left his version of the battle of Chapultepec as a crude lithograph, possibly printed in Mexico City, that depicts his unit and some others ready to assault the seemingly impregnable fortress. The standard in the foreground may well be his unit's own; if so, it was to earn a special place in the victory. "The gallant New York Regiment claims for their standard the honor of being the first waved from the battlements of Chapultepec," wrote General Quitman in his official report.[27] One can well imagine the proud English-born volunteer returning to the scene of his unit's glory soon after the fall of Mexico City, to commemorate the battle for his fellow soldiers.

In the absence of a daguerreotypist, many soldiers probably contrived to have visual souvenirs made for their friends and family, not necessarily intended for a larger audience. Jacob Oswandel, a corporal in the Pennsylvania Volunteers, was not an artist, but he recorded in his diary for February 23, 1848: "At noon I informed my friend, Alburtus Welsh, of our Company, who was on guard at the time, that I would stand guard for him; providing he would make me a drawing of the castle of Chapultepec, to which he cheerfully consented, and was glad of the relief from guard." Oswandel was pleased to receive his "capital drawing" a short time later.[28] To celebrate the heroic exploits of his particular unit, Private James T. Shannon of the Pennsylvania Volunteers left a fragmentary sketchbook and a detailed lithograph of one of the last military actions of the Mexican War. Private Jason D. Polhemus also has given historians a rare glimpse of American forces during the period of the occupation. A sign and ornamental painter by trade, he recorded in his diary that he executed a "regimental portrait," commissioned by his commanding officer, prior to the unit's departure for home. Where they were stationed there were no battles to commemorate, but Polhemus, like his fellow artists, managed to preserve a single moment at a time when such moments were often lost to history, before the final ascendancy of photography.[29]

*T*he artists were only partially responsible for the prints of the Mexican War; the visual record also owes much to the printers and publishers who manufactured and disseminated them. The prints examined in this study were published, over a five-year period, by approximately twenty-five firms in ten cities. Almost half the entire number were produced in New York City, while smaller numbers were made in Philadelphia, Cincinnati, and New Orleans. Isolated examples were brought out in Hartford and Baltimore. Surprisingly, nearly twenty prints were manufactured in Mexico City, for a predominantly English-speaking audience, during the months after hostilities ceased.

The dominance of New York City in the production and dissemination of Mexican War prints is not surprising. While cities like Philadelphia also had active and innovative lithography firms, New York had more of them; moreover, the city had become the principal marketing and communication center for the nation as a whole. This development was quickened by the newspapers, which helped pioneer a new era of journalism and technology. The most progressive penny press newspapers instinctively recognized the insatiable public demand for firsthand news of the war in Mexico and entered into fierce competition for the latest dispatches from eyewitness correspondents. One of these was the New York *Herald,* whose editor, James Gordon Bennett, was a major figure in the history of American journalism. Under Bennett's guidance, the *Herald* was the first newspaper to adopt many modern features, including daily money market and stock reports, and among the first to make extensive use of the telegraph. Bennett was also a tireless supporter of ocean steam navigation, which could speed information from distant places. He often characterized the ongoing revolution in communications as "the annihilation of time and space," which he foresaw would result in "a greater change in some of the social institutions than anyone now imagines." As the telegraph wires began to connect the major cities of the North and inched their way towards the southern coast, he prophesied that the instantaneous transmission of the news would cause "a unity of thought and action throughout the whole republic, similar to that exhibited by a single community."[30]

The *Herald* not only brought an unprecedented amount of news to the American public; it sought to shape the news in its own image. Bennett saw his mission as a "manufacturer of public opinion" for the "great popular masses." His was a journalism that "informs, instructs, guides and governs the public mind"[31]— an attitude shared by many of his contemporaries. In striving for greater circulation and advertising revenue, Bennett also realized the power of sensationalized news reportage. Before the conflict with Mexico, the *Herald* was already publishing accounts of lurid crimes taken from police reports and was following court trials that revealed the darker side of criminal behavior, and during the war, Bennett and his fellow editors were not above printing detailed descriptions of a battle's more sanguine or emotional aspects.

These stories, together with the more official reports of the war's events, were obtained by the *Herald* and the other major newspapers in a competitive atmosphere that was unprecedented in the history of journalism. News of the war reached New Orleans first and was transmitted to other principal cities in various ways. Overland express or steamships carried dispatches to a point where the newly erected telegraph lines could convey them to their destinations. Many newspapers arranged their own express systems to speed the eyewitness accounts along, going to great lengths to beat out their rivals, even by a few hours. The New York *Herald* kept a small vessel at sea to intercept any steamship bearing news, which was then raced to dockside and the waiting typesetters. The New Orleans *Picayune* went this one better, installing a typesetter aboard their ship so the report could be sent immediately to the press.

Indeed, the competition to hit the city streets first with the latest news became something of an obsession. If the news was deemed at all important, the newspaper printed a special edition, an "extra," to be sent through the newsboys to the waiting public. The *Herald* published as many as four editions in a single day, and on more than one occasion an entire edition of an extra sold out within a few hours. There were risks, however, in the desire for speed; time and again a newspaper editor was forced to admit that a lead story had turned out to be filled with incorrect information. In the stiff competition among the newspapers, accuracy was also essential, and editors relied on eyewitness reports by trusted correspondents, among them George Wilkins Kendall of the *Picayune*. Such reports from the field were valued above all others and copied verbatim as soon as they arrived, and papers like the *Herald* usually reprinted more complete accounts from rival newspapers.[32]

Kendall's pioneering efforts still await proper investigation by historians. The recent rediscovery of the Kendall family papers, which have not been seen by scholars for nearly fifty years, sheds new light on his pivotal role as an eyewitness reporter, as well as on his contribution to American printmaking as the author of the finest contemporary illustrated record of the Mexican War.[33] A native of upstate New York, Kendall worked for several newspapers before journeying to New Orleans in 1835. Two years later he co-founded the *Picayune,* setting the type himself. An innovative proprietor, Kendall quickly realized the advantage of covering events in the Republic of Texas. The *Picayune,* under his energetic lead, became a fervent organ for annexation and expansion at the expense of Mexico. In May 1846, with the news of hostilities on the Rio Grande, Kendall rode quickly south to cover the action. He joined Taylor's army in Matamoros, set up a field office, and began his duties as a war correspondent. Soon his desire to be at the forefront of the action caused him to link up with a company of Texas Rangers, and he rode with them through the northern part of the campaign. According to another correspondent, Kendall adopted "the garb and appearance" of his escort and lost no opportunity to see the surrounding country with his wilder compatriots. "Though I did not examine his baggage, I am willing to venture a small wager that he is accompanied with the materials whereon to write, and that many a bright *Picayune* will be made by his present excursion," the correspondent wrote admiringly.[34] A daguerreotype portrait (fig. 4), apparently taken shortly after the war, depicts the intrepid reporter whom a family member described as "a law unto himself."

On May 9, 1847, the editor of the New York *Herald* noted its desire to convey the leading stories of the day as "daguerreotype reports" — written accounts with the accuracy

Figure 4
Photographer Unknown
Portrait of George Wilkins Kendall
Copy print from a daguerreotype taken c. 1848
Courtesy of Kendall Family

and immediacy of a photographic view. Kendall was a "daguerreotype reporter" of the first order; the same issue of the *Herald* carried his first dispatches of the battle of Cerro Gordo. Throughout the southern campaign to Mexico City, when communication to the coast was often completely cut off by enemy activity, Kendall penned his reports on an hourly basis. He went to great lengths to insure the safe delivery of these dispatches to his editors back home, and in retrospect his rate of success was extraordinary. He kept his own string of horses to carry him quickly and efficiently to various points along the American lines, and he frequently copied his dispatches in triplicate, sending two or three separate express riders with identical packets through hostile country back to Veracruz. His efforts paid off; while he lost some riders to guerrilla activity, the majority got through.[35]

Even today, Kendall's dispatches bear a striking directness and immediacy. "I write this in great haste, and with noise, confusion, and everything else around me," he recorded at four o'clock in the afternoon, April 18, 1847, after a successful engagement with Mexican forces on the national highway. "You cannot appreciate the victory. To describe the ground and fortifications of the enemy, the difficulty of turning their outer works, and the toll and peril undergone by the troops were impossible."[36] Even though he filed more detailed follow-up reports of the battles, he never failed to send his initial eyewitness impressions, laden with excitement. He was the first correspondent in the field to publish the results of the great battles of Contreras and Churubusco, near the Mexican capital. Like all his reports, these masterpieces of dramatic narrative include human-interest sidelights to give greater weight to the large events. The dispatches on Contreras and Churubusco were accompanied by a carefully rendered map of the sites, obtained from military sources, as well as detailed casualty lists that Kendall compiled himself by riding to each unit command post.[37] These lists frequently appeared far in advance of those issued by the government and were usually more accurate.

Following the fall of Mexico City, Kendall monitored the peace negotiations and interpreted scores of reports from both sides, which he distilled and sent to his editors at the *Picayune*. Although Kendall was diligent in supplying maps and sketches for reproduction in the newspaper, the technological barriers that prevented rapid translation of a drawing to the printed page must have seemed especially troublesome when competitive advantages were measured in hours. On one occasion the *Picayune* stated that it had received "a fine map of the field of battle" from their indefatigable correspondent; they added apologetically that they would publish it "as soon as it comes from the engraver's hands—in the course of the week, we hope."[38]

Such delays must have seemed especially galling in an age that witnessed perfection of the steam-driven rotary press. In October 1847, for example, the New York *Herald* became the first newspaper in the world to attain a capacity of twenty-five thousand printed sheets per hour, following the introduction of an eight-cylinder press invented by Richard Hoe of New York City. Newspapers in Philadelphia and New Orleans quickly followed suit.[39] Although it would take until the 1850s for perfection of a rotary press process that could utilize lithographs as well, editors such as James Gordon Bennett still recognized the need for illustrations of the war in their newspapers. The *Herald's* pioneering activity in this endeavor presaged the rise of pictorial newspapers in the following decade. As early as November 1846, Bennett reminded his readers that "we have regularly published the views of the principal cities, towns, fortresses, and places of interest.... We need hardly say that our efforts to please our patrons in this respect have been attended with a great outlay of money. . . . We have recently placed in the hands of our artists many additional sketches and views of Mexico, taken on the spot by men of talent, which we shall give, from time to time, as the war proceeds. The public may rely on their being strictly accurate."[40] The *Herald* published many wood engravings of such views, but the results were often disappointing when their crudeness was compared with the far more facile efforts of the lithographers. Nevertheless, they were apparently popular enough to warrant reprinting together on a special sheet, which was marketed by the newspaper as an "extra" to its readers, an "Illustrated History of the Mexican War."[41]

No such technological limitations hampered Nathaniel Currier, whose lithography firm was located a few blocks from the *Herald* offices; he published a total of seventy lithographs depicting scenes from the Mexican War. Currier had begun his apprenticeship in the fledgling business of lithography in 1828; seven years later, at the age of twenty-two, he founded his own shop in New York. Although his famous partnership with James Ives, established in 1852, has obscured Currier's earlier achievements, he was an innovative lithographer. He standardized the production process, developed new techniques in the creation of the prints themselves, and invented new types of lithographic crayons to broaden the range of possible effects.[42] Above all, he revolutionized the marketing and distribution practices for such work. As early as 1838 Currier maintained a storefront for selling his prints to the public. In January 1840, he demonstrated the possibilities of collaboration between lithography and newspapers when his depiction of a steamboat disaster accompanied a special edition of the New York *Sun*. Currier initiated the concept of "rush stock," cheaply printed lithographs that were generated quickly after an event to capitalize on its public interest. (Prints that were made and sold over a longer period of time were referred to as "stock prints.") With the outbreak of the Mexican War, Currier almost single-handedly created a market for popular prints of its events, and just as the penny press newspapers had adopted the British newsboy system, so Currier eventually established his own cadre of pushcart salesmen to hawk the prints in the city streets.[43]

Such marketing tactics made good sense, since the popularity of a current-events print was sometimes short-lived. There are no sales figures or audience profiles for these lithographs, but their success can be measured by the number of Mexican War scenes that appeared during the period. Evidence suggests that many of Currier's Mexican War prints were published very soon after each event; different examples of the same subject show variations that point to the use of more than one stone to print an edition quickly for distribution. Currier hired many talented artists to work for his firm, and several of these broke away in turn to establish rival firms of their own. Consequently, there are many lithographs of Mexican War subjects by lesser firms that copied Currier's designs, and Currier himself was not above appropriating the designs of others for his own ends. One indication of Currier's business success during this period was the fact that his chief rivals deferred to him for distribution rights. Such important prints as Henry Walke's *Naval Portfolio* or James Walker's magisterial *Battle of Chapultepec* were marketed by Nathaniel Currier as "sole agent."[44]

Currier's Mexican War prints were drawn from eyewitness reports that appeared in the New York *Herald* and other newspapers, as demonstrated in a comparison of three lithographs of the same battle. In 1846, Currier chronicled the heroic exploits of Captain Charles

THE BRILLIANT CHARGE OF CAPT. MAY.

BATTLE OF RESACA DE LA PALMA MAY 9TH 1846.
Capture of Genl. VEGA by the gallant Capt. MAY

CAPTURE OF GENl LA VEGA BY THE GALLANT CAPT MAY
AT THE BATTLE OF RESACA DE LA PALMA MAY 9TH 1846.

Figure 5   Top
Artist Unknown
The Brilliant Charge of Capt. May
Lithograph, hand colored, 1846
Lithographed and published by Nathaniel Currier, New York
Amon Carter Museum [163.83]

Figure 6   Above
Artist Unknown
Battle of Resaca de la Palma May 9th 1846
Lithograph, hand colored, 1846
Lithographed and published by Nathaniel Currier, New York
Amon Carter Museum [64.70]

Figure 7   Right
Artist Unknown
Capture of Genl. La Vega by the Gallant Capt. May
Lithograph, hand colored, 1846
Lithographed and published by Nathaniel Currier, New York
Amon Carter Museum [66.71]

A. May at the battle of Resaca de la Palma. These prints appear to have been done at roughly the same time. The one bearing the lowest inventory number beneath its inscription is titled *The Brilliant Charge of Capt. May* (fig. 5) and depicts the attack of the Second Dragoons on a Mexican artillery unit that was inflicting serious losses on the American troops. May is shown charging ahead of his men toward the enemy batteries in the distance. The print appears to echo a sketch of the colorful officer that a correspondent to the New York *Herald* reported seeing shortly after the battle. "It is a most spirited and lifelike thing," he wrote. "May is in advance of them all, on his noble black steed, standing up in the stirrups, his head bent forward, his long hair streaming out behind, like the tail of a comet, and his whole appearance, viewed from the head, looking like one of those celestial visitants."[45] Even if Currier did not see the original sketch, the correspondent's description was sufficient for him to attempt a visual equivalent.

As further reports of the battle arrived, Currier may have decided that he had chosen the wrong moment to glorify, and he produced two further prints that depict the dashing captain capturing a Mexican general. The first of these, titled *Battle of Resaca de la Palma May 9th 1846* (fig. 6), depicts a clean-shaven May with idealized features charging directly over a cannon to grasp the arm of the surprised general. The third lithograph, which seems to be a later version of the second, bears a more specific title: *Capture of Genl. La Vega by the Gallant Capt. May* (fig. 7). Overall, this print more accurately reflects the eyewitness accounts, and it is much better from an artistic standpoint. Moreover, Captain May is shown charging back from the opposite direction, and his features are much more individualized. Reports from the battlefield stated that "his beard falls below his swordbelt, and his mustache is unshorn."[46] Eyewitness reports had indicated that the dragoons' charge upon the artillery positions was so rapid that they overshot their objective and had to wheel sharply around to return to the line of artillery. According to these same reports, General Rómulo de la Vega was surprised from behind as he was exhorting his troops; he subsequently offered his sword to the victorious captain. In Currier's new version, May assumes the guise of a fire-eyed Captain Blackbeard as he dashes from the rear to grab the general's arm. Although even later reports disputed this version of the story, it nevertheless made great copy for the newspapers and lithography firms.[47]

Further evidence that Currier depicted May's purported heroism from eyewitness accounts can also be found in the third print's portrayal of General de la Vega in a slightly more favorable light, with features that seem more individualized. Soon after the captured Mexican general arrived in New Orleans, his daguerreotype portrait was taken; this was made into a wood engraving and reproduced in the New York *Herald* on June 25, 1846, along with a warm description of the general's gentlemanly qualities.[48] It seems obvious that Currier would have updated his earlier versions to utilize such information; any glaring lack of accuracy, when compared to the eyewitness descriptions of the same event that were appearing in the newspapers, would compromise the marketability of the print with an informed public. The color plate of the final version demonstrates another selling feature that Currier adopted early: each of his prints was hand colored, however sloppily, with bright, sometimes garish colors that must have added to their appeal for the "great popular masses." Currier's success prompted at least one contemporary critic to decry his "lithographed daubs" as expressions of "too much national vanity."[49] Yet their considerable popularity could not be denied.

Two other Currier lithographs depicting the campaign to take the port city of Veracruz bear an identical inventory number but differ in details of subject and handling. The earlier version seems to be the *Bombardment of Vera Cruz. March 25th 1847* (fig. 8), which displays a marked inferiority in execution and very little knowledge of military ordnance. General Winfield Scott is shown astride his horse giving direction to an artillery unit bombarding the city. The officers gathered around him seem oblivious to the battle, as the artillery officer to the right levels his massive siege cannon in a seeming effort to sweep half of them from the scene. The second example of the subject, titled the *Seige of Vera Cruz March 1847* (fig. 9), appears to be an altered state (that is, a revised version done on the same stone); it contains many more details within the image, as well as more information in the inscription beneath, apparently quoted from an eyewitness report. The artillery is more convincingly arranged, and ships can be seen in the distance shelling the fortress in the harbor. But the most obvious change is the inclusion, in the foreground, of the bodies of killed and wounded soldiers, an acknowledgment of the realities of war. This reworked version bears the signature of James Cameron, a skilled Scottish-born artist in Currier's employ, and shows much more careful handling in draftsmanship and composition. Cameron's sense of perspective is more accomplished, and the shading is more carefully rendered, for example, in the areas

BOMBARDMENT OF VERA CRUZ.
MARCH 25ᵗʰ 1847.

Figure 8 Above
Artist Unknown
Bombardment of Vera Cruz. March 25th 1847.
Lithograph, hand colored, 1847
Lithographed and published by Nathaniel Currier, New York
Amon Carter Museum [43.72]

Figure 9 Right
James Cameron after an Unknown Artist
Siege of Vera Cruz March 1847
Lithograph, hand colored, 1847
Lithographed and published by Nathaniel Currier, New York
Courtesy of Missouri Historical Society, St. Louis

beneath General Scott's horse.

A lithograph of the same subject by one of Currier's rival firms, headed by James Baillie, demonstrates how some prints departed from accuracy entirely to embrace the absurd.[50] Baillie's *Bombardment of Vera Cruz* (fig. 10) depicts the city under siege by a horde of close-ranked riflemen, who blaze away in sheets of smoke that fill up half the image. Over this improbable scene, on horseback, General Scott gestures with a long baton, like the conductor of a grand, patriotic symphony.

Nathaniel Currier published other prints of the action at Veracruz, indicating his keen awareness of the value of eyewitness reportage. When news of the victory reached the American public, the effect was electric. "We were prepared to witness an excitement on the arrival of this intelligence, but we had no idea that it would be so ardent and enthusiastic as it was," stated the editor of the *Herald*. "The moment the news was announced, every kind of business was suspended. The furor was actually terrific. Joy, patriotism and satisfaction were pictured on every countenance... our shipping, steamboats, public hotels, newspaper establishments, and places of amusement, were decorated with flags."[51] Who would not want to take advantage of such an atmosphere? Currier published a grandiose

American Army 12,000 men.
American loss in killed
and wounded about 75 men.

BOMBARDMENT OF VERA CRUZ.

by the American Army, commanded by Genl. Scott.

Mexican Army 9,000 men.
Mexican loss: killed about 1000,
and 4,000 Prisoners.

Agents: J. Bardsley, Cor. of Arch & 2d St Phila. — Joseph Ward, 53 Cornhill, Boston Mass.
G. J. Loomis, No. 9 Washington St. Albany.

Figure 10   Left
"F.K." after an Unknown Artist
Bombardment of Vera Cruz
Lithograph, hand colored, c. 1847
Lithographed and published by James Baillie,
New York
Amon Carter Museum [63.71]

Figure 11   Above
Artist Unknown
*Landing of the American Forces Under Genl.
Scott at Vera Cruz March 9th 1847*
Lithograph, hand colored, 1847
Lithographed and published by Nathaniel Cur-
rier, New York
Amon Carter Museum [165.83]

version of the scene titled *Landing of the American Forces Under Genl. Scott at Vera Cruz March 9th 1847* (fig. 11), in which huge ships of the line shell a distant fortress while a number of surfboats disgorge an orderly assembly of American troops in the foreground. But two other Currier prints of the action at Veracruz clearly used sketches furnished by an eyewitness artist. One, titled *Bombardment of Vera Cruz March 1847. Attack of the Gun Boats Upon the City, & Castle of San Juan de Ulloa* (cat. no. 113), is remarkable for its relative objectivity when compared to Currier's other prints. Beneath the caption is the notation, "From a sketch taken on board the Steamer Spitfire, during the action, by J. M. Ladd U.S.N." Although the nature of Midshipman Ladd's role in this arrangement is not known, the fact that he was credited on the lithograph itself suggests the value of eyewitness testimony as a selling point.[52]

Further proof that Currier paid very close attention to the eyewitness reports in news-papers is demonstrated by two prints that he published following the battle of Cerro Gordo. The earlier of the two, titled *Battle of Cerro Gordo April 18th 1847* (fig. 12), bears a long inscription beneath the title, taken almost verbatim from General Scott's official report as it was published in the New York *Herald* on May 11, 1847: "The troops ascended the long

Figure 12 Above
James Cameron after an Unknown Artist
Battle of Cerro Gordo April 18th 1847
Lithograph, hand colored, 1847
Lithographed and published by Nathaniel Currier, New York
Amon Carter Museum [40.72]

Figure 13 Right
Artist Unknown
Storming of the Heights of Cerro Gordo
Lithograph, 1847
Lithographed and published by Nathaniel Currier, New York
Courtesy of San Jacinto Museum of History Association

and difficult slope of Cerro Gordo without shelter, and under the tremendous fire of artillery and musketry, with the utmost steadiness, reached the breastworks, drove the enemy from them, planted the colors of the 1st Artillery, 3d and 7th Infantry—the enemy's flag still flying—and after some minutes of sharp firing, finished the conquest with the bayonet."[53] The inscription lists the enemy materiel, soldiers, and officers captured (including, once again, the hapless General de la Vega) and casualty figures, all demonstrating Currier's continuing adaptation of news reports to his lithographs.

Another lithograph, titled *Storming of the Heights of Cerro Gordo* (fig. 13), identifies Colonel William S. Harney of the Second Dragoons as the principal hero in the victory. A detailed description of the battle by Captain George W. Hughes of the Topographical Corps, published in the New York *Herald* at virtually the same time as General Scott's official report, praised the charge led by the brave officer. "His conspicuous and stalwart frame at the head of his brigade, his long arm waving his men to the charge, his sturdy voice ringing above the clash of arms and din of conflict, attracted the attention and admiration alike of the enemy and our own army," Hughes recorded.[54] Currier's print glorifies this central hero, who plants the flag atop the ridge himself while waving his troops forward with his cap. It is interesting to note that this lithograph exists in an earlier state. In the example illustrated

BATTLE OF SIERRA GORDO, APRIL 17th & 18th 1847, BETWEEN GEN'l. SCOTT AND SANTA ANNA.
Capture of Santa Anna's Carriage, Cash, Papers, Dinner & Wooden leg.

Figure 14   Left
"F.K." after an Unknown Artist
Battle of Sierra Gordo, April 17th & 18th 1847,
Between Genl. Scott and Santa Anna
Lithograph, hand colored, c. 1847
Lithographed and published by James Baillie,
New York
Amon Carter Museum [64.71]

Figure 15   Above
Artist Unknown
The Battle of Cerro Gordo. Fought April
17th-18th 1847.
Lithograph, hand colored, 1847
Lithographed and published by Sarony & Major,
New York
Amon Carter Museum [62.71]

here, Cameron reworked the shading and definition of many figures and erased others completely to allow the composition greater freedom. At the same time, a misspelling in the caption was corrected.

Two other prints depicting events at the battle of Cerro Gordo contrast markedly with these examples. James Baillie, who had started his own firm after working as a colorist for Currier, published a lithograph carelessly titled *Battle of Sierra Gordo, April 17th & 18th 1847, Between Genl. Scott and Santa Anna* (fig. 14), which depicts Santa Anna leading the Mexican army in full retreat over the crest of a hill. The Mexican general's indecorous flight, leaving behind a fully prepared dinner and all of his personal effects, including his artificial leg, was the subject of many popular prints and caricatures. The initial reports of this curious capture of spoils came from George Wilkins Kendall, who mistakenly described Santa Anna's artificial limb as made of wood; later reports correctly described it as made of cork.[55] While the Baillie print seems to have been inspired by Kendall's eyewitness description, little else in the depiction can be regarded as accurate.

Much the same can be said for a lithograph published by Sarony and Major, another rival firm, titled *The Battle of Cerro Gordo. Fought April 17th–18th 1847* (fig. 15). Its inscription lists casualty figures that disagree with official reports but correspond with those given in an April 19 dispatch by James L. Freaner of the New Orleans *Delta,* which in turn was published on May 10 by the New York *Herald.* The scene of the battle itself is quite confusing and not very well executed in comparison to the Currier examples, and there is a distinct difference in technique. Here broad shadings of a brush, rather than a crayon, are evident, along with the noticeable effects of rubbing or scraping the stone to achieve highlights.[56]

*T*he prints of the Mexican War that were intended for a broad audience depicted a wide range of subjects and reflected a number of issues. Not surprisingly, the majority of them depicted battles, and the moment portrayed within each battle generally derived from the accounts published in the newspapers. Sometimes a particular incident that was spotlighted in the press, such as General Santa Anna's precipitous flight at Cerro Gordo, became the subject for a popular lithograph. Prints sometimes commemorated events that had been mistakenly reported: Captain May, for example, apparently did not capture General de la Vega himself. Likewise, the celebrated comment, "A little more grape, Captain Bragg," attributed to General Taylor at Buena Vista, was included in several prints but seems never to have been uttered.[57]

Some subjects harked back to older traditions: the equestrian portraits of "Old Rough and Ready," for example, and the numerous surrender scenes, such as Currier's depiction of General Taylor and his staff at the capitulation ceremony at Monterrey. A number of prints glorified moments of personal heroism and sacrifice: Captain May and Colonel Harney lived to enjoy the adulation, but the heroes who sacrificed their lives to achieve victory were elevated to an even higher status. One of the earliest martyrs was Major Samuel Ringgold, who died at the battle of Palo Alto. Ringgold was a well-liked officer who showed great promise, and his death was widely interpreted as an honored sacrifice at the altar of nationalism. Shortly after the event, Currier published a lithograph titled *Death of Major Ringgold. Of the Flying Artillery...*(fig. 16), which depicted the mortally wounded hero falling from his dying horse into the arms of a comrade. James Baillie and Sarony and Major likewise depicted Ringgold's fall, in even more idealized and overwrought versions. Printmakers also tried to appeal to that segment of the American audience who saw in Ringgold the long tradition of American bravery under fire; in addition to his battlefield version, Currier brought out a more formal equestrian portrait of the dashing officer with his sword raised in glory. The young major was buried on the Mexican prairie near where he fell, and the site, surrounded by a fence his men fashioned from captured Mexican muskets, became a pilgrimage for many observers throughout the period.[58]

The night before the battle of Palo Alto, a young lieutenant with the Eighth Infantry in Taylor's army penned the following lines for the *Spirit of the Times;* although his words left much to be desired poetically, they served as an anthem for those, like Ringgold, who sacrificed their lives:

DEATH OF MAJOR RINGGOLD.
OF THE FLYING ARTILLERY.
AT THE BATTLE OF PALO-ALTO, (TEXAS) MAY 8TH 1846.

DEATH OF COL. PIERCE M. BUTLER,

Figure 16   Left
Artist Unknown
Death of Major Ringgold. Of the Flying Artillery. At the Battle of Palo-Alto, (Texas) May 8th 1846.
Lithograph, hand colored, 1846
Lithographed and published by Nathaniel Currier, New York
Amon Carter Museum [67.71]

Figure 17   Above
James Cameron after an Unknown Artist
Death of Col. Pierce M. Butler, of the South Carolina (Palmetto) Regiment, at the Battle of Churubusco (Mexico) Aug. 20th 1847
Lithograph, 1847
Lithographed and published by Nathaniel Currier, New York
Courtesy of San Jacinto Museum of History Association

But since we cannot fight to-day,
Let's fill for the hope of tomorrow!
And pledge to the true hearts far away,
Whom our absence fills with sorrow.

And if in fight our blood we spill,
'Tis a happy consolation,
To know that for us, an eye *will* fill,
Who died for annexation.[59]

In this vein, Currier published a lithograph commemorating the *Death of Col. Pierce M. Butler, of the South Carolina (Palmetto) Regiment, at the Battle of Churubusco...* (fig. 17). According to the New York *Herald,* Butler was a member of "as noble a race of heroes as any country has produced." The account related how the young officer rose from his sickbed, determined to lead his men in battle; how he was wounded twice, and though faint with loss of blood, continued forward until felled by a musket ball in the temple. "He possessed military qualities of the highest order," James Freaner wrote from the battlefield, "and gave

THE NIGHT AFTER THE BATTLE.
BURYING THE DEAD

Figure 18   Above
Artist Unknown
The Night After the Battle: Burying the Dead
Lithograph, hand colored, 1846
Lithographed and published by Nathaniel Currier, New York
Courtesy of San Jacinto Museum of History Association

Figure 19   Right
James Cameron after an Unknown Artist
Death of Lieut. Col. Henry Clay Jr. of the Second Regiment Kentucky Volunteers at the Battle of Buena Vista Feb. 23rd 1847
Lithograph, hand colored, 1847
Lithographed and published by Nathaniel Currier, New York
Amon Carter Museum [68.71]

DEATH OF LIEUT. COL. HENRY CLAY JR.
OF THE SECOND REGIMENT KENTUCKY VOLUNTEERS
at the Battle of Buena Vista Feb. 23rd 1847.

promise of great success and distinction in a career which, alas, terminated at its very commencement."[60] Thus James Cameron portrays the fallen hero in the flower of youth, sacrificed upon the field of glory, a contemporary version of the Pietà.

One of the few prints that evoked the grimmer aspects of death on the battlefield was Currier's *The Night After the Battle: Burying the Dead* (fig.18), which depicts an officer with a melancholy expression supervising a burial party in a moonlit battlefield strewn with bodies and debris. However, most printmakers preferred to depict the glorious fall of heroes and elevate the tragedy of death to a higher plane, as in the fall of Henry Clay, Jr., the eldest son of the great Kentucky statesman, who lost his life at Buena Vista. As many as seven popular prints of this subject appeared in the period; one of the best examples was issued by Currier as the *Death of Lieut. Col. Henry Clay Jr. of the Second Regiment Kentucky Volunteers* (fig. 19). Here he is shown shortly after he was wounded, urging his retreating comrades to leave him, though that would result in his death from Mexican bayonets. "And what shall I say of Clay—the young, the brave, the chivalrous—foremost in the fight—the soul of every lofty sentiment?" wrote one of his colleagues in an account published in the *Spirit of the Times* soon afterwards. The grief of his father was well publicized and pierced

Third Day of the SIEGE OF MONTEREY. Sept. 23rd 1846.

Figure 20
Artist Unknown
Third Day of the Siege of Monterey. Sept. 23rd 1846.
Lithograph, hand colored, 1846
Lithographed and published by Sarony & Major, New York
Amon Carter Museum [41.72]

the hearts of the public. "I derive some consolation from knowing that he died where he would have chosen," Clay wrote in a letter that appeared in the newspapers, "and where, if I must lose him, I should have preferred: on the battlefield, in the service of his country."[61] Currier's lithograph plays upon such sentiments and effectively mirrors the patriotic feeling that accompanied such magnified incidents of the war. The young hero's grave, like that of Ringgold, became a well-known site and appears as the subject of two surviving daguerreotypes (cat. nos. 60, 61).

Journalists were much more likely than printmakers to report the darker side of warfare. The eyewitness reports of Kendall, Freaner, and others did not shrink from grisly details of death and suffering. "We have ridden over several battlefields," wrote Lieutenant Thomas Mayne Reid to the *Spirit of the Times* following the battle of Churubusco. "They are all the same... Of all pictures, a field of battle, fresh, red, and reeking, is the most horrible to look at, the most frightful to reflect upon."[62]

Some of the more vivid eyewitness dispatches recorded savage house-to-house fighting during the four-day battle for Monterey, and an unusual lithograph published by Sarony and Major, *Third Day of the Siege of Monterey, Sept. 23rd 1846* (fig. 20), conveys the cha-

Figure 21
Artist Unknown
Scene in Vera Cruz During the Bombardment,
March 25th, 1847
Lithograph, hand colored, 1847
Lithographed and published by E.B. &
E.C. Kellogg, Hartford, Connecticut
Amon Carter Museum [9.78]

otic and desperate conditions that prevailed in the streets as the American forces battled their way into the heart of the city. Such brutal scenes of warfare, however, were rarely depicted in lithographs, although they were well known to those who read contemporary descriptions of the action; Samuel Reid, who rode with the Texas Rangers, recalled in his account of the battle for Monterrey:

> The street-fight became appalling... the artillery of both sides raked the streets, the balls striking the houses with a terrible crash, while amid the roar of battle were heard the battering instruments used by the Texians. Doors were forced open, walls were battered down—entrances made through the longitudinal walls, and the enemy driven from room to room, and from house to house, followed by the shrieks of women, and the sharp crack of the Texian rifles. Cheer after cheer was heard in proud and exulting defiance, as the Texians or regulars gained the house-tops by means of ladders, while they poured a rain of bullets upon the enemy on the opposite houses. It was indeed a most strange and novel scene of warfare.[63]

The suffering of innocent civilians was reported on a number of occasions, but nowhere was it recorded more vividly than during the bombardment of Veracruz. A visual representation of this aspect of war is *Scene in Vera Cruz During the Bombardment* (fig. 21), published by the Hartford lithography firm of E. B. and E. C. Kellogg. "The officers on picket last night reported that they could distinctly hear the shells fall through the roofs of the houses, and burst in the interiors," wrote a correspondent to the *Spirit of the Times.* "During the whole night the shrieks of the poor inhabitants could be heard. It was heartrending to hear them." In the print, as shells burst among the buildings, groups of men, women, and children—some wounded or dying—fill the small plaza. George Furber, whose volunteer regiment entered the city shortly after its capitulation, corroborated the destruction shown in the lithograph: "We now found, what we were confident of yesterday, that the bombardment had been productive of the utmost desolation within the walls, tearing the buildings to pieces, and sweeping hundreds,—soldiers, citizens, women and children—into a common grave."[64]

*S*ignificant technical innovations and stylistic achievements marked many of the lithographs chronicling the Mexican War. Beyond Currier, several other lithographic firms deserve special mention for these developments. George Endicott, who had first established a lithography business in New York in 1831, formed a partnership with his brother William in 1845. By the outbreak of the war, G. and W. Endicott already had experience in producing lithographs geared to a fine-arts audience when they received a commission from John James Audubon for work on the octavo edition of *The Birds of America.* In 1847 they brought out Captain Daniel Powers Whiting's *Army Portfolio,* which is notable for its high degree of technical accomplishment and was described at the time as "exceedingly well lithographed, and printed in tints."[65]

This observation needs an explanation. Lithographers in England and France during this period made great technological strides that were eagerly adopted by the American firms. England pioneered the development of topographical lithography, and the Whiting portfolio essentially follows that tradition. Charles Joseph Hullmandel, an English artist who published a very influential treatise on lithographic technique, pioneered the "stump style" of shading on stone, using a variety of leather and chalk implements, to mimic the effects of aquatinting.[66] The prints of the *Army Portfolio* display the sharply delineated outlines and even shading of this influence. Moreover, by the middle 1840s, the process of printing tinted lithographs was being perfected in England; an even color in transparent inks was printed directly on the image after the black impression was made. The use of this "tint stone," as it was called, can be discerned in many of the Mexican War prints. Normally the stones were centered using an English-derived compass-like instrument, which left pinholes at either the opposing corners of the print or, less commonly, along the sides. The Whiting lithographs reveal this technique; all of the lithographs of the *Army Portfolio* are notable for their subtle tones and limpid, evocative color effects.

As mentioned earlier, Whiting's prints emphasize the topography of the region in a picturesque manner. While they are somewhat objective in their rendering, they are also romantic in style. One of the lithographs in this series, a view of the central plaza of the city of Monterrey (cat. no. 11), indicates how Whiting's desire for objectivity could be undermined by a lithographic artist's temptation to be artistic. Several artisans in the Endicott firm were employed to execute Whiting's views; this particular example was transferred to stone by Charles Fenderich, a Swiss-born artist. He inserted the soldier standing at attention in the lower right corner, wearing a uniform wholly out of context in the Mexican War, as if a veteran of the Napoleonic conflicts had suddenly materialized upon the scene. Even more jarring are the two figures to the lower right, comically out of scale, which seem to emulate the picturesque groupings of peasant figures in European-style landscapes after the manner of Claude Lorrain. One might imagine Captain Whiting's irritation, perhaps more genteel than that of an enlisted man like George Furber, but irritation nonetheless.[67]

Further technical innovation can be seen in Lieutenant Henry Walke's *Naval Portfolio,* which was issued by another important New York City firm, Sarony and Major. A native of Quebec, Napoleon Sarony arrived in New York around 1836 and apprenticed himself with several lithographers, including Nathaniel Currier. In 1846 Sarony formed his partnership with Henry B. Major, and the firm produced some of the most notable prints of the Mexican War. From the beginning their efforts seem to have been influenced by the newer technical developments then under way in England and France. Generally, this involved the greater use of painterly effects directly on the stone to emulate painting, watercolor, or freehand drawing. These freer, more expressive techniques contrasted sharply with the ordered, mechanical handling of the older methods of topographical lithography. The differences in these two approaches may be seen in a comparison of the prints of the Whiting and Walke portfolios: where the lithographs of the former are distinguished for their carefully plotted outlines and carefully graduated tones, the latter are striking for their painterly filigree of lines and bold shading achieved by heavily rubbed and scraped stones.[68]

The print depicting *The U. States Steamers Scorpion, Spitfire, Vixen and Scourge...* (cat. no. 119) was executed on stone by Walke himself. A light blue tint stone was employed, and one is struck by the artist's efforts to obtain the transparent effects of watercolor in surf and sky by rubbing away portions of the tint stone and heavily scraping areas on the black stone. The latter effect in particular reflects the realization then current that heavily scraping a lithographic stone would produce a print displaying highlights in slight relief, like those of a charcoal drawing. This and the other lithographs in the portfolio also display register pinholes on opposing corners. There is evidence that Walke learned to draw upon the stone as he went along; the last print in the series, titled *The Capture of the City of Tabasco by the U.S. Naval Expedition...*(cat. no. 123), is by far the most successful. The light buff tint stone was beautifully inked and rubbed to simulate a delicately washed sky. Everywhere Walke's drawing is more assured, especially in the tonal gradations, leading one to surmise that the lieutenant had seen his earlier mistakes and now fully understood the elements of lithographic shading, where the white of the paper is allowed to breathe.[69] Both the Whiting and Walke portfolios were embellished with hand coloring; while Walke's seems to have been less carefully printed, both nevertheless represent a new direction in the field of lithography.

With the advancements in tinting and the inclination for lithography to further emulate the effects of painting, it seems inevitable that a technology would be established to eliminate the need for laborious and inconsistent hand coloring by printing a lithograph entirely in colors. Chromolithography, the technique by which colors were lithographed from at least three separate stones to form part of the image itself, was first introduced in America in 1840. Although the process was known in New York by the outbreak of the Mexican War, when it began to appear in the work of the Endicott firm, it was costly and technically difficult and, not surprisingly, was employed in only a few prints of the Mexican War. However, one chromolithograph stands above all the others: Sarony and Major's magnificent folio-sized example titled *The Storming of Chapultepec* (cat. no. 148), taken from the painting by James Walker that was then in the possession of Captain B. S. Roberts.

This lithograph was printed in 1848 from at least three large stones, each measuring nearly thirty by forty inches. The colors were confined for the most part within the black image; that is, the color imitated hand coloring, as in the uniforms of the soldiers, without blending in any way with the black or other colors to achieve independent effects. Even in this print, chromolithography was still tentative, not exploring the full potential for mixing colors and changing the image, and small highlights in red, yellow, and orange were added by hand. The gradations, especially in the sky, are masterful for such an early attempt, and the movement of color in the print lends a degree of animation that was lost when Walker's image was transferred to stone. Sarony and Major attempted to render the complexity and vibrancy of an oil painting in a lithograph, and for one of the earliest efforts, they were notably successful. The size and quality of the print made it a striking wall piece. From a business standpoint, it must have been quite a gamble, and it is not surprising that they relied on Nathaniel Currier's salesmanship to market it to the public. Whether it was a best-seller or not, *The Storming of Chapultepec* stands as one of the landmark prints of the Mexican War.[70]

Another pioneering lithographer who made his mark on Mexican War prints in the period was Pierre S. Duval. Trained as a lithographer in France, he arrived in Philadelphia in 1831 and worked with a number of important artists and printing firms there. As early as 1842, Duval was actively experimenting with the technique of color printing, and he soon became a worthy rival to the New York lithographers. One important development, separate from those already mentioned, can be seen in a lithograph Duval published in 1847, *The Island of Lobos* (cat. no. 107), which was taken from eyewitness sketches by Lieutenant Charles C. Barton of the U.S. Navy. The print employs the lithotint process, one of the forerunners of chromolithography. First mentioned in the early 1840s, this method involved printing from washes of lithographic inks applied to the stone. This should be considered a separate process from the use of a tint stone, which transferred an even color to a broad surface of the lithograph by means of a separate stone. In Duval's lithotint, the ink seems to have been applied to the black stone in a series of graded washes. The more obvious attempt to echo the effects of aquatinting is also apparent in this print; the hand coloring, with its subservience to the carefully grained shading, seeks to heighten the similarity.[71]

Duval's firm also had a direct role in producing prints for a history of the Mexican War, published in 1849, that may stand as one of the earliest American volumes to contain chromolithographic illustrations. John Frost's *Pictorial History of Mexico and the Mexican War*, published in Philadelphia, contained over six hundred forty pages embellished with five hundred illustrations, many pirated from earlier sources. Frost was an educator who, in the course of his lifetime, authored over three hundred books on various subjects. In 1847 he brought out a popular biography of Zachary Taylor, illustrated with portraits taken in part from eyewitness sketches or daguerreotypes. The following year he published *The Mexican War and Its Warriors,* which went through a variety of printed editions, where the number of illustrations seems to vary. For his *Pictorial History,* Frost apparently lifted his prose from so many other sources that no one of them would find it worthwhile to cry foul. However, the book, for all its shortcomings, contains one entirely new innovation: seven chromolithographs, printed separately and laboriously tipped into the volume.[72]

One of the chromolithographs in Frost's volume served as a fold-out color frontispiece, roughly twelve by eighteen inches; the others measure not quite four by seven inches. Indeed, the six smaller chromolithographs were probably printed on a single stone, then cut apart to be fixed in the book. The frontispiece, titled *Landing of the Troops at Vera Cruz* (cat. no. 111), was printed by P. S. Duval's firm utilizing at least six separate colors, including a rich metallic gold (see plate 11). Unfortunately, the Duval prints were on a rather thin paper, easily damaged by use.

Another example of the same print, now in the collection of the Library of Congress (fig. 22), shows the ruinous effects of refolding. But this impression is important for another reason: it was not done by Duval but by another Philadelphia firm, Wagner and McGuigan. Thomas Wagner had been an employee of Duval's before establishing his own business with James McGuigan, and by 1844 their firm had received a medal from the Franklin Institute for their advances in "polychromatic lithography."[73] However laudable their efforts in this new area, their version of the chromolithographed frontispiece for Frost's book is far inferior to Duval's. Although the two prints are quite similar in composition, variations in many details indicate that the scenes were rendered by two separate artists, perhaps from a master drawing in outline that was furnished to the two firms. The greatest differences can be seen in the effects of shade and texture produced by the color stones, and their combination in the finished print. Duval's example shows more successful pictorial effects achieved by overprinting the color stones. For example, the overprinting of the variegated blue and yellow stones in the foreground provides a green area, which is transformed into purplish shadows under the troops where the yellow gives way to pink. The addition of gold as a

Figure 22
Artist Unknown
Landing of the Troops at Vera Cruz
Chromolithograph, 1849
From John Frost, *Pictorial History of Mexico and the Mexican War* (Philadelphia: Thomas, Cowperthwait & Co. for James A. Bill, 1849), frontispiece
Lithographed by Wagner & McGuigan, Philadelphia
Courtesy of Prints and Photographs Division, Library of Congress

ENTRANCE OF THE ARMY INTO THE CITY OF MEXICO.

Figure 23
Artist Unknown
Entrance of the Army into the City of Mexico
Chromolithograph, 1849
From John Frost, *Pictorial History of Mexico and the Mexican War* (Philadelphia: Thomas, Cowperthwait & Co. for James A. Bill, 1849), plate 6
Lithographed by Wagner & McGuigan, Philadelphia
Courtesy of The Huntington Library, San Marino, California

border and as touches of flame on the distant rooftops of Veracruz lends an extra degree of vibrancy. The regularized textures of the color stones in Duval's print, particularly in the area of the sky, are very reminiscent of a color woodcut. As in the chromolithograph of Chapultepec produced by Sarony and Major, the new medium appears tentative, not quite able to declare its own independence.

It is apparent that the Philadelphia firms of both Pierre Duval and Thomas Wagner were employed to produce the color illustrations for Frost's book. There seems to be no instance where the chromolithographic efforts of the two firms were mixed together in one volume; each book was illustrated with work by one or the other. Even with two firms sharing the workload, it must have been a formidable assignment, and not surprisingly, the other illustrations, which are small to begin with, are not very high in quality. They depict views of the battle of Buena Vista, the bombardment of Veracruz, the battles of Churubusco and Cerro Gordo, the storming of Chapultepec, and General Scott's entry into Mexico City. A comparison of two versions of the latter subject shows very different stylistic approaches by the two Philadelphia firms. One, titled *Entrance of the Army into the City of Mexico* (fig. 23), was executed by Wagner and McGuigan and comes from a copy of Frost's book now in the Huntington Library. The other example is detached from its book and can be found in the collection of the American Antiquarian Society. *The Occupation of the Capital of Mexico by the American Army* (fig. 24) is credited not only to Duval but also to the firm's principal

THE OCCUPATION OF THE CAPITAL OF MEXICO BY THE AMERICAN ARMY.

Figure 24
Christian Schuessele
The Occupation of the Capital of Mexico by the American Army
Chromolithograph, 1849
From John Frost, *Pictorial History of Mexico and the Mexican War* (Philadelphia: Thomas, Cowperthwait & Co. for James A. Bill, 1849), plate 6
Courtesy of The American Antiquarian Society, Worcester, Massachusetts

artist at the time, Christian Schuessele. The latter was a highly trained craftsman who introduced some of the most sophisticated techniques to the burgeoning chromolithographic industry, and his hand is readily visible in this small example. Compared with the Wagner and McGuigan copy, Schuessele's scene is far more detailed and the color stones much more expertly utilized, especially in the shadings of the buildings and the treatment of the sky. In terms of the figures, neither image is very accurate; however, the architecture and setting in the Duval/Schuessele version closely correspond to the view of the Mexican capital illustrated in Carl Nebel's *Voyage pittoresque et archéologique.*

The same year that Frost's ambitious history appeared, Duval provided samples of his efforts in chromolithography to the Commissioner of Patents in Washington, D.C. In a report issued shortly thereafter, the agency praised the development of what they termed "machine painting," predicting that it would soon "rival the finest touches of the old masters, and multiply by millions, their esteemed productions."[74] Such productions, in the hands of firms like Duval or Currier and Ives, were to dominate the commercial print market for the remainder of the century.

*T*he eyewitness prints that must be compared against all others are those produced under the direction of George Wilkins Kendall for his book *The War Between the United States and Mexico Illustrated,* published in January 1851.[75] The book consisted of twelve hand-colored lithographs with explanatory text written by Kendall. The plates, on handmade folio-sized paper, were executed in Paris under the close supervision of the author and the artist he had chosen for the task, Carl Nebel. Kendall was evidently familiar with Nebel's earlier work in Mexico, for he lost no time in coming to an agreement with the artist in the closing months of the war. By April 1848 Kendall was in Paris, writing regular dispatches to the *Picayune* back home concerning the revolutionary turmoil in Europe. It is not known how long Nebel remained in Mexico to sketch or paint the various battle sites, but analysis of individual plates in the catalogue suggests that he probably only visited Cerro Gordo, Veracruz, and sites around Mexico City itself. At some point Nebel returned to Hamburg, where his family resided, and made occasional trips to Paris to oversee the work on the lithographs. The printing process was to take over two years, and at least one letter that survives indicates Kendall's impatience with the artist. On May 26, 1849, Kendall wrote his old friend Thomas Falconer in London that "he is a strange man, is Nebel, and were it not that I am in so deep I should cut loose from him at once. He has great talents, but like all Germans, has some eccentricities and whims that render having anything to do with him in the way of business disagreeable." Kendall complained that he had lost "months and months" on the project because the artist was reluctant to visit Paris during a cholera epidemic. He concluded the letter by saying that Nebel had finally made a quick visit and had "fixed everything right with the lithographers."[76]

The firm in question was that of Rose-Joseph Lemercier, and Kendall could hardly have chosen a better artisan for his efforts. Lemercier was an innovative technician who had developed a number of new processes, including a method of obtaining delicate shadings by spreading powdered lithographic crayon on a stone that had been slightly warmed. By the early 1840s his firm was the center for experimentation among a number of painters who sought to achieve a new range of painterly effects through the medium of lithography. Looking at the prints from Kendall's volume today, one is struck by the soft ink washes and delicate tonal areas that underlie the watercolor. Highlights seem to have been either reserved with a waxen substance (beeswax mixed with turpentine was most often used) or carefully scraped into the surface of the stone to yield understated areas of support for the hand coloring.[77]

In the summer of 1850, Kendall returned to America to make final arrangements for the book's publication. During a visit to New Orleans in July, he displayed the specimen proofs of his illustrations and received lavish praise, including that of his own newspaper:

> We have never seen anything to equal the artistic skill, perfection of design, marvellous beauty of execution, delicacy of truth of coloring, and lifelike animation of figures.... They present the most exquisite specimens ever exhibited in this country of the art of colored lithography; and we think that great praise ought to be awarded to Mr. Kendall for having secured such brilliant and beautiful and costly illustrations for the faithful

record of the victories of the American army. Mr. Kendall's pictures, with all their beauty as finished works of consummate art, are exact delineations of the topography and natural scenery…and true representations in every point of the military positions and movements.…The officers of the army who went through the war assure us that the accuracy of the representation of these famous spots is like daguerreotyping. They are therefore of great historical value, as well as splendid embellishments.[78]

Prior to his stopover in New Orleans, Kendall had signed an agreement with D. Appleton in New York for the publication and distribution of his work. In addition, he made arrangements for the binding to be done by the firm of Matthews and Rider.[79] On his way back to Paris, Kendall stopped in London to sign an agreement with Fred R. Rosenberg "to color a set of prints, embracing a series of twelve battle scenes, (50 of each, 600 in the aggregate), at three shillings for each print, he, the said Rosenberg, farther obligating himself to color them as well, in every respect, as the models furnished him [by] this said Kendall, and which will accompany each sett of 50 prints."[80] It seems likely that Nebel furnished a master copy of each finished print for the colorists to follow. If the various newspaper reports are to be believed, Kendall secured the efforts of colorists in England, France, Belgium, and Germany in order to complete the full edition of five hundred copies. The results, by any standard, are impressive. The coloring in all the copies of the prints that have been examined is uniform in technique and masterly in its effects. Visible touches of brushwork are set against strong areas of pure color, while pale washes give delicate substance to the backgrounds.

Back in Paris by December 1850, Kendall drew up a formal agreement between Nebel and himself whereby the two men would serve as "joint and equal partners in all the profits arising from the work." The document also stated that Nebel was to furnish additional sketches for a more ambitious history of the Mexican War that Kendall was then writing. Although this larger history was never published, the extensive manuscript in the author's meticulous hand survives.[81]

The reviews following publication of *The War Between the United States and Mexico Illustrated* were numerous and uniformly laudatory. Kendall collected copies of most of them and used excerpts in a prospectus that he had printed and circulated. The work was distributed in three formats: "in paper covers, $34; in elegant portfolios, $38; half bound, $40." The subjects of the twelve prints were the battles of Palo Alto, Monterrey, Buena Vista, Veracruz, Cerro Gordo, Contreras, Churubusco, Molino del Rey (two views), Chapultepec (two views), and Scott's entrance into Mexico City. Beyond the appearance of the book itself, Kendall was obsessed with the accuracy of his efforts. "The accounts of every battle, as the reader cannot be but aware, must necessarily be partial," he warned in the preface. "Each witness sees but a part, and often a small part, of the strife around him, while all who participate, being actively engaged and strongly excited, are more or less incapacitated for the cool and steady observation requisite to the acquirement of just impressions of what is passing." Kendall was here emphasizing his role as a synthesizer of the eyewitness record, as well as an interpreter of its larger historical significance. He was justly proud of the illustrations that he had helped create, stating that he had personally examined every battle site save the one at Buena Vista. He concluded by asserting that "no country can claim that its battles have been illustrated in a richer, more faithful, or more costly style of lithography."[82]

Four months after the work's initial publication, Kendall wrote his brother-in-law, William Rix, from New Orleans: "Here in the office we have got rid of nearly 100 copies, and at full prices—no charges for commissions nor any thing of that kind."[83] The author had reason to be pleased with his success; newspapers across the country touted his effort as the finest production of its kind ever to appear in America. "The Mexican War forms an epoch in our national history, and here we have a truthful narrative of the most important events during its progress," declared the Boston *Sentinel,* "valuable to the historian, invaluable to the military man as a study of the topography of the movements of the troops, and most defineable to the man of taste as a beautiful specimen of art."[84]

The reviewer in the *Sentinel,* like many of his colleagues, believed that "the work itself bears witness, that the truly graphic description could only have been accomplished by an observer, and that an acute, accurate and impartial one." In several cities the testimony of veteran officers of the war was solicited. One group greatly admired "the correctness in the position of the troops—the topography of the field," together with the "striking resemblance of the different strongholds and fortifications." In addition, many agreed with the assessment in the *Knickerbocker* that the natural scenery in Nebel's prints was represented "with the faithfulness of a daguerreotype reflection." A writer for the New Orleans *Crescent* claimed that "they are the first battle pictures we ever saw, which had individuality. Usually, they look as if made to order, and would suit one battle just as well as another. But a glance satisfies the mind that these are copies after nature." Many of the reviews extolled the portfolio as a memento of national achievement. The editor for the Louisville *Daily Gazette* proclaimed: "What American, with an American heart, does not love to dwell on those scenes, where our countrymen covered our arms with glory, and won for themselves immortal fame? Who would not rather ornament his walls with these magnificent pictures of Kendall's—each one alive with glorious memories,—rather than with unmeaning sketches or colored views, with which are connected no dear recollections?"[85]

A writer to the New Orleans *Delta*, while readily acknowledging the historical accuracy of the portfolio, was more captivated by the plates as works of art in themselves. "I have never seen so much done in so small a space, without violating in some measure, the rules of art," he wrote admiringly. "The easy grace and boldness of objects in the foreground,—the extraordinary power of perspective,—the endless variety and beauty of the sky" made the illustrations among the finest that he had ever seen. The writer described the beauty of the coloring that infused every print with a "glowing, yet mellow light," that lent a "warm, dreamy hue to even the rudest objects." The romantic aspects of Nebel's vision of the Mexican landscape, qualities that had also been invoked by many other artists and writers, struck the reviewer with particular forcefulness. "I have never been in Mexico," he admitted, "but the peculiarity of the light, and the gorgeous coloring of the vegetation, forcibly reminded me of some oriental scenes, whose beauty both poets and painters have delighted to dwell upon."[86]

The historical content of the prints in *The War Between the United States and Mexico Illustrated* is treated in detail in the catalogue section. For the most part, Kendall deserves high praise for his efforts. He attempted to depict every battle from a neutral viewpoint, and although he displayed a nationalist bias in his interpretation of the war, he also sought to place the event in a broader historical perspective. In a similar fashion, Nebel's prints depict the battles in broad tableaus, comparable to grand-manner history painting.

The War Between the United States and Mexico Illustrated represents the climax of the confluence of journalism and lithography on the prints of the Mexican War. "The incidents of no war of the same extent since the world has been peopled, ever have been so accurately and so universally known as this war would be," declared the editor of *Niles' National Register*.[87] Indeed, the period of the Mexican War brought Americans new standards by which to judge the timeliness and veracity of visual reportage. Moreover, this development occurred at the very moment that photography began to be utilized to record current events, including the war itself. The prints of the Mexican War thus heralded a new age of visual communication, as well as technological achievement, that carried into the modern era.

Notes

1. There is as yet no adequate overview of American lithography as it was practiced prior to the Civil War. One of the best introductions to the subject is provided in Wendy Wick Reaves, "Portraits for Every Parlor," in *American Portrait Prints: Proceedings of the Tenth Annual Print Conference* (Charlottesville: University Press of Virginia, for the National Portrait Gallery, Smithsonian Institution, 1984), pp. 83-134. Still a useful source is Nicholas B. Wainwright, *Philadelphia in the Romantic Age of Lithography* (Philadelphia: The Historical Society of Pennsylvania, 1958). As a warning to potential scholars, Peter C. Marzio has asserted that, after a careful search of major manuscript collections in Washington, Baltimore, New York, and Philadelphia, and after correspondence with more than forty other libraries and historical societies, the material "concerning lithography before the Civil War has vanished. Only the lithographs remain." See his essay, "American Lithographic Technology Before the Civil War," in John D. Morse, ed., *Prints in and of America to 1850* (Charlottesville: University Press of Virginia, 1970), p. 254.

2. Michael Twyman, *Lithography, 1800-1850: The Techniques of Drawing on Stone in England and France and Their Application in Works of Topography* (London, New York, and Toronto: Oxford University Press, 1970). The history of chromolithography is presented in Peter C. Marzio, *The Democratic Art: Pictures for a Nineteenth-Century America* (Boston: David R. Godine, in association with the Amon Carter Museum of Western Art, Fort Worth, 1979).

3. There are a number of sources for the history of journalism in this period. See, for example, Culver H. Smith, *The Press, Politics, and Patronage: The American Government's Use of Newspapers, 1789-1875* (Athens: University of Georgia Press, 1977); Michael Schudson, *Discovering the News: A Social History of American Newspapers* (New York: Basic Books, 1981); Dan Schiller, *Objectivity and the News: The Public and the Rise of Commercial Journalism* (Philadelphia: University of Pennsylvania Press, 1981); and Alexander Saxton, "Problems of Class and Race in the Origins of the Mass Circulation Press," *American Quarterly* 36 (1984): 211-34. For the Mexican War, an excellent source is Thomas William Reilly, "American Reporters and the Mexican War, 1846-1848" (Ph.D. diss., University of Minnesota, 1975). For a technological overview, see Calder M. Pickett, "Six New York Newspapers and Their Response to Technology in the Nineteenth Century" (Ph.D. diss., University of Minnesota, 1959), and Robert Luther Thompson, *Wiring a Continent: The History of the Telegraph Industry in the United States, 1832-1866* (Princeton: Princeton University Press, 1947).

4. New York *Herald*, Sept. 16, 1845, p. 2. See also Joseph J. Matthews, *Reporting the Wars* (Minneapolis: University of Minnesota Press, 1957), p. 53.

5. Reilly, "American Reporters and the Mexican War," pp. 453-67.

6. *Niles' National Register* 21 (Sept. 25, 1847): 53, and 21 (May 8, 1847): 155. The achievements of Kendall, Haile, and Freaner are chronicled in Reilly, "American Reporters and the Mexican War"; see also Fayette Copeland, *Kendall of the Picayune* (Norman: University of Oklahoma Press, 1943).

7. Ronnie C. Tyler, *The Mexican War: A Lithographic Record* (Austin: Texas State Historical Association, 1973), p. 62.

8. There is to date no unified study on Walker's life and work. For information on his service in the Mexican War, see Marian R. McNaughton, "James Walker—Combat Artist of Two American Wars," *Military Collector & Historian* 9 (Summer 1957): 31-35. McNaughton mentions twelve small paintings now in the possession of the United States Army, which now hang in the Army Art Collection, U.S. Army Center for Military History, Alexandria, Virginia. There are also four paintings at West Point; these are illustrated in Milton F. Perry, "Four Walker Paintings," *Military Collector & Historian* 9 (Winter 1957): 109-10.

9. The whole episode is recounted in the *Autobiography of the Late Col. Geo. T. M. Davis, Captain and Aid-de-Camp, Scott's Army of Invasion (Mexico), from Posthumous Papers* (New York: Jenkins and McCowan, 1891), pp. 263-65. For a full account of Walker's views of Chapultepec, see cat. no. 148.

10. This information is taken from an unpublished typescript copy of Captain Roberts's diary in the United States Military Academy Library, West Point, pp. 87-90.

11. A.T. [Albert Tracy], U.S.A., "Three Pictures. With a Glance at their History," *Army and Navy Journal*, no. 465 (Dec. 23, 1882): 2-3.

12. Ibid.

13. Ibid. The other paintings Tracy produced were a rendition of the battle of Churubusco, which was less elaborately prepared but "generally faithful and correct," and a portrait of General Worth, field glasses in hand, with the battle of Molino del Rey in the background. The latter had apparently been requested by Worth's supporters back home, who wished to place his name in contention for the Presidency.

14. *Daily National Intelligencer*, Sept. 15, 1847, p. 3; *Literary World* 53 (Feb. 1848): 12-13.

15. William Seaton Henry, *Campaign Sketches of the War with Mexico* (New York: Harper & Brothers, 1847), preface.

16. Eugene Current-Garcia, "Thomas Bangs Thorpe and the Literature of the Ante-Bellum Southwestern Frontier," *Louisiana Historical Society* 39 (April 1956): 209-13; Milton Rickels, *Thomas Bangs Thorpe, Humorist of the Old Southwest* (Baton Rouge: Louisiana State University Press, 1962), p. 121.

17. Thomas Bangs Thorpe, *"Our Army" at Monterey* (Philadelphia: Carey and Hart, 1847), preface.

18. George C. Furber, *The Twelve Months Volunteer; or, Journal of a Private in the Tennessee Regiment of Cavalry, in the Campaign in Mexico, 1846-7...* (Cincinnati: J. P. Jones, 1857), pp. 356-59. Furber credits an illustration of the battleground of Buena Vista facing page 460 to "Lieutenant Gray, adjutant third regiment, Ohio." Furber was amused at the inaccuracy of an illustration depicting the return march of the Volunteers but allowed it to stand because "it would strike the minds of his former comrades in the same manner" (pp. 614-15).

19. For example, this description in *Niles' National Register* 20 (Aug. 29, 1846): 401-2: "Cast the eye beyond Monterey, and the sublime presents itself in lofty upreared pyramids of adamantine stone, tinged with crimson red, where the creeping vine cannot be found, and where the cedar and pine—children of the alpine heights—have never dared to rear their heads—the sides and summits of these vast mountains presenting nothing to view but the bare and glistening stone...."

20. *Knickerbocker* 30, no. 5 (Nov. 1847): 464; New Orleans *Picayune*, Aug. 28, 1847, p. 2; *Daily National Intelligencer*, June 24, 1847, p. 3 (final two quotations).

21. *Daily National Intelligencer*, June 24, 1847, p. 3.

22. Samuel C. Reid, Jr., *Scouting Expeditions of McCulloch's Texas Rangers* (Philadelphia: G. B. Zieber and Co., 1847), pp. 225-26; Henry T. Tuckerman, "William Beckford and the Literature of Travel," *Southern Literary Messenger* 16 (Jan. 1850): 10.

23. The portfolio was advertised in the New York *Herald*, April 12, 1848, p. 3. See the discussion of Walke's watercolors as a basis for the prints of the *Naval Portfolio* under cat. nos. 112, 114, 119, 121, 123.

24. For Paldi's biography and his views, see cat. no. 4; for those of Hill, see cat. nos. 8-10.

25. The eyewitness account of Major Luther W. Giddings, who served in Hill's regiment, recalled that the division remained in line "anxiously watching a scene so novel to volunteers, their hearts beating with wild enthusiasm"; *Niles' National Register* 21 (Nov. 14, 1846): 167-68.

26. For Brydolf's reminiscences, see George S. May, ed., "An Iowan in the Mexican War," *Iowa Journal of History* 3, no. 2 (1955): 173.

27. New York *Herald,* Nov. 18, 1847, p. 1.

28. J. Jacob Oswandel, *Notes of the Mexican War, 1846-47-48* (Philadelphia: n.p., 1885), p. 489.

29. For more on Shannon and his print, see cat. no. 160; for Polhemus, see cat. nos. 161, 164.

30. New York *Herald,* Sept. 6, 1845, p. 1. See also Pickett, "Six New York Newspapers and Their Response to Technology," pp. 163-64. For a biography of Bennett, see Oliver Carlson, *The Man Who Made the News: James Gordon Bennett* (New York: Duell, Sloan & Pearce, 1942).

31. New York *Herald,* Sept. 1, 1845, p. 2; Sept. 2, 1845, p. 2; Sept. 9, 1845, p. 2.

32. Reilly, "American Reporters and the Mexican War," pp. 18-22, 30-47.

33. The Kendall papers were originally described in some detail by Fayette Copeland in his 1943 biography *Kendall of the Picayune,* pp. 321-23. Shortly after Kendall's death in 1867, his family began collecting material on his life. The papers apparently were first kept by Kendall's son, Henry Fletcher Kendall (1855-1913), before being passed on to his sister, Georgina de Valcourt Kendall (1850-1947), who had married Eugene J. Fellowes in 1873. Copeland transcribed the Kendall material for his biography while the papers were in Mrs. Fellowes's possession in San Antonio, Texas. For unknown reasons, Mrs. Fellowes never acceded to a number of requests that her father's papers be deposited in an archive, where they would be protected. After Mrs. Fellowes's death, the papers were first passed to the daughter of Henry Fletcher Kendall, Mrs. Adeline Kirby. Following her death in 1968, the papers went to her brother, William Henry Kendall, who passed away in 1970. Through the efforts of Milan Hughston, Associate Librarian of the Amon Carter Museum, the papers were located in private hands, and the owners graciously allowed the author and Mr. Hughston full access to them. Unfortunately, though the surviving family papers contain many remarkable items, a number of objects had been destroyed by poor storage conditions; moreover, many of the documents cited by Copeland, including a twelve-volume diary of Kendall's years in Texas, remain missing. It is hoped that further searching will yield these important historical items.

34. New York *Herald,* Sept. 2, 1846, p. 1.

35. New York *Herald,* May 9, 1847, p. 2. See also the New York *Herald,* Sept. 16, 1847, p. 1; Reilly, "American Reporters and the Mexican War," pp. 310-11.

36. New York *Herald,* May 9, 1847, p. 2.

37. New York *Herald,* Sept. 17, 1847, p. 2. A wood engraving of Kendall's map, credited as having been executed by "Lieutenant Beauregard of the Corps of Engineers," appeared in the New York *Herald,* Sept. 23, 1847, p. 2.

38. Quoted in the New York *Herald,* Sept. 17, 1847, p. 2.

39. See the report in the New York *Herald,* Oct. 30, 1847, p. 2. A writer for the New Orleans *Picayune* described it as follows: "From ten to twelve thousand copies of a newspaper can be printed upon it in one hour, and the principle is capable of indefinite extension, by the multiplication of a number of distributing cylinders....Each of these small cylinders throws off nearly three thousand impressions per hour, and by increasing their number, three thousand more impressions are secured for every cylinder." (New York *Herald,* Oct. 29, 1847, p. 2.)

40. New York *Herald,* Nov. 20, 1846, p. 2.

41. New York *Herald,* Dec. 9, 1846, p. 2.

42. Harry T. Peters, *Currier and Ives: Printmakers to the American People* (Garden City, N.Y.: Doubleday Doran Company, 1942), p. 7.

43. For a complete list of prints of Mexican War subjects produced by Currier, see Frederick G. Ruffner, ed., and Bernard F. Reilly, Jr., *Currier & Ives: A Catalogue Raisonné* (Detroit: Gale Research Company, 1984).

44. See Currier's ad in the New York *Herald,* April 12, 1848, p. 3.

45. New York *Herald,* June 7, 1846, p. 2.

46. Ibid.

47. May's charge was the subject of at least ten different prints in the period. For the initial reports on his exploits, see the New York *Herald,* May 29, 1846, p. 1; *Niles' National Register* 19 (May 30, 1846): 201, and 19 (June 20, 1846): 252. May's charge was also depicted in a crude wood engraving by Samuel Putnam Avery in the New York *Herald,* June 28, 1846, p. 1, and in a more finished steel engraving by Tompkins Matteson in the *Columbian Magazine* 6 (Sept. 1846): 143. Currier's changes to his composition were well-advised in such a competitive market. Sarony and Major, for instance, were noted as having published a colored lithograph of Captain May's capture of General de la Vega less than three weeks after news of the battle had reached New York. See the New York *Herald,* June 16, 1846, p. 1.

48. New York *Herald,* June 25, 1846, p. 2.

49. Charles Lanman, "On the Requisites for the Formation of a National School of Historical Painting," *Southern Literary Messenger* 14 (Dec. 1848): 728.

50. Baillie worked for Nathaniel Currier as a colorist from 1843 until 1847. He apparently did not draw any designs on stone himself. See Harry T. Peters, *America on Stone* (Garden City, N.Y.: Doubleday, Doran & Co., 1931), pp. 84-85.

51. New York *Herald,* April 11, 1847, p. 1.

52. See Donald H. Mugridge, *An Album of American Battle Art, 1755-1918* (Washington: U.S. Government Printing Office, 1947), pp. 136-37.

53. New York *Herald,* May 11, 1847, p. 1.

54. Ibid.

55. Kendall's initial reports are given in the New York *Herald,* May 10, 1847, p. 1, and May 15, 1847, p. 1. Several versions of this subject were published by R. Magee in Philadelphia but are decidedly inferior in style. More interesting was a caricature drawn by Edward W. Clay, who is known to have done work for James Baillie. It was published by Henry W. Robinson and titled *Santa Anna Declining a Hasty Plate of Soup at the Battle of Cerro Gordo.* This print shows Santa Anna's cork leg accurately.

56. Freaner's dispatches appeared in the New York *Herald,* May 10, 1847, p. 1, and May 11, 1847, p. 1. Sarony and Major's activity in this period remains to be examined. See the comments in Peters, *Currier and Ives,* p. 13, and Marzio, *The Democratic Art,* pp. 49-51.

57. Bragg's disclaimer can be found in the New Orleans *Picayune,* Jan. 23, 1849, p. 1.

58. New York *Herald,* May 25, 1846, p. 1, and June 2, 1846, p. 1. A crude wood engraving of the fall of Ringgold appeared in the *Herald* on June 28, 1846, p. 1; a highly romanticized engraving by Tompkins Matteson appeared in the *Columbian Magazine* 6 (Aug. 1846): 92-93. Ringgold as a hero is also examined in Robert W. Johannsen's excellent study, *To the Halls of the Montezumas: The Mexican War in the American Imagination* (New York: Oxford University Press, 1985), p. 124.

59. *Spirit of the Times* 16 (Sept. 5, 1846): 332.

60. New York *Herald,* Sept. 18, 1847, p. 1.

61. *Spirit of the Times* 17 (April 24, 1847): 101; *Niles' National Register* 21 (Aug. 7, 1847): 363, also 21 (April 17, 1847): 98. Another account of Clay's death appears in *Sartain's Magazine* 1 (July 1847): 44-45.

62. *Spirit of the Times* 17 (Dec. 18, 1847): 507. George Furber is one eyewitness who cannot refrain from grisly descriptions of corpses after the battles; see *The Twelve Months Volunteer,* pp. 532-33, 598-99. A newspaper account that was published at approximately the same time as the Currier print described the mangled and rotting remains on the battlefield of Palo Alto; see *Niles' National Register* 19 (June 27, 1846): 264.

63. Reid, *Scouting Expeditions of McCulloch's Texas Rangers,* p. 192.

64. *Spirit of the Times* 17 (April 17, 1847): 91; Furber, *The Twelve Months Volunteer,* pp. 544-45.

65. *Knickerbocker* 30 (Nov. 1847): 464. See also Georgia Brady Bumgardner, "George and William Endicott: Commercial Lithography in New York, 1831-51," in David Tatham, ed., *Prints and Printmakers of New York State, 1825-1940* (Syracuse: Syracuse University Press, 1986), pp. 43-66.

66. Hullmandel (1789-1850) was a major figure in the history of lithographic technology. His treatise was doubtless known to the American lithographers: *The Art of Drawing on Stone, Giving a Full Explanation of the Various Styles, of the Different Methods to Be Employed to Ensure Success, and of the Modes of Correcting, as Well as of the Several Causes of Failure* (London, 1824; 2d ed., 1833; 3d ed., 1835). His accomplishments are described by Twyman; for his shading method, see *Lithography, 1800-1850,* pp. 119-24. Twyman lists Hullmandel's patent for 1840 that described "a new effect of light and shadow, imitating brush or stump drawing," p. 267.

67. Whiting's brother-in-law, Lt. Napoleon J.T. Dana, gave some hints of this irritation; see cat. no. 1.

68. See Twyman, *Lithography, 1800-1850,* pp. 156-60, 201-2.

69. "Both paper and stone could be scratched away with the knife or scraper for effects such as rain and spray, or for highlights, but where rather larger light areas were needed lithographers adopted a technique... to reserve the light areas of a drawing with a mixture of beeswax and turpentine, which was coloured with flake white and applied with a brush" (ibid., p. 179).

70. Twyman ascribes the initial development of the chromolithographic process to another pioneering artist, Godefroy Engelmann (1788-1839), who published a treatise titled *Album chromo-lithographique ou recueil d'essais du nouveau procede d'impression lithographique en couleurs,* which was published in Paris around 1838. See Twyman, *Lithography, 1800-1850,* pp. 160-62. For the background of the process in America, see Marzio, *The Democratic Art,* pp. 8-20. Marzio, however, mistakenly assigns the Walker chromolithograph to Henry Walke; see pp. 49-50.

71. Lithotinting is also evident in the prints of the *Naval Portfolio.* Although there seems to have been much confusion over the term (since the processes were kept secret by Hullmandel and others), the general principle remains that the effects are achieved at the printing stage of the lithograph. An original source describes it as follows: "Lithotint, indeed, is only a modification of the process of lithography, made for the purpose of obtaining impressions from graduated tints of liquid ink applied to the stone with a brush, in the same way as India ink or sepia drawings are made on paper" (Twyman, *Lithography, 1800-1850,* p. 149).

72. Mugridge, *Album of American Battle Art,* pp. 135-36. Editions of Frost's books were examined at the Huntington Library. The author is indebted to Marni Sandweiss for her assistance with the Huntington copy of Frost's *Pictorial History.*

73. Marzio, *The Democratic Art,* p. 24.

74. Ibid., pp. 24-26, 231.

75. George Wilkins Kendall, *The War Between the United States and Mexico Illustrated* (New York: D. Appleton & Co., 1851). See cat. nos. 5, 16, 38, 115, 125, 134, 136, 140, 141, 146, 152, 159.

76. George Wilkins Kendall to Thomas Falconer, London, May 26, 1849, in the Western Americana Collection, Beinecke Rare Book and Manuscript Library, Yale University. The author is indebted to the research of Ron Tyler for this citation. The Kendall family papers contain a scrapbook of miscellaneous newspaper clippings from the period, as well as a prospectus for *The War Between the United States and Mexico Illustrated* that contains undated excerpts from newspaper reviews. Kendall's movements to and from Paris are recorded in his passport, which also survives.

77. See Twyman, *Lithography, 1800-1850,* p. 140. By the early 1840s the French painter Eugène Isabey "was experimenting with new techniques at Lemercier's in order to realize the full painterly potentialities of the medium" (ibid., p. 241).

78. New Orleans *Picayune,* July 15, 1850, p. 2.

79. A typescript of the agreement between Kendall and his publisher is in the Fayette Copeland papers, Western History Collections, University of Oklahoma. Receipts for the binding costs from Matthews and Rider are preserved in the Kendall family papers.

80. A typescript of this agreement was made by Fayette Copeland and is now in the Western History Collections of the University of Oklahoma. A search of the Kendall family papers has not yielded the original.

81. The manuscript is in the collection of the Eugene C. Barker Texas History Center, University of Texas at Austin.

82. Kendall, *The War Between The United States and Mexico Illustrated,* preface.

83. George Wilkins Kendall, New Orleans, to William Rix, Mobile, April 21, 1851, Western Americana Collection, Beinecke Rare Book and Manuscript Library, Yale University.

84. Boston *Sentinel,* undated clipping in the Kendall scrapbook, Kendall family papers.

85. All these reviews are preserved in the Kendall family papers. The clippings from the Boston *Sentinel,* New Orleans *Delta,* and New Orleans *Crescent* (all undated) and from the Louisville *Daily Gazette* (dated April 11, 1851) are found in the Kendall scrapbook; the *Knickerbocker's* review is quoted in the printed prospectus for Kendall's illustrated history.

86. New Orleans *Delta,* undated clipping, Kendall scrapbook, Kendall family papers.

87. *Niles' National Register* 21 (May 8, 1847): 155.

Daguerreotypes of the Mexican War

Martha A. Sandweiss

Sometime around 1927 H. Armour Smith, later director of the Yonkers Museum of Science and Arts, acquired for his personal collection a group of twelve sixth-plate daguerreotypes neatly labeled and mounted in a handmade walnut case. Ten of the daguerreotypes were made in or around Saltillo, Mexico, most probably in 1847 or early 1848, during the American occupation of the town. The remaining two depicted Fort Marion and the neighboring community of St. Augustine, Florida, a jumping-off point for soldiers moving to and from the Mexican battlegrounds. In 1938 Robert Taft described these daguerreotypes in his pioneering book, *Photography and the American Scene,* and reproduced the most dramatic of the images, a view of General John E. Wool and his troops pausing in their march down a Saltillo street. Taft cited these images as the only known photographs of the Mexican War and, indeed, the world's first photographs of war. "The historic value of these photographs would repay an extended study," he concluded.[1]

The photographs promised to shed light on the development of photojournalism and the early practice of photography in Mexico and in America's frontier west. They offered evidence that just eight years after Louis Jacques Mandé Daguerre announced his marvelous new discovery to the world, an enterprising photographer or photographers had traveled to the interior of Mexico to record a newsworthy event. In an age when more than ninety-five percent of daguerreotypes were studio-made portraits, this man had worked outdoors in an occupied military zone with uncertain access to supplies, making views of military activities on silver-plated copper daguerreotype plates.

Technological limitations, of course, made it impossible to photograph action. The long exposures required made even a portrait sitting an arduous event: heavy metal clamps on

Figure 25   Opposite
Photographer Unknown
General Wool and Staff in the Calle Real, Saltillo
Sixth-plate daguerreotype
Cat. No. 53
Amon Carter Museum [81.65/22]

specially fabricated portrait stands held the sitter's head rigid and still for the camera. Outside of a studio, where animate subjects could not easily be immobilized, one could not be sure of obtaining a clearly focused view of people at all. There was no way to capture the heat of battle on a photographic plate. At best, one could capture troops standing in a street or pausing astride their horses far from the chaos of actual warfare.

Before this unknown daguerreotypist went to Mexico only a few photographers had ever used a camera to record an event — as opposed to a person, a building, a static street view, or an unpeopled landscape — and it is doubtful that any of them had made such an extended series of views documenting a particular activity.[2] Had this photographer perceived a new market for photography as a medium capable of purveying topical news and pioneered a new use for the burgeoning art? Had he deliberately fashioned himself the world's first photojournalist? Or was he merely an energetic adventurer caught up in a more haphazard enterprise?

Numerous mysteries have surrounded the Smith daguerreotypes since their first publication in Taft's book. Neither their maker nor their original collector has ever been identified. Precisely where Smith found them is unknown, and when and why he or his estate disposed of such widely recognized and important photographs is similarly uncertain. Around 1960 Archibald Hanna, Jr., Curator of Western Americana at Yale's Beinecke Library, found the framed daguerreotypes at Whitlock's Book Barn in Bethany, Connecticut, and purchased them for the library collection.[3] There they have remained, the subject of ongoing speculation as to their collector, their maker, and their documentary importance. Numerous daguerreotype portraits of Mexican War figures — virtually all made in the United States — have long been known to students of military and photographic history. But no additional outdoor views showing troops or Mexican War battle sites were known to exist until 1981, when thirty-eight daguerreotype portraits and views of Mexican War scenes were discovered in a Connecticut barn and acquired for the Amon Carter Museum.

The thirty-eight images, both sixth- and quarter-plates, are part of a collection that also includes seven daguerreotypes that were made in the United States and eight that are so obscured as to yield no information about the image. Five related daguerreotypes of American and unidentified images were subsequently acquired from the same source. The Mexican daguerreotypes include thirteen military portraits, two portraits of Mexican citizens, two portraits of unidentified civilians (which may or may not have been made in Mexico), two views identified as being of Durango, one of Parras, one image of sailing ships at an unidentified port, one post-mortem view, two pictures of graves, four views of American troops, and a number of images of Saltillo street scenes, buildings, and the town's environs. Considering the variety of scenes portrayed in contemporary prints of the war, the remarkable similarity of the subject matter represented in the Yale and Amon Carter daguerreotype collections is notable. The Carter collection includes a reversed image of General Wool and his troops (fig. 25), made within a few moments of the Yale view on the same Saltillo street; a view of Major Lucien Webster's artillery battalion in a mountain pass near Saltillo, a scene also depicted in one of the Yale views; and variations of some of the Saltillo street scenes also found in the Yale collection. Additional views and portraits in the Carter collection further support the probability that Saltillo was the base of operations for the unidentified photographer or photographers. One Carter view depicts the grave of Henry Clay, Jr., felled at the battle of Buena Vista on February 23, 1847, and temporarily interred at a special military cemetery south of Saltillo before being transported home to Kentucky by his comrades. The identified military officers in the Carter portraits all served in American-occupied Saltillo during the year following the United States' decisive victory at the nearby Buena Vista battlefield. The Mexican village of Parras, shown in one daguerreotype, is just ninety miles to the west, and Wool and his troops passed through there on their way to Saltillo. There is nothing to prove that the Mexican views and portraits in the two collections were made by the same photographer. But the coincidence of subjects and the predominance of Saltillo-related scenes suggests that at least some views in both collections were made by the same elusive figure, and that the views and portraits taken in American-occupied Saltillo were made between the time of the American victory at Buena Vista on February 23, 1847, and the departure of the American troops in June 1848.[4]

Neither the plates at Yale nor those at the Amon Carter Museum yield any obvious clues as to the photographer's or photographers' identity. Even basic provenances for the collections are problematic. The Yale daguerreotypes are all labeled in the same neat hand. Only the inclusion of the two views of Fort Marion and St. Augustine suggests that the collector of the plates might have passed through Florida on his way to or from Mexico and acquired these two pictures as further souvenirs of his wartime travels.

Found in the barn of a Connecticut family with no known connections to the Mexican War, the images in the Amon Carter collection offer a few more visual clues as to their probable collector. A plate subsequently identified as the earliest known photograph of Wilmington, North Carolina, suggests a possible connection with that state.[5] More suggestive are three unidentified views of an extraordinary romanesque house unlike anything troops might have encountered in Mexico. The house proves to be Oaklands, built by the prominent architect Richard Upjohn in 1835-36 for Robert Hallowell Gardiner of Gardiner, Maine. Gardiner, a wealthy landowner and active leader in local affairs, was not himself a photographer. But the Amon Carter daguerreotype collection includes three views of his house; a street scene of his home town of Gardiner; a heretofore unrecorded portrait of President James Knox Polk, who visited Oaklands on a campaign tour in July 1847; a portrait of Gardiner's neighbor and associate, Maine Senator George Evans; and a daguerreotype copy of a naval print of the Battle of the Nile, a battle in which Gardiner's cousin, Captain Benjamin Hallowell, was distinguished for gallant conduct. Gardiner — or someone close to him — seems likely to have assembled the collection.[6]

The most likely collector is his son, John William Tudor Gardiner (1817-79; fig. 26), a graduate of the United States Military Academy and a first lieutenant with Company D of the First Dragoons during the war with Mexico. Arriving in Mexico on December 15, 1847, Gardiner remained there until June 1848 when he was reposted to Fort Snelling, Minnesota. He later served on Isaac Stevens's 1853 survey of possible routes for a Northern Pacific railway, where he worked with John Mix Stanley, an artist and photographer whose daguerreotype record of the expedition has long since been lost.[7] In December 1853 Gardiner sailed for a new posting in California on the steamer *San Francisco,* narrowly escaping death when the ship went down off the Capes of the Delaware. "My preservation at the time of the wreck was marvelous," Gardiner wrote a few months later. "Out of nearly 200 persons in the after part of the upper cabin I was the only person who did not go overboard."[8] Major John M. Washington — veteran of the Mexican War, former military governor of New Mexico Territory, and subject of one of the Amon Carter daguerreotypes — was not so for-

Figure 26
Artist Unknown
John William Tudor Gardiner
Lithograph
Courtesy of Gardiner Family Archives, Gardiner, Maine

tunate. As the handwritten label affixed to the back of his daguerreotype image notes, he was "lost with his Reg in steamer San Francisco en route for California."[9] The label suggests that the collector of the daguerreotypes was well acquainted with Washington's fate. Certainly Gardiner was. The label is not in his hand, but it establishes one more possible link between him and the collection.

When Gardiner finally got to California in 1855 he made use of the local daguerreotypists to keep in touch with his family in Maine. Writing to his mother from Fort Tejon in 1856 with news of his young child, he noted, "I sent you a daguerreotype of him from Los Angelos. It ought to be received with this."[10]

Circumstantial evidence, then, establishes Gardiner as the likely collector of the largest extant collection of Mexican War daguerreotypes. He had an interest in photographic imagery, served in Mexico at or shortly after the time the Mexican views were made, and had a clear interest in owning photographic images of his family homestead. As the label on the verso of the Washington portrait illustrates, the labels affixed to fourteen of the Mexican images in the Amon Carter collection were written at least several years after the war. Whether Gardiner acquired the Mexican images in Mexico or at some later point is impossible to learn.

If the identity of the collector of the Amon Carter daguerreotypes seems fairly certain, the photographer of these images and those at Yale does not. When Taft published one of the Yale daguerreotypes in 1938, he wrote, "It seems more reasonable to assume that they were made by a local daguerreotypist than it is to assume that any hardy United States daguerreotypist set out with intent to photograph the Mexican War."[11] That, indeed, could have been the case. But scattered newspaper accounts and other contemporary sources unknown to Taft suggest that a number of American and American-trained photographers did travel south to photograph the war and its participants. With little knowledge of Mexico and, in some cases, a dubious knowledge of photographic technique, they documented the people and events of the war and made architectural views to sell to American soldiers.

The first daguerreotype camera arrived in Mexico as early as March 1840. But the earliest photographer with an American connection to work there was probably Fanny Calderón de la Barca. Born in Scotland in 1804 and a resident of Boston and New York from 1831 to 1838, the former Frances Irskine Caldwell was living in Mexico with her husband, Spanish diplomat Angel Calderón de la Barca, in October 1840 when she received a daguerreotype camera as a gift from the Boston historian William Hickling Prescott. Prescott ordered the apparatus for Calderón in April, and writing in anticipation of its receipt she told him, "I think there are few areas of the world where it can be used to more advantage." Calderón and her husband made their first recorded photographic expedition to Chapultepec on November 21, 1840, and subsequently sent a less than satisfactory example of their daguerreotype work back to Prescott in Boston.[12]

Though a prolific journal and letter writer, Calderón left little documentation of her photographic efforts. John Lloyd Stephens, who carried a daguerreotype camera obtained in New York with him on his second voyage to Yucatán in 1841, left a better record of the experiments he conducted with his expedition artist George Catherwood. Immediately upon their arrival at Uxmal, Catherwood began making daguerreotype views of the ruins, "but the results were not sufficiently perfect to suit his ideas. At times the projecting cornices and ornaments threw part of the subject in shade, while others were in broad sunshine; so that, while parts were brought out well, other parts required pencil drawing to supply their defects." Catherwood resorted to making careful drawings with a pencil and his more trustworthy camera lucida, abandoning the daguerreotype camera to Stephens and their companion, Dr. Cabot, who continued making daguerreotypes to "ensure the utmost accuracy" of the plates that would be engraved to illustrate the expedition report.[13]

Catherwood, Stephens, and Cabot had somewhat more success when they went into business in Mérida "as ladies' Daguerreotype portrait takers. It was a new line for us, and rather venturesome, but not worse than for the editor of a newspaper to turn captain of a steamboat; and, besides, it was not like banking — we could not injure any one by a failure." By displaying their successes and hiding their failures, they managed to stay in business for a few days until on one distressing morning the daguerreotype apparatus "seemed bent upon confounding us; and, covering our confusion as well as we could, we gathered up our Daguerreotype and carried ourselves off." After an equally brief career as surgeons operating on crossed eyes, they returned to their chief business of investigating the antiquities of the Yucatán peninsula.[14]

If inexperience and the unreliability of early daguerrian equipment made photography an uncertain profession, so did the difficulty of obtaining supplies in Mexico, particularly after the onset of war in 1846. The experience of Richard Carr, a remarkable young man who traveled through Mexico making photographs from late 1845 until late 1847, suggests the extent of the problem. Born in England in 1818, Carr came to America in 1837. On July 28, 1845, he went to New York and paid forty dollars to the prominent photographer John Plumbe "to learn me to take daguerreotype portraits." By late October he was in New Orleans, where on the twenty-sixth of the month he opened a daguerrian portrait studio. But just two weeks later he wrote to his brother, "I have had very bad success at my new undertaking have not cleared half my expenses, as such must try it else w[h]ere." On December 1, he boarded a schooner and sailed for Veracruz.

Carr seems to have spent most of his time in Mexico *avoiding* political turbulence and military activity, but he could not escape the economic ramifications of current events. After establishing himself in Veracruz, he sent an order for one hundred dollars' worth of supplies to Langenheim and Company in Philadelphia, but it is not clear that these supplies ever arrived. In May 1846, with two donkeys to carry his baggage, he left Veracruz for Orizaba, a town to the west with about 25,000 inhabitants, and in July he moved on to Oaxaca. There he "was several times employed to take the likenesses of females that [the priests] told me was their scister, or niece, but have afterwards been told by others it was their sweathearts or children." By November, Carr had exhausted his supplies. In his journal he noted, "Left Oaxaca for Campeachy [Campeche] in Yucatan having disposed of all my cases and plates, am not able [to] buy any in this country — nor can I import any on account of the blocade, I find it necessary to undertake this long journey."

After a journey of nearly two months, Carr arrived in Campeche and in early January "was able to obtain a small supply of Daguerreotype articles, such as I stood most in need of, commenced taking portraits, in the mean time sent to the United States for a further supply."[15] But after waiting for three and a half months and doing barely enough business to meet his expenses, he resolved that the best way to get his supplies "is to go after them." He sailed for New Orleans, spent a week there buying the needed materials, and returned to Mérida to set up a business. Apparently it did not thrive. After several months he left the city for an extended tour of Yucatecan villages and in November 1847 left Mexico and sailed for Belize. He traveled through Nicaragua, Panama, and Ecuador. While in Guayaquil, he received word of the California gold strike and news that labor there would be paid "at a most exorbitant price." "I have got to leave here," he wrote in his journal, "and phraps shall do better their than elsewere though the Americans I detest." He sailed for California and on January 1, 1849, walked ashore in San Francisco, where there was "scarsely a sober man to be found," and became the first photographer in town.[16]

None of the American photographers documenting war activities or American troops left such a detailed account of their business problems. But their frequent changes of address, the seeming brevity of their careers, and the frequency with which one finds ads for used daguerrian equipment in Mexico's English-language papers all testify to their difficulties.

The most successful, or at least the most long-lived, American photographer documenting wartime activities in Mexico was A. J. Halsey, who established himself in Mexico City in September 1845, eight months before the United States declared war on her southern neighbor. Like Carr, Halsey had a peripatetic career. With an American partner named Saad, he had opened the first daguerrian portrait studio in Montreal in September 1840 and in early October had moved on to establish a studio in Québec. The two men must have counted on the extreme interest and gullibility of their clients, for contemporary accounts suggest they actually knew little about the daguerrian process. Indeed, their pictures faded on exposure to light. By the time Halsey arrived in Mexico he was presumably more skilled as he boasted of his four years of experience and his superior new machines and offered to give instruction in the art of daguerreotypy.[17]

Halsey advertised in Mexico City's Spanish-language papers in the spring of 1846 and in early 1847. But after General Scott's entry into Mexico City in September 1847 he switched audiences and began advertising his services in the unoffical American army paper, the *Daily American Star*. His standard ad read:

> Portraits by the Daguerreotype with Colors
> A. J. Halsey respectfully announces to the public and officers of the U.S. Army, that he is now prepared to take miniatures by the above process in first rate style, which can compete with any taken in the city, price $5. Views of churches, castles, public buildings, &c., taken at a short notice on large size plates. Hotel of the National Theatre, No. 21.

A further note in the paper of October 26, 1847, added: "A few views of the Cathedral, taken from nature for sale in his rooms. Also, miniatures on ivory copied from those of the daguerreotypes. A perfect likeness guaranteed, otherwise no charge."[18]

A man of commerce rather than politics, Halsey resumed his Mexican-oriented practice after the war. He maintained his studio in Mexico City into the 1860s, becoming a supplier of photographic supplies and specializing in city views and flattering soft portraits that appeared to "diminish" a person's age.[19]

Most of the other American daguerreotypists seeking to capitalize on the war had briefer careers. A Mr. Palmer from New Orleans — presumably the J. R. Palmer who operated a daguerrian gallery on Canal Street — arrived in Matamoros in June 1846 and advertised that "he is prepared to take likenesses in the latest and most approved style of the art." Apparently he soon changed professions, for the Matamoros paper, *American Flag,* carried a brief story on October 14, 1846 stating, "We are happy to inform our friends, who have been disappointed in obtaining Daguerreotype likenesses from one of us, since entering upon another vocation, that Chas. J. Betts, a Daguerreotype artist, has recently taken rooms in the upper story of the Resaca House, and takes miniatures in the most improved style of the art. Pictures of General Vega and other distinguished individuals may be seen at his rooms."[20] The paper's oblique reference to Palmer was probably clear to its readers, for he had apparently joined the newspaper's staff. By March 3, 1847, J. R. Palmer was coeditor of the *American Flag.*

Unlike Halsey, who settled down to business in a single place, Palmer's successor Betts followed the American army from city to city. An item in the Matamoros paper of September 21, 1846, announced his imminent departure for Monterrey. Betts himself noted in the October 24 issue that "he will remain but a short time," and four days later he advertised "A first-rate apparatus with cases, chemical &c complete. The whole, together with instructions for taking pictures with all the latest improvements, will be sold cheap for cash." On December 5, he published an announcement "that he will remain in this city but 3 or 4 days longer, and all those wishing Daguerreotypes had better call soon." On December 19 he announced he "will remain but a few days longer, positively."[21]

By April 1847 Betts was with the American army in Veracruz, where for "two weeks only" he was prepared to take portraits and, on request, would "go to residences to take miniatures of the dead and wounded." Veracruz "has been in our hands only 20 days," boasted Lt. Arthur M. Manigault on April 19, 1847, "and there is an American Theater open, a newspaper, daguerreotype taker and several coffee houses kept by Americans." Betts left the town along with the troops. In July he followed Scott's army from Jalapa to Puebla. A Mr. L. H. Polock had passed through Puebla a few weeks earlier and operated a daguerrian studio for several days. But Betts must have perceived still more opportunity, for he set up a studio with J. C. Gardiner just one block from Scott's headquarters.[22]

John Charles Gardiner merits attention because he was a distant cousin of John William Tudor Gardiner, the probable collector of the Amon Carter daguerreotypes. But he was a scoundrel who practiced dentistry in Mexico under his brother's license and, with this brother George, defrauded the United States government of more than four hundred thousand dollars. Daguerreotypy seems to have been just another short-lived money-making scheme to him, and there is nothing to suggest that he actually knew his more honorable military cousin or pursued photography for more than a very brief time.[23] Either Betts or Gardiner advertised an "excellent DAGUERREOTYPE APPARATUS for sale" in late July, and by September Betts (apparently without his former partner) was settled in Mexico City along with Scott and his army.[24]

Aiming his business towards the American troops (just as his rival A. J. Halsey did), Betts advertised in the American paper: "C. S. Betts respectfully informs the citizens of this city, as well as the officers etc. of the U. S. Army, that he has taken rooms in the second story of the building situated at the corner of Calle de Plateras and Calle de Refugio at the sign of the 'WHITE FLAG' and one square from the plaza, here he is prepared to take miniatures in every style, with all the improvements. Satisfaction shall be given or no charge made." His portrait studio featured a large painting of Chapultepec that formed a scenic backdrop for his portrait studies.[25]

Betts apparently changed or disbanded his studio in mid-December, for his last adver-

Figure 27
Photographer Unknown
Col. Hamtramck, Virginia Vol.
Quarter-plate daguerreotype
Cat. No. 68
Amon Carter Museum [81.65/3]

tisement ran in the *American Star* of December 17. On January 11, 1848, the paper ran a notice advising the public that C. S. Betts and A.L. Cosmes de Cosio had disbanded their partnership. Cosmes de Cosio, who had been practicing daguerreotypy in Mexico City since the preceding September, would henceforth be "ready to serve his patrons, in the street of San Jose del Real, No. 5, every day, from 9, A. M. to 4, P. M. Persons wishing to have their likenesses taken, will find that those he takes are of superior quality, and lower price than others. The coloring of the back ground in the portraits done gratis." With this notice, Mr. Betts disappears from the records. Inconclusive evidence suggests that Cosmes de Cosio later pursued his craft in Spain.[26]

In September 1847, not long after Betts left Veracruz to follow General Scott on his march toward Mexico City, another American daguerreotypist moved into the port city to set up a studio. A local editor invited the public to become acquainted with George Noessel, recently from New Orleans and the only daguerrian artist in town, an "expert" craftsman, "and what is better than that, a perfect gentleman with whom they will be happy to become acquainted." In November, Noessel moved his studio from the "Palace" to a private home and advertised that "as it is a family residence he hopes that the ladies of Vera Cruz who felt a delicacy in going to the Palace will now honor him with a call." The New Orleans *Picayune* informed its readers that Noessel was succeeding in "picking up interesting subjects with whose portraits to enrich his gallery," and gave particular notice to his portrait of Colonel Dominguez, the commander of a spy company under General Scott, that emphasized the colonel's "coarse sensuality." But by February 1848 Noessel, too, was on his way out of Veracruz and the daguerrian trade. In mid-February he served as the principal conductor of a merchants' caravan from Veracruz to Mexico City. After that, nothing more is known either of him or his business career.[27]

No circumstantial evidence exists to link any of these photographers to the daguerreo-type records of the Mexican War currently held by Yale and the Amon Carter Museum. While these men worked in the port cities of Matamoros and Veracruz and followed Scott's army to Mexico City, the photographer who made the surviving images was with Taylor's army in the north. If documentation of the southern photographers is scant, information on those working with the northern army is scarcer still.

There was at least one photographer known to be at the battle of Buena Vista and with Wool's troops in Saltillo during 1847 and 1848, and he kept meticulous records of all of his activities. Through an unfortunate set of circumstances, however, he did not have his camera with him. Thus there are no Mexican War photographs by the great southwestern writer (and amateur daguerreotypist) Josiah Gregg.

Gregg left Independence, Missouri, in June 1846 with a trading caravan bound for New Mexico along the Santa Fe Trail. Before leaving, he wrote to a correspondent in St. Louis: "I have just perceived, that in giving you a description of the daguerreotype plates I wanted, I set down their dimensions at '3⅜ by 4⅛ inches' instead of '2¾ by 3¼ inches', as it should have been. The price I gave '$3.50 per dozen' was correct for the size last mentioned, as stated to me by Mr. Miller the daguerreotypist. I hope my mistake will have occasioned no incon-venience, as the price will have shown the size I wanted. The large size would be too large for my instrument." Gregg added that his friend John Mix Stanley, the painter and photog-rapher, would pick up the new daguerreotype plates for him.[28]

But en route to Santa Fe, Gregg received a message from his friend Colonel Yell of the

Rancheros, - Gregg's
"Commerce of Prairies"

Arkansas Volunteers urging him to accompany the United States Army into Mexico. Gregg went back to Independence, then headed south toward Mexico, while the wagon carrying his scientific instruments and supplies (presumably including his daguerreotype apparatus) continued west to Santa Fe. In Mexico, Gregg settled in Saltillo with Taylor's army and was an observer at the battle of Buena Vista fought nearby in February 1847. It was April of that year before he recovered his scientific equipment in Chihuahua.[29]

Gregg spent the winter of 1847-48 practicing medicine in Saltillo, where, as he notes in his journal, he knew many of the subjects of the Amon Carter daguerreotypes. General Wool seemed "an amiable gentlemanly man; yet I fear rather crabid and petulant, and perhaps... old womanish — more efficient in minutiae and details than in grand and extensive operations." Col. John Francis Hamtramck (fig. 27) had a "tyrannical temperament." "For pomposity, vanity and parade, he was not even excelled by Gen. Wool. He was in almost daily habit of riding about town, in full uniform, with a long tail of guard in his wake, putting on airs which General Taylor never thought of."[30]

But Gregg, an obsessive note-taker, makes no mention of making daguerreotypes in Mexico. While he carefully records barometric readings and temperatures, latitudes and rainfall, unusual animals and exotic plants, he says nothing of photographic experiments. It therefore seems unlikely that he actually had his camera with him in Mexico. Perhaps it is just an odd coincidence that the most unusual of the daguerreotypes in the Yale collection is a hand-colored daguerreotype of a painting or lithograph with a script label "Rancheros — Gregg's Commerce of Prairies" (fig. 28). The ultimate source of the image, a Carl Nebel painting of two traditionally costumed Mexican women framed in a doorway, is now lost. Lithographed first for Nebel's 1836 publication *Voyage pittoresque et archéologique dans la partie la plus intéressante du Mexique*, it was later adapted for an illustration in George Wilkins Kendall's 1844 *Narrative of the Texan Santa Fe Expedition* (fig. 29), another travel narrative the daguerreotype owner apparently confused with Gregg's *Commerce of the Prairies* (which also came out in 1844).[31]

There is some inconclusive evidence that Nebel himself might have been familiar with the operation of a daguerreotype camera as early as 1840, when he accompanied Frances Calderón de la Barca on her photographic excursion to Chapultepec.[32] Nebel's possible familiarity with photography might explain the daguerreotype of his painting, but there is nothing to suggest that he used a daguerreotype camera during the war or that he used daguerreotype studies for his sketches and prints of battle scenes. Kendall's preface to his and Nebel's great collaborative work, *The War Between the United States and Mexico Illustrated*, emphasizes the care with which the illustrations were composed. Kendall makes no mention of photographic studies for the prints and, with his great concern for fidelity and accuracy, it seems likely that he would have noted any daguerreotype views had he known they existed. Indeed, Nebel's prints are far more grand in scope and richly detailed than any daguerreotypes could have been.

Only two working photographers (and they may be one and the same) can be placed in or near Saltillo in 1847. A lithographic portrait of Zachary Taylor published in New York in 1847 carries the printed legend, "Fac simile of Gl. Zach. Taylor from a Daguereotype full lenght likeness taken at Buena Vista, by J. H. Wm. Smith" (fig. 30). Smith is an elusive figure not found in military records or American military newspapers, but his presence at the Buena Vista campground suggests that he might have been based in Saltillo, the town closest to

Figure 28   Opposite
Photographer Unknown
Rancheros — Gregg's Commerce of Prairies
Hand-colored sixth-plate daguerreotype of a
lithograph
Cat. No. 66
Courtesy of Yale Western Americana Collection,
Beinecke Rare Book and Manuscript Library

Figure 29   Above
A. Halbert
Mexican Girls
Engraving
From George Wilkins Kendall, *Narrative of the
Texan Santa Fe Expedition* (New York: Harper
and Brothers, 1844)
Amon Carter Museum Library

Figure 30
After a daguerreotype by J. H. Wm. Smith
Rough and Ready As He Is
Lithograph
Cat. No. 44
Courtesy of Special Collections Division, The
University of Texas at Arlington Libraries,
Arlington, Texas

the battle site. He may be the Philadelphia daguerreotypist named William H. Smith who is credited with making the photographic image from which a later mezzotint of Taylor was made in 1848.[33]

There is also an unnamed daguerreotypist referred to in the correspondence of Captain Kenton Harper and Brevet Major John Fulton Reynolds. Harper, a member of the First Virginia Volunteer Regiment, was stationed in and around Saltillo in 1847 and 1848. On June 15, 1847, he wrote his wife from Camp Buena Vista, telling her that he was sending home a "likeness." A month later he wrote that he "had three likenesses taken to send home," all "thought to be excellent," but could not find a reliable way to transport them to Virgina. On October 7, he had yet another portrait made in Saltillo, which the accommodating daguerreotypist delivered to him several days later at Camp Buena Vista. The different images presented him in different moods, Harper wrote his wife, and provided a topic of conversation around camp. The third, he told her, is "thought here to be decidedly the best of all."[34]

An avid letter writer, Harper seems to have intended for his portraits to provide his family a visual analogue to his written reports. On December 9, 1847, he responded to his wife's comments on the first picture she had received. "I do not think there is the change in my appearance which you conclude has taken place from my daguerreotype. Perhaps when you get the other likenesses sent, this may be corrected. I know I have been in better health generally than when at home, but it is true I have been subjected to a great many cares and harrassments, and they may have left their impress upon my features."[35]

Reynolds, a member of the Third U.S. Artillery recognized for his gallantry at the battle of Buena Vista, was apparently photographed by the same unidentified photographer, and his correspondence provides the only evidence that the man was, indeed, an American. Writing to his sister from Camp Buena Vista on July 25, 1847, just a few weeks after Harper first mentioned the Saltillo photographer, Reynolds noted that he had had his "daguerreotype taken by a Yankee in Saltillo." He thought it rather "cross-looking" but promised to send it along as soon as he could find a reliable courier. He finally found a willing messenger in September and in February 1848 received confirmation of the daguerreotype's receipt from his sister in Pennsylvania. "I am glad to hear that it reached you in safety," Reynolds wrote. "I have had an other and larger one taken which I hope may please you better."[36]

Harper's and Reynolds's correspondence provides the only known literary references to the likely daguerreotypist of the Amon Carter and Yale images. The possibility that the daguerreotypist they saw actually took the other images is suggested by the coincidence of place and time and by a brief and tantalizing reference in Harper's letter of January 29, 1848, "Colonel Hamtramck has heard of the receipt of his [daguerreotype], sent at the same time." The whereabouts of Harper's portraits are unknown, but a daguerreotype of Hamtramck is included in the Amon Carter collection (cat. no. 68).[37]

By the time of the Mexican War, portrait daguerreotypes were a ubiquitous feature of American life, and it is not surprising that American troops should patronize the "Yankee" photographers who followed them to Mexico. Indeed, a popular print of 1846 (fig. 31) suggests that many military men had their portraits made before leaving for Mexico to leave behind as mementoes for loved ones. In the print, a young man who has joined the New York volunteers to escape his debts bids farewell to his sweetheart on the eve of his departure for Mexico and the West. "Good bye Liz! Here's my doggerotype likeness! I'd stand treat but I haint got the ghost of a real cent left, our uniforms is so very expensive."[38] A photographic

ONE OF THE CALIFORNIAN BO-HOYS TAKING LEAVE OF HIS GAL.

Figure 31
Edward W. Clay
One of the Californian Bo-Hoys Taking Leave of His Gal
Toned lithograph (hand colored) by Henry R. Robinson, 1846
Amon Carter Museum [24.77]

Figure 32
Photographer Unknown
Exeter, N.H., Volunteers
Quarter-plate daguerreotype, c. 1846
Amon Carter Museum [79.33]

journal relates the story of another dissolute volunteer, determined to leave a daguerreotype with his "lady-love," who showed up drunk at a photographic studio on a gray, cloudy day. The resulting daguerreotype had a "dark and misty" appearance. But the operator assured the young man that "when the weather became clear and his head also the picture would assume a clearness not then discernable, which fully satisfied the soldier and he departed for Mexico."[39] On occasion, large groups of soldiers were photographed upon their departure. Daguerreotypes like the Amon Carter Museum's image of the Exeter, New Hampshire, volunteers beginning their long trip south (fig. 32), were intended to serve less as private mementoes than as historic documents.[40]

If some soldiers left daguerreotypes at home as a kind of hedge against the threat of mortality, others carried daguerreotypes into the field as keepsakes. Colonel Robert Treat Paine, commanding officer of the North Carolina Volunteers and the subject of one of the Amon Carter daguerreotypes (fig. 33), showed daguerreotypes of his wife and daughter to the wife of the gardener at Arispe's Mills, a flour mill near Saltillo where Paine and his regiment were stationed through late 1847. The woman requested to see Mrs. Paine's likeness so often, Paine finally wrote his wife, that "I cannot consent to submit you too frequently to

Figure 33
Photographer Unknown
Col. Paine, N. C. Reg. in Mexican War
Quarter-plate daguerreotype
Cat. No. 73
Amon Carter Museum [81.65/17]

the gaze of strangers."[41] Daguerreotype portraits of sweethearts (whether real or imagined) were valued just as much as those of wives. In late 1846, a volunteer from the Kentucky regiment wrote to a friend at home, "I miss one thing very much out here, and if you have a chance, you must send me one — that is the daguerreotype likeness of some pretty girl. I am not very particular which one. Almost all the boys have one with the exception of myself, and it puts me to considerable trouble borrowing them, so that I will not forget what our girls look like. If you can find any young ladey who will send me a copy, do so by all means and if I ever reach Kentucky, I will reciprocate the favor."[42]

The advertisements of photographers such as Halsey and Betts suggest a market in souvenir daguerreotypes of notable architectural sites, particularly churches and palaces, and post-mortem views. While copy work was not advertised, it seems to have been sought after by at least some Americans familiar with this use for daguerreotypy. Artillery officer Robert Anderson wrote to his wife of a "lovable" painting that he had seen on exhibition in Tacubaya. "If I can get a good daguerreotypist here," he wrote, "I will endeavor to bring you a view of this charming work."[43]

Nonetheless, it seems safe to surmise that most of the daguerreotypes made by Americans in Mexico during the war, like those made at home, were portraits. Kenton Harper may have been unusual in being photographed so many times. But his interest in sending home a daguerreotype portrait to assure his wife of his physical well-being, much as a modern-day soldier might telephone home to give reassurance that all is well, suggests why American troops sought the services of the itinerant daguerreotypists floating through Mexico.

Ultimately, despite the scant trails of evidence left by a number of daguerreotypists working in Mexico between 1846 and 1848, there is nothing to connect a particular, named figure to the surviving images of the Mexican War, the world's first photographs of war. More important, perhaps, is to know what impact these daguerreotypes had on an American public that hungered for accurate visual images of the war; to understand what kind of audience they had, what influence they had on popular perceptions of the war, and how they influenced other graphic representations of military activity.

Americans' visual knowledge of the war came from four main sources: individually issued prints, paintings, the sketchy renderings reproduced in newspapers and books, and, finally, daguerreotypes. Accuracy was an important standard of judgment for images in any of these media, as Rick Stewart's analysis of printed war imagery suggests, and great importance was placed on the impressions of the eyewitness observer who could record what he actually saw.

American newspapers avidly followed the activities of artists who went to Mexico, for their work promised to include the most complete and detailed information. The New Orleans *Daily Picayune* wished good luck to painter William Garl Brown, Jr., as he set off for Monterrey in the spring of 1847 to capture a likeness of General Taylor, and in frequent dispatches to the paper the *Picayune's* Mexico correspondent, J. E. Durivage, charted Brown's progress. "Although you cannot get a glimpse of the general *in propria persona* before the end of November," he wrote in early July, "you will soon see his 'picture in little.' A very accurate likeness of him has been taken by Mr. Brown." Reporting later on a painting of Taylor and his staff, Durivage noted, "the figures are all in miniature, and executed with a most life-like faithfulness and exquisite finish." The portraits, along with Brown's painting of the Buena Vista battle scene, would make a "very handsome and interesting" exhibition upon the artist's return to the United States. When Brown returned to his home town of Richmond, Virginia, in September 1847, curiosity about his paintings was piqued when it was learned that Taylor himself had pronounced Brown's portrait "*the best* likeness that has been taken of him." And, indeed, the paintings earned praise from the crowds that paid twenty-five cents a head to see them in a rented exhibition hall.[44]

The work of the Philadelphia painter Jesse Atwood generated similar enthusiasm. The army newspaper *American Pioneer* followed his trip to Monterrey in May 1847 and reported that his two portraits of General Taylor were "excellent likenesses." Taylor himself provided the artist with a testimonial letter, thanking him for "the undeserved compliment you have paid me in the danger, fatigue, labor and trouble you have undergone and encountered in traveling from the City of Philadelphia to this place for the purpose of painting my portrait." When Atwood's paintings were exhibited to paying crowds in New Orleans and New York during the summer of 1847, they met with mixed reviews. But it was generally agreed that Atwood deserved special recognition for his efforts. The New York *Herald* noted, "The artist who encountered the toil and dangers of a journey to Monterey, for the purpose of getting a true likeness of the old hero ought to be well repaid for his outlay of money and labor."[45]

The public seemed fascinated with every sort of on-the-spot visual reportage. Two French painters, intent on creating a large painting of the battle of Resaca de la Palma, were praised because their "chief personages on the scene will be a foot and a half high which will amply suffice to preserve the resemblance."[46] The misadventures of another Frenchman were also followed in the New Orleans press. The supply wagon of a sculptor named Garbeille was ambushed while the artist was en route to Monterrey to do a bust of General Taylor. Garbeille lost all of his supplies and was forced to use sculpting tools carved from mules' bones. Apparently, though, he did not lose his sense of humor. The sign on his studio door read, "The unfinished mouth and nose of Gen. Taylor compose part of our present stock."[47]

The accuracy of these renderings was of great interest to the troops in Mexico as well as to the Americans back home. The Saltillo *Picket Guard* made no mention of the daguerreotypes apparently made in that town in 1847, but the unofficial army paper heaped ridicule on the images published in a New York paper that were clearly *not* based on eyewitness views. General Taylor's "common soldier's light blue overalls" were transformed into a full military suit with "huge epaulettes," and a picture of a Mexican crowd, it said, looked more like "a group of Swiss emigrants just landed at the wharf."[48]

In view of such interest in accuracy and the attention given to the artists who traveled to Mexico, braving physical and financial hardships to get eyewitness views of the war, it is noteworthy that the activities of American daguerreotypists in Mexico received no attention in the American press. They, of course, were capturing the most accurate eyewitness images of all, recording the minute details of faces, uniforms, city streets, and regional geography on the polished surface of the daguerreotype plate.

In contrast, the American press and public gave great attention to the work of the daguerreotypists who photographed the Mexican War heroes as they returned home. Lieutenant Colonel Charles A. May, a hero of the battle at Resaca de la Palma, "was nearly run down by the daguerreotypists in Philadelphia, who were anxious to get his likeness" when he passed through town in the summer of 1847. Photographers lucky enough to gather a sufficient number of portraits staged public exhibitions, similar to those of painters like Atwood or Brown. In Richmond, Virginia, for example, William Pratt advertised a "SPLENDID EXHIBITION OF THE STATESMEN AND HEROES OF THE MEXICAN WAR," featuring General Taylor, Santa Anna, President Polk, and "other celebrated individuals from all parts of the world." The arrival of a new daguerreotype of Taylor "FROM NEW ORLEANS, BY EXPRESS!" merited a special notice in the paper.[49]

Likewise, while only one daguerreotype made in Mexico served as the basis for an American print (J. H. William Smith's portrait of Taylor at Buena Vista), many more American-made daguerreotypes of war figures served as the basis for the woodcuts that appeared in contemporary books.[50]

Although no extant newspaper illustrations based on Mexican War daguerreotypes have been located, the possibility that some might exist is suggested by a satirical passage in an 1862 novel by Albany Fonblanque, Jr. A fictional correspondent for the *New York Illustrated Thunder* tells a friendly maid how he obtained his successful daguerrian views of the Mexican War. "Between you and me, I was only one day and night in the Filibuster's camp; but there was an old ruin, a village and a forest near at hand, so I took 20 views of each from different points, and one or the other did very well for every place mentioned in the news. No one in New York knows the difference. It was much the safest way of doing business and saved travelling expenses."[51]

Testimony given more than thirty years after the fact suggests that the military painter James Walker may have made daguerrian studies for his large canvases of battle scenes. General James T. Shields, who appears in the several versions of Walker's painting *The Storming of Chapultepec,* recalled in 1878, "We were taken just as we stood, by a photographer who followed the army to take sketches whenever he could. It was afterwards transferred to canvas. . . . The artist happened to get his camera in focus just while I was talking to Gen. Quitman, and so I apprehend it [the painting] a more correct battle-piece than the most of those that ornament our public buildings." While Walker may have been making pencil sketches with the aid of a camera obscura, Shields's testimony (possibly clouded by his experiences in more frequently photographed Civil War battles) suggests that the artist was making quick views of complex scenes, something that could be accomplished only with a photographic camera. If so, Walker's paintings would be the only ones known to have been made with the aid of a daguerreotype view.[52]

The fact that there are no known American exhibitions of daguerreotypes made in Mexico during the war, and only one recorded print made after one of these photographs, suggests that the photographers themselves had a limited awareness of the potential market for their work. The daguerreotypist of the Saltillo views in the Yale and Amon Carter collections must have had some sense of the timeliness of his pictures, as indicated by his variant views of such noteworthy subjects as Webster's battalion and Wool's march. But there is no indication that he ever reached beyond a purely local market to forge connections with the journalists and printmakers who could make his work better known. Nor is there any suggestion that he had a flair for self-promotion. Perhaps he and his counterparts lacked the financial means to gather a large collection of images, return to the United States, and hire an exhibition hall. Perhaps they had no sense of the tremendous American interest in eyewitness views of the war. They seem simply to have created an immediate customer demand, filled it, then gone on to other projects. The brief, elusive careers of most of the

American photographers working in Mexico suggests that most of these men were not committed to the photographic profession. Photography was a trial venture, an occasional sideline that supplemented their work as dentists or merchants.

American public attitude may also have contributed to the lack of a demand or market for the Mexican War daguerreotypes. Although Americans valued the seemingly accurate visual representations of the war they could see in painting or daguerreotype exhibitions, prints, newspapers, or books, no "truthful" rendering of the war or its heroes ever excited as much passion as a kind of purely patriotic painting used in popular celebrations of military victories. Called "transparencies," these were large painted images on window shades or wax-primed sheets of linen or cotton, hung from the sides of buildings and lit from behind with hundreds or even thousands of candles. This was ephemeral art: the paintings on fabric frayed and, not infrequently, caught on fire. While none of the transparencies are known to survive, it is clear that they played an important role in establishing popular images of the war. They created a grandly scaled iconography that had little to do with the small, finely detailed images of military people and events preserved on a daguerreotype plate.

The transparencies were made as part of "illuminations," large public celebrations held to mark the country's military triumphs. These popular political demonstrations, including parades, public speeches, bonfires, and fireworks, were part of a well-established Anglo-American tradition. American colonists had used transparencies painted with popular political cartoons and icons during the demonstrations that preceded the American Revolution.[53]

The most popular Mexican War transparencies invoked the same symbols made familiar in prints. The Baltimore papers reported that the favorite subject for that city's illumination in April 1847 was an illustration of General Taylor's oft-quoted words, "A little more grape, Capt. Bragg," though another transparency received more attention because it managed to combine so many potent political symbols into a single image. The painting depicted "Gens. Taylor and Scott on horseback, with the fields of Buena Vista and Vera Cruz, in the background, also, the castle of San Juan de Ulua, with the American flag flying from the turrets and receiving a salute from the United States fleet. . . . The whole is surmounted by an American eagle, whose widespread wings open to warrant protection in the whole country so bravely won." A similar transparency, measuring twenty by seventeen feet, was featured in a Philadelphia illumination along with canvases depicting the charge of "Old Rough and Ready" at Buena Vista, the battle of Monterrey, and an image of General Taylor on horseback trampling a Mexican flag in the dust. In Washington, D.C., the transparencies were equally patriotic if a bit more partisan. Senator Thomas Hart Benton decorated his house with transparencies featuring the adventures of the volunteers from his home state of Missouri and a flag carried to a peak in the Rocky Mountains by his son-in-law J. C. Frémont. An ornate transparency placed on the New Orleans Municipal Hall placed Scott and Taylor squarely within the pantheon of American heroes. Between full-length likenesses of the two generals was a tablet recording the battles of the American Revolution and the War of 1812, and presiding over all was a painted bust of the original American military hero, George Washington.[54]

The illuminations were elaborately orchestrated and were obvious fire hazards. For an illumination in New York in the spring of 1847, the owners of one building reportedly lit twelve hundred candles in seven seconds. To encourage widespread public participation in the New Orleans illumination of May 1847, a local insurance company assured its customers that "the contemplated illumination...*is not considered as an infringement of the policies.*" The bureaucrats in Washington were more cautious. A reporter noted that "it was considered best not to illuminate the offices of the public department, because they contain the valuable records of the government, and most of them are not fire-proof, and it was not considered proper to make any discrimination between them." But not all federal buildings were sacred, for "the President's House was brilliantly illuminated."[55]

These illuminations provided occasions for mass gatherings, speeches, music, and fervent expressions of patriotism. Despite the American public's avowed taste for truthful artistic representations of wartime events, the evocative symbols depicted in the illuminations proved tremendously popular. How could daguerreotypes compete for the interest of the general public? They were small, difficult to see, and best viewed privately with carefully controlled light. Instead of a melange of patriotic symbols, they depicted tiny, unidentifiable soldiers, unpeopled city views, formal portraits, or Mexican churches. No slogans or titles or detailed keys clarified their meaning or their journalistic importance. They were incapable of inspiring the kind of patriotism evoked by the large, boldly painted banners that lined public streets during the mass gatherings of the illuminations. The very thing that made daguerreotypes attractive to particular viewers — their literal accuracy — made them unappealing to a vast public audience that also demanded a patriotic symbology of the war.

Thus while the surviving daguerreotypes of the Mexican War are the world's first photographs of war and represent the first extensive photographic coverage of a newsworthy event, they do not mark the birth of modern photojournalism or the end of the lithograph's importance as a conveyor of news and information. Even prints based on eyewitness views were veiled, as Rick Stewart suggests, in the romantic spirit of the age. Sketch artists and printmakers had a free hand to embellish; they could add American flags, create heroic poses, elaborate on military scenes to enhance an impression of American invincibility and patriotic nationalism. Even as these prints conveyed relatively accurate information about uniforms or troop formations or the topography of the battlefield, they catered to a public that insisted on seeing the war in more grandiose, symbolic terms as an expression of America's manifest destiny. They thus mediated between the public's interest in accurate eyewitness accounts and its concurrent interest in a romantic, more symbolic rendering of the war and its heroes.

The very process of daguerreotypy denied photographers the opportunity to mediate between these two poles of public sentiment. What the photographer saw was what appeared on the daguerreotype plate. He might add hand-applied coloring to emphasize particular features of the scene. But unlike a printmaker, he had no way of altering facial expressions, rearranging poses, or adding patriotic accoutrements to the scene once it was recorded. Moreover, he had no way to attach language to his picture. The creators of illuminated transparencies could use words to reiterate the connection between Mexican War heroes and their forebears of the American Revolution, and printmakers could use elaborate captions to supply a stirring, patriotic context for their scenes of battle. Likewise, the authors of books and publishers of newspapers could supply literary captions for their reproductions of Mexican War scenes, portraits, and maps to shape public understanding of the imagery. At best, a daguerreotypist could only glue a small identifying caption to his image or its protective case.

By the early 1850s, the most ambitious daguerreotypists documenting American expansionism in California and the West had learned to overcome the inherent drawbacks of the small and private daguerrian image by presenting their work to the public in rented halls with themselves present to describe scenes or even deliver narrative lectures. If grandiose ideas could not be conveyed by the image they could at least be suggested by a published brochure or the spoken word.[56] The American daguerreotypists working in Mexico during the war were not so resourceful. They never found a way to create an audience for their work either through public presentations or graphic reproductions.

Yet only a decade and a half later, as Americans took up arms in a vast civil war, the possibilities of photography as a tool of journalism were firmly established. In 1855, Roger Fenton and James Robertson had shown the British public the potential uses of wartime photography with their paper prints of Crimean War scenes. They made use of a new technology that allowed photographers to record their images on glass plate negatives from which countless paper prints could be made. This negative/positive process had important repercussions for the photographer and the popularity of the photographic print. The ability to make numerous prints from a single negative made photographers more willing to take risks in securing remote or dangerous views because the potential payoff in terms of commercial sales was much increased. The existence of multiple views permitted the photographer to market single images or elaborate albums, and the common practice of mounting paper photographs on stiff paper or boards permitted him to add a title, description, or evocative text to shape the viewer's understanding of the image. By the 1860s, the American photographer also had more opportunity to reproduce his work in other media. The ease with which a photographic image on paper could be viewed (in contrast to the mirror-like image of the daguerreotype) increased the appeal of the photograph as a source for the engraver or lithographer, and the growth of America's illustrated press provided a new outlet for these graphic reproductions of photographic imagery. Indeed, the subsequent rise of photography as the most important visual medium for the timely dissemination of news and the concurrent decline in the importance of sketchbook journalism directly parallel the increasing sophistication of photographic reproduction technologies in the late nineteenth and early twentieth centuries.

Photography has become central to our understanding and recollection of recent wars, allowing us to "remember" events we never experienced through the searing images of pain and heroism branded upon our collective memory. The world's first photographs of war had no such power. Neither the daguerreotypists working in Mexico during the war of 1846-48, nor their audience, had any sense of the potential uses for the craft of photography or the potential impact of the photographic image.

Notes

1. Robert Taft, *Photography and the American Scene: A Social History, 1839-1889* (1938; rpt., New York: Dover Publications, 1964), p. 485 n. 246a. More detailed descriptions of these daguerreotypes can be found in the catalogue. A recent scholar of the history of war photography continues to name the Mexican War daguerreotypes as the earliest photographs of war. See Frances Fralin, *The Indelible Image: Photographs of War, 1846-Present* (New York: Harry N. Abrams for the Corcoran Gallery of Art, 1985), p. 12.

2. Extant examples from this period of other daguerreotypes documenting scenes for their news value are extremely scarce. One notable example is Carl Ferdinand Stelzner's daguerreotype of the ruins of Hamburg following the great fire of May 1842 (Staatliche Landesbildstelle, Hamburg).

3. George Miles to the author, Sept. 6, 1983. One story suggests that Smith found the daguerreotypes "in a wooden case in the attic of an old mansion in Yonkers, N. Y." See James D. Horan, *Mathew Brady: Historian with a Camera* (New York: Crown Publishers, 1955), p. 90. Queries to the Hudson River Museum (formerly the Yonkers Museum with which Smith was affiliated) have not yielded any further information on the daguerreotypes.

4. Detailed information on the content and dating of these images is included in the catalogue.

5. See cat. no. 93 and Houston G. Jones, *North Carolina Illustrated* (Chapel Hill: University of North Carolina Press, 1983), p. 222.

6. For further information on the plates, see the catalogue. For information on Gardiner, see Robert Hallowell Gardiner, *Early Recollections of Robert Hallowell Gardiner, 1782-1864* (Hallowell, Maine: Printed for R. H. Gardiner and W.T. Gardiner, 1936) and Rt. Rev. George Burgess, D.D., "Notice of Robert Hallowell Gardiner," *Collections of the Maine Historical Society,* vol. 7 (Bath: Published for the Society, 1876), pp. 403-28. The earliest published view of Oaklands is taken from a daguerreotype by C. T. Rogers and appears in J. W. Hanson, *History of Gardiner and Pittston* (Gardiner: Wm. Palmer, 1852), p. 221. A contemporary view of Oaklands, which is still owned and lived in by the Gardiner family, can be found in Wayne Andrews, *Architecture in America* (New York: Atheneum, 1960), p. 52.

7. Information on John William Tudor Gardiner's military service can be found in his official service record in the National Archives (Records of the Adjutant General's Office, 1780s-1917, RG 94, CB Files: G378 CB 1866) and in the voluminous papers generated by his widow Annie's 1879 claim for a military pension. See also J. W. T. Gardiner to [Geo. Brook?], March 26, 1847, in "Letters Received by the Adjutant General," National Archives microfilm M567, roll 377; and George W. Cullum, "John W. T. Gardiner, Class of 1840," undated typescript, Gardiner Family Archives, Gardiner, Maine.

8. Tudor [John William Tudor Gardiner] to Frederick, July 13, 1854, Gardiner Family Archives.

9. See cat. no. 58. Gardiner maintained a clippings file on the shipwreck that is preserved in the family archives.

10. Tudor [John William Tudor Gardiner] to Mother, May 31, 1856, Gardiner Family Archives.

11. Taft, *Photography and the American Scene,* p. 485 n. 246a. Richard Rudisill called attention to the presence of three itinerant American photographers in wartime Mexico in his book *Mirror Image: The Influence of the Daguerreotype on American Society* (Albuquerque: University of New Mexico Press, 1971), p. 131. However, until now the most thorough consideration of American photographers in Mexico during this time has been the excellent but virtually unknown essay by Arthur Woodward, "Our First Military Photographers," in *The Westerners New York Posse Brand Book* 12, no. 3 (1965): 62-66. Mr. Woodward's research cards, on deposit in the Amon Carter Museum Library, proved an excellent starting point for my own research.

12. Howard T. Fisher and Marion H. Fisher, eds., *Life in Mexico: The Letters of Fanny Calderón de la Barca* (Garden City, N.Y.: Doubleday, 1966), pp. 356-57, 748.

13. John Lloyd Stephens, *Incidents of Travel in Yucatan,* 2 vols. (1843; rpt., New York: Dover, 1963), 1:100.

14. Ibid., pp. 54-64.

15. E. White and Co. in New Orleans advertised that they would ship photographic supplies to any part of the United States, Mexico, or the West Indies; see New Orleans *Picayune,* Feb. 25, 1848.

16. "Diary of Richard Carr," Archives of British Columbia, references courtesy Peter Palmquist, Arcata, California. See also Palmquist's article "An Account of California's First Photographer" in Peter E. Palmquist, ed., *Photography in the West* (Manhattan, Kans.: Sunflower University Press, 1987), pp. 102-5.

17. *El Siglo XIX,* Sept. 11, 1845 (citation courtesy Rosa Casanova); Ralph Greenhill and Andrew Birrell, *Canadian Photography: 1839-1920* (Toronto: The Coach House Press, 1979), pp. 24-25. Some evidence suggests that Halsey may have known Richard Carr. Carr's journal entry of August 12, 1846, notes that he wrote to "Mr. Alsey" on the tenth of the month. He received a reply from "Mr. Halsey" on the twenty-seventh. Carr was living in Oaxaca at the time and it seems possible that he may have met Halsey or learned that he was a possible source of supplies.

An Andrew J. (or alternatively "I") Halsey was interviewed in Mexico City in 1852 as part of the United States government's inquiry into the complicated and questionable business affairs of George A. Gardiner and his brother, the occasional photographer John Charles Gardiner (see below, n. 23). A deposition from another informant in the case suggested that George Gardiner had lived in Veracruz in 1840 with "a writing-master by the name of Halsey, whose given name I think was J[ohn] B." Such connections suggest the possibility that Halsey may have had a brother who preceded him to Mexico. See the following correspondence in papers relating to the Gardiner case at the Beinecke Library, Yale University (WA MSS S-544): P. R. Fendall to J. Prescott Hall, June 7, 1852; Fendall to Daniel Webster, March 19, 1852; Fendall to [?], April 20, 1852. See also the deposition from C. Markoe in "The Gardiner Investigation" [Rep. No. 1 to accompany bill H. R. 326, 32nd Congress, 2nd Session], p. 125.

18. *Diario Oficial,* May 3-11, 1846; *Diario del Gobierno,* Feb. 15, 1847, and periodically until April 1, 1847; *Daily American Star,* Sept. 12, Oct. 26, 1847.

19. *El Siglo XIX,* Dec. 12, 1850; *Diario de Avisos,* April 22, 1858; *Mexican Extraordinary,* Aug. 1861; citations courtesy Rosa Casanova. Although none of Halsey's American military portraits have been identified, two of his Mexican portraits survive. His photographic portraits of General Llave and Cosme Varela are in the National Museum of History, Mexico City (Rosa Casanova to the author, June 29, 1986).

20. *Republic of Rio Grande and Friend of the People,* June 16, 1846; *American Flag,* Oct. 14, 1846, March 3, 1847; Margaret Denton Smith and Mary Louise Tucker, *Photography in New Orleans: The Early Years, 1840-1865* (Baton Rouge: Louisiana State University Press, 1982), p. 167.

21. *American Flag,* Sept. 21, Oct. 24, Oct. 28, Dec. 5, Dec. 19, 1846.

22. Veracruz *American Eagle,* April 6, 1847; "A Letter from Vera Cruz in 1847," *Southwestern Historical Quarterly* 18 (Oct. 1914): 217; Puebla *American Star No. 2,* July 15, 1847. Polock's studio is noted in the *American Star No. 2,* June 20, 1847. His subsequent fate is unknown, though two other references bear investigation. A photographer named "H. Pollack" is noted in Baltimore in 1854 (see *Humphrey's Journal,* March 1, 1854, p. 352), and "Lewis Pollack" is noted as a photographer in the 1868 New Orleans city directory (see Smith and Tucker, *Photography in New Orleans,* p. 168).

23. Gardiner's photographic activities are noted in the Puebla *American Star No. 2,* July 15, 1847. His fraudulent dental practice is noted in the *National Intelligencer,* May 2, 1853. John Charles Gardiner was implicated in the case against his brother George, who was found to have submitted false claims to the Board of Commissioners established to settle claims from Americans who had lost property in Mexico during the war. George Gardiner received an initial settlement of $428,750. Further investigations, however, concluded that Gardiner's claim was fraudulent; that the mine he claimed to have lost had never, in fact, existed. Gardiner's claim was the subject of a Congressional investigation ("The Gardiner Investigation," Rep. No. 1 to accompany HR No. 326, 32nd Congress, 2nd Session) and a subsequent trial for perjury in the circuit court of the District of Columbia (*The United States* vs. *George A. Gardiner,* 1853). Upon being convicted of criminal charges in a Washington court in March 1854, George A. Gardiner swallowed strychnine. He died a few hours later in his jail cell. (See New York *Times,* March 6, 1854.) Unfortunately, the voluminous testimony collected in his various trials reveals nothing about his brother's brief photographic activities.

24. *American Star No. 2,* July 25, 1847; Mexico City *American Star,* Sept. 28, 1847.

25. *American Star,* Oct. 5, Oct. 29, 1847.

26. *American Star,* Dec. 17, 1847; *Diario del Gobierno,* Sept. 1-6, 1847; *American Star,* Jan. 11, 1848. Kenneth Finkel, in *Nineteenth-Century Photography in Philadelphia* (New York: Dover, 1980), notes a [John] Betts in partnership with Frederick DeBourg Richards in Philadelphia from 1854 to 1857. In conversation with the author (July 7, 1988) he suggests an uncertainty as to Betts's first name, but notes that the quality of Richards's collaborative work with Betts hints of Betts's prior photographic experience. A daguerreotype (c. 1857) by the Wilmington firm of [Benjamin] Betts and [Nelson] Carlisle in the collection of the J. Paul Getty Museum, Malibu, California, is misattributed to Charles J. Betts. See the museum's *Journal* 14 (1986): 268, and Jon M. Williams, "Daguerreotypists, Ambrotypists, and Photographers in Wilmington, Delaware, 1842-1859," *Delaware History* 18 (Spring-Summer 1979): 191. The proximity of Philadelphia and Wilmington suggests that John and Benjamin Betts may be one and the same. A. L. Cosmes de Cosio may be the Antonio Cosmes referred to in Lee Fontanella, *La Historia de la Fotografía en España desde sus Orígenes hasta 1900* (Madrid: El Viso, 1981), pp. 79, 132, 163, 215, 255. A man identified only as "M. Cosmo of Cossio" is cited as the inventor of a glass transparency process in the *Photographic Art Journal,* Nov. 1852, p. 322.

27. Floyd Rinhart and Marion Rinhart, *The American Daguerreotype* (Athens: University of Georgia Press, 1981), p. 403; Veracruz *Sun of Anahuac,* Sept. 17, 1847 (citation courtesy Art Woodward reference collection, Amon Carter Museum); Veracruz *Free American,* Nov. 22, 1847; New Orleans *Picayune,* Jan. 1, 1848; *Daily American Star,* Feb. 10, 1848. A handwritten label affixed to the inside of the case of a daguerrian portrait of Captain George

Ellis Pugh (collection of Dr. William Schultz, Olmstead Township, Ohio) notes that the image was made in Veracruz on September 16, 1847. The coincidence of dates suggests that this portrait might be by Noessel. If so, it would be the only known daguerreotype attributable to him. Two wood engravings done from daguerreotypes Noessel made in New Orleans of Samuel Walker and Benjamin McCulloch appear in Samuel C. Reid, Jr., *Scouting Expeditions of McCulloch's Texas Rangers* (Philadelphia: G. B. Zieber & Co., 1847).

28. *Diary and Letters of Josiah Gregg,* edited by Maurice Garland Fulton, 2 vols. (Norman: University of Oklahoma Press, 1941-44), 2:188-89.

29. Gregg, *Diary and Letters,* 1:198-99, 2:106.

30. Ibid., 1:218, 2:213-14.

31. George Wilkins Kendall, *Narrative of the Texan Santa Fe Expedition* (New York: Harper & Bros., 1844), opp. p. 324.

32. The evidence for Nebel's presence on this excursion is problematic. The original edition of Calderón de la Barca's memoirs, published in London in 1843, omits many proper names. The entry for November 21, 1840 reads, "Yesterday we went to Chapultapec, C____n and I, M. de G____, and M. de N____, to take views with the Daguerreotype." The editors of the modern English-language edition of the text relied on a hand-annotated copy of the first American printing to fill in many of the blank names. They had "no doubt" that the annotations originated with the author herself, and they identified the mysterious M. de N____as Carl Nebel. (Fisher and Fisher, *Life in Mexico,* pp. 679-80 n. 16, p. 748 n. 3.) Nebel, who lived in Mexico from 1829 to 1834, was back in Mexico City in 1840 prosecuting a lawsuit against a publisher who had brought out an unauthorized version of his work. The editor of the modern Mexican edition of the text, however, identifies M. de N____as M. de Normoso. No source for this name is given. (Felipe Teixidor, ed., *La Vida en Mexico Durante una Residencia de Dos Anos en Ese Pais por Madame Calderón de la Barca* [Mexico City: Editorial Porrua, 1959], 2:305.)

33. John Sartain's mezzotint of "Major-General Zachary Taylor/President of the United States" is in the Amon Carter Museum collection (8.82). William H. Smith, daguerreotypist, is listed in *McElroys Philadelphia Directory for 1849* (Philadelphia: Edward C. and John Biddle, 1849).

34. Captain Kenton Harper's papers are in the Southern Historical Collection, University of North Carolina, Chapel Hill. These references from letters to his wife Eleanor Calhoun Harper of June 15, July 25, Oct. 7, and Oct. 19, 1847 (and all subsequent references from these papers) were provided to me through the courtesy of Tom Kailbourn, Wellsville, N.Y.

35. Harper to Eleanor Calhoun Harper, Dec. 9, 1847.

36. John Fulton Reynolds to Kate Reynolds, July 25, Sept. 5, 1847, Feb. 13, 1848. Reynolds's papers are in the archives of Franklin and Marshall College, Lancaster, Pennsylvania; citations provided by Tom Kailbourn. A daguerreotype of Reynolds in the college archives bears conflicting notations indicating that it was made in Saltillo in 1847 and in Mexico City in 1848. A note indicating that it was "sent 9-12-1847" suggests that it might, indeed, be the daguerreotype Reynolds refers to in his letter of Sept. 5, 1847, when he notes that he had just located someone to transport a daguerreotype home.

37. Harper to Eleanor Calhoun Harper, Jan. 29, 1848. A review of the Hamtramck Papers at Duke University yields no mention of a daguerreotype or daguerreotypist.

38. See the reproduction in David Nevin, *The Mexican War* (Alexandria, Va.: Time-Life Books, 1978), p. 117.

39. N. G. Burgess, "Amusing Incidents in the Life of a Daguerrian Artist," *Photographic and Fine Art Journal,* June 1855, p. 190.

40. A similar group daguerreotype, known through literary references only, was made of Company D of the Third Regiment of Missouri Mounted Volunteers in St. Charles, Missouri, in June 1847 as they began their march to Santa Fe. (Ken Cooper to the author, July 28, 1988.)

41. Colonel Robert Treat Paine to Lavinia Paine, Sept. 15, Sept. 30, 1847, Paine Papers, Southern Historical Collection, University of North Carolina at Chapel Hill. Citations courtesy Tom Kailbourn.

42. Liberty, Missouri, *Weekly Tribune,* Dec. 5, 1846, p. 1; citation courtesy Art Woodward reference collection, Amon Carter Museum.

43. Robert Anderson, *An Artillery Officer in the Mexican War, 1846-7* (1911; rpt., Freeport, N.Y.: Books for Libraries Press, 1971), p. 304. Reference courtesy Tom Kailbourn.

44. New Orleans *Daily Picayune,* June 3, July 6, Aug. 3, 1847; Richmond *Enquirer,* Sept. 14, Sept. 21, 1847. The painting of Taylor and his staff is now in the collection of the National Portrait Gallery, Washington, D. C.

45. Monterrey *American Pioneer,* May 31, 1847; New York *Herald,* Aug. 12, 1847. Other reviews are in the New Orleans *Daily Picayune,* June 20, June 23, 1847, New York *Herald,* Aug. 18, 1847, and Richmond *Enquirer,* Aug. 13, 1847. Taylor's letter to the painter is reproduced on a lithographed version of one of the portraits, published by P. S. Duval of Philadelphia in 1847 (cat. no. 43).

46. *American Flag,* Aug. 14, 1846. The painting was subsequently displayed in New Orleans for 50¢ admission fee. See *Daily Picayune* supplement, Dec. 3, 1847. (For more on this painting, see cat. no. 43, note 5.)

47. *Daily Picayune,* Sept. 7, Aug. 27, 1847.

48. Saltillo *Picket Guard,* May 3, 1847.

49. *Daily Picayune,* July 17, 1847; Richmond *Enquirer,* May 26, April 18, Feb. 25, 1848.

50. See Fayette Robinson, *An Account of the Organization of the Army of the United States* (Philadelphia: E. H. Butler & Co., 1848), opp. title page, and John Frost, *Pictorial History of Mexico and the Mexican War* (Philadelphia: Charles Desilver, 1848), p. iv.

51. Albany Fonblanque, Jr., *The Filibuster* (London: Ward and Lock, 1862), p. 55.

52. For a fuller discussion of Walker's paintings and the chromolithograph derived from one of them, see cat. no. 148.

53. Kenneth Silverman, *A Cultural History of the American Revolution* (New York: Thomas Y. Crowell, 1976), p. 96.

54. Richmond *Enquirer,* April 23, April 24, 1847; Washington *Union,* May 8, 1847; New Orleans *Daily Picayune,* May 16, 1847.

55. *Daily Picayune,* April 22, May 15, 1847; Washington *Union,* May 8, 1847.

56. Robert Vance presented his collection of 300 full-plate daguerreotypes entitled "Views in California" in New York City during the fall of 1851. He provided viewers with a printed brochure and was often present himself to give anecdotal information about the views. J. Wesley Jones made an astonishing 1500 daguerreotypes documenting the California gold fields and the overland route from California to the Missouri River in the summer and fall of 1851. He later converted his daguerreotypes into a painted panorama (a telling example of a daguerreotypist's own lack of confidence in the dramatic appeal of his work), which he presented around the eastern United States with a narrative lecture as accompaniment.

Catalogue of Prints and Daguerreotypes

Ben W. Huseman

*I*n the early years of this project the author, under the direction of Ron Tyler, compiled a working catalogue of all prints relating to the Mexican War, including popular prints, sheet music covers, and book illustrations of all kinds. As the working catalogue grew to unmanageable proportions, a more narrow focus was deemed necessary. When the Museum acquired a significant group of Mexican War daguerreotypes in 1981, we decided to examine the prints and daguerreotypes of the war together, focusing on a comparative study of eyewitness views. While the very nature of the medium implies the eyewitness veracity of the daguerreotype views included here, not all prints can claim such accuracy. The prints selected for the present catalogue were chosen because they were taken from sketches by eyewitnesses or because they may initially have given the appearance of eyewitness veracity. An analysis of the prints' historical content has revealed varying degrees of accuracy: some prints may be regarded with certain allowances as among the best of primary sources; some are questionable and others wholly fictitious despite the initial illusion of truth. Prints of questionable authenticity have been included in the hope that other scholars will bring further knowledge to bear upon them.

The prints are arranged chronologically according to subject, with the incidental result that a history of the war emerges through the pictorial images. The daguerreotypes, most apparently made around the time of the battle of Buena Vista, have been inserted in a separate section at the end of the northern and western campaigns, basically in keeping with the chronological arrangement of the prints. Although some prints with rare or unusual subject matter have been included to give greater historical breadth to the catalogue, the reader must realize that this pictorial history is by no means a balanced account of the war. The vast majority of prints in this catalogue were produced by or for Americans, often from patriotic or nationalistic motives, with the result that the Mexican side does not receive equal treatment. Repeatedly the American prints stress the heroism and triumph of American arms at the expense of Mexico, and they generally do not attempt to portray any incident or action that would be seen as dishonorable to the United States. Certain geographic areas of the war received no attention from printmakers, and many incidents or occurrences may have seemed too mundane, uninteresting, or violent to suit the nineteenth-century notion that a history picture should be morally uplifting. The activities of the daguerreotypists in Mexico were even more haphazard, and the daguerrean images presented here document only a narrow geographic region.

A NOTE ON THE USE OF THIS CATALOGUE

Each entry in the catalogue contains standard curatorial data:

Printmaker and/or artist or photographer (if known)

Title (Original misspellings in titles and inscriptions have been retained, without [*sic*]. Modern titles for daguerreotypes have been enclosed in brackets[]. Some abbreviations in the inscriptions on the daguerreotypes have been spelled out in the titles.)

Medium

Size (For prints, size refers to image size [minus inscriptions], except where noted as comp. [composition, which includes inscriptions]. For daguerreotypes, size refers to plate size.)

Inscription locations are abbreviated as follows:
u.l. = upper left		l.l. = lower left
u.c. = upper center		l.c. = lower center
u.r. = upper right		l.r. = lower right

Capitalization has been standardized, but punctuation has not.

Location (if in the Amon Carter Museum, the accession number is included)

Biographies of artists and printmakers appear in footnotes scattered among the print entries, usually at the first appearance of their work. The index provides the best method for retrieving information on a particular artist.

Certain place names, among them Veracruz and Monterrey, were spelled differently in the nineteenth century or were consistently misspelled by American printmakers. Though such spellings have been retained in the curatorial data and in quotations, they have been silently corrected in the catalogue discussion.

FREQUENTLY CITED WORKS

Alcaraz, Ramon, et al. *Apuntes para la historia de la guerra entre Mexico y los Estados-Unidos.* Mexico: Payno, 1848. Translated and reprinted as *The Other Side: or, Notes for the History of the War Between Mexico and the United States....* New York and London: J. Wiley, 1850; reprint, New York: Burt Franklin, 1970.

Alessio Robles, Vito. *Saltillo en la historia y en la leyenda.* Mexico City: A. del Bosque, 1934.

Ballentine, George. *Autobiography of an English Soldier in the United States Army.* Edited by William H. Goetzmann. Chicago: R.R. Donnelley & Sons, 1986. (First published, New York: Stringer and Townsend, 1853.)

Balbontín, Manuel. *La invasión americana, 1846 á 1848. Apuntes del subteniente de artilleria Manuel Balbontín.* Mexico City: printed by Gonzalo A. Esteva, 1883.

Bauer, K. Jack. *The Mexican War, 1846-1848.* New York: Macmillan, 1964.

Bauer, K. Jack. *Surfboats and Horse Marines: U.S. Naval Operations in the Mexican War, 1846-48.* Annapolis: U.S. Naval Institute, 1969.

Carleton, James H. *The Battle of Buena Vista, with the Operations of the "Army of Occupation" for One Month.* New York: Harper and Brothers, 1848.

Chamberlain, Samuel E. *My Confession.* Edited by Roger Butterfield. New York: Harper & Brothers, 1956.

Connelley, William Elsey. *Doniphan's Expedition and the Conquest of New Mexico and California.* Kansas City, Mo.: the author, 1907.

Copeland, Fayette. *Kendall of the Picayune.* Norman: University of Oklahoma Press, 1943.

Cullum, George W. *Biographical Register of the Officers and Graduates of the U.S. Military Academy at West Point, N.Y.* 7 vols. Boston and New York: Houghton, Mifflin and Company, 1891-1930.

Dictionary of American Biography. Edited by Allen Johnson and Dumas Malone. 12 vols. New York: Charles Scribner & Sons, 1959-73.

Furber, George C. *The Twelve Months Volunteer; or Journal of a Private, in the Tennessee Regiment of Cavalry, in the Campaign, in Mexico, 1846-7.* Cincinnati: J.A. & U.P. James, 1848.

Giddings, Luther. *Sketches of the Campaign in Northern Mexico. In Eighteen Hundred Forty-Six and Seven. By an Officer of the First Regiment of Ohio Volunteers.* New York: For the author by G. P. Putnam and Co., 1853.

Grant, Ulysses S. *Personal Memoirs of U.S. Grant.* New York: Charles L. Webster & Company, 1894.

Gregg, Josiah. *Diary and Letters of Josiah Gregg.* Edited by Maurice Garland Fulton. Norman: University of Oklahoma Press, 1944.

Groce, George C., and David H. Wallace. *The New-York Historical Society's Dictionary of Artists in America, 1564-1860*. New Haven: Yale University Press, 1957.

Heitman, Francis B. *Historical Register and Dictionary of the United States Army, From Its Organization, September 29, 1789, to March 2, 1903*. 2 vols. Washington, D.C.: Government Printing Office, 1903.

Henry, William Seaton. *Campaign Sketches of the War with Mexico*. New York: Harper & Brothers, 1847.

Hughes, George Wurtz. *Memoir Descriptive of the March of a Division of the United States Army, Under the Command of Brigadier General John E. Wool, from San Antonio de Bexar, in Texas, to Saltillo, in Mexico*. Senate Executive Document 32, 31st Congress, 1st Session, 1850.

Jacobsen, Jacques Noel, Jr., comp. and ed. *Regulations and Notes for the Uniform of the Army of the United States, 1847*. Staten Island, N.Y.: Manor Publishing, 1977.

Kendall, George Wilkins. *The War Between the United States and Mexico Illustrated, Embracing Pictorial Drawings of All the Principal Conflicts*. New York: D. Appleton & Company, 1851.

Mahé, John II, and Roseanne McCaffrey, eds. *Encyclopaedia of New Orleans Artists, 1718-1918*. New Orleans: The Historic New Orleans Collection, 1987.

Moore, H. Judge. *Scott's Campaign in Mexico*. Charleston: J. B. Nixon, 1849.

Mugridge, Donald H. *An Album of American Battle Art, 1755-1918*. Washington, D.C.: U.S. Government Printing Office for the Library of Congress, 1947.

Nebel, Carl. *Voyage pittoresque et archéologique dans la partie la plus intéressante du Mexique*. Paris: M. Moench, 1836.

Nevin, David. *The Mexican War*. Alexandria, Va.: Time-Life Books, 1978.

Oswandel, J. Jacob. *Notes of the Mexican War, 1846-47-48*. Philadelphia: n.p., 1885.

Parker, William H. *Recollections of a Naval Officer, 1841-1865*. New York: Charles Scribners' Sons, 1883.

Peterson, Harold L. *The American Sword, 1775-1945*. New Hope, Pa.: The River House, Robert Halter, 1954.

Phillips, John, and Alfred Rider. *Mexico Illustrated in Twenty-six Views*. London: E. Atchley, Library of Fine Arts, 1848.

Semmes, Raphael. *Service Afloat and Ashore*. Cincinnati: Wm. H. Moore and Co., 1851.

Smith, George Winston, and Charles Judah, eds. *Chronicles of the Gringos: The U.S. Army in the Mexican War, 1846-1848: Accounts of Eyewitnesses and Combatants*. Albuquerque: University of New Mexico Press, 1968.

Smith, Justin H. *The War with Mexico*. 2 vols. New York: The Macmillan Company, 1919; reprint, Gloucester, Mass.: Peter Smith, 1963.

Thorpe, Thomas Bangs. *"Our Army" on the Rio Grande*. Philadelphia: Carey & Hart, 1846.

Tyler, Ronnie C. *The Mexican War: A Lithographic Record*. Austin: Texas State Historical Association, 1973.

Wallace, Lee A. "The First Regiment of Virginia Volunteers, 1846-1848." *Virginia Magazine of History and Biography* 77, no. 1 (1969): 46-77.

American city directories through 1860 are available in a microfiche collection published by Research Publications, Inc., New Haven, Conn., based on Dorothea N. Spear, *Bibliography of American Directories Through 1860* (Worcester, Mass.: American Antiquarian Society, 1961).

Some of the more obscure references were found through Seymour V. Connor and Odie B. Faulk, *North America Divided: The Mexican War 1846-1848* (New York: Oxford University Press, 1971), analytical bibliography, pp. 185-276; and Norman E. Tutorow, *The Mexican-American War: An Annotated Bibliography* (Westport, Conn.: Greenwood Press, 1981).

Battalion of Artillery. — 8th Infantry. — 2nd Dragoons. — 7th Inf. — 5th Inf. — Light Artillery. — 3d Inf. — 4th Infantry. — Town

1st Brigade.
GEN⁰ WORTH.

COL TWIGGS Lᵗ COL Mᶜ INTOSH

2nd Brigade.

3d Brigade.
COL WHISTLER.

Birds-eye view of the
CAMP OF THE ARMY OF OCCUPATION,
COMMANDED BY GEN⁰ TAYLOR.

Near Corpus Christi, Texas, (from the North) Oct. 1845.

PLATE 1   CAT. NO. 1
CAMP OF THE ARMY OF OCCUPATION, NEAR CORPUS CHRISTI

Battle of Palo alto
May 8, 1846

PLATE 2   CAT. NO. 5
BATTLE OF PALO ALTO

76

1. *Sierra Madre.*
2. *Mitre Mountain.*
3. *Height on Federation Hill.* Carried by Storm on the 21st Sep.t
4. *Fort Soldado.* by part of the 2d Division.
5. *Height from which shot was thrown from one of the captured nine pounders of the Redoubt, into the main Plaza on the 23d* By part of the 2d Division.
6. *Height on Independence Hill, taken at daylight on the 22d*

MONTEREY,

As seen from a house-top in the main Plaza, (to the West.)

October, 1846.

Entered according to Act of Congress in the year 1847 by C.P.Whiting in the Clerks Office of the Southern District of New York.

PRINTED IN COLORS BY G. & W. ENDICOTT NEW YORK.

7. *Bishop's Palace, or Castle and Fort, Stormed on the 22d by part of the 2d Division.*
8. *City Police Offices and Prison.*
9. *Pass leading to Saltillo. Occupied by the 2d Division on the morning of the 21st after the action of St. Jeronimo.*
10. *Captured Mexican Cannon.*
11. *Quarters of the 7th Infantry.*
12. *Convent of St. Francisco.*

[Nº 1. of a Series]

PLATE 3   CAT. NO. 11
MONTEREY FROM THE MAIN PLAZA

1. Independance (or Castle) Hill.
2. Lt. Col. Duncan's Battery of Light Artillery throwing shells at the routed Mexican Cavalry.
3. City of Monterey.
4. "Sierra Silla." Saddle Mountain.

HEIGHTS OF MONTEREY,

from the Saltillo road looking towards the City. (from the West)

"Worth's Division" moving into position under the guns of the enemy, after the action of "St. Jeronimo," on the morning of 21st Sept. 1846.

LITH'D PRINTED IN COLORS BY G. & W. ENDICOTT, NEW YORK.

5. Rancho. (or village) of St. Jeronimo.
6. Federation Hill. First position carried by assault on the afternoon of 21st Septr.

N.B. The second Division was composed of one Regt. of Texan Cavalry, two Cos. of Texn. Rangers, two Batteries of Lt. Artillery, the "Artly. Battalion", the 5th, 7th and 8th Regts. of Infantry, and one Company of Louisiana Volunteers.

(No 2)

PLATE 4   CAT. NO. 12
HEIGHTS OF MONTEREY, FROM SALTILLO ROAD

BY MORTON, CAPT. 7TH INF. DEL.

ON STONE BY E. WEBER.

1. Mountains of the "Sierra Madre". 8 Miles distant.
2. Part of "Federation Hill" Position and Breast work, first carried by assault, on the 21st Sepr. 1846.
3. Road to Saltillo, with the rear guard and wagon-train coming in to the Castle, after its capture on the 22nd.

VALLEY TOWARDS SALTILLO,

From near the base of "Palace Hill", at Monterey.

(Looking to the S. West.)

Entered according to act of Congress in the year 1847 by D. P. Whiting in the Clerks Office of the District Court of the Southern District of N. York.

G. & W. ENDICOTT LITH N.Y.

4. Village of "San Pedro".
5. "Spur" of "Mitre Mountain," around which the first action with the Mexican Cavalry was fought, on the morning of the 21st September.
6. Part of the "base of "Mitre Mountain."

[No. 3.]

PLATE 5   CAT. NO. 13
Valley Towards Saltillo, from Monterey

1. *"Sierra Silla".* [Saddle Mountain, about 7 Miles distant.]
2. *Village of "Guadaloupe".*
3. *Citadel,* [in possession of the Mexicans, firing upon Gen.' Taylor's position on the eastern side of the City.]
4. *Cathedral.*

5. *Cemetery.*
6. *Gen.' Arista's Palace and Garden.*
7. *Part of Federation Hill,* [shewing the point occupied by Major Scott, with the 5.th Inf.y with one of the captured guns throwing shot into the "Main Plaza".]

MONTEREY,

From Independence Hill, in the rear of the Bishop's Palace.

As it appeared on 23.d September, 1846 [Looking East.]

Entered according to Act of Congress in the year 1851 by D. P. Whiting in the Clerks Office of the District Court of the Southern District of New York.

LITH. & PRINTED IN COLORS BY G. & W. ENDICOTT, NEW YORK.

[No 4.]

PLATE 6   CAT. NO. 14
MONTEREY, FROM INDEPENDENCE HILL

Capture of Monterey
Sept. 1. 22 23 + 24 1846

PLATE 7   CAT. NO. 16
Capture of Monterey

BATTLE OF BUENA VISTA.

VIEW OF THE BATTLE-GROUND AND BATTLE OF "THE ANGOSTURA" FOUGHT NEAR BUENA VISTA, MEXICO FEBRUARY 23RD 1847. (LOOKING S. WEST.)

PLATE 8   CAT. NO. 36
Battle-Ground of "The Angostura," Near Buena Vista

Battle of Buena Vista
Feby 22 + 23 1847

PLATE 9   CAT. NO. 38
BATTLE OF BUENA VISTA

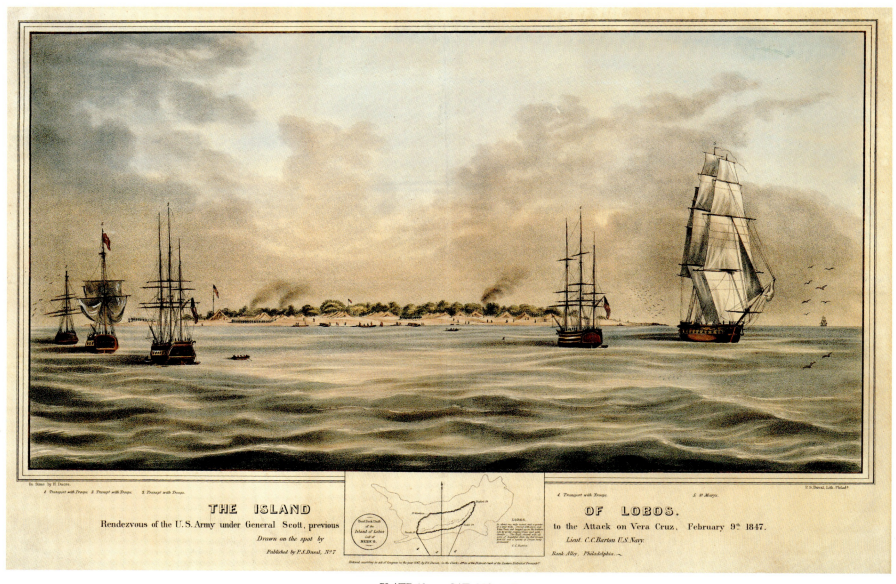

On Stone by H. Dacre.

1. Transport with Troops.   2. Transport with Troops.   3. Transport with Troops.

4. Transport with Troops.   5. St Marys.

P.S.Duval, Lith. Philad²

THE ISLAND

Rendezvous of the U.S. Army under General Scott, previous

Drawn on the spot by

Published by P.S.Duval, N° 7

OF LOBOS.

to the Attack on Vera Cruz, February 9ᵗʰ 1847.

Lieut. C.C.Barton U.S.Navy.

Bank Alley, Philadelphia.

Entered according to act of Congress in the year 1847, by P.S Duval, in the Clerks office of the District Court of the Eastern District of Pennsylvania

PLATE 10   CAT. NO. 107
ISLAND OF LOBOS: RENDEZVOUS OF U.S. ARMY

84

LANDING OF THE TROOPS AT VERA CRUZ.

PLATE 11   CAT. NO. 111
LANDING OF THE TROOPS AT VERA CRUZ

Lith of Sarony & Major

Entered according to Act of Congress in the year 1847 by Sarony & Major in the Clerks Office of the District Court of the Southern District of New York.

Illustrated by H. Walke L.T. U.S.N.

THE U. S. STEAM FRIGATE MISSISSIPPI, COMᴿᴱ M. C. PERRY.

Going out to the relief of the American Steamer Hunter a French Bark (her prize) and an American Pilot Boat wrecked on Green Island reef near Vera Cruize March 21ˢᵗ 1847.

Published by Sarony & Major 117 Fulton St New York.

PLATE 12   CAT. NO. 112
U.S. STEAM FRIGATE *Mississippi*

Bombardment of Vera Cruz

PLATE 13   CAT. NO. 115
BOMBARDMENT OF VERA CRUZ

THE U. STATES STEAMERS, SCORPION, SPITFIRE, VIXEN AND SCOURGE; WITH 46 BARGES IN TOW, CROSSING THE BAR AT THE MOUTH OF TOBASCO RIVER, (MEXICO.)

COMᵈᵍ M.C. PERRY IN COMMAND. SUPPORTED BY THE COMMᵈᵍˢ OF CAPTAINS. J. MAYO, S.L. BREEZE, F. FORREST. COMMANDERS Wᵐ J. Mᶜ CLUNEY, A. BIGELOW, F. BUCHANAN, H.A. ADAMS, A.S. MACKENZIE G. A. MAGRUDER, G. J. VAN BRUNT. LIEUᵗⁿ COMMANDING S.S. LEE, S. LOCKWOOD AND J. M. BERRIEN. JUNE 14ᵗʰ 1847.

Published by Sarony & Major, 117 Fulton St. New York.

PLATE 14   CAT. NO. 119
U.S. Steamers Crossing the Bar, Tobasco River

88

THE LANDING, OF THE NAVAL EXPEDITION, AGAINST TABASCO. (MEXICO.) COMᴰᴿᵉ M.C. PERRY IN COMMAND.

WITH DETACHMENTS OF OFFICERS, SEAMEN, AND MARINES, FROM THE U.S. STEAMER FRIGATE MISSISSIPPI, CAPᵗ MAYO, COMᴰᴿᵉ MACKENZIE, AND ADAMS, U.S. SHIP, ALBANY, CAPᵗ BREESE, FRIGATE RARITAN, CAPᵗ FORREST. U.S. SHIP, JOHN ADAMS, COMᴰᴿᵉ Wᵐ J. McCLUNEY. U.S. SHIP GERMANTOWN, COMᴰᴿᵉ BUCHANAN. U.S.SHIP DECATER, COMᴰᴿᵉ PEARSON BOMB BRIG, STROMBOLI, COMᴰᴿᵉ WALKER, BOMB BRIG, VESUVIUS, COMᴰᴿᵉ MAGRUDER BOMB BRIG, ETNA. COMᴰᴿᵉ VAN BRUNT. MARINES COMᴰ BY CAPᵗ EDSON.

The landing was effected in 3 minutes, after the Comᴰᴿᵉ gave the order, (in the face of the enemy, intrenched,) by about 1000, American Seamen and Marines, armed with muskets, and 10 Brass field pieces which were served upon the enemy, after they had been driven from their works by the heavy guns of the Steamer Scorpion Comᵈᵉʳ Bigelow, Steamer Spitfire Lieut. Comᵈᵗ S.S. Lee. Steamer Vixen Lieut. Comᵈᵗ Smith. Steamer Scourge Lieut. Comᵈᵗ S. Lookwood, and the Schooner Bonita Lieut. Comᵈᵗ Birrien; which Covered the landing.

Published by Sarony & Major 117 Fulton Street N.Y.

PLATE 15   CAT. NO. 122
LANDING OF NAVAL EXPEDITION AGAINST TABASCO

Battle of Cerro-gordo

PLATE 16   CAT. NO. 125
BATTLE OF CERRO GORDO

Assault at Contreras

PLATE 17   CAT. NO. 134
ASSAULT AT CONTRERAS

Battle at Churubusco
Aug 20 1847

PLATE 18   CAT. NO. 136
BATTLE AT CHURUBUSCO

Molino del Rey — attack upon the molino
Sept. 8th 1847

PLATE 19   CAT. NO. 140
MOLINO DEL REY — ATTACK UPON THE MOLINO

Molino del Rey — attack upon the cas-mata

Sept 8. 1847

PLATE 20   CAT. NO. 141
MOLINO DEL REY — ATTACK UPON THE CASA MATA

Storming of Chapultepec — Pillow's attack
13th 1847

PLATE 21   CAT. NO. 146
STORMING OF CHAPULTEPEC — PILLOW'S ATTACK

THE STORMING OF CHAPULTEPEC SEPT! 13TH 1847.

PLATE 22   CAT. NO. 148
Storming of Chapultepec

96

PLATE 23   CAT. NO. 152
STORMING OF CHAPULTEPEC — QUITMAN'S ATTACK

PLATE 24   CAT. NO. 159
GENL. SCOTT'S ENTRANCE INTO MEXICO

Part One:

Prints of Northern Mexico and the West

*P*rints of the war with Mexico may be divided into two geographical groups, coinciding with two generally distinct phases of the war. The first group of prints illustrates the period from the beginning of the war to February 1847, when major movements and actions took place along the Rio Grande River and in areas that today comprise the American Southwest and northern Mexico. The second group contains prints pertaining to the campaign in central and southern Mexico later in the war.

The numerous causes of the war and the political incidents that led to its beginning are beyond the focus of this catalogue. While an understanding of some of these factors is necessary, an attempt to explain them here can only be superficial. The most immediate causes of the war were diplomatic hostilities that arose between Mexico and the United States when the latter annexed Texas in 1845 and the ensuing boundary dispute (Mexico claimed the Nueces River as the boundary; the United States claimed the Rio Grande). The westward movement of Anglo-Americans into the sparsely settled northern Mexican frontier aggravated political and economic instabilities within Mexico, and the weakness of Mexican control over the frontier areas encouraged the expansionist designs of many Americans. President James K. Polk late in 1845 offered to purchase New Mexico and California from Mexico, a proposal which incensed many Mexicans.

In January 1846 President Polk asserted American claims along the disputed border by ordering a small army under Major General Zachary Taylor to advance to the north bank of the Rio Grande. The Mexican government felt it had to respond, and soon the first clashes occurred. As word of American casualties reached Washington, Polk advised Congress that a state of war existed. Congress formally declared war on May 13.

After receiving word of Taylor's victories along the Rio Grande, the American government ordered Taylor to invade northern Mexico with the goal of overawing the Mexicans and inducing them to come to terms. Simultaneously, General Stephen Watts Kearny was to seize New Mexico and California and hold it as an indemnity, and the U. S. Navy was to blockade Mexican ports on both the Pacific and the Gulf of Mexico. Brigadier General John E. Wool led a division from San Antonio, Texas, across the Rio Grande near Presidio and Colonel Alexander W. Doniphan led a separate column of volunteers from Missouri through New Mexico; both Wool and Doniphan intended to seize Chihuahua. The Americans achieved all of these objectives except two: Wool was diverted from Chihuahua to support Taylor, and the Mexican government refused to come to terms.

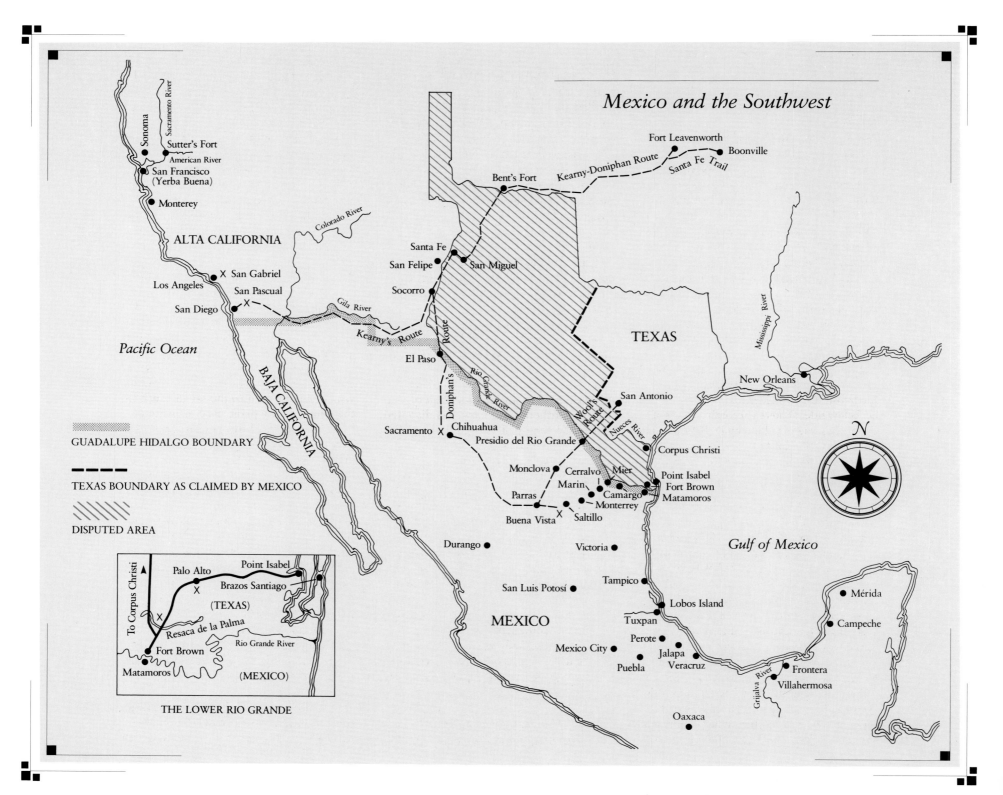

Mexico and the Southwest

Sacramento River

Sonoma
Sutter's Fort
American River
San Francisco
(Yerba Buena)
Monterey

ALTA CALIFORNIA

Colorado River

X San Gabriel
Los Angeles
San Pascual
San Diego X

Pacific Ocean

Gila River

Kearny's Route

Fort Leavenworth
Boonville
Kearny-Doniphan Route
Santa Fe Trail

Bent's Fort

Santa Fe
San Felipe
San Miguel
Socorro

Route

El Paso

Rio Grande River

TEXAS

Mississippi River

New Orleans

San Antonio

Doniphan's Route

Sacramento X   Chihuahua
Presidio del Rio Grande

Wool's Route

Nueces River

Corpus Christi

GUADALUPE HIDALGO BOUNDARY

TEXAS BOUNDARY AS CLAIMED BY MEXICO

DISPUTED AREA

BAJA CALIFORNIA

Monclova
Parras

Cerralvo   Mier
Marin
Camargo
Monterrey
Buena Vista X   Saltillo

Point Isabel
Fort Brown
Matamoros

Gulf of Mexico

Durango

Victoria

San Luis Potosí

MEXICO

Tampico

Lobos Island

Tuxpan

Perote

Mexico City   Jalapa
Puebla   Veracruz

Mérida

Campeche

Grijalva River

Frontera
Villahermosa

Oaxaca

To Corpus Christi
Palo Alto   Point Isabel
X   Brazos Santiago
(TEXAS)
X
Resaca de la Palma
Fort Brown
Rio Grande River
Matamoros   (MEXICO)

THE LOWER RIO GRANDE

N

Corpus Christi

1. See Plate 1
Charles Parsons after Daniel Powers Whiting
BIRDS-EYE VIEW OF THE CAMP OF THE
ARMY OF OCCUPATION, COMMANDED
BY GENL. TAYLOR. NEAR CORPUS
CHRISTI, TEXAS, (FROM THE NORTH)
OCT. 1845.
Toned lithograph (hand colored), 1847
12-3/8 x 19-3/8 in. (31.4 x 49.2 cm.)
l.l.: "D. P. Whiting Capt. 7th Inf. Del."
l.c.: "Lith. and Printed in Colors by G. & W.
Endicott N. York."
l.r.: "On Stone by C. Parsons."
l.c.: "Battalion of Artillery. — 8th. Infantry
— 2nd. Dragoons. — 7th. Inf. — 5th. Inf. —
Light Artillery. — 3d. Inf. — 4th. Infantry —
Town. / 1st. Brigade. 2nd. Brigade. 3d. Bri-
gade / Genl. Worth. Col. Twiggs Lt. Col.
Mc.Intosh. Col. Whistler."
l.c. below title: "Entered according to act of
Congress in the year 1847 by D. P. Whiting in
the Clerks Office of the district Court of the
Southern district of New York."
ACM 2.74/1

Among the best-known prints relating to the Mexican War are the series of lithographs titled *Army Portfolio*, after sketches by U. S. Army Captain Daniel Powers Whiting (1808-92).[1] Whiting's first print depicts General Zachary Taylor's camp at Corpus Christi, Texas, about seven months before the first major battles were fought. Captain Whiting, in command of Company K of the Seventh Infantry, arrived at the village of Corpus Christi on August 28, 1845,[2] a month behind the lead units of General Taylor's "Army of Observation," as it was originally styled. By October, when Whiting's view was taken, the Army of Occupation consisted of General William Jenkins Worth's first brigade, which included the Eighth Infantry and twelve companies of artillery actually serving as infantry and termed the "artillery battalion"; the second brigade under Lieutenant Colonel J. S. McIntosh, consisting of the Fifth and Seventh Infantry; the third brigade under Colonel William Whistler, which included the Third and Fourth Infantry; the Second Dragoons under Colonel David E. Twiggs; field artillery, including some New Orleans volunteers; and some Texas Rangers.[3] As the print's inscriptions are not keyed to the image, it is difficult to determine which tents belong to which units.

The army was there to protect the frontiers of the newly annexed state. Hostilities between Texas and Mexico had continued long after the battle of San Jacinto in 1836. Each side invaded the other's territory, and the location of Texas's southern boundary was disputed; indeed, Mexico still refused to recognize Texas's independence. Annexation shifted most of Texas's defense burden and boundary problem to the United States and further angered Mexico. Taylor's army at Corpus Christi was poised just south of the Nueces River in territory claimed by both Texas and Mexico.

The magazine *Niles' National Register* published a rather flattering description of the camp, from a letter dated August 30:

> A thousand spotless white tents, along the shelly margin of the shore of Corpus Christi Bay...are pitched on a piece of table land that reaches about a quarter of a mile to a range of hills....
>
> The commanding general has thrown up a field work, a wall of shells and sand, six feet thick and three hundred yards in length on his right.... The whole length of the line along the shore occupied, appears to be about one mile and a half....
>
> The only drawback to continuing this encampment is the scarcity of wood and water — the former, the troops haul about three miles, and the latter is quite brackish — though I believe there are one or two small wells in camp which supply a very fair beverage.[4]

But other sources mentioned additional problems at the camp. Sudden changes in weather brought piercing northers and sultry heat. Rattlesnakes infested the tents. At some time nearly twenty percent of the men were on the sick list.[5]

William Seaton Henry, an officer in the Third Infantry, described the town, which may be seen in the far distance in the center of the print, as consisting of "some twenty or thirty houses, partly situated on a shelf of land, elevated some six or eight feet above the water, about two hundred yards broad, and on a bluff which rises from the plain to the height of one hundred feet."[6] In the print a pier is visible; one of the small vessels in the bay is a steamer, several of which were used as lighters to ferry the troops and supplies from deeper-draft ships anchored beyond the coastal islands in the Gulf. One such steamer at Corpus Christi, the *Dayton*, burst her boiler on September 12, killing and wounding several soldiers. The Mexican War was the first major American war in which steamships were used, and they were still not without their risks.

After months of threats, failed negotiations, and rumors, the U. S. government ordered Taylor to advance south to the Rio Grande to back up the U. S. claims to the disputed territory. On March 8, 1846, the army began the long march. Captain Henry, who was among the last to leave, noted that "Corpus Christi looked perfectly deserted; the field of white canvas was no longer visible; the camp-ground looked like desolation itself; but the bright waters of the bay looked as sweetly as ever."[7]

Whiting's view of the encampment was first issued separately in a slightly different version, drawn on stone by lithographer Charles Fenderich and printed by Edward Weber of Baltimore.[8] The version here, drawn on stone by Charles Parsons and printed by the firm of George and William Endicott in New York, was published as part of the *Army Portfolio* and was first available in the summer of 1847.[9] Two reasons for the separate printings of the view are suggested in a letter by Whiting's brother-in-law, Lieutenant Napoleon J. T. Dana, who also served with the Seventh Infantry. Writing his wife on February 16, 1847, Dana mentioned that "by the last arrival Whiting received four engravings [sic] of his drawing of the Corpus Christi encampment. Two hundred copies have as yet been printed. He is very unfortunate, for his brother is unable to raise the requisite funds to bring them out, and I am afraid the publication of his pieces will be delayed. He is not at all pleased with this first engraving, for the artist has not done it justice."[10] The Endicott series, however, received enthusiastic reviews from several newspapers and periodicals when it came out; the *Knickerbocker* called the Corpus Christi view "a very full composition, admirably drawn, and unmistakably faithful to the scene."[11]

Whiting's view was not the only eyewitness sketch of Corpus Christi to appear in print, and other amateur artists may also have been sketching at the camp. On March 15, 1846, the New York *Herald* published an engraving on its front page showing Corpus Christi and Taylor's camp from the south. A similar view appears as the frontispiece to Captain W. S. Henry's *Campaign Sketches*, first published in the summer of 1847.[12]

1. A native of Troy, New York, Whiting graduated from the U.S. Military Academy at West Point in 1832. While there he received training in topographical drawing. A career army officer, he was promoted to captain shortly before the outbreak of the Mexican War. During the war he participated in the defense of Fort Brown (see cat. no. 3), fought at Monterrey, and was breveted major for gallant and meritorious conduct in the battle of Cerro Gordo. After the war he spent considerable time in the West, serving at Jefferson Barracks, Missouri, at Forts Towson, Arbuckle, and Washita, Indian Territory, and in the Utah expedition of 1858-59. During the Civil War he commanded at Fort Garland for a year for the Union. (See Mugridge, *Album of American Battle Art*, p. 128; Cullum, *Biographical Register*, 1:520-21; and Returns of the Seventh Infantry Regiment, May 1845-March 1846, RG 94, M665, roll 79, National Archives, Washington, D.C.)

For the rest of the *Army Portfolio* see cat. nos. 11-14. The location of Whiting's original sketches for the prints is not known. According to Whiting family sources, recorded in the acquisition files for the *Portfolio* in the Archives of the U.S. Military Academy, drawings originally intended to continue the series beyond Monterrey were lost when a steamboat sank en route to New York.

2. Returns of the Seventh Infantry Regiment, July-September 1845.

3. Smith, *War with Mexico*, 1:143; Henry, *Campaign Sketches*, pp. 17-53. On p. 39 Henry lists the order of the troops.

4. *Niles' National Register*, Sept. 20, 1845, p. 36.

5. Smith, *War with Mexico*, 1:143-44. Eyewitness accounts of the camp at Corpus Christi include Ethan Allen Hitchcock, *Fifty Years in Camp and Field*, ed. W. A. Croffut (New York and London: G. P. Putnam's Sons, 1909), pp. 193-210, and Ulysses S. Grant, *The Papers of Ulysses S. Grant*, ed. John Y. Simon, 10 vols. (Carbondale and Edwardsville: Southern Illinois University Press, 1967), 1:53-75.

6. Henry, *Campaign Sketches*, p. 17.

7. Ibid., pp. 52-53.

8. Impressions of this version are located in the Prints and Photographs Division of the Library of Congress and the Bowdoin College Art Museum. The Fenderich and Weber version differs from the Parsons and Endicott version mainly in the treatment of the sky and in the ships in the gulf. The former version has clouds and a few more ships; it was entered by Whiting in the copyright clerk's office in the District of Columbia. (See cat. no. 11 for more on Charles Fenderich.)

9. Parsons (1821-1910) was born in England and brought to the United States at age nine. In 1833 he was apprenticed in New York to George Endicott, the first of a number of Endicotts in the lithography business; Parsons remained associated with the Endicott firm until 1860. He was also a marine and landscape painter in oil and watercolor and an Associate of the National Academy of Design and member of the American Watercolor Society. (On Parsons, see Groce and Wallace, *Dictionary of Artists in America*, p. 489; Harry T. Peters, *America on Stone* [Garden City, N.Y.: Doubleday, Doran and Co., 1931], pp. 30-89; and John W. Reps, *Views and Viewmakers of Urban America* ... [Columbia: University of Missouri Press, 1984], pp. 196-98. On the Endicotts, see Groce and Wallace, p. 213; David Tatham, ed., *Prints and Printmakers of New York State, 1825-1940* [Syracuse: Syracuse University Press, 1986], pp. 43-65; and Frances Phipps, "Connecticut Printmakers: The Kelloggs of Hartford," *Connecticut Antiquarian* 21 [June 1969]: 19-26.)

10. Napoleon J. T. Dana to his wife Sue, Feb. 16, 1847, Archives of the U.S. Military Academy, West Point, N.Y. Thanks to Robert H. Ferrell of Indiana University for transcriptions of Dana's letters.

11. *Knickerbocker* 30, no. 5 (Nov. 1847): 464. See Rick Stewart's essay for further discussion of the *Army Portfolio* and its critical reception.

12. The young engraver for the *Herald*, Samuel Putnam Avery, did not identify his source, but the engraving must have been ultimately derived from a sketch by someone who had drawn it on the spot. Henry's frontispiece credits neither the engraver nor the artist but may have been copied from the Avery engraving, the narrow horizontal composition of which it condenses. The Spanish translation of Henry's book, *Apuntes de campaña en la guerra con México* (Mexico: Imprenta de la Voz de la Religion, 1848), in turn has a lithograph copy of the second engraving entitled *Corpus Christi. Campamento de Taylor*. It was issued by the Mexico City lithographer Plácido Blanco.

The Campaign on the Rio Grande

2.
After an unknown artist
POINT ISABEL, FROM BRASOS SANTIAGO
Engraving, 1846
3-1/2 x 6 in. (8.9 x 15.2 cm.)
l.l. in image: "Gilbert & Gihon"
From Thomas Bangs Thorpe, *"Our Army" on the Rio Grande* (Philadelphia: Carey & Hart, 1846), opposite p. 14
Courtesy of Special Collections Division, The University of Texas at Arlington Libraries, Arlington, Texas

POINT ISABEL, FROM BRASOS SANTIAGO.

2. POINT ISABEL, FROM BRASOS SANTIAGO

Marching south from Corpus Christi, one of the lead columns of General Taylor's army reached the small village of Frontón de Santa Isabela on Point Isabel on March 25, 1846. The town was located on "a bluff some fifteen or twenty feet high" overlooking a harbor just north of the mouth of the Rio Grande, near Matamoros. Transports carrying supplies for the army arrived at Brazos Santiago, a pass through which ships from the Gulf entered the bay of Point Isabel. The town's sixty Mexican inhabitants burned the customs house and fled. The Americans turned the village into a fortified supply base, occupying the remaining huts and constructing other rude shelters and sheds.[1]

This engraving appeared in a book titled *"Our Army" on the Rio Grande*, published in Philadelphia in 1846. In the preface, dated August 1846, author Thomas Bangs Thorpe claims that "the illustrations of the work are from nature, save the one representing the death of Major Ringgold; that is an attempt to embody the scene from descriptions of eye witnesses."[2] Most of the plates for the

book, including this one, were engraved by Gilbert & Gihon, a Philadelphia partnership of wood engravers Reuben S. Gilbert and William B. Gihon.[3] The text does not name the artist or artists whose drawings were the basis for the engravings, but Thorpe, a journalist and landscape and portrait painter who traveled to the Rio Grande to see the army's operations firsthand, may have supplied some of the sketches himself.[4]

This print of Point Isabel, taken from a view probably drawn on the spot, shows the base at the height of its activity in 1846, with American steamships and sailing vessels in the harbor and tents set up on the left. Thorpe's book also contains an engraved view of Brazos Santiago.[5]

1. Thorpe, *"Our Army" on the Rio Grande*, pp. 14-15, 45-48, 60; Bauer, *Mexican War*, pp. 37-39.
2. Thorpe, *"Our Army" on the Rio Grande*, p. iii.
3. Reuben Gilbert and William B. Gihon were active together in Philadelphia from 1846 until the 1850s. Reuben Gilbert began wood engraving around 1833, and his work is sometimes confused with that of another wood engraver named George Gilbert, whose name appears in Philadelphia city directories from 1818 until 1846. (See Sinclair Hamilton, *Early American Book Illustration 1670-1870*, 2 vols. [Princeton, N.J.: Princeton University Press, 1968], 1:xxxiv; Groce and Wallace, *Dictionary of Artists in America*, pp. 258, 259.)
4. Thorpe (1815-78) showed an early interest in history painting and studied art under the brilliant and eccentric painter John Quidor. A native of Massachusetts, Thorpe went to Louisiana in 1836 and pursued both painting and writing, winning acclaim for his short stories of local color and western humor. He also wrote for several Louisiana newspapers and briefly reported on the war for the New Orleans *Daily Tropic* while gathering materials for *"Our Army" on the Rio Grande* in May and June 1846. (See Milton Rickels, *Thomas Bangs*

Thorpe: Humorist of the Old Southwest [Baton Rouge: Louisiana State University Press, 1962]. Shorter biographies are in the *DAB*, 9:509, and Groce and Wallace, *Dictionary of Artists in America*, pp. 628-29.) Thorpe's Mexican War books are discussed in Rick Stewart's essay.

5. Thorpe, *"Our Army" on the Rio Grande*, opp. p. 45. A lithographed copy of the view of Point Isabel appeared in Cincinnati lithographer Emil Klauprecht's illustrated German-language news journal *Fliegende Blätter*, Dec. 3, 1846, opp. p. 252. Another engraved view of Point Isabel by "C. B." after Lieutenant Alfred Sully appeared in 1847 in Henry's *Campaign Sketches*, opp. p. 86. A lithograph titled *The United States Squadron, Landing Its Seamen & Marines, at the Brazos de Santiago, May 8th. 1846* depicts several ships of the U.S. Navy's Home Squadron landing troops near the mouth of the Rio Grande to aid Taylor's army; it served as a folding frontispiece for Rev. Fitch W. Taylor's *The Broad Pennant* (1848). Drawn on stone by Francis Michelin of New York, it is perhaps based on an eyewitness sketch by Taylor, who served as chaplain with the Home Squadron.

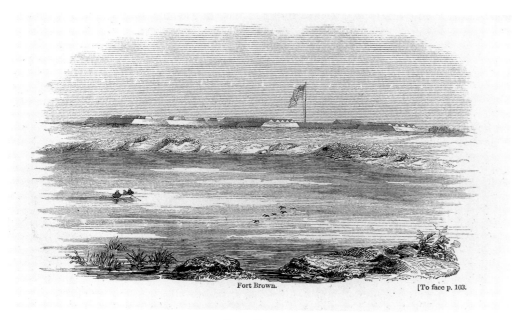

3. FORT BROWN

3.

After Joseph Horace Eaton?
FORT BROWN
Engraving, 1847
3-1/2 x 5-1/2 in. (8.9 x 14.0 cm.)
From William Seaton Henry, *Campaign Sketches of the War with Mexico* (New York: Harper & Brothers, 1847), opposite p. 103
Courtesy of Special Collections Division, The University of Texas at Arlington Libraries, Arlington, Texas

Taylor's army reached the north bank of the Rio Grande opposite the Mexican town of Matamoros on March 28. There the Americans hoisted the Stars and Stripes and erected a camp, while they sent word to the Mexican commander at Matamoros, General Francisco Mejía, that their intentions were peaceful. Mejía, facing overwhelming numbers of American troops, began constructing fortifications. The Americans in turn constructed Fort Texas, a star-shaped earthwork for eight hundred men.

The fort was at the center of the first hostilities of the war. The Mexican force was reinforced, and on April 24 a large body of Mexican cavalry crossed the river several miles west of Matamoros and ambushed an American patrol that was sent to investigate. On May 3, Taylor marched with the bulk of his forces back east to Point Isabel to protect his communications and supply line. Left to defend Fort Texas were Major Jacob Brown and about five hundred men of the Seventh Infantry Regiment, with four eighteen-pounders and a field battery. For six days Mexican guns from Matamoros bombarded the fort; on May 8 and 9 Brown and his men could also hear the guns in the heavier battles to the northeast at Palo Alto and Resaca de la Palma. The fort's defenders suffered only light casualties except for Major Brown, who was mortally wounded. The site, renamed Fort Brown in his honor, is now in the city of Brownsville, Texas.[1]

In his preface to the book containing this engraved view of Fort Brown, Captain William Seaton Henry acknowledges "his obligations to Lieutenant A. Sully, of the army, for his spirited embellishments; and to Major J. H. Eaton, to whom he is indebted for a few designs."[2] Since Sully's name appears on several of the plates but Eaton's never does, it is possible that the uncredited plates, like the view of Fort Brown, were taken from Eaton's designs. On the other hand, the view could have been copied from a virtually identical engraving by Samuel Putnam Avery that appeared in the New York *Herald* and *Weekly Herald* in July 1846 — or Avery, too, may have worked from a design by Eaton.[3]

1. Henry, *Campaign Sketches*, pp. 103-4; Bauer, *Mexican War*, pp. 39, 41-52. See also Thorpe, *"Our Army" on the Rio Grande*, pp. 26, 49-51, 53-72, 105-7; the title page has a view of the *Interior of Fort Brown* after an unknown artist, showing the "Graves of Major Brown and Lieut. Stevens at the Foot of the Flagstaff."

2. Henry, *Campaign Sketches*, pp. v-vi. For more on Eaton, see cat. no. 36, note 1.

3. New York *Weekly Herald*, July 18, 1846, p. 1; New York *Herald*, July 21, 1846, p. 1. For more on Avery, see cat. no. 7.

4.
Emil Klauprecht (?) after Angelo Paldi
BATTLE OF RESACA DE LA PALMA, MAY 9TH 1846. BATTLE OF PALO ALTO, MAY 8TH 1846.
Lithograph, 1847
14-7/8 x 19-1/4 in. (37.7 x 49.0 cm.), two views on one sheet
below upper print, l.c.: "Genl. Taylor's Staff"
below lower print, l.l. to l.r.: "J 2d. Dragoons H 8th. Infantry G Duncan's Art. F 4th Infantry E 2 18 pound D 3rd Infantry C Ringgold's Art. B 5th Infantry A Walker's Rangers"
l.c. below lower title: "From Drawings Taken on the Day of the Respective Battles by Ange Paldi 5th. Inf. U. S. A. and Respectfully Dedicated to the Colonel of His Regiment General Geo. M. Brooke."
l.l.: "Lith. by Klauprech & Menzel, Corner of Fifth & Vine St. Cincinnati"
l.r.: "Published by Wm. Wiswell"
Courtesy of Prints and Photographs Division, Library of Congress, Washington, D.C.

On May 8 Taylor's army, returning to Fort Texas from Point Isabel, sighted the Mexican army under Major General Mariano Arísta drawn up in a line of battle nearly a mile long, blocking their path. The two armies bombarded each other in the sanguinary battle of Palo Alto, and when dawn came the next day the Americans discovered that the Mexican army had withdrawn farther down the road toward Fort Texas. The Mexicans again assumed a defensive position, this time where the road crossed a dry ravine or resaca. In an even bloodier battle, the Americans broke through the Mexican line, sent Arísta's army reeling in panic back across the Rio Grande, and relieved the defenders of Fort Texas.

"Ange" (Angelo) Paldi, an Italian-born principal musician in the Fifth U. S. Infantry Regiment, witnessed the battles of Palo Alto and Resaca de la Palma and

sketched them on the spot.[1] The Fifth Infantry was on the right flank at Palo Alto, as depicted in these prints, but the view is taken from the center rear of the American lines. It is possible that Paldi, as a bandsman, was not deployed with the regular foot soldiers in his regiment, had time on his hands, and recorded the scene from this vantage point; or he may have made part of his sketch during a lull in the battle, when the dry grass between the two armies caught fire from the shell bursts and oppressive heat and smoke temporarily obscured the view for both forces. More likely, he drew on his knowledge of the battle to complete a sketch (or sketches) immediately after the event, since the Fifth Infantry encamped on the battlefields on the night after each battle. He was on furlough from May 15 to September 15, 1846, during which time he could have finished the sketches and personally delivered them to the lithographers in Cincinnati. (Even if Paldi did not make his sketches on the days of the battles, as claimed, he would still have had ample opportunity to record the actions from memory in their proper terrain, since his regiment was camped again in the area the next year, from January 23 or 25 until February 15.) Brigadier General George Mercer Brooke, to whom Paldi dedicated the print, was technically the regimental colonel of the Fifth Infantry but was not present at the battles; he spent most of the war in Louisiana, where on June 2, 1846, he replaced Brigadier General Edmund P. Gaines as commander of the U.S. Army's Western Division.[2]

Since the battle of Palo Alto was almost entirely an artillery duel with both armies basically static, Paldi did not have to portray complicated maneuvers. Unlike most popular lithographic prints of the battle, his view does not single out General Taylor or portray the wounding of Major Samuel Ringgold, whose flying artillery was recognized as a deciding factor in the American victory and whose death made him a national hero.[3]

From right to left, Paldi shows the mounted Texas Rangers under Samuel Walker, the Fifth Infantry Regiment commanded by Lieutenant Colonel James S. McIntosh, Ringgold's battery of artillery, the Third Infantry Regiment, Lieutenant William H. Churchill's two eighteen-pounder siege guns, the Fourth Infantry Regiment, Captain James Duncan's artillery, the Eighth Infantry Regiment, and the Second Dragoons. Five covered wagons in the left foreground of the print are meant, no doubt, to suggest the army's large, cumbersome baggage and supply train. As reported by other eyewitnesses, the flat, grassy middle distance between the armies is entirely devoid of bushes and includes the grass fires. Among General Arísta's more numerous Mexican troops in the distance may be distinguished, from right to left, General Anastasio Torrejón's lancers, on horseback with their lances held vertically and pennants waving; several masses of infantry separated by four batteries of artillery with three guns each; and, on the Mexican right, more cavalry. The distant background is flat with a few small trees. Accounts of the battle generally agree with one another and corroborate the details of the print.[4] In keeping with common artistic practice, Paldi reduced somewhat the number of soldiers in each infantry unit. (A full-strength American regiment at this time seems to have had around five hundred men.)

Paldi's view of the battle of Resaca de la Palma is more difficult to decipher, and an assessment of its accuracy is more complicated. No descriptive key is furnished, with the exception of the inscription "Genl. Taylor's Staff" (which alludes to three mounted officers in silhouette in the foreground). The action at Resaca de la Palma took place on obstructed terrain amidst general confusion and ended in a complete rout of the Mexican forces; thus it was far less orderly than Palo Alto and presented Paldi with a much more difficult subject.[5] At the beginning of the engagement, chaparral and small trees obstructed the Americans' view of the battlefield except along a road through the ravine at the center of the Mexican line. Major Thomas Staniford, second in command of Paldi's regiment (the commander, Lieutenant Colonel McIntosh, was severely wounded twice in the battle), later reported that the Fifth Infantry

> was ordered into the chaparral on the left of the road, and directed to advance as skirmishers, and push for the enemy. The chaparral at first was dense, almost impassable; consequently the regiment became much separated and extended, rendering it impossible to advance with much regularity. A severe cannonading from both sides now began, mingled with tremendous fire of musketry. In a few moments the order was given to charge the enemy's batteries, which was promptly done by cavalry and infantry, and the enemy's guns were all captured.[6]

Even if Paldi and his fellow musicians were at the rear of all of this, it is highly unlikely that he could have made anything more than quick, cursory sketches, if indeed he made any at all at this time. The artist therefore must have drawn his view immediately after the battle (if we are indeed to trust the inscription of the English edition claiming that it was made on the day of the battle). Paldi probably relied on his own recollections and those of his comrades, and he may have deliberately distorted the scene and eliminated some of the trees and underbrush to present a fuller account to the viewer.

The focus of the print is just to the left of center, along the road through the ravine, where a squadron of the U. S. Second Dragoons charges the batteries of the Mexican center. None of the American cavalrymen is specifically discernible as Captain Charles A. May, whose "brilliant charge" at Resaca de la Palma was celebrated by numerous popular prints.[7] Just to the left, in front of another Mexican cannon, appears to be an officer who wears a cockade and raises his sword; this might represent Mexican General Rómulo Díaz de la Vega, who was captured in the battle shortly after the charge of the dragoons. A body of Mexican infantry, protected by the cover of a thicket, fires at the enfilading American infantry at the far left.

The view seems to have been taken from a position on the left of the road, where part of Paldi's regiment would have been. The American infantrymen in the left foreground, some in silhouette, could represent part of the Fifth Infantry emerging from the chaparral into the open ground around the Mexican positions. If so, they are in position to take the cannons if the cavalry charge only temporarily dislodges the Mexican gunners.[8] One has to doubt that General Taylor's staff had such a fine view of the scene at such close range to the Mexican cannon; perhaps this effective and not uncommon compositional device of silhouetted foreground figures was added by the lithographer. Accurately, however, only one American cannon, commanded by Lieu-

BATTLE OF RESACA DE LA PALMA,
MAY 9TH 1846.

BATTLE OF PALO ALTO,
MAY 8TH 1846

FROM DRAWINGS TAKEN ON THE DAY OF THE RESPECTIVE BATTLES BY ANGE PALDI 5TH INF U S A AND RESPECTFULLY DEDICATED TO THE COLONEL OF HIS REGIMENT GENERAL GEO. M. BROOKE.

Lith by Klauprech & Menzel Corner of Fifth & Vine St. Cincinnati

Published by W. Wiswell

4. Battle of Resaca de la Palma / Battle of Palo Alto

tenant Randolph Ridgely, is shown on the far right, while further Mexican batteries may be barely seen in the distance at left, masked among the trees.[9] In the left middle distance, a body of Mexican lancers appears in full retreat; in the left and center horizon appear lines of Mexican infantry. At right, somewhat awkwardly, another body of American cavalry charges into the picture; in the distant right behind them, trees and thickets almost obscure several lines of U. S. infantry.

Sometime before August 28, 1847, Emil Klauprecht, the editor of the German literary journal *Fliegende Blätter* and partner with Adolphus Menzel in the Cincinnati lithography firm of Klauprecht & Menzel, obtained Angelo Paldi's sketches from the front.[10] Klauprecht & Menzel (who anglicized the firm's name to Klauprech & Menzel on some of their prints) issued two editions of lithographs after Paldi's sketches. One presented views of both battles on a single sheet, with titles and inscriptions in English. Another edition, probably from the same stone or stones, was actually printed on two separate sheets, one for Palo Alto and another for Resaca de la Palma; these had German titles and inscriptions and appeared as illustrations in *Fliegende Blätter* in August and September 1847.[11] Along with the illustrations, Klauprecht published a German translation of Thomas Bangs Thorpe's descriptions of the battles from *"Our Army" on the Rio Grande*, which had appeared in August 1846. If Paldi did not label his sketch, it is possible that Klauprecht & Menzel supplied the identifying inscriptions for Paldi's Palo Alto view from Thorpe's account of that battle. How faithfully the lithographers adhered to the original sketches cannot be determined, since the sketches have not been located.

1. Paldi was born in Mortara in the Kingdom of Sardinia (now part of Italy) on January 21, 1805. Sometime afterwards he went to France, where he became known as André Paldi, worked as a house painter, and married. The date of his emigration to America is not known, but on July 2, 1841, Paldi enlisted with the U. S. Army at Fort Crawford, Wisconsin. As a "principal musician" (sergeant) Paldi might have been a sort of band leader, depending on the instruments of the other regimental musicians. In 1845 he and his unit went south to Corpus Christi, Texas, by way of New Orleans as part of Zachary Taylor's Army of Occupation. His term of enlistment expired on May 2, 1846, the day after his regiment marched to Point Isabel; he reenlisted in time to participate in the battles of Palo Alto and Resaca de la Palma a week later. After this Paldi went on furlough and apparently did not rejoin his regiment (which had meanwhile fought at Monterrey) until October 1846, for "the principal musician" was listed as absent without leave after September 15. The Fifth Infantry was stationed at Saltillo from November 16, 1846, until January 9, 1847; later they marched in Winfield Scott's campaign from Veracruz to Mexico City. Paldi himself, however, probably returned to the States sometime after April 15, 1847; the regimental returns list two principal musicians after this date, one of them on detached recruiting service by order of General Worth. Paldi was discharged on January 6, 1848, probably at Fort Gibson, Indian Territory.

Later Paldi settled in Detroit and became a practicing architect and draftsman. From 1853 until 1859 he was employed in this capacity with the Detroit City Water Works and advertised regularly in the Detroit city and business directories for the execution of plans for public and private edifices. During the Civil War he served as a major with the First Michigan Cavalry, after the war returning to Detroit. In 1872 he left his wife and family, went to Albion, New York, and contracted a bigamous marriage. In Albion he assumed the name of "Michael" as a prefix on account of what one acquaintance described as his "wonderful skill in painting" and his admiration for Michelangelo. Neither wife knew of the other's existence until after Paldi's death, c. 1879, when both women filed for Mexican War veteran's widow's pensions. (For biographical sources see Certificate of Marriage of Ange, André Paldi to Marie Honorine Philippe, dated May 4, 1836, Montesson, Canton d'Argenteuil, France, copy and translation in Paldi's Mexican War Veterans Pension Claim, RG 15, National Archives, Washington, D.C.; *Registers of Enlistments in the United States Army, 1798-1914* [Washington, D.C.: National Archives Microfilm Publications], vols. 43-44, 1840-June 1846, M233, roll 21; Returns of the Fifth Regiment of Infantry, U. S. Army, May 1846-January 1848, RG 94, M665, roll 55, National Archives; Detroit City and Business Directories, 1852-59, entries for Paldi and for Detroit City Water Works; Heitman, *Historical Register*, 2:134.)

2. Bauer, *Mexican War*, p. 58; Fayette Robinson, *An Account of the Organization of the Army of the United States; with Biographies of Distinguished Officers of All Grades*, 2 vols. (Philadelphia: E. H. Butler & Co., 1848), 1:325-27.

3. In 1846 Nathaniel Currier published three versions of *General Taylor at the Battle of Palo Alto* and two versions of *The Death of Major Ringgold of the Flying Artillery at the Battle of Palo Alto* (see fig. 16); lithographers James Baillie and the Kelloggs of Connecticut also published prints of these subjects. All were composed back east as news of the events on the Rio Grande reached the home front.

4. For a description of the battle of Palo Alto, see Thorpe, *"Our Army" on the Rio Grande*, pp. 73-88. On pp. 202ff. Thorpe published the official reports of several of the commanding officers, including General Taylor. Also see Henry, *Campaign Sketches*, pp. 90-95, map opp. p. 90; Kendall, *War Between the United States and Mexico Illustrated*, pp. 1-3; Smith, *War with Mexico*, 1:164-69.

5. For eyewitness descriptions of the battle of Resaca de la Palma, see Thorpe, *"Our Army" on the Rio Grande*, pp. 89-111, 202ff. (official reports); also see Henry, *Campaign Sketches*, pp. 96-102, especially map opp. p. 96. Secondary accounts are in Smith, *War with Mexico*, 1:170-76; Kendall, *War Between the United States and Mexico Illustrated*, pp. 3-4.

6. Report of Major T. Staniford to Col. D. E. Twiggs, May 10, 1846, published in Thorpe, *"Our Army" on the Rio Grande*, pp. 215-16.

7. For a discussion of these prints see Rick Stewart's essay. Captain May had a very distinctive appearance, with long, dark hair and beard.

8. A controversy developed as to who actually captured de la Vega and his guns. Although May took credit, the infantry claimed that May's charge was not completely successful and that the Mexican gunners, including General de la Vega, dodged the cavalrymen and returned to their guns. After the dragoons' charge had lost its momentum deep inside the Mexican lines, the American Eighth Infantry and part of the Fifth followed up and captured the guns. A bugler is said to have captured General de la Vega. See Smith, *War with Mexico*, 1:467, n. 16; C. A. May's report of May 10, 1846, in Thorpe, *"Our Army" on the Rio Grande*, pp. 218-20.

9. See Ridgely's report printed in Thorpe, *"Our Army" on the Rio Grande*, pp. 216-18. After Major Ringgold was mortally wounded at Palo Alto, Ridgely assumed command of his battery of the Flying Artillery. This battery was the only American artillery that engaged the enemy at Resaca de la Palma.

10. Klauprecht (1815-96), a native of Mainz, reportedly came to America in 1832. The source of his lithographic training is unknown, but by 1837 he had established a lithography business in Cincinnati. Sometime before 1840 he formed his partnership with Menzel. At least one print they produced during the 1840s has Klauprecht's own signature on the stone (see cat. no. 40). Klauprecht also had literary interests; besides the *Fliegende Blätter*, he was editor or coeditor of three other German newspapers in Cincinnati: the *Deutsche Republikaner* (1849-51, 1852-56), the *Westliche Blätter* (1851-52), and the *Volksblatt* (1856-64). He evidently left the lithography business sometime in the mid-1850s, Menzel carrying it on in his own name after 1853. (See *Lithography in Cincinnati, Part I: To the Advent of the Steam Press* [Cincinnati: Young & Klein, 1956], n.p.; Peter C. Marzio, *The Democratic Art: Chromolithography 1840-1900; Pictures for a Nineteenth Century America* [Boston: David R. Godine, 1979], pp. 131, 254 nn. 6, 8; Robert E. Ward, *A Bio-Bibliography of German-American Writers, 1670-1970* [White Plains, New York: Kraus International Publications, 1985], p. 155.)

11. *Fliegende Blätter* (Cincinnati), Aug. 28, 1847, foldout betw. pp. 234 and 235; Sept. 4, 1847, after p. 242.

5. See Plate 2

Adolphe-Jean-Baptiste Bayot after Carl Nebel
BATTLE OF PALO-ALTO
Toned lithograph (hand colored), 1851
11 x 16-11/16 in. (27.9 x 42.4 cm.)
l.l.: "C. Nebel fecit."
l.r.: "Bayot lith."
From George Wilkins Kendall, *The War Between the United States and Mexico Illustrated* (New York: D. Appleton & Company, 1851), plate 1
ACM 186.72/1

This print is the first in the monumental series of twelve lithographs for Carl Nebel and George Wilkins Kendall's *War Between the United States and Mexico Illustrated*. The author, George Wilkins Kendall of the New Orleans *Picayune*, probably first met German-born artist Carl Nebel in Mexico City during the American occupation.[1] Although Kendall himself was present at many of the battles and had "personally examined the ground on which all save that of Buena Vista were fought," it is less clear that Nebel witnessed the battles or (in some cases) examined the sites.[2]

In the preface to the album Kendall says little concerning the artist's working methods, but he does carefully state Nebel's intentions:

Of the twelve illustrations accompanying this work... the greater number were drawn on the spot by the artist. So far as regards the general configuration of the ground, fidelity of the landscape, and correctness of the works and buildings introduced, they may be strictly relied upon. Every reader must be aware of the impossibility, in painting a battle scene, of giving more than one feature or principal incident in the strife. The artist has ever cho-

sen what he deemed the more interesting as well as exciting points of each combat, and trusts that the public may excuse any errors which may be discovered. Something the painter is always compelled to sacrifice for effect, but in the present series of illustrations the greatest care has been taken to avoid inaccuracies.

Kendall emphasized his concern for even the small details: "The soldiers of the United States have been painted in their ordinary fatigue caps and dresses—such as they always wore during the war. More effect might have been produced by arraying them in their full uniforms, but this would have been deviating from the truth and was avoided."[3]

Several American reviewers in 1851 went a step further than Kendall, implying that Nebel had accompanied the reporter in all of the battles and had drawn every picture on the spot. They also emphasized Kendall's impartiality as an observer, although it is obvious today that Kendall's judgment was clouded by the patriotism that inspired him to create the book and by his earlier experiences as a prisoner in Mexico after the failed Texan Santa Fe expedition of 1841.[4]

In fact, Nebel probably never visited Palo Alto, during the battle or on any occasion.[5] Kendall himself was not at the battle but later visited the site and obtained official battle accounts. He must have provided Nebel with the best sources, possibly including Thorpe's *"Our Army" on the Rio Grande* and Klauprecht & Menzel's lithograph(s) of Angelo Paldi's sketch of the battle.

In Nebel's reconstruction, the American army in the foreground faces the Mexican army in the distance, which blocks the road from Point Isabel (behind the viewer) to Fort Texas opposite Matamoros (out of view in the distance). In the foreground along the road, two teams of oxen with ammunition caissons have unlimbered the two eighteen-pounders seen firing in the center of the print. In the right foreground, surrounded by his staff, is an American officer on a white horse, probably intended to represent General Taylor on "Old Whitey." Just beyond him is the Third Infantry and beyond them a squadron of the Second Dragoons. To the dragoons' right, the Fifth Infantry is formed in a square to repel Mexican lancers attacking from the right distance. Directly beyond the dragoons, Major Ringgold's battery of the Flying Artillery assists the Fifth against the Mexican lancers. To the left of the eighteen-pounders are several lines of American infantry, probably representing the Fourth and Eighth Infantry and a battalion of artillery acting as infantry. Beyond them, on the left, are another squadron of the Second Dragoons and Captain Duncan's battery of light artillery. Along the Mexican line in the distance, long lines of infantry alternate with batteries of artillery, except where smoke from the grass fire has obscured the view.

The details of the uniforms are generally correct, as Kendall and the artist intended. The troops wear blue fatigues with forage caps or straw panama hats, which a few men adopted for hot climates. Enlisted men and lower-grade officers wear shell jackets, while others wear the long frock coats prescribed for officers.[6]

While he kept close to his historical sources, Nebel also exercised a certain amount of artistic judgment. He broke up what could have been a very long, flat, and uninterestingly horizontal scene by introducing foreground details such as the oxen, the dead and wounded, and the

mounted officers. He also incorrectly added hills on the horizon.[7] (The artist may have gotten the impression that the area around the battlefield was hilly from an engraving titled *Battle Field, Palo Alto — Mexican Army Drawn up in Battle Array* that appeared in Thorpe's *"Our Army" on the Rio Grande.* Thorpe's print may have been done from an eyewitness sketch, but the engraver drew groves of trees that could be construed as an escarpment in the distance.[8]) For pictorial and narrative reasons, Nebel also condensed the number of men in the units and perhaps deepened their ranks to include as much of the American line as possible. Where Angelo Paldi's view was adapted to a three-page foldout, Nebel had to restrict himself to a more conventional format.

It is significant that Nebel did not illustrate the battle of Resaca de la Palma. Kendall called the second battle "but a sequel or supplement" to the first, adding: "No drawing of the [second] could possibly be taken, owing to the broken nature of the ground and the dense cover in which the battle was fought."[9] This is curious, in light of Paldi's sketch, and may indicate that Paldi eliminated a considerable amount of trees and brush from his view;[10] or perhaps Kendall and Nebel ignored the second battle because they had insufficient knowledge of the battlefield.

1. Kendall, his role in Mexican War journalism, and the production and reception of his and Nebel's illustrated history are discussed in Rick Stewart's essay.

Nebel (1805-55) was particularly suited to the task of illustrating Kendall's great work. He reportedly completed his collegiate education, including the study of engineering, at "one of the German Universities," and "further perfected himself in architecture and drawing in Paris and Italy." During a five-year residence in Mexico, from 1829 until

1834, he sketched and painted Mexican costumes, cities, buildings, landscapes, and archaeological sites, which he later had lithographed in Paris for his album *Voyage pittoresque et archéologique dans la partie la plus intéressante du Mexique* (Paris, 1836). With an introduction by the renowned Prussian geographer Alexander von Humboldt, the work was also published in Spanish in 1840 as *Viaje pintoresco y arqueológico sobre la parte más interesante de la República mexicana, en los años transcurridos desde 1829 hasta 1834.* Although rare in the United States because of its one-hundred-dollar price, it was widely recognized then and now as one of the finest illustrated works on that country.

Little is known about Nebel until 1847, when he was again in Mexico City. On November 22, 1847, during the American occupation, Colonel James E. Duncan wrote to Kendall that "I see Navel [*sic*] on the street[.] he says he is getting on well with his pictures — now that I am in limbo I cannot go to see them, or I should give you some account of them" (Kendall Family Papers). Nebel was in Paris during part of the time that his Mexican War lithographs were being printed by Lemercier; he died there on June 4, 1855. (See Pourade, *Sign of the Eagle*, p. 165; Tyler, *Mexican War: A Lithographic Record*, pp. 18-19; Kendall Correspondence, Beinecke Rare Book and Manuscript Library, Yale University; New Orleans *Daily Picayune*, July 14, 1850, p. 2, Jan. 1, 1851, p. 2; Emanuel Benezit, *Dictionnaire critique et documentaire des peintres, sculpteurs, dessinateurs et graveurs de tous les temps et de tous les pays ....* Nouv. ed., 8 vols. [Paris: Librairie Gründ, 1948-55, 1966], 6:323; Ulrich Thieme and Felix Becker, *Allgemeines Lexikon der Bildenden Künstler von Antike bis zur Gegenwart,* 38 vols. [Leipzig: Verlag von E. A. Seeman, 1907-26, 1942, 1947; reprint by F. Ullmann, 1965], 25:370-71.)

Lithographer Adolphe-Jean-Baptiste Bayot (1810-after 1866) was born in Alessandria, Italy, to French parents. He exhibited works at the Paris salons from 1836-1866. (See Benezit, *Dictionnaire*, 1:484; Thieme and Becker, *Allgemeines Lexikon*, 3:104.) Peters, *America on Stone*, p. 91, claims that Bayot came to the United States, but this is unlikely.

2. Ron Tyler went a long way toward defining Nebel's qualifications as an eyewitness; see his *Mexican War: A Lithographic Record*, pp. 18ff.

3. Kendall, *War Between the United States and Mexico Illustrated*, pp. iii, iv.

4. Mexican War scrapbook, pp. 5, 10, 15, 17, 21, 22, 27, in Kendall Family Papers, clippings credited to Boston *Atlas*, probably Feb. 1851; Boston *Saturday Evening Gazette*, Feb. 1, 1851; New Orleans *Crescent*, n.d.; Boston *Sentinel*, probably Feb. 1851; Boston *Transcript*, probably Feb. 1851; and "M.F.W.," correspondent to the New Orleans *Delta*, n.d. For Kendall's adventures in the Santa Fe expedition, see Copeland, *Kendall of the Picayune*, pp. 57-108, and Kendall, *Narrative of the Texan Santa Fe Expedition* (New York: Harper and Brothers, 1844).

5. This was pointed out by Pourade, *Sign of the Eagle*, p. 165, and by Tyler, *Mexican War: A Lithographic Record*, p. 20.

6. See *Regulations for the Uniform and Dress of the Army of the United States* (Washington, D.C.: Adjutant General's Office, printed by J. Gideon, June 1839), General Order No. 36 of 1839.

7. Pourade, *Sign of the Eagle*, p. 165.

8. Thorpe, *"Our Army" on the Rio Grande*, opp. p. 74.

9. Kendall, *War Between the United States and Mexico Illustrated*, p. 4.

10. Thorpe, *"Our Army" on the Rio Grande*, opp. p. 92, contains an engraving of the battlefield of Resaca de la Palma. Probably made from a drawing by an eyewitness, perhaps Thorpe himself, it shows dense chaparral, as reported.

6.
After John Phillips
MATAMORAS
Toned lithograph (hand colored), 1848
10-3/8 x 15-3/8 in. (26.4 x 39.1 cm.)
l.r.: "Day & Son Lithrs. to the Queen"
From John Phillips and Alfred Rider, *Mexico Illustrated in Twenty-six Views* (London: E. Atchley, Library of Fine Arts, 1848), plate 26
ACM 10.79/26

Matamoros surrendered to General Taylor on May 17, 1846, several days after the battle of Resaca de la Palma. Until the end of the war it remained under American control as an important supply base and collecting point for thousands of American volunteer troops.[1] Englishman John Phillips apparently traveled to Matamoros sometime before the war, when he made the original sketch or sketches for this view. The print is the last in a series by Phillips and lithographer Alfred Rider for an album titled *Mexico Illustrated in Twenty-six Views*, published in London in 1848, which apparently sold in the United States for one hundred dollars.[2]

In his text accompanying the view of Matamoros Phillips acknowledged that the town "has recently come into notice from being the place where hostilities commenced between the Mexican and American troops.... Like most Mexican towns, the houses seldom exceed two stories in height, and are strongly built of stone or sunburnt bricks. There is a large square, part of one side of which is occupied by the cathedral, a heavy unfinished building."[3]

Exact dates for Phillips's original sketches have not been determined, but Richard F. Pourade states that the artist "saw Matamoros before the ravages of the great hurricane of 1844." Phillips's print differs considerably from an engraved view of Matamoros, taken from the north or northeast, that appeared in the New York *Herald* on July 29, 1846.[4] No cupolas or domes appear in the *Herald* view, whereas Phillips's contains several.

Engraved copies of Phillips's views, including this one, appeared in Brantz Mayer's two-volume history, *Mexico, Aztec, Spanish and Republican* (1850). Most of these plates are signed "Bobbett & Edmonds Sc." and give no credit to Phillips.[5]

Prints after sketches made by Americans in Matamoros also appeared in illustrated newspapers, journals, and books. In addition to their 1846 view, the New York *Herald* published a *View of the Market Plaza in Matamoros* on March 8, 1847. Thorpe's *"Our Army" on the Rio Grande* (1846) contains engravings after eyewitness sketches of Taylor's headquarters tents near Matamoros, a *View of Matamoros from Fort Brown* (fig. 2), views of private residences, the "unfinished" cathedral, the *Halls of Justice and Head Quarters of Our Troops*, the *Chapel de la Capilla*, and the Mexican barracks.[6]

One other note may be of interest: the flags in the Amon Carter Museum's impression of Phillips's print are hand-colored red, white, and green for Mexico, but a close examination of the flag on the square-rigged vessel suggests that the artist or lithographer originally intended it to be the Stars and Stripes. This suggests an appeal to the American market by either Phillips or his lithographer.

1. See Smith and Judah, *Chronicles of the Gringos*, pp. 71-74, and Bauer, *Mexican War*, pp. 81-88.

2. There is some confusion about John Phillips. Simon Houfe, *The Dictionary of British Book Illustrators and Caricaturists 1800-1914* (Woodbridge, England: Antique Collector's Club, 1978), lists a

6. MATAMORAS

John Phillips (1800-74) who was Keeper of the York Museum, 1825-40, Professor of Geology at Trinity College, Dublin, 1844-53, and Keeper of the Ashmolean Museum, Oxford, 1854-70. He illustrated a number of books on the English countryside, but there is no mention of his having gone to Mexico. In 1846 a *Descriptive Notice of the Silver Mines and Amalgamation Processes of Mexico, Extracted from the Railway Register* was published in London, with the author listed as John Phillips, "Secretary to the Real del Monte Mining Company." Perhaps coincidentally, a contemporary named John Arthur Phillips wrote a number of books on metallurgy. See *British Museum General Catalogue of Printed Books to 1955* (Readex Microprint Corporation, 1967), 20:225, cols. 69-71, 75, 77. Thanks to Ann-Marie Logan and Ethel Symolon of the Yale Center for British Art, New Haven, Connecticut, for information on Phillips. Nothing is known about Phillips's collaborator on *Mexico Illustrated*, Alfred Rider.

Day & Son was an important English lithography firm, established before 1830 by William Day, Sr. (1797-1845). Day's eldest son, William Jr., was head of the firm in 1848. After 1867 the firm became known as Vincent Brooks, Day & Son. (See Ronald Russell, *Guide to British Topographical Prints* [North Pomfret, Vt.: David & Charles, 1979], p. 105; Michael Twyman, *Lithography 1800-1850* [London: Oxford University Press, 1970], pp. 208-9.)

A reviewer of Kendall's *War Between the United States and Mexico Illustrated* wrote, "Some English Historian has issued a work upon the same subject, which sells for $100, while Mr. Kendall's is sold at $40, and much more handsomely bound." (Unidentified clipping from a Mobile, Alabama, newspaper, Mexican War scrapbook, p. 23, Kendall Family Papers.)

3. Phillips, *Mexico Illustrated*, text accompanying plate 26.

4. Pourade, *Sign of the Eagle*, p. 16; New York *Herald*, July 29, 1846, p. 1. The *Herald*'s engraver, Samuel Putnam Avery, gives no credit to the artist, but the caption claims the view is "a faithful representation as from the point where it was taken." Compare also the "Plan of Matamoros, Fort Brown, and surrounding country" in Thorpe, *"Our Army" on the Rio Grande*, p. 50.

5. Brantz Mayer, *Mexico, Aztec, Spanish and Republican*, 2 vols. (Hartford: S. Drake and Company, 1853, copyright 1850), 1: opp. p. 337.

6. New York *Herald*, March 8, 1847, p. 1; Thorpe, *"Our Army" on the Rio Grande*, illustrations on pp. 137, 139, 140, 143, 147, 149, 150, and tipped in opp. 125, 129, 140, 142.

7.
Samuel Putnam Avery after an unknown artist
VIEW OF THE PLAZA OF CAMARGO, MEXICO
Engraving, 1847
l.r. in image: "Saml. Avery, Sc."
l.c.: "The Camp of the Seventh Regiment of the United States Infantry, August 19th, 1846."
From the New York *Herald*, January 30, 1847, p. 1

Preparing for an attack on the Mexican interior, Taylor sent the Seventh Infantry over two hundred miles up the winding Rio Grande to its junction with the Rio San Juan near the town of Camargo, one of the last points along the great river that could be reached by steamboats. The Seventh reached Camargo on July 14 and 15, followed shortly by General Worth and the Fifth Infantry, and established another supply base and staging point.[1] Captain W. S. Henry, who arrived with the Third Infantry on August 3, just a few days before the sketch for this print was taken, wrote disparagingly:

> Camargo is a dilapidated-looking town…. It boasts, like all Mexican towns, of a grand Plaza and a Cathedral, a few low stone buildings, of very thick walls and flat roofs, a great many miserable "jacals," not a few donkeys, and any number of dogs and chicken-cocks. The 7th Infantry, under the command of Captain Miles, was encamped in the Plaza…. The Cathedral is of no particular architectural beauty; it has a cupola and two bells.[2]

This is one of a number of views of Mexican towns, cities, battles, and portraits of prominent soldiers engraved by Samuel Putnam Avery for the New York *Herald*.[3] Many of the Mexican War maps and plans that appeared in the paper without credit were probably engraved by Avery, although by 1847 he had a fourteen-year-old apprentice named Isaac Pesoa who could have done a few of these. The original artists never were credited.

Another engraving of the plaza and cathedral, taken from almost the same angle, appears in Henry's *Campaign Sketches*. It also shows tents in the plaza but has added a mortar, four field guns with limbers, and an ox cart.[4] The *Herald* had earlier published a "strictly accurate" *View of Camargo, Looking South*, "drawn by an accomplished officer of the regular Army." Captain D. P. Whiting was attached to the Seventh Infantry and was a capable artist, but so were many regular army officers and no firm attribution can be made for these views.[5]

1. Bauer, *Mexican War*, pp. 87-89; Smith, *War with Mexico*, 1:211-12, 356, 493.

2. Henry, *Campaign Sketches*, pp. 152-54. See also Luther Giddings's description quoted in Smith and Judah, *Chronicles of the Gringos*, pp. 289-90.

3. Samuel Putnam Avery (1822-1904), a native of New York City, was apprenticed to a bank note engraving company in his late teens. In 1844 he opened his own engraving office and the next year began to furnish engravings for the New York *Herald* and *Weekly Herald*. After the Mexican War Avery furnished engravings for books and magazines. Isaac Pesoa, Avery's former apprentice, eventually took over the engraving business as Avery, who had established an extensive network of friendships with many prominent American artists and collectors, became one of the most successful and respected art dealers in the country. (See Ruth Sieben Morgan, "Samuel Putnam Avery (1822-1904), Engraver on Wood; A Bio-Bibliographical Study," M.L.S. thesis, Columbia University, 1940; revised, with additions, 1942. Also see *Editorials and Resolutions in Memory of Samuel Putnam Avery* (New York: privately printed, 1905).)

4. Henry, *Campaign Sketches*, p. 153.

5. Avery engraved a view of Marin—a town on the march from Camargo to Monterrey—that appeared in the *Herald*, March 15, 1847, p. 1. A similar engraving, from the same viewpoint, appeared in Reid, *Scouting Expeditions*, opp. p. 133.

THE NEW YORK HERALD.

Vol. XIII. No. 29—Whole No. 4626.

NEW YORK, SATURDAY MORNING, JANUARY 30, 1847.

Price Two Cents.

VIEW OF THE PLAZA OF CAMARGO, MEXICO.

The Camp of the Seventh Regiment of the United States Infantry, August 19th, 1846.

THE NEW YORK HERALD.

JAMES GORDON BENNETT, PROPRIETOR.

Circulation---Forty Thousand.

The Mexican War.

[Correspondence of the Charleston Courier.]

New Orleans, Jan. 15, 1847.

Colonel Totten, Chief Engineer, of the United States, arrived here to-day from Washington. The Rocket and double Howitzer Brigade is expected daily. The regiments of Louisiana, Pennsylvania and Mississippi, are about being embarked, and will take 90 days rations with them. These troops are supposed to be destined for Tuspan, where they will be joined by the Massachusetts, North and South Carolina, Virginia, Illinois, and second Pennsylvania regiments.

AFFAIRS IN ALBANY.

LEGISLATIVE PROCEEDINGS.

TELEGRAPHIC.

Albany, January 29, 1847.

Senate.

The resolution was adopted to raise a select committee in regard to the Geological survey, with power to send for persons and papers.

Assembly.

Vice Chancellor's Court.

Before Vice Chancellor Sandford.

LEGISLATIVE PROCEEDINGS.

Albany, Jan. 28 1847.

Senate.

7. Plaza of Camargo, Mexico

Monterrey

8.
After Stephen G. Hill
VIEW OF MONTEREY — FROM THE
HEIGHTS SOUTH OF THE CITY.
Lithograph, 1846
8-11/16 x 16 in. (22.1 x 40.6 cm.)
l.c.: "Silver & Rowse, Lith., College Building,
Cin. O."
l.l. to l.r.: "Bishop's Palace. Orange Grove.
Arista's Garden. Black Fort. Cathedral and
Grand Plaza."
l.c. below title: "Drawn by Stephen G. Hill, of
1st. Reg. Ohio Volunteers. / Entered accord-
ing to Act of Congress, in the year 1846, by
Stephen G. Hill, in the Clerk's Office, of the
United States' District Court of the District of
Ohio."
Courtesy of Prints and Photographs Division,
Library of Congress, Washington, D.C.

Monterrey, capital of the state of Nuevo León, was the key objective in Taylor's campaign in northern Mexico. In 1846 it contained about 10,000 inhabitants and was defended by an almost equal number of soldiers—survivors of Arísta's army plus other reinforcements, all under the command of General Pedro Ampudía. Recognizing its military importance, the Mexicans had fortified the city strongly.

This lithograph is the first of a series of views of the battle of Monterrey after drawings by Private Stephen G. Hill of the Ohio Volunteers. Hill's first view was taken "from the heights south of the city" soon after its surrender, probably near a captured Mexican redoubt that stood on part of Federation ridge. The artist employed a somewhat primitive perspective, exaggerating the size of certain important landmarks and diminishing distances. Nonetheless the print provides an excellent overview of the topography, the Mexican defenses, and the points of the American attack in the four-day battle.[1]

The American army approached Monterrey on September 19 along the road from Marín to the northeast, which, if visible, would be in the far right distance. After receiving fire from Mexican guns they retired to the Bosque de Santo Domingo, which they called Walnut Grove or Walnut Springs, and established a camp. The fork of the road from Marín, seen in the distant middle right, was the approximate point from which the American army began its attack the next day. An American mortar set up in this vicinity serves as an important point of reference for orientation with other views of the city.[2]

On September 20, General Worth's division crossed the plain in the distance just in front of the conical hill (in the center left distance) in a sweeping march that took them beyond Independence Hill (at far left) on which the Bishop's Palace sits. The next day they captured the Saltillo Road and Federation ridge, most of which extends out of the picture to the left. Early the next morning (September 22) Worth's division stormed the highest part of Independence Hill and shortly afterwards captured the Bishop's Palace.

In the meantime, beginning on the twenty-first, troops under Generals Twiggs and Butler concentrated their efforts on the eastern part of the city, seen at the right. The American troops avoided the "Black Fort," in the center of the print; Taylor and his officers presumed, no doubt correctly, that this fortification directly north of the city could not be taken without heavy losses.[3] In spite of this precaution, the assaulting Americans in the eastern sector received almost constant fire from the Black Fort. The artist's regiment, the Ohio Volunteers, attacked the northeast side of town, seen just beyond the cathedral in the right of the print; Hill drew another view of this part of the battle (cat. no. 9). At far right are two horseshoe shapes, the one farthest right representing Fort Tenería, the nearer one Fort Diablo. The Americans took Tenería on the twenty-first, but with frightful loss; not until the evening of the twenty-second did the Mexicans evacuate Fort Diablo.

The attack in the eastern end was finally relieved on the twenty-third as Worth's division closed in from the west. While some of Worth's men trained captured Mexican guns (some from the heights from which this view was taken) on the cathedral and main plaza (seen at right), the rest advanced into the orange grove and through "Arista's palace and garden" (identified in the print on the left side of the city). Inside the city they fought their way from house to house east toward the main plaza, which is bounded on the right by the cathedral's facade and two towers. The building on the western side of the plaza was the prison, near where the artist took his third view; the adjacent building on the southern side of the plaza served as quarters for the Seventh Infantry after the battle. Just in front of this building and to the right rises a tiny tower belonging to the Convent of San Francisco. The empty square to the left of the prison is the market plaza. In the foreground is the Santa Catarina River, bounding the southern part of the city.

Hill was a grocer from Cincinnati who enlisted as a musician (bugler) in the First Regiment of Ohio Volunteer Infantry. He may have been wounded in the capture of Monterrey; his service

BISHOP'S PALACE.   ORANGE GROVE.   ARISTA'S GARDEN.   BLACK FORT.   CATHEDRAL AND GRAND PLAZA.

Silver & Rowse, Lith., College Building, Cin. O.

VIEW OF MONTEREY—FROM THE HEIGHTS SOUTH OF THE CITY.

Drawn by Stephen G. Hill, of 1st. Reg. Ohio Volunteers.

Entered according to Act of Congress, in the year 1846, by STEPHEN G. HILL, in the Clerk's Office, of the United States' District Court of the District of Ohio.

8. MONTEREY — FROM THE HEIGHTS SOUTH OF THE CITY

record indicates that he was discharged there on October 24 on a surgeon's certificate of disability.[4]

He may have returned to Cincinnati at this time with his sketches, which were soon lithographed by the Cincinnati firm of Silver & Rowse.[5]

1. Among the numerous accounts of the struggle for Monterrey are Kendall, *War Between the United States and Mexico Illustrated*, pp. 5-10; Smith, *War with Mexico* 1:230-61, including maps on pp. 232, 240; Thomas Bangs Thorpe, *Our Army at Monterey* (Philadelphia: Carey and Hart, 1847), with map opp. p. 9; and Henry, *Campaign Sketches*, pp. 190-216, and map betw. pp. 192 and 193. For the historical context of the battle see Bauer, *Mexican War*, pp. 86, 89; Smith, *War with Mexico*, 1:230-34, 493-95.

2. To the right of the fork in the road appears a wooded hill, which Carl Nebel used as a vantage point for his view of the battle (cat. no. 16). Stephen Hill's second view was probably taken just to the left of the fork in the road. The mortar appears in both of these views. The views can be usefully compared with the map "Monterey and Its Approaches" lithographed by Jules Manouvrier and Perez Snell for the New Orleans *Daily Picayune*, Nov. 19, 1846 (extra), p. 2.

3. Smith, *War with Mexico*, 1:233, 495 n. 16, gives a detailed description of this fort based on contemporary Mexican and American sources. He notes that it was known variously as "the citadel," the "Old Colored Gentleman," and by its Mexican name "Fort Independencia," which is not to be confused with the fort on Independence Hill.

4. Cincinnati Directory for 1846, p. 203; *Official Roster of the Soldiers of the State of Ohio in the War of the Rebellion, 1861-1866, and in the War with Mexico, 1846-1848* (Norwalk, Ohio: The Laning Company, for the Ohio State General Assembly, 1895), pp. 406, 407; envelope containing compiled service record for Stephen G. Hill of Company K, First Regiment of Ohio Infantry, RG 94, National Archives, Washington, D.C. Hill was born about 1819 and enlisted on June 9, 1846, in Captain William H. Ramsey's Company K of the First Ohio; he is probably the artist "S. G. Hill" who painted an undated oil on canvas view of the Platte River, in Colorado. (Rudolf Wunderlich, "The Things that Were: 19th and 20th Century Paintings of the American West," *Kennedy Quarterly* 8 [June 1968], p. 55.) A cabinet maker named S. G. Hill is listed in the Cincinnati Directory for 1849-50, p. 137.

5. Silver & Rowse, located at the "College Building" or "College Hall" on Walnut Street in Cincinnati, existed only briefly in 1846 and 1847. Silver may perhaps be Thomas J. Silver, who is listed as a painter in the Cincinnati city directories for 1842, 1843, and 1846. J. B. Rowse appears in the city directory for 1848-49. About the same time that he was working with Silver, he was also associated with a Sherer (or Scherer) in the same building. (See *Lithography in Cincinnati, Part I*, n.p.)

9.
After Stephen G. Hill
A VIEW OF THE BATTLE OF MONTEREY, SEPT. 21, 1846.
Lithograph, 1846
10-1/2 x 18-3/4 in. (26.7 x 47.6 cm.)
l.l. to l.r.: "Miss. and Tenn. Volunteers. Gen. Taylor and Staff. First Reg. O. V. [Silver & Rowse, Lith. College Building, Cin. O.] Mortar. Louisville Legion. Gen. Worth Storming the Heights. / Cathedral. Gen. Hamer. Black Fort. Bishop's Palace."
l.c. below title: "From a Drawing by Stephen G. Hill, of the 1st Reg. Ohio Volunteers. / Entered according to an act of Congress, in the District Court of the United States for the district of Ohio, by Stephen G. Hill, in the year 1846."
ACM 79.87

This view of the attack on Monterrey from the east corresponds exactly with a description of the topography and battle by Major Luther Giddings, an officer in Hill's regiment. The correspondence is so close that either Giddings or Hill may have used the other's work to aid in recollecting the scene, or the two may even have collaborated.

Giddings describes the regiment's position at the beginning of the battle, looking on from north or northeast of the city:

> A gently ascending slope, covered in places with chapparal — with here and there a field of corn or sugar cane, spreads itself before the town. The road by which our army approached, descends over this plain into the centre of the city....
>
> In front of the city, and about one fourth of a mile out, upon the plain, stands, solitary and alone, an immense fort, covering 3 or 4 acres of ground. It is built of solid masonry, with bastions, ditches

&c.— and is one of those strong holds which, in the opinion of our military engineers, can only be taken by what they call regular approaches. This fort is pierced for 32 guns, and commands every avenue, to the city, over the plain upon the east. It throws both shot and shells from its walls; and it was this fort...that fired upon our advanced division on the day of our arrival.

In the rear, or west of the city, rises, ridge after ridge, and peak over peak, the lofty Sierra Madre. On the north, [sic, west] of the city is a deep gorge in the mountain, through which is the road to Saltillo and Mexico. This pass and the approaches to Monterey upon that side, are defended by a series of batteries placed upon peaks jutting out from the sides of the great Sierra, and by a strong and elevated fortress, located about half way between the pass and town — known as "the Bishop's palace." It was through this pass alone, that the Mexican army could receive reinforcements or retreat with safety.[1]

At far left in Hill's print, a body of troops representing Brigadier General John A. Quitman's brigade, composed of the First Mississippi and First Tennessee Regiments of volunteers, attacks a small fort flying a Mexican flag. This is undoubtedly Fort Tenería. Puffs of smoke to the right of the fort indicate areas of heavy fighting in the eastern portion of the city, already under attack by the regulars of Brigadier General David E. Twiggs's First Division. In this stage of the fighting Twiggs's division found itself in a very tight spot, caught between two Mexican batteries.

The mounted officers in the left foreground represent General Taylor and his staff; Taylor is the third from the left. Just to Taylor's right, a line of troops files toward the center of town, denoted by the dome of the cathedral. These troops represent the artist's own regiment, the First Ohio Volunteers, who were sent to relieve Captain Braxton Bragg's battery. Bragg's was one of three American batteries at work on the east side of the city and was in some danger of being captured. The long line of men in the right foreground is the "Louisville Legion" of Kentucky Volunteers, guarding the mortar commanded by Captain Ramsey (which belches a puff of white smoke in the center foreground). Another of the mounted officers in the foreground is identified as Brigadier General Thomas L. Hamer, whose brigade consisted of the First Ohio Volunteers and the Louisville Legion.

In the distance, just to the right of center, smoke billows from the Black Fort, whose walls and parapets may be barely distinguished to the right of the smoke. On a hill to the right of the Black Fort is the Bishop's Palace, behind which are the fortifications on Federation Hill. At far right, the Second Division under General William Jenkins Worth marches off into the distance; Mexican lancers are shown attacking the head of this column. The lancers were driven back by the Texas Rangers accompanying Worth's division (see cat. no. 12).

The attack on Monterrey from the east achieved little despite its heavy cost to the Americans. Mexican defenders fired through loopholes in stone walls and from masked batteries, redoubts, and other fortifications. Almost every street was barricaded and raked by field pieces, and the houses themselves, with their thick walls and flat roofs, were readily defended. Hill's own regiment penetrated the city's streets but could not maintain its position against so many well-fortified houses.[2] Had General Quitman's troops not managed to take the Tenería redoubt, the entire attack in the east would have faltered.

1. Major [Luther] Giddings, 1st Ohio Volunteers Camp near Monterey, Mexico, to "Messrs. Comly," publishers of the Dayton (Ohio) Journal, cited in Niles' National Register 21 (Nov. 14, 1846): 167. Giddings later wrote an expanded account of his experiences in Sketches of the Campaign in Northern Mexico in Eighteen Hundred Forty-Six and Seven; compare the map on p. 149 of that work with Stephen Hill's view.

2. Besides Giddings's, eyewitness accounts of the fighting in the eastern and northern sector of the city include Henry, Campaign Sketches, pp. 206-9; Electus Backus's journal quoted in Smith and Judah, Chronicles of the Gringos, pp. 79-82; Manuel Balbontín, La invasión americana, pp. 24-35; and Grant, Personal Memoirs, pp. 67-73. Apparently no prints after eyewitness views exist that show street fighting in the eastern sector. Reid, Scouting Expeditions, contains an excellent engraving titled Street Fight on General Worth's Side (opp. p. 192).

MISS. AND TENN. VOLUNTEERS.   GEN. TAYLOR AND STAFF.   FIRST REG. O. V.   [Silver & Rowse, Lith. College Building, Cin. O.]   MORTAR.   LOUISVILLE LEGION.   GEN. WORTH STORMING THE HEIGHTS.

CATHEDRAL.   GEN. HAMER.   BLACK FORT.   BISHOP'S PALACE.

A VIEW OF THE BATTLE OF MONTEREY, SEPT. 21, 1846.

From a Drawing by STEPHEN G. HILL, of the 1st Reg. Ohio Volunteers.

Entered according to an act of Congress, in the District Court of the United States for the district of Ohio, by STEPHEN G. HILL, in the year 1846.

9. BATTLE OF MONTEREY

10.
After Stephen G. Hill
A FRONT VIEW OF THE CATHEDRAL,
FROM THE MAIN PLAZA, MONTEREY.
Lithograph, 1847
7-3/8 x 13-1/16 in. (18.7 x 33.2 cm.)
l.c. below title: "Drawn by Stephen G. Hill, of
First Reg. Ohio Volunteers. / Entered accord-
ing to act of Congress, in the year 1847, by
Stephen G. Hill, in the Clerk's Office of the
United States District Court of the District of
Ohio. / Silver and Rowse, Lith., College
Building, Cin., O."
ACM 78.87

On September 24 the battle ended, the
Americans having fought their way to
within one block of this plaza. Over the
next several days the Mexican defenders
withdrew to the south under the terms of
an armistice, and the Americans occupied
Monterrey. The Ohio Volunteers
remained in the American camp at Santo
Domingo (Walnut Grove) after the battle.[1]
Private Hill may have been quartered in
the city on account of his "disability." At
any rate, probably before his discharge
on October 24, he found time to visit the
city and complete several sketches.

The North American captors of
Monterrey were charmed by its main
plaza and have left sketches and descriptions of its appearance.[2]

This view by Hill was apparently
taken from the prison looking toward
the east. Behind the cathedral is the Cerro
de la Silla (Saddle Mountain). To the left
of the cathedral is the building from the
rooftop of which Captain Whiting took
his view of the main plaza looking west
(cat. no. 11). The round building behind
the cathedral may be a baptistry. The
buildings on the far right served as
quarters for the Seventh Infantry after the
battle; in front of them are captured
Mexican cannon.

Captain Henry of the Third Infantry
wrote:

Into this large square most of the
enemy had been driven before they
sent in a flag of truce. On one side
ranged the captured artillery. Some
twelves and nines were beautiful
pieces, of English manufacture, and
of as late date as 1842. On the eastern side of the Plaza is the Cathedral.
It is an immense pile, of no particular
order of architecture. Its front is
richly ornamented with elaborate
stucco-work; its chime of bells is
melodious, and an excellent clock
warns the citizens of the flight of
every quarter of an hour. . . .

When I first visited it, religion
had fled from its walls; it was used
as a depot for ammunition; the
quantity is immense, of every kind
and description. . . . Two of our shells
exploded in the Plaza on the night
of the 23d, and killed and wounded
many. Had one exploded in the
church, there is no describing the
terrible loss that might have ensued.[3]

T. B. Thorpe considered the cathedral "one that would ornament any city
on our continent" and mentioned that the
clock tower also contained a barometer.
He also recorded that the building was
"surrounded by a heavy stone wall, which,
besides its handsome gateway, is elaborately ornamented with figures in stucco,
mostly in basso-relievo, illustrating leg-
ends of the Spanish church." The American chaplains held their own services in
the cathedral after its capture. Captain
Henry attended several of these including
a high mass, at which he noted, "I do not
think there were twenty souls present;
and they, in the immensity of the Cathedral, were hardly noticed. War had caused
its solemn aisles to be deserted."[4]

1. Giddings, *Sketches of the Campaign in Northern
Mexico*, pp. 220ff., describes the regiment's activities following the battle.
2. Compare, for example, Private Samuel Chamberlain's watercolor views of *The Grand Plaza at Monterey* and *Street Fighting in the Calle de Iturbide*, in
Chamberlain, *My Confession*, betw. pp. 86 and
87. Chamberlain arrived at Monterrey just after the
battle (see pp. 55-56).
3. Henry, *Campaign Sketches*, pp. 221-22.
4. Thorpe, *Our Army at Monterey*, pp. 114-15;
Henry, *Campaign Sketches*, p. 256. The cathedral
was begun in 1603 but not completed until 1851;
the south tower was enlarged sometime after the
war. Compare the photograph in *Baedeker's Mexico*
(Englewood Cliffs, N.J.: Prentice-Hall, 1987), pp.
189, 190.

A FRONT VIEW OF THE CATHEDRAL, FROM THE MAIN PLAZA, MONTEREY.

DRAWN BY STEPHEN G. HILL, OF FIRST REG. OHIO VOLUNTEERS.

Entered according to act of Congress, in the year 1847, by Stephen G. Hill, in the Clerk's Office of the United States District Court of the District of Ohio.

SILVER AND ROWSE, LITH., COLLEGE BUILDING, CIN., O.

10. Cathedral, from the Main Plaza, Monterey

11.   See Plate 3

Charles Fenderich after Daniel Powers Whiting
MONTEREY, AS SEEN FROM A HOUSE-
TOP IN THE MAIN PLAZA, (TO THE
WEST.) OCTOBER, 1846.
Toned lithograph (hand colored), 1847
Size: 13 x 18-13/16 in. (33.0 x 47.8 cm.)
l.l.: "D. P. Whiting Del Capt. 7th. Inf. Del."
l.r.: "On Stone by Chas. Fenderich."
l.c., below title: "Entered according to Act of
Congress in the year 1847 by D. P. Whiting in
the Clerks Office of the District Court of the
Southern District of New York. / Printed in
Colors by G. & W. Endicott New York."
l.l.: "1. Sierra Madre. / 2. Mitre Mountain. /
3. Height on Federation Hill Carried by Storm
on the 21st. Sept. / 4. Fort Soldado by part
of the 2d. Division. / 5. Height from which
shot was thrown from one of the captured /
nine pounders of the Redoubt, into the main
Plaza on the 23d. By part of the 2d. Division.
/ 6. Height on Independence Hill, taken at
daylight on the 22d."
l.r.: "7. Bishop's Palace, or Castle and Fort,
Stormed on the 22d. by part of the 2d. Division
/ 8. City Police Offices and Prison. / 9. Pass
leading to Saltillo. Occupied by the 2d. Division on the / morning of the 21st. after the
action of St. Jeronimo. / 10. Captured Mexican Cannon. / 11. Quarters of the 7th.
Infantry. / 12. Convent of St. Francisco."
l.r. below key: "[No. 1 of a Series.]"
ACM 2.74/2

This lithograph and the three other Monterrey views that follow, along with the
artist's view of the encampment at Corpus
Christi (cat. no.1), were issued as a set
entitled *Army Portfolio*. Captain Whiting's regiment, the Seventh Infantry, was
quartered in the city from shortly after
its surrender on September 23 until
December 13 and again from December
20 to 28.[1] During this time he sketched a
series of views of the battle, probably in
watercolor; his progress can be followed

in letters written by his brother-in-law,
Lieutenant Napoleon J. T. Dana, also
with the Seventh Infantry. Dana wrote on
November 1 that Whiting had just finished this first view of Monterrey and that
he would send the series of "pictures" back
to the "engraver" (i.e., lithographer) at
Washington, D. C. "I have no doubt that
W. will succeed admirably well in this
undertaking and I feel very sure that he
will make himself quite independent. I
believe he will realize $10,000 if he carries
the thing out.... General Worth has
excused Whiting from all duty to enable
him to take three views and has autho-
rized him to take a public horse to go out
in the hills with."[2]

By June 24, 1847, the prints were
available to the American public. The
editors of the *Daily Picayune* in New
Orleans noted on August 28:

We had the pleasure of examining
several of the original pictures as
they passed through this city on their
way to Washington, and can bear
testimony to the spirit and fidelity
with which they have been copied
upon stone.... We have had opportunity to verify the fidelity of these
views by repeated inquiries of those
who have visited the country. All
attest Capt. Whiting's strict adherence to nature. All written narratives
give an inadequate idea of the situation of Monterey and the natural
difficulties which our army encountered. A half hour's study of Capt.
Whiting's sketches will elucidate
better than a volume of written
description the movements of Gen.
Worth's column in the great days of
September; and no other sketch
impresses the mind palpably with
the powers of resistance to assaults

which a Mexican town presents in
its mode of construction.... [The
sketches] are singularly beautiful,
too, as drawings from nature of some
of the finest scenery upon the
continent.[3]

Whiting's first view in Monterrey was
taken from the flat roof or azotea of a
building just north of the cathedral, looking west over the main plaza. The picturesque view contains all of the landmarks
of the city's west side, where General
Worth's Second Division — including
Whiting's company of the Seventh
Infantry — fought from September 21
through 23. One reviewer commented:
"While looking at this picture we can
imagine ourselves in the city of Monterey,
with its flat-roofed houses, each surrounded with a heavy parapet of stone
pierced with holes, intended originally to
carry off the rain, but which could easily
be used as loopholes for musketry; and
we realize the statement that every house
was a fortress, and our surprise is no
longer at the terrible carnage among our
men who penetrated the streets, but that
they were able to penetrate them at all."[4]

The inscriptions on this and the
other prints, contemporary written
accounts, maps, and other views help
identify the details and demonstrate
Whiting's care and accuracy in recording
the scenes around the city. The buildings
on the left of the square were the quarters
of the artist's regiment following the battle, with the captured Mexican artillery
pieces ranged in front. Behind the buildings, at the left, are the tower and elaborate pediment of the Convent of San
Francisco. Directly opposite the viewer
on the west side of the square are the city
police offices (or halls of justice) and
prison, and beyond them are the market

plaza (not visible), the west side of town, Arista's palace and garden (not visible among the trees), and the pass to Saltillo. Just to the right of the pass, rising above the trees, is Independence Hill, the lower portion crowned by the Bishop's Palace. The imposing mass of Miter Mountain rises above it to the right, while to the left of the pass rises Federation Hill, with its small fortification on top. On a lower portion of the hill sits Fort Soldado, and further left on the same ridge is the "height from which shot was thrown from one of the captured nine pounders of the Redoubt, into the main Plaza on the 23d." Beyond these heights extend the still greater heights of the Sierra Madre in the left distance.

T. B. Thorpe was one of many Americans who described the main plaza:

Opposite the cathedral are the halls of justice and the prisons. They have a dreadful appearance; the heavy massive walls and crowded grated windows give fearful evidence of the narrow cells within, and the hopelessness of escape, except in death. High above, on the wide parapet, walked day and night the lone Mexican sentinel, giving additional repulsiveness to the building....

The faces of the plaza, at right angles with the cathedral and halls of justice, were occupied by the fashion stores and offices of various kinds, and must, in the "piping time of peace," have presented a gay appearance, when filled with costly goods, blazing with light, and thronged with *signoras* and gay *cavalleros*.[5]

A daguerreotype in the collection of Dr. William Schultz reproduces an almost identical sketch of this view, apparently a watercolor, and is an interesting example of the use of photography to reproduce works of art. Whether or not the daguerreotype reproduces Whiting's original is difficult to tell. The image in the daguerreotype is reversed. The cannons and buildings on the south side of the square are missing, but the daguerreotype may have cropped the original drawing or painting. Instead of the peasants and guard in the foreground of the print, the daguerreotype shows two soldiers sitting on the ledge and facing the plaza; the two views also show different figures in the plaza. Inscriptions at the base of the image read: "Plaza. Monterey Nov. 5", followed by what are possibly the initials "J.R.V." or "J.B.V." where one would expect Whiting's initials. Perhaps the picture is a copy, or Whiting's original, or an original drawing by another American soldier who sketched from the same roof.[6]

The incongruous pastoral figures in the right foreground of the print were probably introduced by Charles Fenderich, the Swiss-American artist who copied Whiting's original on stone in Edward Weber's lithography studio in Baltimore.[7] Fenderich probably also introduced the guard in the left foreground, since his uniform and shako are incorrect for the Mexican War era. These alterations no doubt irked Whiting, and they offer further clues as to why the rest of his series was lithographed by the Endicotts in New York rather than by Weber.

1. Returns of the Seventh Infantry Regiment, August 1846-January 1847, RG 94, M665, roll 79, National Archives, Washington, D.C.

2. Lt. Napoleon J. T. Dana to his wife Sue, Nov. 1, 1846, Archives of the U. S. Military Academy, West Point, N.Y.

3. New Orleans *Daily Picayune*, Aug. 28, 1847, p. 2. The earliest known review is in the *Daily National Intelligencer*, June 24, 1847, p. 3. Similarly the *Knickerbocker* reported that the prints' "entire faithfulness is attested in the strongest terms by General Worth, and other officers of the army" (30, no. 5 [Nov. 1847]: 464); Major Luther Giddings of the First Ohio Volunteer Infantry commented that the lithographs taken from Whiting's views "correctly and beautifully represented" the mountains around Monterrey (*Sketches of the Campaign in Northern Mexico*, p. 137).

4. *Daily National Intelligencer*, June 24, 1847, p. 3.

5. Thorpe, *Our Army at Monterey*, pp. 114-15.

6. Thomas Kailbourn has suggested that "J.R.V." might stand for Captain John Rogers Vinton of the Third Artillery, who was breveted major for gallant conduct at Monterrey and was killed at the siege of Veracruz. John Frost, *Life of Major General Zachary Taylor, with Notices of the War in New Mexico, California, and in Southern Mexico...* (New York: D. Appleton & Co., 1847), contains an engraved frontispiece after a sketch by Major Vinton.

7. Fenderich was born in 1805 and came to America around 1830. Settling in Philadelphia around 1833, he was associated with landscape artist and lithographer John Caspar Wild in 1833-34 and with Lehman & Duval and P. S. Duval (mostly doing political portrait work) from 1835 to 1837. From 1837 until 1843 he made political portraits in Washington, D. C., and military and naval views for Edward Weber of Baltimore, for whom he also drew on stone a version of Whiting's view of Corpus Christi (see cat. no. 1) and a portrait of General William Jenkins Worth. In 1849 he went to California, working in San Francisco as a portrait painter until after 1887. (See Groce and Wallace, *Dictionary of Artists in America*, p. 222; *A. Hoen on Stone: Lithographs of E. Weber & Co. and A. Hoen & Co., Baltimore, 1835-1969* [Baltimore: Maryland Historical Society, 1969], p. 15; Jeanne Van Nostrand, *The First Hundred Years of Painting in California 1775-1875* [San Francisco: John Howell Books, 1980], pp. 100-101; Edan Milton Hughes, *Artists in California 1786-1940* [San Francisco: Hughes Publishing Company, 1986], pp. 152-53; Nicholas B. Wainwright, *Philadelphia in the Romantic Age of Lithography* [Philadelphia: Historical Society of Pennsylvania, 1958], pp. 22, 34, 38, 49, 183, 191.)

12. See Plate 4

Frederick Swinton after Daniel Powers Whiting
HEIGHTS OF MONTEREY, FROM THE
SALTILLO ROAD LOOKING TOWARDS THE
CITY. (FROM THE WEST.)
Toned lithograph (hand colored), 1847
12-11/16 x 19-1/2 in. (32.2 x 49.5 cm.)
l.l.: "D. P. Whiting Capt. 7th Inf. Del."
l.r.: "On Stone by F. Swinton."
l.c. below title: "(Worth's Division" moving
into position under the guns of the enemy, after
the action / of "St. Jeronimo," on the morning
of 21st. Sepr. 1846) / Entered according to
Act of Congress in the year 1847 by D. P.
Whiting in the Clerks Office of the District
Court of the Southern district of New York. /
Lith. & Printed in Colors by G. & W. Endicott, New York."
l.l.: "1. Independance (or Castle) Hill. / 2. Lt.
Col. Duncan's Battery of Light Artillery
throwing shells / at the routed Mexican Cavalry. / 3. City of Monterey. / 4. "Sierra Silla,"
"Saddle Mountain."
l.r.: "5. Rancho, (or village) of St. Jeronimo.
/ 6. Federation Hill; First position carried by
assault on the / afternoon of 21st. Septr. /
N.B. The second Division was composed of
one Regt. of Texan Cavalry; / two Co's. of
Texn. Rangers, two Batteries of Lt. Artillery,
the "Arty. / Battalion", the 5th. 7th. and 8th.
Reg'ts. of Infantry, and one Company / of
Louisiana Volunteers."
l.r. below key: "(No. 2)"
ACM 2.74/3

In this view, U. S. regular infantry and
a battery of light artillery of General
Worth's division move west along the Saltillo Road on September 21 as they prepare to attack the western defenses of
Monterrey. The city is barely discernible
in a valley behind a tree in the middle left.
Minutes earlier along this road, Mexican
lancers had fought a sharp engagement
(which Whiting refers to as "St. Jeronimo") with Texas Rangers; the body of a
slain Mexican lancer lies to the left of the
road, while a few of his comrades escape
over the field in the middle left distance.[1]
George Wilkins Kendall, riding with
Captain McCulloch's Texas Rangers at
the head of Worth's division, noted the
regulars' movement along this stretch of
road:

A few scattered jacales were found
at the junction of the roads, built at
the edge of the cornfields which
extended towards the Rio San Juan
de Monterey, and hardly had our
light batteries taken a position, and
commenced firing upon the sand-bag
breast work upon the crest of Independence Hill [the hill at left in
Whiting's view], before a battery of
two heavy guns, which had previously been concealed, was opened
on our column with round shot from
the height to the right...known as
Loma de Federación, or Federation
Hill — a high summit immediately
overlooking Gen. Worth's position.
It was a plunging fire, the balls
striking directly among our men;
and with such precision did the
Mexicans serve their guns that the
commanding general at once
advanced the main part of his division to a sugar house in the direction
of Saltillo...completely out of reach
of the enemy's cannon.[2]

Besides the action of the morning of
the twenty-first, this print records the setting of Worth's subsequent attack on the
fortified heights west of town. Later that
day, a part of Worth's division, including
Captain Whiting's company, returned and
stormed Federation Hill (the hill second
from right in the print).[3] Estimated by
some accounts as over 800 feet high, Federation Hill — actually part of a ridge
extending far behind what could be seen
from this angle — proved to be a weak
and isolated link in the city's defenses.
From the crest of the hill, Worth's men
turned captured Mexican cannon on a fort
known as El Soldado, located farther
down the ridge, and quickly overran it.
According to Mexican sources, only about
175 troops had been posted on the entire
ridge.[4] At three o'clock on the following
morning, General Worth sent part of his
force to take the crest of Independence
Hill, seen at left, which they accomplished
with surprising speed in spite of the
almost vertical ascent; the Mexicans had
only posted one gun and around fifty or
sixty men at the crest.[5]

Although this view is labeled as
number two of Whiting's series, the letters
of Lieutenant Dana suggest that the artist
painted the sketches in a different order.
On November 1, 1846, reporting the
completion of the view of the main plaza
(cat. no. 11), Dana wrote that the artist's
"next view will be from the first captured
redoubt looking at the Bishop's Palace
and repeating the battle scene when it was
taken," clearly a reference to number four
of the Monterrey views (cat. no. 14).
Later, on November 16, Dana reported
Whiting at work on the view of the heights
from the Saltillo Road: "Whiting has progressed a good way with another picture
which will be a very beautiful one. The
view is taken from where our column
stood in the road under the cannonade of
the two hills where Captain McKavett
was killed. The column will be represented in the picture and will of course
make it more interesting." On November
30 Dana wrote more ambiguously that
Whiting was "nearly finished with a third
piece of painting."[6]

According to their inscriptions, this

lithograph and the last of the series (cat. no. 14) were drawn on stone by F. Swinton, an employee of G. & W. Endicott. He is probably Frederick Swinton of Staten Island, New York, who exhibited watercolors at the American Institute in 1842.[7]

1. An engraving, probably after an eyewitness sketch, of the *Cavalry Charge on the Morning of the 21st* is included in Reid, *Scouting Expeditions*, opp. p. 156.

2. New Orleans *Picayune*, Nov. 19, 1846 (extra), p. 1. Certainly Kendall's account and Whiting's view complement one another; they were probably acquainted, for Kendall was a friend of Forbes Britton, a captain of the Seventh Infantry like Whiting (Copeland, *Kendall of the Picayune*, p. 166).

3. An engraving of the *Storming of Federation Hill and Fort Soldada*, probably taken from an eyewitness sketch, is included in Reid, *Scouting Expeditions*, opp. p. 162. It is similar to Whiting's view. See also the account of this action in a letter of Lieutenant Edmund Bradford, Sept. 27, 1846, in Smith and Judah, *Chronicles of the Gringos*, p. 87.

4. Smith, *War with Mexico*, 1:244-46, 498 n.8.

5. Ibid., 1:246-47. For eyewitness accounts see Reid, *Scouting Expeditions*, pp. 181-83; Bradford, in *Chronicles of the Gringos*, p. 88.

6. Lt. Napoleon J. T. Dana to wife Sue, Nov. 1, Nov. 16, Nov. 30, 1846, Archives of the U. S. Military Academy, West Point.

7. Groce and Wallace, *Dictionary of Artists in America*, p. 617.

13.   See Plate 5

Charles Parsons after Daniel Powers Whiting
VALLEY TOWARDS SALTILLO, FROM NEAR THE BASE OF "PALACE HILL," AT MONTEREY. (LOOKING TO THE S. WEST.)
Toned lithograph (hand colored), 1847
12-7/16 x 19-7/16 in. (31.6 x 49.4 cm.)
l.l.: "D.P. Whiting Capt. 7th. Inf. Del."
l.r.: "On Stone by C. Parsons"
l.c. below title: "Entered according to act of Congress in the year 1847 by D. P. Whiting in the Clerks Office of the district Court of the Southern district of New York / G. & W. Endicott Lith. N.Y."
l.l.: "1. Mountains of the "Sierra Madre" 8 Miles distant. / 2. Part of "Federation Hill" Position and Breast work, / first carried by assault, on the 21st. Sepr. 1846. / 3. Road to Saltillo, with the rear guard and wagon train / coming in to the Castle, after its capture on the 22nd."
l.r.: "4. Village of "San Pedro" / 5. "Spur" of "Mitre Mountain," around which the first action / with the Mexican Cavalry was fought, on the morning / of the 21st. September. / 6. Part of the base of "Mitre Mountain." "
l.r. below key: "(No. 3.)"
ACM 2.74/4

Sketching after the battle, Captain Whiting left a very personal pictorial record, apparently recording only scenes and actions that he had seen himself. This print reproduces the view he saw on the morning of September 23 from the base of Independence or Palace Hill, after its capture the previous day. According to inscriptions, the tallest mountain at left and those in the distant center represent the Sierra Madre. The smaller hill at left is the part of Federation Hill first carried on September 21. In the right distance rise what appear to be two hills or mountains (both parts of Miter Mountain), around the nearer of which was fought the opening action between the Mexican lancers and the Texas Rangers on the morning of the twenty-first. In the valley below the viewer, the rear guard and wagon train move along the Saltillo Road on their way into the captured Bishop's Palace. Parallel to the road runs the Santa Catarina River, its presence noted by a small ditch around the base of Federation Hill. Several tiny jacales appear along the road, the first of them labeled as the village of San Pedro.

Samuel Reid of the Texas Rangers, like the artist, returned to Independence Hill after the battle and contemplated the beauty of the view to the west, where "the Saltillo road wound itself along a chain of hills, dotted here and there with jacales and ranchos, as far as the eye could reach, until it lost itself into a broad plain."[1]

1. Reid, *Scouting Expeditions*, p. 226.

14.   See Plate 6

Frederick Swinton after Daniel Powers Whiting
Monterey, from Independence Hill,
in the Rear of the Bishop's Palace.
As it appeared on 23d. September,
1846. (Looking East.)
Toned lithograph (hand colored), 1847
12-7/16 x 19-7/16 in. (31.6 x 49.4 cm.)
l.l.: "D.P. Whiting Del Capt. 7th. Inf."
l.r.: "On Stone by F Swinton."
l.c. below title: "Entered according to Act of
Congress in the year 1847 by D. P. Whiting in
the Clerks Office of the district Court of the
Southern District of New York. / Lith. &
Printed in Colors by G. & W. Endicott, New
York."
l.l. "1. "Sierra Silla," (Saddle Mountain, about
7 Miles distant.) / 2. Village of "Gaudaloupe."
/ 3. Citadel, (in possession of the Mexicans,
firing upon Genl. Taylor's / position on the
eastern side of the City.) / 4. Cathedral."
l.r. "5. Cemetery. / 6. Genl. Arista's Palace
and Garden. / 7. Part of Federation Hill,
(shewing the point occupied by Major Scott,
/ with the 5th Infy. with one of the captured
guns / throwing shot into the Main Plaxa.")"
l.r. below key: "(No. 4.)"
ACM 2.74/5

Independence Hill and the Bishop's Palace
were the keys to Monterrey's western
approach. After taking the redoubt on
the crest of the hill early on September
22, General Worth's men began to bombard the fortified Bishop's Palace with a
twelve-pounder howitzer that they had
disassembled and dragged up to the crest.
Within a few hours, they captured the
palace. This print shows the view from
the crest of Independence Hill on the following, climactic day of the battle. At the
far left in the distance, almost on the
border of the print, is the "Citadel" or
Black Fort, which remained in the hands
of the Mexican defenders and hampered
Taylor's operations on the eastern side of

the city. Beyond the Black Fort, at the far
left, lies a tiny town labeled as the village
of "Gaudaloupe." In the city may be seen
the cathedral, and forward and to the
right of it the cemetery, surrounded by a
wall. Just to the left of the Bishop's Palace,
on the plain, are Arista's palace and garden, and beyond them the Santa Catarina
River. At the far right is part of Federation
Hill. A puff of smoke and a line of troops
at its top indicates the point where the
Fifth Infantry, under Major Martin Scott,
fired a captured Mexican gun directly
into the main plaza of the city.[1]

Lieutenant Dana's letters record
Whiting's work on this view; on
November 9 he wrote: "He has been out
for five days sketching among the hills.
Three days I went with him."[2] Many of
the American troops, like Whiting and
Dana, retraced their steps after the battle,
and the view of Monterrey from the
Bishop's Palace was a favorite vantage
point. Samuel Reid of the Texas Rangers
wrote of visiting the Bishop's Palace:

This building...had been built
some fifty years ago, as a residence
for the bishop of the diocese, who
had selected the position on account
of its romantic and beautiful site. It
is said to have been once very splendid, but by neglect has fallen to
decay. The walls of the main building alone were standing, with a par-
terre in front, and a high flight of
stone steps leading to the grand
entrance, from which could be seen
traces of its former magnificence;
the fortifications around, lately made
by the Mexicans, gave it the appearance of some old feudal castle....

Below, was the city with its lofty
steeples, its beautiful white houses
and lovely gardens, with the Monte

Sillo, or saddle mountain on the
right, (which takes its name from
two peaks of the mountain, forming
the shape of a saddle,) at whose
base murmured the limpid stream of
the rapid San Juan, with its pebbled
and rocky shores, while far to the
left, [sic, right] rose the high peaks
of the *Sierra del Madre*, towering to
the vault of heaven. To the east lay
the lovely green valley with its fields
and woods, before so beauteous,
now sad to look upon from the dread
carnage of the late battle.[3]

Reid's book contains a number of
intriguing engraved views taken around
Monterrey, including a view of the
Bishop's Palace "from a drawing by Lieut.
J. P. McCown, 4th Artillery" and another
depicting the capture of the palace.[4] The
New York *Herald* published an engraved
view of Monterrey from the Bishop's Palace that concurs essentially with Whiting's
view.[5] Another soldier who visited this
site was Private Samuel Chamberlain of
the First Dragoons, whose private memoirs describe how he obtained a watercolor view of the city from the Bishop's
Palace and shot a Mexican who attempted
to steal his horse while he was sketching.[6]
If Chamberlain's tale is true, Whiting was
prudent to have his brother-in-law
accompany him in the hills around
Monterrey.

1. Smith, *War with Mexico*, 1:247-48; Reid, *Scouting Expeditions*, pp. 190-91. For descriptions of the cemetery and Arista's palace and garden, see Giddings, *Sketches of the Campaign in Northern Mexico*, pp. 237-38.

2. Lt. Napoleon J. T. Dana to wife Sue, Nov. 9, 1846, Archives of the U.S. Military Academy, West Point. See cat. no. 12 for a discussion of the sequence of Whiting's sketches.

3. Reid, *Scouting Expeditions*, pp. 225-26.

4. Ibid., opp. pp. 156, 162, 185, 192, 225. John Porter McCown (1815-79), a West Point graduate, was an artillery lieutenant in Worth's division at Monterrey. (Returns of the 4th Regiment of U.S. Army Artillery, March 1846-Aug. 1848, RG 94, M727, roll 27, National Archives, Washington, D.C.; Cullum, *Biographical Register*, 2:31-32.)

5. New York *Herald*, Nov. 14, 1847, p.1. A similar engraved view appeared in Mayer, *Mexico, Aztec, Spanish and Republican* (1850), 1: opp. p. 344.

6. Chamberlain, *My Confession*, pp. 200-203; this incident takes a whole chapter, entitled "The Picture That Cost a Life." The watercolor is reproduced between pp. 86 and 87.

15.

Fd. Bastin after an unknown artist
HÉROICA DÉFENSA DE LA CIEUDAD DE MONTEREY CONTRA EL EGERCITO NORTE AMERICANO, EL 23 DE SEPTIEMBRE 1846.
Toned lithograph (hand colored), c. 1850
8-1/16 x 12-7/16 in. (20.5 x 31.7 cm.)
l.r. on stone: "Fd. Bastin"
u.l.: "No. 1"
l.l.: "Julio Michaud y Thomas Mexico"
From *Album Pintoresco de la República Méxicana* (Mexico City: Estamperia de Julio Michaud y Thomas, c. 1850)
Courtesy of Fikes Hall of Special Collections and DeGolyer Library, Southern Methodist University, Dallas, Texas

The largest single source of printed images based on the Mexican view of the war is contained in a picture book titled *Album Pintoresco de la República Méxicana*, published in Mexico City about 1850 by Julio Michaud y Thomas. Of these forty-five lithographed plates (including several chromolithographs), six depict battle scenes from the war between Mexico and the United States. A number of the plates not related to the war were drawn on stone by Urbano López, probably in Mexico City, but others, signed by Pierre-Frédéric Lehnert and Ferdinand (?) Bastin, may have been executed in Paris, where they were printed by the Lemercier firm (which also produced the lithographs for Kendall and Nebel).[1] As most of the forty-five plates were copied from earlier sources such as Nebel's *Voyage pittoresque* and John Phillips's *Mexico Illustrated*, there is reason to believe that all of the plates may have been pirated.

This view of street fighting during the third day of the siege of Monterrey is similar to a lithograph produced in 1846 by Sarony & Major (fig. 20). It may ultimately derive from a European source; Ron Tyler has pointed out the similarities between the Sarony & Major print and the works of Eugène Delacroix that depict the fighting on the barricades during the revolution of 1830.[2] Bastin's work is so generalized that there is no likelihood that it was taken from an on-the-spot sketch.

1. Nothing is known about Bastin. Lehnert is listed in Benezit, *Dictionnaire...des Peintres, Sculpteurs, Dessinateurs et Graveurs* (1966), 5:488, as a watercolorist, pastel painter, engraver, and lithographer who was known for his depictions of animals and hunting scenes. He was born in Paris in 1811.

2. See Tyler, *Mexican War: A Lithographic Record*, p. 24, plates 13-15.

HÉROICA DÉFENSA DE LA CIEUDAD DE MONTEREY

contra el Egército norte Américano,

El 23 de Septiembre 1846

15. HÉROICA DÉFENSA DE MONTEREY

16.   See Plate 7
Adolphe-Jean-Baptiste Bayot after Carl Nebel
CAPTURE OF MONTEREY
Toned lithograph (hand colored), 1851
10-13/16 x 16-3/4 in. (27.5 x 42.6 cm.)
l.l.: "C. Nebel fecit"
l.r.: "Bayot lith."
l.l. stamped: "Entered / According to Act / of
Congress"
From George Wilkins Kendall, *The War
Between the United States and Mexico Illus-
trated* (New York: D. Appleton & Company,
1851), plate 2
ACM 186.72/2

The capture of Monterrey offered artists many choices for a vantage point, since it actually consisted of several different battles and smaller struggles fought over several days in a variety of picturesque terrain. George Wilkins Kendall had gone to Monterrey with McCulloch's Texas Rangers to report firsthand for the *Picayune*. Kendall and C. M. Haile, another reporter for the *Picayune*, accompanied Worth's division at Monterrey and did not witness the fighting in the eastern sector. Both gave excellent accounts of the fighting in the west, but the *Picayune* received criticism for not covering the terrible fighting in the eastern and northern part of the city, where American casualties were highest and American successes much less spectacular.[1] In assembling his material for *The War Between the United States and Mexico Illustrated*, Kendall was careful to include this aspect of the battle and may have directed Nebel to concentrate on this general view from the north. The view is not much different from the Americans' first glimpse of the city on September 19 as they approached on the road from Marin and Cerralvo. Kendall wrote:

In the foreground of the picture may be seen General Taylor himself, with the column of attack marching down to the eastern edge of the city; the smoke from the Black Fort, as well as from the town itself, showing that the invaders were under fire from the first. In the middle ground, a little to the right of the Black Fort which looms up prominently in advance of the city, may be seen the Hills of Independence and Federation, the San Juan running between. On the lower points of these hills are the Bishop's Palace and the work of La Soldada, while the smoke upon the crests to the right indicates the position of the batteries which opened upon Worth's division on the morning of the 21st of September, his troops at the time concealed in the valley on the west. The towering mountains of the Sierra Madre form the background of the picture, the opening directly beyond the Bishop's Palace being the gap through which the road runs towards the Rinconada and Saltillo. The artist could not well select any one incident of the contest as the subject of his drawing; no effort of the pencil could give effect to the hard fighting within the streets, and to take up the storming of one of the western heights would shut out the city from the view. He therefore preferred giving the reader an outline of Monterey, with its defences and approaches, and in this, although the position of some of the hills may have been slightly changed, he has been successful.[2]

Kendall's description may hint at how Nebel created this view. Although

he ranged over much of Mexico in the years before the war, we have no proof that the artist actually witnessed the capture of Monterrey or that he ever visited Monterrey with the intent of painting this scene. Kendall's statements that "it was found impossible to offer other than a general view" and that "the position of some of the hills may have been slightly changed" may imply that the artist could not visit the site. No single view could show both Worth's attack in the west and Taylor's in the east, as Kendall writes, but at the more accessible battle sites of Molino del Rey and Chapultepec, Nebel rendered two paintings of each battle to show different aspects of the fighting.

Nebel apparently reconstructed the scene in his studio after the war, and no doubt his best source must have been Kendall's own account. Topographical accuracy would have been one of the most difficult aspects of such a reconstruction. Kendall could provide Nebel with numerous eyewitness descriptions of Monterrey from the north from contemporary books and newspapers, which often contained maps of the city and even printed views of Monterrey from this angle.[3] Finally, contemporary lithographs were available, including Whiting's and Hill's views.

Nebel evidently used his sources carefully. The mortar being fired in the center of his view, for example, is thoroughly documented as being to the right of the fork in the road on September 21.[4] The solitary tree, on the other hand, may be a compositional device, derived from descriptions of the nearby walnut grove. The activities of the figures in the foreground demonstrate not only Nebel's knowledge of American uniforms and military operations, but his superior technical skills.

1. Copeland, *Kendall of the Picayune*, pp. 158, 170-84.

2. Kendall, *War Between the United States and Mexico Illustrated*, p. 10.

3. Compare the view with the account by Major Luther Giddings quoted in cat. no. 9 and that by Thorpe, *Our Army at Monterey*, pp. 45ff., 100-101. Maps of the battle site were published in Thorpe, *Our Army at Monterey*, opp. p. 9 (drawn by a Lieutenant Benjamin; see also the engraving of the city opp. p. 70); New Orleans *Picayune,* Nov. 19, 1846 (extra), between pp. 1 and 2; New York *Herald*, Nov. 12, 1846, p. 1; and Reid, *Scouting Expeditions*, pp. 146-47 (drawn by Lieutenant George Meade of the U.S. Topographic Engineers).

4. The mortar appears in Stephen Hill's view (cat. no. 9) and on the maps of Lieutenants Benjamin and Meade cited in the preceding note.

17.

After John Phillips

PASS IN THE SIERRA MADRE — NEAR MONTEREY

Toned lithograph (hand colored), 1848
10-7/16 x 15-1/2 in. (26.5 x 39.4 cm.)
l.r.: "Day & Son, Lithrs. to the Queen."
From John Phillips and Alfred Rider, *Mexico Illustrated in Twenty-six Views* (London: E. Atchley, Library of Fine Arts, 1848), plate 25
ACM 10.79/25

The exact date that John Phillips made the original sketch for this view is not known, nor is the exact location depicted. However, the print may represent Rinconada Pass, approximately thirty miles west of Monterrey, along the road to Saltillo. After the surrender of Monterrey, General Ampudia's defeated Mexican army marched through this pass in its withdrawal to Saltillo. Later, American troops under Worth, advancing on that city, discovered uncompleted, abandoned fortifications along the pass.[1] Although Phillips probably sketched the view before the war, he may later have added the infantry, heavy artillery, and a couple of covered vehicles to evoke the more recent event.[2]

Although the coloration on several sets of Phillips's prints is superb, it is not always accurate. In the impression of this lithograph illustrated here, the flag in the distance has been colored red, white, and blue for the Stars and Stripes. However, Phillips no doubt intended the troops to be Mexican since most wear shakos, which American troops apparently never wore in Mexico. In light of this, Kendall and Nebel were quite prudent in their later decision to supervise carefully the coloration of their lithographs.

1. Smith, *War with Mexico*, 1: 262-65.

2. Pourade, *Sign of the Eagle*, p. 57, comments that the view was done "a number of years before the war." It would be an understatement to add that in time of war it would be dangerous for a foreigner like Phillips to sit and sketch an army on the move.

17. Pass in the Sierra Madre — Near Monterey

Wool's March

18.
After an unknown artist
San Antonio de Bexar. 1846
Lithograph, 1850
4-1/16 x 6-5/8 in. (10.3 x 16.8 cm.)
l.r.: "C. B. Graham Lithog"
From George Wurtz Hughes, *Memoir Descriptive of the March of a Division of the United States Army, Under the Command of Brigadier General John E. Wool, from San Antonio de Bexar, in Texas, to Saltillo, in Mexico*, Senate Ex. Doc. 32, 31st Congress, 1st Session (1850), after p. 67
Amon Carter Museum Library

In August 1846 a division of the U. S. Army under Brigadier General John E. Wool concentrated at the town of San Antonio de Bexar, in Texas. Known as the Centre Division, it consisted of about 3,400 men plus staff. Wool was directed to lead his division on an expedition against the western Mexican city of Chihuahua; in the course of the march this objective was abandoned as unrealistic, and they reinforced Worth in Saltillo instead.

One of Wool's officers, Captain George Wurtz Hughes, had instructions from the Topographical Bureau "to collect information in reference to the habits and disposition of the people, the geography, natural history, resources, military strength, statistics, and political history of the countries through which we might march."[1] Captain Hughes compiled this information into a government report titled *Memoir Descriptive of the March of a Division of the United States Army, Under the Command of Brigadier General John E. Wool, from San Antonio de*

SAN ANTONIO DE BEXAR.
1846

C.B.Graham. Lithog

18. San Antonio de Bexar

Bexar, in Texas, to Saltillo, in Mexico, published in Washington, D.C., in 1850.

In addition to maps, Hughes's report contains seven printed views lithographed by Curtis Burr Graham, a Washington lithographer originally from New York.[2] Of these, four—including an interior and an exterior view of the Alamo, a view of Mission San José, and a view of Mission Concepción—are taken from sketches by Sergeant Edward Everett, which are now in the Amon Carter Museum.[3] No artist is credited for the remaining three views, however, and no original sketches are known to survive. Everett could have made the sketch for this general view of San Antonio but not for the two views taken in Mexico, since he never arrived there.

Recognizable in this lithograph of San Antonio is the San Antonio River and the domed church of San Fernando.[4]

1. Hughes, *Memoir Descriptive*, pp. 8-10. On Wool's expedition, see also Bauer, *Mexican War*, pp. 150-51, 204-5; Smith, *War with Mexico*, 1:267-69.
2. Graham (1814-90) worked in the lithography business in New York with his brother, John Requa Graham, and later with John Price. In 1842 Graham moved to Washington, D.C., where he furnished lithographic and engraving work, mostly for the U.S. government, consisting of maps, charts, and views. (See Richard Eighme Ahlborn, *The San Antonio Missions: Edward Everett and the American Occupation, 1847* [Fort Worth: Amon Carter Museum, in cooperation with Los Compadres de San Antonio Missions National Historical Park, 1985], pp. 12, 20–21, 43, 47; Groce and Wallace, *Dictionary of Artists in America*, p. 216.)

3. Everett (1818- after 1900) was born in London, where he may have learned the basics of drawing and watercolor. He settled in Quincy, Illinois, with his parents in 1840 and worked as a mechanic and engineer there before joining a volunteer company, the Quincy Riflemen, that was soon involved in the Mormon War in Illinois in 1845-46. At the opening of the Mexican War he and his unit were inducted into federal military service and sent to Texas.

4. Hughes described San Antonio at this period in *Memoir Descriptive*, pp. 9-10.

19.

After Edward Everett

RUINS OF THE CHURCH OF THE ALAMO, SAN ANTONIO DE BEXAR.

Lithograph, 1850

4-1/16 x 6-11/16 in. (10.3 x 17.0 cm.)

l.l.: "Drawn by Edwd. Everett"

l.r.: "C.B. Graham Lithog"

l.c. below title: "Scale 10. feet to an Inch"

From George Wurtz Hughes, *Memoir Descriptive of the March of a Division of the United States Army, Under the Command of Brigadier General John E. Wool, from San Antonio de Bexar, in Texas, to Saltillo, in Mexico*, Senate Ex. Doc. 32, 31st Congress, 1st Session (1850), after p. 67

Amon Carter Museum Library

19. RUINS OF THE CHURCH OF THE ALAMO, SAN ANTONIO DE BEXAR

Everett, like Hughes, was ordered to collect information on the history and customs of places on the line of march, but he was also ordered to make drawings of buildings and objects of interest. Several of the eighteenth-century Spanish missions in and around San Antonio—the Alamo, Concepción, and San José—attracted Everett's attention. Hughes described the missions as "monastic fortresses, whose stately and melancholy ruins attest to their former magnificence and grandeur."[1] The Alamo, of course, was remembered as the site of the 1836 defeat and annihilation of Texan troops by a Mexican army under General Antonio López de Santa Anna.[2]

Everett began his drawings of the Alamo and Mission San José with enthusiasm, but while on guard duty he was wounded during a disturbance in a gambling house. His wound confined him to bed for a month and prevented him from proceeding to Mexico with the greater part of General Wool's division, which departed San Antonio in late September 1846. Beginning in the spring of 1847 Everett participated in the army's renovation and conversion of the Alamo complex to a supply depot with offices, workshops, and stabling yards. He resumed his drawings of the missions later that year and made duplicates of them for Graham while in Washington in 1848.[3]

Of Everett's two views of the eighteenth-century mission chapel, this one depicts the facade in a state of disrepair, while the other shows a rare glimpse of the ruined interior. Graham's lithographs adhere closely to Everett's original watercolors.[4] Hughes's published report also contains a lithographed plan of the mission's surviving structures, after an original sketch (now unlocated) by Everett. The mission chapel, never completed and neglected for years by the Spanish government, had suffered damage in the March 6, 1836, battle. Santa Anna ordered it razed after the Mexican defeat at San Jacinto on April 21. Notably absent in Everett's view is the pediment that was later added to the top of the facade. In later years, Everett commented, "I regret to see by a late engraving of this ruin, tasteless hands have evened off the rough walls... surmounting them with a rediculous scroll, giving the building the appearance of the headboard of a bedstead." He was glad, however, to see that some restoration work had been done.[4]

1. Hughes, *Memoir Descriptive*, p. 10.
2. See Susan Prendergast Schoelwer and Tom W. Gläser, *Alamo Images: Changing Perceptions of a Texas Experience* (Dallas: DeGolyer Library and Southern Methodist University Press, 1985). Also see Schoelwer, "The Artist's Alamo: A Reappraisal of Pictorial Evidence, 1836-1850," *Southwestern Historical Quarterly* 91 (April 1988): 403-56.
3. Ahlborn, *San Antonio Missions*, pp. 5-21, 41-58.
4. Edward Everett, "A Narrative of Military Experience in Several Capacities,"quoted in Ahlborn, *San Antonio Missions*, p. 17.

20.
After an unknown artist
CHURCH NEAR MONCLOVA
Lithograph, 1850
4-1/16 x 6-11/16 in. (10.3 x 17.0 cm.)
l.r.: "C.B. Graham Lithog"
From George Wurtz Hughes, *Memoir Descriptive of the March of a Division of the United States Army, Under the Command of Brigadier General John E. Wool, from San Antonio de Bexar, in Texas, to Saltillo, in Mexico,* Senate Ex. Doc. 32, 31st Congress, 1st Session (1850), after p. 67
Amon Carter Museum Library

Marching into the state of Coahuila, Wool's division reached Monclova, a town of about 8,000 inhabitants, around October 30. Although the municipal authorities were not openly hostile, Wool formally occupied the town on November 3 and established his headquarters in the governor's palace, remaining until November 24.[1]

Hughes's report has two illustrations of buildings labeled "near Monclova," one a "watch-tower," the other this church. Unfortunately he describes neither in his text.

1. Bauer, *Mexican War*, pp. 146-50.

CHURCH NEAR MONCLOVA.

20. CHURCH NEAR MONCLOVA

The Seizure of California

21.
After Joseph Warren Revere
Monterey — Capitol of California
Lithograph, 1849
3-3/8 x 6 in. (8.6 x 15.2 cm.)
u.r.: "Page 24."
l.l.: "Sketched by J. W. Revere U. S. N."
l.r.: "Lith. of Wm. Endicott & Co. N. York."
l.c. below title: "Published by C. S. Francis &
Co N. York."
From Joseph Warren Revere, *A Tour of Duty
in California*, ed. Joseph N. Balestier (New
York: C. S. Francis & Co., Boston: J. H.
Francis, 1849), p. 24
Courtesy of Special Collections Division, The
University of Texas at Arlington Libraries,
Arlington, Texas

21. Monterey — Capitol of California

California, New Mexico, and the land in between saw several important actions during the Mexican War, but the forces involved were small, and there were few pitched battles. There were fewer artists to record the events in these distant places, and communications back to the East were slow and difficult: in any case, relatively few prints were made relating to the western campaigns. The best known images of the war in California are a series of twenty-eight watercolors by William H. Meyers, a gunner on the U.S. sloop-of-war *Dale*. Meyers recorded the battles of San Pascual, Santa Clara, and San Gabriel and other actions in both Alta and Baja California. His sketches were not published in the nineteenth century, however, and are therefore not included in this catalogue.[1]

Lieutenant Joseph Warren Revere (1812-80), the artist of this and the following lithograph, played a prominent part in the U. S. Navy's wartime operations in California. At the opening of the war Lieutenant Revere was serving with the Pacific Squadron on board the U. S. sloop-of-war *Portsmouth*. *A Tour of Duty in California* (1849), taken from the journal he had written, contains six lithographs by William Endicott & Co. after sketches by the author. Besides the views of Monterey and Sutter's Fort, these include *Quicksilver Mine Near Santa Clara, Monte Diablo, A Pui Day*, and *A Ranchero Feat*.[2]

The Mexican government's weak control over sparsely settled Alta California encouraged the American government to seize the territory, where an increasing number of Americans had settled in the years before the war. Tensions between the two countries had already been so high that in October 1842 an American naval commander, thinking that a state of war existed between them, had seized the port of Monterey. He had withdrawn as soon as he realized his error, but the U. S. Navy's Pacific Squadron continued to maintain an ominous presence off California's coast.[3]

The American seizure of California began with a revolt by American settlers in the Sacramento and Napa valleys, partly fomented by Captain John Charles Frémont of the U.S. Army Engineers, who had led an expedition of sixty-two armed men to California in late 1845. The revolutionaries seized Sonoma on June 10 or 14, 1846, and declared their independence on July 4. Frémont assumed leadership of the "Bear Flag Revolt." After he learned of the first battles on the Rio Grande, Commodore John D. Sloat, commander of the Pacific Squadron, ordered the U. S. frigate *Savannah* and the sloops-of-war *Cyane* and *Levant* to seize Monterey, which they did without incident on July 7. Two days later, the *Portsmouth* (Revere's ship) seized San Francisco.[4]

California art historian Jeanne Van Nostrand noted that Revere could have made his sketches of the Monterey area as early as April or May 1846, when the *Portsmouth* was there awaiting Commodore Sloat's arrival. But she also notes that the presence of the U. S. flag over the government building in the right foreground suggests that the sketch for the print was made after the occupation began on July 7.[5] Some ships of the Pacific Squadron may be distinguished in the harbor; the largest of these may be a frigate, perhaps the *Savannah* or *Congress*. The latter arrived at Monterey on July 15 carrying Commodore Robert F. Stockton, who became commander of the operations ashore and later succeeded Sloat as commander of the Pacific Squadron.[6] The old Spanish fort may be atop a distant hill at far left in the print. Just below it are some tents, perhaps belonging to American troops. The Monterey customs house stands on the wharf near the center of the picture; here the American sailors and marines first landed.[7] The timber ribs of an old wrecked ship jut out of the water at far right — a curious detail that also appears in two views of Monterey in 1842, drawn on stone by Charles (Karl) Gildemeister and lithographed by Francis D'Avignon of New York. The separately lithographed keys to these prints, prepared with the help of the U. S. Consul at Monterey, Thomas O. Larkin, label the detail "Wreck Com. Rogers"; these keys also help to identify the owners of some buildings in Revere's view.[8]

The New York *Herald* on January 10, 1847, also published a view of Monterey engraved by Samuel Putnam Avery.

The view, which was printed on two blocks, has a fair degree of accuracy, depicting the shoreline from the presidio and chapel to the Mexican fort. The uncredited artist of the original sketch may have been an American sailor.[9]

1. Meyers's original watercolors are in the Franklin Delano Roosevelt Library at Hyde Park, N.Y. They are reproduced in Dudley W. Knox, *Naval Sketches of the War in California* (New York: Random House, 1939), with an introduction by Franklin D. Roosevelt.

2. Jeanne Van Nostrand, *A Pictorial and Narrative History of Monterey, Adobe Capital of California, 1770-1847* (San Francisco: California Historical Society, 1968), pp. 92-94; Jeanne Van Nostrand, *First Hundred Years of Painting in California*, pp. 12, 118-19. None of Revere's original sketches are known to be extant.

Revere was a grandson of Paul Revere of American Revolution fame. According to Van Nostrand, the artist was born in Boston, trained at the U. S. Naval School at New York, and made his first voyage, to the Pacific, at sixteen. After the Mexican War he briefly worked as a government timber agent in California, resigned his commission in the navy, and engaged in the coastal trade with Mexico. He later served in the Mexican army, having secretly purchased a large estate in that country, then served in the Civil War as colonel (later general) of the Seventh New Jersey Volunteers. At his death, his home in Morristown, New Jersey, contained numerous oils and frescoes that he had painted.

3. See Gene A. Smith, "The War That Wasn't: Thomas apCatesby Jones's Seizure of Monterey," *California History* 66 (June 1987): 104-13, 155, 157. In 1842, William H. Meyers was a gunner aboard the U. S. frigate *Cyane*; his journal, which he illustrated with several watercolor sketches of this incident, is today in the Bancroft Library.

4. Bauer, *Mexican War*, pp. 164-67, 168-69; Bauer, *Surfboats and Horse Marines*, pp. 149-57. See Allan Nevins, *Frémont, Pathmarker of the West*, 2 vols. (1939; rpt., New York: Frederick Ungar, 1961), 1: 217-342.

5. Van Nostrand, *Monterey, Adobe Capital of California*, pp. 74, 94. Also see Jeanne Van Nostrand and Edith M. Coulter, *California Pictorial: A History in Contemporary Pictures, 1786 to 1859* (Berkeley and Los Angeles: University of California Press, 1948), pp. 43, 50-51. The government building or cuartel was originally a barracks for Mexican soldiers. After modifications it became headquarters for the U.S. Army. Alfred Sully of the U. S. Army depicted it in an 1847 watercolor.

6. Bauer, *Surfboats and Horse Marines*, pp. 245, 246.

7. Ibid., p. 152.

8. Reproduced in Van Nostrand, *Monterey, Adobe Capital of California*, pp. 64-67. The same book, p. 75, reproduces an engraving of Monterey by George Measom from Frederick Walpole, *Four Years in the Pacific in H. M. Ship Collingwood, from 1844 to 1848*, 2 vols. (London, 1850), 2: 205.

9. New York *Herald*, Jan. 10, 1847, p. 1.

22.

After Joseph Warren Revere
SUTTER'S FORT — NEW HELVETIA
Lithograph, 1849
3-3/8 x 5-7/8 in. (8.5 x 15 cm.)
u.r.: "Page 72."
l.l.: "Sketched by J. W. Revere U. S. N."
l.c.: "Published by C. S. Francis & Co N. York."
l.r.: "Lith. of Wm. Endicott & Co. N. York."
From Joseph Warren Revere, *A Tour of Duty in California*, ed. Joseph N. Balestier (New York: C. S. Francis & Co., Boston: J. H. Francis, 1849), p. 72
Courtesy of Special Collections Division, The University of Texas at Arlington Libraries, Arlington, Texas

Sutter's Fort or New Helvetia, located at the junction of the Sacramento and American Rivers (now the city of Sacramento), was a fortified frontier trading establishment and feudal estate operated by John Augustus Sutter, a German-born Swiss who had arrived in California in 1839 by way of the U.S., Oregon, and Hawaii.[1] After taking Sonoma, Frémont had established his main camp on the American River, a few miles from the fort, and Sutter had opened his gates to the revolutionaries. Not completely trusting Sutter, Frémont had placed one of his lieutenants, topographical engineer and artist Edward Kern, in charge of the fort.

Lieutenant Revere (the artist of this view) was sent to Sonoma with news of the occupation of Monterey; he carried American flags to replace the improvised Bear Flag of the revolt. Although he sent one of the American flags to be raised at Sutter's Fort on July 11, he did not reach the fort himself until later that month. At that time he helped assemble a mixed force of Californians, Americans, foreigners, and Indians in expectation of an attack from a band of hostile Walla Walla Indians.[2] Later Sutter's Fort became a major post and assembly point for recruits for the California Battalion during the campaign in the south.[3]

Revere described Sutter's Fort as

a parallelogram enclosed by adobe walls, fifteen feet high and two feet thick, with bastions or towers at the angles, the walls of which are four feet thick, and their embrasures so arranged as to flank the curtain on all sides. A good house occupies the centre of the interior area, serving for officer's quarters, armory, guard and state rooms, and also for a kind of citadel. There is a second wall on the inner face, the space between it and the outer wall being roofed and divided into work-shops, quarters, &c., and the usual offices are provided, and also a well of good water. Corrals for the cattle and horses of the garrison are conveniently placed where they can be under the eye of the guard. Cannon frown (I believe that is an inveterate habit of cannon,) from the various embrasures, and the *ensemble* presents the very ideal of a border fortress.[4]

In both the view of Monterey and that of Sutter's Fort, the distances and proportions of the objects appear to have been condensed, presumably by the lithographer. The large tree in this view of the fort is probably also a lithographer's exaggeration, since such a tree would seriously interfere with defense.[5]

22. SUTTER'S FORT — NEW HELVETIA

1. See Oscar Lewis, *Sutter's Fort: Gateway to the Gold Fields* (Englewood Cliffs, N.J.: Prentice-Hall, 1966), n.p. On January 24, 1848, less than ten days before the signing of the Treaty of Guadalupe Hidalgo, which officially ended the war, one of Sutter's employees, James W. Marshall, discovered gold at a sawmill fifty miles from the fort, sparking the 1849 gold rush.

2. Revere, *A Tour of Duty*, p. 152.

3. Bauer, *Mexican War*, pp. 169, 173; Lewis, *Sutter's Fort*, p. 130.

4. Revere, *A Tour of Duty*, p. 74.

5. Compare the photographs in Lewis, *Sutter's Fort*, between pp. 96 and 97. William Rich Hutton made a drawing of the fort, today in the Huntington Library, in April 1847, but apparently it was not reproduced until much later. Also compare a lithograph of *Sutter's Fort, Sacramento, Cal. 1847* inscribed "D. W. Smith, Agent" (cropped in the Amon Carter Museum impression), published c. 1860 by Britton & Co., San Francisco; a sign for "S. Brannan & Co." is visible at the right. Another impression is at the California Historical Society.

23.

Read after an unknown artist
VIEW OF THE TOWN OF YERBA BUENA, OR SAN FRANCISCO, CALIFORNIA.
Engraving, 1847
l.r. just below image: "Read."
From the New York *Herald*, July 14, 1847, p. 1

This curious view of San Francisco appeared in the New York *Herald* in July of 1847 with the caption:

> The above is an accurate engraving of the town and harbor of Yerba Buena, or San Francisco, California —in presenting it to our readers we do it with the assurance that its accuracy may be relied upon. The sketch from which the engraving was made, was taken on the spot at the time when that place was blockaded by the American squadron, which will account for so many vessels being in the harbor.

The *Herald* follows with a description of the vicinity, reprinted from the *California Star*, the first newspaper to be published in San Francisco.[1] The view is so generalized and the city so distant that little information can be gained from it. The presence of domes and large buildings tends to refute the paper's claim of authenticity. The engraver "Read" is probably Donald F. Read or James Alexander Read, two brothers who worked as wood engravers and magazine illustrators in New York between 1845 and 1860.[2]

Other printed views of San Francisco during the Mexican War include a lithograph after a painting by Victor Prevost. The original oil painting and an impression of the lithograph, published by Sarony & Major, are in the Historical Society of San Francisco.[3] Another lithograph of the town in 1847 or 1848 was made from a sketch by William F. Swasey, who came to California in 1845 with the Snyder-Blackburn party and served with the California Battalion during the war. Swasey's view has a descriptive key that identifies the buildings plus the ships in the harbor, including the U. S. sloop-of-war *Portsmouth* and the three transports that arrived in March and April 1847 with Colonel John D. Stevenson's First Regiment of New York Volunteers. However, the lithograph was not published until 1886 by the Bosqui Engraving and Printing Co., and the original sketch was destroyed in the San Francisco fire of 1906.[4]

1. New York *Herald*, July 14, 1847, p. 1.

2. Groce and Wallace, *Dictionary of Artists in America*, p. 526.

3. The painting is reproduced and discussed in Van Nostrand and Coulter, *California Pictorial*, p. 55.

4. The lithograph is reproduced and discussed in Van Nostrand and Coulter, *California Pictorial*, p. 49. Stevenson's New York regiment, of which many volunteers remained in California as settlers, is depicted in several images produced during the war. The New York *Herald*, Aug. 10, 1846, p. 1, and the *Weekly Herald*, Aug. 15, 1846, p. 1, published engravings by Samuel Putnam Avery depicting *The Encampment of the New York Legion, or the California Regiment, on Governor's Island, in New York Harbor*. Another engraving, inscribed "J. D. S.," of *The Scene of the Presentation of Bibles to the New York Legion, or California Regiment* appears in the *Weekly Herald*, Sept. 5, 1846, p. 1, and the *Herald*, Sept. 6, 1846, p. 1. John McHenry Hollingsworth, a lieutenant in the First New York Volunteers, kept an illustrated diary of his travels and experiences in California. It is published in *California Historical Quarterly* 1 (Jan. 1923): 207-70, and in *The Journal of Lieutenant John McHenry Hollingsworth of the First New York Volunteers* (San Francisco: California Historical Society, 1923).

THE NEW YORK HERALD.

Vol. XIII. No. 192—Whole No. 4780

NEW YORK, WEDNESDAY MORNING, JULY 14, 1847.

Price Two Cents.

THE NEW YORK HERALD
ESTABLISHMENT,
North-west corner of Fulton and Nassau sts

JAMES GORDON BENNETT, PROPRIETOR.

CIRCULATION—FORTY THOUSAND.

VIEW OF THE TOWN OF YERBA BUENA,

OR SAN FRANCISCO, CALIFORNIA.

23. Yerba Buena, or San Francisco, California

24.
After James W. Abert
SAN MIGUEL
Engraving and etching, 1848
4-3/16 x 7-3/8 in. (10.6 x 18.7 cm.)
From James W. Abert, *Report of Lieut. J. W. Abert, of his Examination of New Mexico, in the Years 1846-'47*, House Ex. Doc. 41, 30th Congress, 1st Session (Washington: Wendell and van Benthuysen, Printers, 1848), opp. p. 445
ACM 65.75/4

SAN MIGUEL.

24. SAN MIGUEL

In June 1846, Colonel (soon promoted Brigadier General) Stephen W. Kearny and an army of only 1,458 men left Fort Leavenworth, in Indian Territory, with orders to invade Mexican California and to secure New Mexico for the United States. His force, styled the "Army of the West," included several topographical engineers under Lieutenant William H. Emory, who had orders to collect data on the regions traversed. After an exhausting 537-mile march to Bent's Fort, in southwestern Colorado, the army moved south through Raton Pass into New Mexico on August 7.[1] Meeting no resistance, it soon reached the village of Las Vegas, where the general addressed the populace, promised them good government and protection of their freedoms, and administered the oath of allegiance to the principal citizens. On August 16, Kearny repeated this ceremony at the town of San Miguel del Vado, seen in this print from Lieutenant James W. Abert's official report of his examination of New Mexico, published for the U. S. government.[2]

Located along the Pecos River a few miles southeast of Santa Fe, San Miguel was an important stop on the Santa Fe Trail. In 1841 members of the Texan Santa Fe expedition had been captured and imprisoned at the town before they were sent to Mexico City.[3]

Lieutenant Abert, one of the topographical engineers, was among a number of troops who had remained behind at Bent's Fort with a "dangerous" illness.[4] Upon his recovery he was ordered to reconnoiter New Mexico while Kearny headed west to California. Included in Abert's report for the government are some of the earliest known views of New Mexico, taken from original sketches that he made along with a diary. On Friday, September 25, Lieutenant Abert recorded: "About one o'clock, having marched 12 miles, we arrived at San Miguel.... In the evening we made a visit to the village. Here is a good-sized church, built somewhat after the style of the cathedrals in the Old Country. I made a distant sketch of the town and then a nigh one of the church. The whole structure is of adobes."[5]

There were at least two different editions of the plates for Abert's *Report*. The House edition illustrated here contains all engravings and etchings by an unknown printmaker with the exception of two lithographs of Indians. It was bound together with William H. Emory's *Notes of a Military Reconnoissance...* (see cat. nos. 27-29). A Senate edition of Abert's report (also from 1848) contains lithographs by the firm of C. B. Graham in Washington, D. C.[6]

1. Bauer, *Mexican War*, pp. 127-31; Smith, *War with Mexico*, 1:284-97. An engraving of Bent's Fort appears in John T. Hughes, *Doniphan's Expedition* (Cincinnati: J.A. & U.P. James, 1848), reprinted in Connelley, *Doniphan's Expedition*, p. 206. The New York *Weekly Herald*, May 1, 1847, p. 1, published a similar engraving. A fine plan and elevation of the fort also appeared in James William

Abert, *Journal of Lieutenant James W. Abert, from Bent's Fort to St. Louis in 1845*, Senate Ex. Doc. 438, 29th Congress, 1st Session (1846).

2. Bauer, *Mexican War*, p. 133; George Rutledge Gibson, *Journal of a Soldier Under Kearny and Doniphan, 1846-1847*, ed. Ralph P. Bieber (Glendale, Calif.: Arthur H. Clark, 1935), pp. 195–200.

3. Andrew K. Gregg, *New Mexico in the Nineteenth Century: A Pictorial History* (Albuquerque: University of New Mexico Press, 1968), p. 44.

4. James William Abert (1820-97) graduated from Princeton in 1838 and in 1842 from West Point, where he studied drawing under Robert W. Weir. His father, John James Abert, was the first commander of the Corps of Topographical Engineers. The younger Abert set out with Frémont's third exploring expedition in 1845; he led a detachment of Frémont's men from Bent's Fort through Kiowa and Comanche country along the Canadian River, ultimately reaching Fort Gibson in Indian Territory. (See *Through the Country of the Comanche Indians in the Fall of the Year 1845: The Journal of a U.S. Army Expedition led by Lieutenant James W. Abert . . .*, ed. John Galvin [San Francisco: John Howell Books, 1970] .) His published *Report* of this expedition contains some lithographs after his own sketches. After his 1846 reconnaissance of New Mexico with Lieutenant Warren G. Peck, he returned to St. Louis along the Santa Fe trail in a grueling midwinter ordeal. For a good general account of this expedition, the resulting publication, and other biographical information, see William H. Goetzmann, *Army Exploration in the American West 1803-1863* (New Haven: Yale University Press, 1959), pp. 116-18, 123-27, 130, 134, 144-49. Also see Groce and Wallace, *Dictionary of Artists in America*, p. 1; Peggy and Harold Samuels, *Illustrated Biographical Encyclopedia of Artists of the American West* (Garden City, N.Y.: Doubleday, 1976), p. 1; and Cullum, *Biographical Register*, 2: 151-52.

5. *Western America in 1846-1847: The Original Travel Diary of Lieutenant J. W. Abert*, ed. John Galvin (San Francisco: John Howell Books, 1966), p. 33. The "nigh sketch" mentioned by Abert is reproduced in Galvin's book, opp. p. 32.

6. The Senate edition is *Report of Lieut. J. W. Abert of His Examination of New Mexico in the Years 1846-47*, Senate Ex. Doc. 23, 30th Congress, 1st Session (Washington, D. C., 1848). It is described in Henry R. Wagner & Charles L. Camp, *The Plains & the Rockies: A Critical Bibliography of Exploration, Adventure and Travel in the American West, 1800-1865*, 4th ed., ed. by Robert H. Becker (San Francisco: John Howell Books, 1982), pp. 301–2. Copies of the lithographed plates are reproduced in Gregg, *New Mexico in the Nineteenth Century*.

25.

After James W. Abert

SANTA FE

Engraving and etching, 1848

4-3/16 x 7-15/16 in. (10.6 x 20.2 cm.)

From James W. Abert, *Report of Lieut. J. W. Abert, of his Examination of New Mexico, in the Years 1846-'47*, House Ex. Doc. 41, 30th Congress, 1st Session (Washington: Wendell and van Benthuysen, Printers, 1848), opp. p. 419

ACM 65.75/1

On August 18, two days after it had occupied San Miguel, the American army entered Santa Fe, as described in the diary of Private John Taylor Hughes of the Missouri Volunteers:

> The day was cloudy until evening, when the sun broke out just as we entered Santa Fé. Gen. K. came in advance & entered the town with ten companies, in fine array & banners streaming in the breeze, behind them the Artillery, which halted on the hill, and the Volunteers under Col. Doniphan marched next in order through the various crooked streets of the town; their banners gaily flown to the breeze, while the batteries fired a salute of near 20 guns. The American flag was erected in the public square so as to wave over the Palace Royal or Gov. Armijo's Residence.[1]

General Manuel Armijo, the New Mexican governor and commandante, had disbanded his small army and fled south to Chihuahua. Acting Governor Juan Bautista Vigil y Alarid welcomed General Kearny, and Santa Fe was peacefully occupied. Over the next several days, Kearny announced the United States'

SANTA FE.

25. SANTA FE

annexation of the territory and oversaw the establishment of a new civilian government.[2] On September 27 the convalescent Lieutenant Abert finally arrived from Bent's Fort. "About 5 o'clock I came in sight of a few houses and beyond them beheld a distant line of hills and felt almost disheartened, when all at once I caught sight of the American flag waving proudly over some low flat-roofed buildings that lay in a deep valley. I knew this must be Santa Fe."[3]

Abert's view, taken from the south, corresponds closely to a plan of Santa Fe that appeared in John T. Hughes's *Doniphan's Expedition*.[4] Fort Marcy, flying the American flag, may be seen on the heights overlooking the town. In the center of the picture, the American flag flies from the main plaza. The long building just behind it is the Governor's Palace, while the building just beneath the flag is the chapel. The tall building to the right of the flag is the Parroquia, or parish church. Abert featured some native plants in the foreground, probably sotol and a variety of prickly pear.

1. Diary of John T. Hughes, Aug. 18, 1846, in Connelley, *Doniphan's Expedition*, p. 62.
2. Bauer, *Mexican War*, pp. 134-35.
3. Abert, *Western America in 1846-1847*, p. 34.
4. Reprinted in Connelley, *Doniphan's Expedition*, p. 210.

26.
After James W. Abert
FORT MARCY AND THE PARROQUIA — SANTA FÉ.
Engraving and etching, 1848
4-1/4 x 7-7/16 in. (10.8 x 18.9 cm.)
From James W. Abert, *Report of Lieut. J. W. Abert, of his Examination of New Mexico, in the Years 1846-'47*, House Ex. Doc. 41, 30th Congress, lst Session (Washington: Wendell and van Benthuysen, Printers, 1848), opp. p. 454 [misprinted 754]
ACM 65.75/7

Fort Marcy, seen at left in this print after Lieutenant Abert, was, according to John T. Hughes,

> laid off by Lieutenant Gilmer, of the topographical corps, and L. A. Maclean, a volunteer of Reid's company; and built by the volunteer

troops, a certain number of men being detailed each day for the purpose.... The figure of this fort is that of an irregular tridecagon, and is sufficiently ample to mount a great number of cannon and accommodate 1000 soldiers. Its walls are massive, thick and strong, and are built of adobes two feet long, one foot broad, and six inches thick. It is a strong fortress, and perpetuates the name of the present Secretary of War.[1]

In his diary entry for October 3, Lieutenant Abert wrote:

> In the evening we visited Fort Marcy, which is situated on a prominent point of bluffs commanding the whole city. The distance to the flagstaff in the centre of the Plaza is but

26. FORT MARCY AND THE PARROQUIA — SANTA FÉ

664 yds. The whole interior is defiladed from all surrounding heights within range, and the only approachable side guarded by a blockhouse. Ten guns may be brought to bear upon the city. The slopes are revetted with adobes. Fine pine logs are easily obtained that will answer for the construction of the magazine and blockhouse.[2]

General Kearny made a point of attending mass in the Parroquia to emphasize to the inhabitants that the U.S. government would respect the rights of Catholics. Abert also attended a service at the Parroquia and left a description of the interior. On October 4 he recorded: "In the evening I made a sketch of the Parroquia. Though mud walls are not generally remarkable for effect, still the great size of the building compared with those around produces an imposing effect. The fort is seen lying close by on the top of a high bluff, and behind it one sees the tops of distant mountains. The house of the priest, on the right-hand side of the capilla, is whitewashed in front and looks remarkably neat."[3]

During his reconnaissance of New Mexico, Lieutenant Abert made numerous other sketches that were printed in his *Report*. Many of them relate to the Indian civilization of the region, both past and contemporary; they include views of the ruins of Pecos and Abó, the Gold Mountains near Tuerto, San Felipe, the Pueblos of Santo Domingo, Santa Anna, and Acoma, a view of Valverde and other landscapes, and portraits of Indians.

1. Connelley, *Doniphan's Expedition*, pp. 245-46. See also Colonel William H. Emory, *Notes of a Military Reconnoissance, from Fort Leavenworth, in Missouri, to San Diego, in California...*, Senate Ex. Doc. 7, 30th Congress, 1st Session (Washington: Wendell and Van Benthuysen, Printers, 1848), p. 32, who notes that he also helped select and survey the site of Fort Marcy. Emory also notes that after August 31, twenty Mexican masons were added to the construction crew of the fort. On L. A. Maclean, see cat. no. 30, note 3.

2. Abert, *Western America in 1846-1847*, pp. 39-40.

3. Ibid., p. 40.

27.
After John Mix Stanley
SAN FELIPPE NEW MEXICO
Lithograph, 1848
4-1/8 x 6-11/16 in. (10.5 x 17.1 cm.)
l.r.: "C. B. Graham's Lith"
From William H. Emory, *Notes of a Military Reconnoissance, from Fort Leavenworth, in Missouri, to San Diego, in California, including part of the Arkansas, Del Norte, and Gila Rivers*, House Ex. Doc. 41, 30th Congress, 1st Session (Washington: Wendell and Van Benthuysen, Printers, 1848), opp. p. 38
ACM 66.75/3

General Kearny determined that the forces under his command were more than sufficient to garrison New Mexico, and he planned to send Colonel Doniphan and his troops south to rendezvous with General Wool's troops in Chihuahua. Kearny himself left Santa Fe for California on September 26 with three hundred men of the First Dragoons. Also accompanying him was a fourteen-man topographical unit led by Lieutenant William H. Emory and including artist John Mix Stanley.[1] Stanley, a civilian, had arrived in Santa Fe on August 31 with a trading caravan, and Emory had hired him as a replacement for Lieutenant G. W. Peck of the topographical engineers, who like, Abert, had fallen behind sick at Bent's Fort.[2]

Stanley was to draw Indian and Spanish ruins, landscape views, vegetation, animals, and Indians encountered during the grueling journey to California.[3] He made small sketches, from which he later made more complete oil sketches. These were lithographed to illustrate Emory's *Notes of a Military Reconnoissance, from Fort Leavenworth, in Missouri, to San Diego, in California*, published by the government in 1848. The *Notes* appeared in numerous issues and editions (one bibliographer noted twenty-

SAN FELIPPE   NEW MEXICO.

27. SAN FELIPPE, NEW MEXICO

one such issues). The plates shown here were lithographed by the firm of C. B. Graham in Washington, D.C., and bound with Abert's report; other editions have plates lithographed by Edward Weber's firm in Baltimore.[4]

One of Stanley's first views was of the village of San Felipe on the Rio Grande, seen in this lithograph. Emory, who had first visited the site on September 3, characterized it as a "pretty village... overhung by a steep craggy precipice, upon the summit of which are the ruins of a Roman Catholic church, representing in the landscape sketch the appearance of the pictures we see of the castles of the Rhine."[5]

1. Goetzmann, *Army Exploration*, pp. 127-44. Also see Goetzmann's *New Lands, New Men: America and the Second Age of Discovery* (New York: Viking Penguin, 1986), pp. 173-74.

2. Stanley (1814-72) worked in early life as a house and sign painter and received some artistic instruction from James Bowman, a portrait painter who had studied in Italy. Stanley spent some time painting portraits in the East and Midwest, but he is better known for his Indian portraits and scenes and as a western expeditionary artist. In the late 1830s he did some work among the Sioux at Fort Snelling, Minnesota. In 1842 he went to Fort Gibson, Indian Territory, where he set up a studio and for three years visited and painted various tribes during treaty councils. After his work with the Kearny expedition Stanley went on to Oregon in 1847 and to Hawaii in 1848-49. Throughout these travels he sketched and painted (also taking daguerreotypes of many of his subjects), and in 1850-52 he displayed his works in eastern cities and the Smithsonian Institution. He offered to sell his collection to the U. S. Government, but Congress refused. In 1853 Stanley served as artist for Isaac I. Stevens's northwestern railway survey expedition, working up his sketches as lithographed illustrations for the official report of the expedition. A large collection of his original Indian paintings were destroyed in the January 1865 fire at the Smithsonian. (See Robert Taft, *Artists and Illustrators of the Old West, 1850-1900* [New York: Charles Scribner's Sons, 1953], pp. 1-21, 269; Peggy and Harold Samuels, *Illustrated Biographical Encyclopedia*, p. 460; New York *Times*, April 14, 1872, p. 2. The best source on Stanley is Julia Ann Schimmel, "John Mix Stanley and Imagery of the West in Nineteenth-Century American Art," Ph.D. diss., New York University, 1983, esp. pp. 63-70, 259-65.)

3. Emory, *Notes of a Military Reconnoissance*, p. 45.

4. See Wagner and Camp, *The Plains and The Rockies*, pp. 315–20.

5. Ibid., p. 38. The Stark Museum of Art, Orange, Texas, owns the preparatory painting for this lithograph (oil on board, 10 x 12-3/4 in.). The locations of other Stanley originals for Emory's *Notes of a Military Reconnoissance* are noted in Schimmel, "John Mix Stanley," pp. 400-403.

28.
After John Mix Stanley
MOUTH OF NIGHT CREEK
Lithograph, 1848
4-1/8 x 6-3/4 in. (10.5 x 17.2 cm.)
l.r.: "C. B. Graham's Lithy."
From William H. Emory, *Notes of a Military Reconnoissance, from Fort Leavenworth, in Missouri, to San Diego, in California, including part of the Arkansas, Del Norte, and Gila Rivers*, House Ex. Doc. 41, 30th Congress, 1st Session (Washington: Wendell and Van Benthuysen, Printers, 1848), opposite p. 61
ACM 66.75/9

Before leaving New Mexico, Kearny's army encountered Kit Carson, who had just arrived from California with the news that the territory had already surrendered. Thinking he would not need them, Kearny sent two hundred dragoons back to Santa Fe, while he, Carson, and the remainder continued on. They headed west past the valley of the Mimbres River until they struck the Gila River, then roughly followed the Gila down to its junction with the Colorado River at present-day Yuma, Arizona.[1]

Among the numerous illustrations of Emory's report is this view after Stanley, depicting Kearny's mule train passing obstacles near the mouth of Night Creek, a tributary of the Gila, on October 20.[2] The print gives some idea, however small, of the enormous difficulties Kearny and his men faced. Emory's *Notes* supplement this print:

> We wended our way through the narrow valley of the Night creek. On each side were huge stone buttes shooting up into the skies. At one place we were compelled to mount one of these spurs almost perpendicular. This gave us an opportunity of seeing what a mule could do. My

conclusion was, from what I saw, that they could climb nearly as steep a wall as a cat. A pack slipped from a mule, and though not shaped favorably for the purpose, rolled entirely to the base of the hill, over which the mules had climbed.[3]

1. Goetzmann, *Army Exploration*, pp. 134-36; Emory, *Notes of a Military Reconnoissance*, pp. 39-99.
2. Schimmel, "John Mix Stanley," p. 402, lists the original oil sketch for the lithograph as in the collection of Mrs. Dean (Alice Stanley) Acheson, in Washington, D.C.
3. Emory, *Notes of a Military Reconnoissance*, p. 61.

29.
After John Mix Stanley
SAN DIEGO FROM THE OLD FORT
Lithograph, 1848
4-1/8 x 6-11/16 in. (10.5 x 17.0 cm.)
l.r.: "C. B. Graham, Lithr."
From William H. Emory, *Notes of a Military Reconnoissance, from Fort Leavenworth, in Missouri, to San Diego, in California, including part of the Arkansas, Del Norte, and Gila Rivers*, House Ex. Doc. 41, 30th Congress, 1st Session (Washington: Wendell and Van Benthuysen, Printers, 1848), opposite p. 128
ACM 66.75/24

Reaching eastern California, Kearny and his men discovered to their shock that the Californianos had revolted against the American occupation forces in southern California. Kearny's little force continued

28. MOUTH OF NIGHT CREEK

SAN DIEGO FROM THE OLD FORT

29. SAN DIEGO FROM THE OLD FORT

Emory also mentioned that on December 28, Captain Dupont of the sloop-of-war *Cyane*, which was also lying off San Diego, insisted that "Mr. Stanly" should go on board his ship so that he could pursue his work "unmolested."[3] Stanley was probably already working on sketches for the illustrations in Emory's report. By April 1847 Stanley was in San Francisco, where another traveler, Edwin Bryant, saw the artist at work on the oil sketches for the report: "Mr. Stanley, the artist of the Kearny expedition completed his sketches in oil, at San Francisco; and a more truthful, interesting, and valuable series of paintings, delineating mountain scenery, the floral exhibitions on the route, the savage tribes between Santa Fe and California — combined with camp-life and marches through the desert and wilderness — has never been, and probably never will be exhibited."[4]

1. Van Nostrand and Coulter, *California Pictorial*, p. 47.

2. Emory, *Notes of a Military Reconnoissance*, p. 113.

3. Ibid., p. 114. See also Goetzmann, *Army Exploration*, pp. 138-44.

4. Edwin Bryant, *What I Saw in California* (New York and Philadelphia: D. Appleton & Co. and G. S. Appleton, 1849), pp. 435-36, quoted in Schimmel, "John Mix Stanley," p. 68. About this time Stanley painted a small watercolor sketch of what is probably San Francisco Bay. (Schimmel, "John Mix Stanley," p. 70, states that this watercolor is in the collection of Mrs. Carl S. Dentzel.)

through the Colorado Desert on the most exhausting leg of the journey. After a costly skirmish on December 6 near the Indian village of San Pascual, the beleaguered Army of the West at last arrived at San Diego, where the American navy had a garrison, on December 12.

Artist John Mix Stanley had stayed behind with the supply train during the skirmish at San Pascual, so he did not record this action. He did, however, complete a view of San Diego, which was made into one of the few prints of California illustrating the Mexican War. According to Jeanne Van Nostrand and Edith M. Coulter, Stanley's view shows Old Town, San Diego, with "a few homes grouped around the plaza, those of José

Antonio Estudillo, Juan Bandini, and Juan Machado being the most prominent."[1]

Lieutenant Emory, who was breveted captain for meritorious conduct at San Pascual, described in his official report a "view of the fort overlooking the town of San Diego and the barren waste which surrounds it.... The town consists of a few adobe houses, two or three of which only have plank floors. It is situated at the foot of a high hill on a sand flat, two miles wide, reaching from the head of San Diego bay to False bay. A high promontory of nearly the same width, runs into the sea four or five miles and is connected by the flat with the main land."[2]

BATTLE OF SACRAMENTO, FEB. 28TH 1847,
TERRIFIC CHARGE OF THE MEXICAN LANCERS.
Drawn from a sketch taken on the battle ground by E. B. Thomas, U. S. A.

American Army 924 men.

Mexican Army 4220 men

LITH. & PUB. BY N. CURRIER,

182. NASSAU ST. COR. OF SPRUCE ST. N. Y.

30. Battle of Sacramento, Terrific Charge of the Mexican Lancers

30.
Robert Telfer after Elihu Baldwin Thomas
BATTLE OF SACRAMENTO, FEB. 28TH.
1847, TERRIFIC CHARGE OF THE
MEXICAN LANCERS.
Lithograph (hand colored), 1847
9-1/4 x 12-11/16 in. (23.6 x 32.2 cm.) comp.
l.l. on stone: "R. Telfer, del."
l.l.: "American Army 924 men."
l.c. below title: "Drawn from a sketch taken
on the battle ground by E.B. Thomas, U.S.V.
/ no. 539"
l.r.: "Mexican Army 4220 men."
Courtesy of Prints and Photographs Division,
Library of Congress, Washington, D.C.

This Currier lithograph depicts a battle
that occurred during the campaign
of Colonel Alexander Doniphan and his
force of Missouri Volunteers in the state
of Chihuahua.[1] Kearny had sent Doniphan's regiment across mountains and
desert to join General Wool's division in
the city of Chihuahua, but unknown to
them, Wool had been diverted to Saltillo
(see cat. no. 18). Doniphan had 924 soldiers, equipped with four six-pounder
field guns and two twelve-pounder howitzers. They were accompanied by about
three hundred traders and teamsters and
more than three hundred wagons.

Traveling along the El Paso road a
few miles north of the city of Chihuahua,
they discovered that a Mexican force
under Brigadier General José A. Heredia
had erected strong fortifications on a plateau in front of the Sacramento River
crossing. On the morning of February
28, 1847, Doniphan formed his wagons
into four columns, with the remainder of
his command between, except for two
hundred cavalry. Before reaching the
Mexican fortifications, the columns made
a sharp right turn off the road and then
crossed a deep, dry creek bed. They
reached the high ground of the plateau

on the Mexican left while the Mexican
cavalry, led by Brigadier General Pedro
Garcia Condé, maneuvered to oppose
them. Part of the wagon columns, having
reached the plateau, may be seen at far
right in the print.

According to Private John T. Hughes:

In passing the Arroyo the caravan
and baggage trains followed close
upon the rear of the army. Nothing
could exceed in point of solemnity
and grandeur the rumbling of the
artillery, the firm moving of the caravan, the dashing to and fro of
horsemen, and the waving of banners
and gay fluttering guidons, as both
armies advanced to the attack on the
rocky plain; for at this crisis General
Condé, with a select body of twelve
hundred cavalry, dashed down from
the fortified heights to commence the
engagement. When within nine
hundred and fifty yards of our align-
ment, Major Clark's battery of six
pounders, and Weightman's section
of howitzers opened upon them a
well directed and most destructive
fire, producing fearful execution in
their ranks. In some disorder they
fell back a short distance, unmasking
a battery of cannon, which immediately commenced its fire upon us. A
brisk cannonading was now kept up
on both sides for the space of fifty
minutes. . . . In this action the enemy,
who were drawn up in columns four
deep, close order, lost about twenty-
five killed, besides a great number of
horses. The Americans who stood
dismounted, in two ranks, open
order, suffered but slight injury.[2]

After Condé fell back to his fortified
positions, the Missourians rushed the

Mexican guns directly in their front, with
Captain John W. Reid's cavalry taking
the lead.[3] These guns are seen at left in
the print. Even after American horsemen
took the fort, the Mexican battery across
the river, perhaps seen in the distant
right, continued to bombard the Americans until Captain R. H. Weightman took
his guns across the river and more American cavalry flanked that position. The
Mexicans then abandoned the field, and
Doniphan's men entered the capital city
of Chihuahua.

It is significant that Private Elihu
Baldwin Thomas, the artist whose sketch
served as the model for this lithograph,
chose to depict the moment in the battle
when the American artillery broke up the
Mexican cavalry charge. Thomas was in
Major Clark's Battalion of Light Horse
Artillery and was therefore recording his
own unit's part in the battle.[4] As the
inscription states, Thomas's sketch was
taken on the battleground, probably soon
after the battle.

After a brief occupation of
Chihuahua in March and April, the
Missourians marched another five
hundred miles to join Worth at Saltillo
and then, no longer needed, began their
return to the States.[5] Thomas and his
company mustered for discharge in New
Orleans on June 24, 1847. Probably at
this time his sketch of the battle made its
way to Nathaniel Currier's shop in New
York, where it was copied on stone by
R. Telfer.[6]

1. The best source on Doniphan's expedition and the battles of Brazito and Sacramento is Connelley, *Doniphan's Expedition*, which contains extensive notes and official reports as well as a reprint of John T. Hughes's *Doniphan's Expedition*. Also see Bauer, *Mexican War*, pp. 151-59. An engraving of Colonel Doniphan's army marching through the Jornada del Muerto in southern New Mexico appears in William H. Richardson, *Journal of William H. Richardson, a Private Soldier in the Campaign of New and Old Mexico* (New York: the author, 1848). The engraving is also reproduced in Connelley, *Doniphan's Expedition*, p. 368. Richardson's book also contains extremely rare genre scenes of soldiers engaged in camp activities. One, *A Camp Washing Day*, is reproduced and discussed in Mugridge, *Album of American Battle Art*, pp. 132–33.

2. Connelley, *Doniphan's Expedition*, p. 409.

3. Ibid., p. 413, contains an engraving by Horace Grosvenor showing *The Charge of Captain Reid, at Sacramento*. The original sketch for this engraving is in the Amon Carter Museum. Author John Taylor Hughes credits his "valued and esteemed friend, L. A. Maclean, of the Missouri Horse Guards, who generously and gratuitously furnished most of the designs which embellish this work." Lachlan Allan Maclean (c. 1822–1864), born in Scotland, was a corporal in Captain John W. Reid's Company D, First Regiment of Missouri Mounted Volunteers. In Santa Fe, he had helped to design and construct Fort Marcy (see cat. no. 26). Maclean was severely wounded at the battle of Sacramento; although it is possible that he made his drawing of the "Charge of Captain Reid" in the field, it is more likely that he drew it from memory after his unit was discharged in New Orleans in June 1847. A Missouri school-teacher, Maclean later served and died in the Confederate army. (See Connelley, *Doniphan's Expedition*, pp. 118, 245, 386, 405, 416, 547, 548; Compiled Service Record for Mexican War Volunteers [Lachlan A. Maclean, Corporal, Co. D, First Regiment Doniphan's Missouri Mounted Infantry], RG 94, National Archives, Washington, D.C.; General Index to Compiled Service Records, Civil War, Confederates, RG 109, M253, roll 296, National Archives.)

4. Elihu Baldwin Thomas (before 1828-1910) enlisted June 8, 1846, in St. Louis as a private in Captain Weightman's Company A of Major Clark's Battalion of Light Horse Artillery, Missouri Volunteers. Thomas married in St. Louis on April 7, 1852, and worked there as a printer (compositor). The Mexican War Pension Claim, application no. 19555, certificate no. 15458, filed by his widow Imogine Y. Thomas on May 2, 1910, also states that Thomas died in St. Louis on April 25, 1910 (RG 15, National Archives). See also Connelley, *Doniphan's Expedition*, pp. 574, 576.

5. An engraving of Texas Rangers shooting a Mexican guerrilla in the presence of Colonel Doniphan's troops, near the Rio Grande, appears in Richardson, *Journal of William H. Richardson*; it is reproduced in Connelley, *Doniphan's Expedition*, p. 489.

6. "R. Telfer" may be Robert Telfer, a wood engraver active in Philadelphia from 1849 to 1857. Associated with Alexander Lawrie in the engraving firm of Telfer & Lawrie, he was listed in the Philadelphia city directory of 1849. From 1852 to 1854 he was associated with David Scattergood, a wood engraver and bookseller, in the firm of Scattergood & Telfer. From 1850 to 1858 a John R. Telfer as active in Cincinnati as a wood engraver. (See Groce and Wallace, *Dictionary of Artists in America*, pp. 561, 621, citing Philadelphia City Directories for 1849-57.)

31.

Fd. Bastin after an unknown artist
BATALLA DEL SACRAMENTO, TERRIBLE CARGA DE LOS LANCEROS MEXICANOS, CONTRA EL EGERCITO NORTE AMERICANO, EL 28 DE FEBRERO, 1847.
Toned lithograph, c. 1850
7-7/8 x 12-3/8 in. (20.0 x 31.5 cm.)
l.l. on stone: "Fd. Bastin"
u.r.: "No. 1"
l.l.: "Julio Michaud y Thomas, Mexico."
From *Album Pintoresco de la República Méxicana* (Mexico City: Estamperia de Julio Michaud y Thomas, 1850)
Courtesy of Fikes Hall of Special Collections and DeGolyer Library, Southern Methodist University, Dallas, Texas

This lithograph of the battle of Sacramento for an album published in Mexico City demonstrates how widely different artists' interpretations of an event may vary. In this lithograph by Ferdinand (?) Bastin, General Condé's Mexican lancers are shown overwhelming the Missouri artillery, with the bodies of dead and wounded Americans being trampled in the foreground. In the background, Mexican infantry are shown pursuing a body of American infantry in full retreat. According to all American accounts, however, the charge of the Mexican lancers was broken up before they reached the American guns, and it was the Mexicans who turned and ran.

The lithograph was probably produced in Paris in 1850 by the firm of Lemercier, although it was published in Mexico by Julio Michaud y Thomas. Nothing is known about Bastin, but judging from the quality of his work he was a very skilled draftsman, unlike his American counterpart who produced the previous print for Nathaniel Currier. Bastin may have worked as a lithographer in Paris for Lemercier.

BATALLA DEL SACRAMENTO

terrible Carga de los Lanceros Mexicanos, contra el Egercito norte Americano

El 28 de Febrero. 1847.

31. Batalla del Sacramento, Terrible Carga de los Lanceros Mexicanos

32.
Henry after an unknown artist
MANOEUVRES AT SAN LUIS POTOSI
Engraving, 1847
6-7/8 x 7-3/4 in. (17.3 x 19.7 cm.)
From *Brother Jonathan* (New York: Wilson
and Company, 1847), p. 8
Courtesy of Yale Western Americana Collection, Beinecke Rare Book and Manuscript
Library

Exiled Mexican general Antonio López
de Santa Anna returned to Mexico in
mid-August 1846. He had convinced the
Polk administration that he would seek a
settlement with the U.S. if he could return
to power, but once back in Mexico he
immediately began efforts to repel the
American invaders. At the city of San Luis
Potosí, about three hundred miles south
of Monterrey, he collected over 18,000
troops.[1]

In 1847 *Brother Jonathan*, an irregularly issued illustrated magazine, published this engraving of Santa Anna
drilling his new troops. According to the
caption, the "engraving, by Henry, from
a sketch made by an American spy, represents a drill-parade, forming a grand
spectacle of one of the largest and most
splendidly uniformed corps ever beheld
on this continent." Though the engraving
appears to have been made by an eyewitness, it conflicts somewhat with an
account by Manuel Balbontín:

> The troops were drilled with frequency. The infantry, by brigades,
> under the command of its respective
> generals; but they never saw a general
> drill, not even by division. The cav-

MANŒUVRES AT SAN LUIS POTOSI.

Drilling of the Mexican Troops by Santa Anna, previous to marching upon Gen. Taylor at Saltillo and Buena Vista.

Santa Anna, on his return from exile, in 1846, immediately repaired to San Luis Potosi with all the force he could muster, and here filled up his army to the number of about twenty-four thousand. His troops suffered much for means of subsistence; but finally, by pledging his own private credit, as he himself states, he raised one hundred and eighty thousand dollars—sufficient to last two weeks—by which means he was enabled to take up his long delayed march upon General Taylor. The above engraving, by Henry, from a sketch made by an American spy, represents a drill-parade, forming a grand spectacle of one of the largest and most splendidly uniformed corps ever beheld on this continent.

32. MANOEUVRES AT SAN LUIS POTOSI

alry manoeuvred only by regiments. The artillery were rarely accustomed to manoeuvre and never fired blanks. The general in chief never appeared in the camp of instruction, by luck, because he could not appreciate the respective quality of the corps which were under his command....

During the months of November and December, reenforcements arrived for the army. Also the troops raised in the states of Guanajuato and Jalisco arrived. These troops were in general badly armed: there were corps in which were seen arms of all sizes, and a large number of them without bayonets, — one noted many guns held together with leather straps or with cords instead of braces.[2]

In late January and early February this force left San Luis Potosí on a long march northward, intending to strike Taylor's forces and retake Saltillo.

1. Bauer, *Mexican War*, p. 201. American accounts generally estimate their number at 20,000; but Ramón Alcaraz estimates 18,000.
2. Manuel Balbontín, *La invasión americana*, pp. 55-62. See also cat. no. 131, n. 1.

33.
After George C. Furber
VICTORIA — MOUNTAINS — CAMP OF GEN. PATTERSON'S DIVISION.
Engraving, 1848
3-7/8 x 6-1/2 in. (9.8 x 16.5 cm.)
From George C. Furber, *The Twelve Months Volunteer; or, Journal of a Private, in the Tennessee Regiment of Cavalry, in the Campaign, in Mexico, 1846-7* (Cincinnati: J. A. & U. P. James, 1848), opposite p. 318
Courtesy of Special Collections Division, The University of Texas at Arlington Libraries, Arlington, Texas

While Santa Anna trained his army in San Luis Potosí, American troops occupied the northeastern Mexican state of Tamaulipas. The scene of little fighting, the region received scant attention from American printmakers. However, views of Tamaulipas do appear in George C. Furber's *The Twelve Months Volunteer; or, Journal of a Private, in the Tennessee Regiment of Cavalry, in the Campaign, in Mexico, 1846-7*, first published in Cincinnati in 1848 and, according to the title page, "embellished with correct engravings, from drawings by the author." Furber was a practicing lawyer from Germantown, Tennessee, who had determined at the outbreak of the Mexican War "to throw aside Blackstone and Chitty and take up the sword and carbine."[1] In his preface, the author-artist described his efforts to leave an authentic record, adding that he had included twenty-three engravings rather than the six he originally intended.

As historical documents of the war, Furber's book and its illustrations are in a class by themselves. Although the engravings (another edition has lithographs) are amateurish and leave much to be desired aesthetically, Furber's vivid written descriptions from his journal complement and augment the illustrations even more than Nebel's and Kendall's great collaborative effort. Furber went to uncommon lengths to describe every physical, topographical, botanical, architectural, or other detail he included in his pictures, even noting occasionally when the engraver had strayed from his (Furber's) original sketches.[2]

Furber's unit, part of a division of volunteers under Generals Robert Patterson and Gideon J. Pillow, traveled overland from Matamoros to Ciudad Victoria, the capital of Tamaulipas, arriving on January 4, 1847. The encampment there also included troops who had fought at Monterrey, accompanied by Zachary Taylor.[3] The entry in Furber's journal for January 7 gives a voluminous description of the view of camp and city as seen in the engraving:

Two feet beyond these men [a sentinel and a Mexican *caballero* looking for a horse], reader, is the edge of the precipice, which falls off perpendicularly perhaps a hundred and fifty feet. You see the creek, or little river, running along over its rocky bed; — beyond this, on the right, you observe the camps of the two Illinois regiments of infantry: you see the men drawn out on parade. — The camp on the left, with the chapparal between it and the river, is that of our regiment; but the men are drawn up in solid square beyond. — The wagon train that accompanied our division from Matamoras, you perceive in its regular lines: they look like a considerable number; but could you see them strung out on the march, you would suppose that number to be greater than it really is. — Between the train and the tents

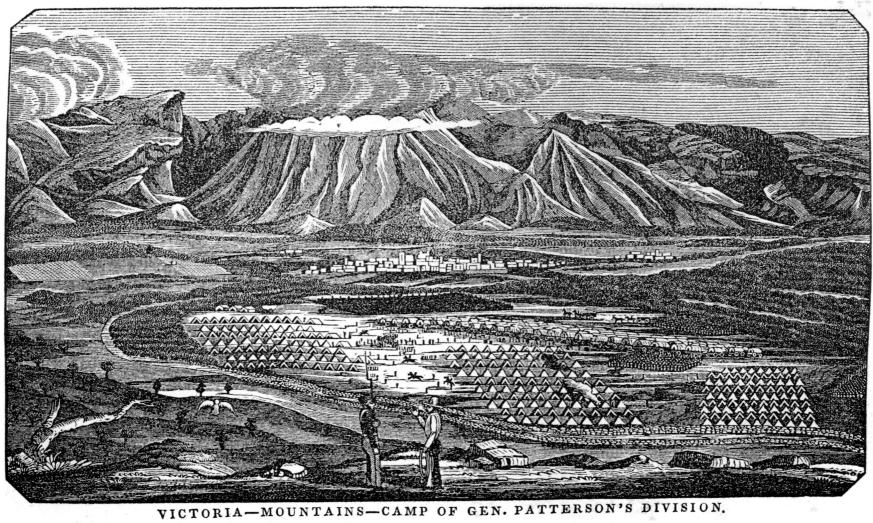

VICTORIA—MOUNTAINS—CAMP OF GEN. PATTERSON'S DIVISION.

33. Victoria — Mountains — Camp of Gen. Patterson's Division

of our regiment, you can observe the crowds around the commissaries, who are issuing the rations. — In front of the regiment of cavalry, as they are drawn out there, you see the marquee of General Patterson, and those of his aids. General Pillow's is within the chapparal, and is hid from view. — You see a wagon, by the general's tent: that is but one; but these generals, when on the march have more: — General Patterson has three for himself and staff....

Over the wagon train, to the right, you perceive two wagons going towards town. — They are part of a large number that go in every day, to bring corn for our horses; which General Taylor has obliged the alcaldes of the town to have brought in from the country around.... Over the body of cavalry, towards the town, you see first the stone wall of the cemetery or consecrated burial ground; *campo santo* (sacred ground) the Mexicans call it. There are many fine tombs and much ornamented stone-work over the dead there; but these are too small to be seen at this distance....

Beyond this cemetery, on the next hill, you see one end of the town of Victoria, with its white buildings of *tunastate* rock. — The town is much larger than you would think, from the view in this direction; for it runs up along the creek, back towards the mountains, for more than a mile; all this is rather down a slope, and is concealed from your view; you look on the narrow end. — It contains about eight thousand inhabitants.[4]

1. Furber, *Twelve Months Volunteer*, title page, p. 15; see also Hamilton, *Early American Book Illustrators and Wood Engravers*, 1:132. Furber was thirty-two years old at the time of his enlistment in Memphis, Tennessee, as a private in Company G ("The Eagle Guards") of the First Tennessee Mounted Infantry on May 29, 1846. (Compiled Military Service Records of Soldiers in the Mexican War Who Served from the State of Tennessee, RG 94, M638, roll 4, National Archives, Washington, D.C. His journal begins in Tennessee and chronicles his trip across Arkansas and Texas. Opposite p. 150 he includes an engraved view of the ruins of Goliad, a quite rare view of the site where 350 Texan troops under Colonel James W. Fannin were massacred during the Texas Revolution.

2. See Rick Stewart's essay for an example of this. Hamilton, *Early American Book Illustrators and Wood Engravers*, p. 132, notes that George K. Stillman's name appears on a number of the plates as the engraver and that four of these illustrations appeared again in Furber's later book, also published in Cincinnati: *Ike McCandliss, and Other Stories; or Incidents in the Life of a Soldier* (Cincinnati: J. A. & U. P. James, 1853). In addition to Stillman's name in the plates, some have the initials "S. B. G."

3. Smith, *War with Mexico*, 1: 266-67, 351, 356-62. An engraving after Lieutenant Alfred Sully depicting *The Sierra Madre, 15 miles from Monterey* appears in Henry, *Campaign Sketches*, p. 269. The original sketch was apparently taken on the march to Victoria from Monterrey.

4. Furber, *Twelve Months Volunteer*, pp. 321-24.

34.
After George C. Furber
CITY OF TAMPICO FROM FORT ANDONEGA
Engraving, 1848
3-7/8 x 6-3/8 in. (9.8 x 16.2 cm.)
From George C. Furber, *The Twelve Months Volunteer; or, Journal of a Private, in the Tennessee Regiment of Cavalry, in the Campaign, in Mexico, 1846-7* (Cincinnati: J. A. & U. P. James, 1848), after p. 393
Courtesy of Special Collections Division, The University of Texas at Arlington Libraries, Arlington, Texas

On November 15, 1846, a U.S. naval squadron under Commodore David Conner had seized the city of Tampico, the principal town in the state of Tamaulipas, and after Veracruz the chief port of Mexico on the Gulf Coast. Earlier, the city had been abandoned by Mexican forces. By November 23 a force of 650 U. S. Army regulars had been brought in by sea to garrison the town, which became a gathering point for the troops in northern Mexico, including General Patterson's, for the upcoming campaign against Veracruz and central Mexico. George Furber's unit arrived at Tampico at the end of January 1847, camping there for forty days before embarking on transport ships for the Veracruz expedition.[1]

In his journal entry for February 4, Furber described two views that he sketched from Fort Andoñega, which stands on a hill commanding the city.

In the first view, reader, imagine yourself standing on this old fort, looking towards the southwest. — As you see in the picture, the wall is in front of you; this wall is of stone and cement, and is about eight feet thick, sloped off on the top....

Over the lake, on the hill, you see the city. — You observe that it

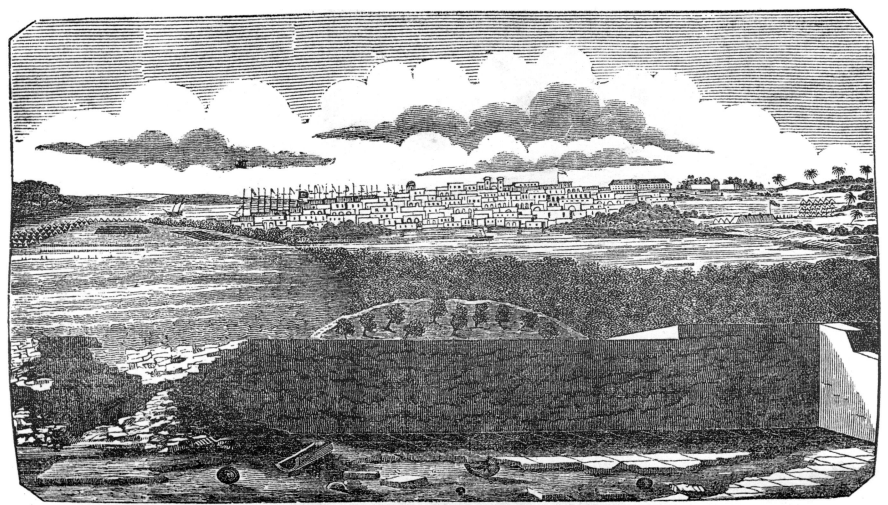

CITY OF TAMPICO FROM FORT ANDONEGA.

34. City of Tampico from Fort Andonega

falls off from the centre, down to the river, on the left. At the right extremity you observe a tall building, with a flag over it. It has been turned into a fort, and has artillery mounted on its flat roof, though the pieces are not to be perceived at this distance. — To the right of that, you see a large building; that is the military hospital; built and used as such, by the Mexicans, and appropriated by our forces to the same purpose. The road from the interior, by which we entered the city, comes in there. To the right of that, is the *campo santo*, or cemetery, with its stone walls and lofty gate. There is another to its left, but it is concealed from view by the hospital. Nearly between you and the cemetery, and not far from the edge of the lake, you see a new fort, with a flag above it; it is yet unfinished.... To the right of these, and farther up, you see the tents of part of Gen. Shields' brigade....

On the left of the picture, from Fort Andonega, you see, first, part of the extensive plain...on the farther extremity of which the Tennessee brigade, under Gen. Pillow, is encamped; the tents of the first regiment of which can be seen.... Beyond the camp you see the river, that flows round from the other side of the city; over the lower part of which can be seen the numerous masts of the vessels there at anchor. A large flag can be seen over this part of the city. It is on the flagstaff in the *plaza de Comercio*, or the lower plaza, adjoining the river.[2]

1. Smith, *War with Mexico*, 1: 276-83, 362-69; Bauer, *Surfboats and Horse Marines*, pp. 52-57; Furber, *Twelve Months Volunteer*, pp. 391-93.
2. Furber, *Twelve Months Volunteer*, pp. 394-400.

35.
After George C. Furber
MOUTH OF PÁNUCO RIVER, FROM FORT ANDONEGA
Engraving, 1848
3-3/4 x 6-3/8 in. (9.6 x 16.2 cm.)
From George C. Furber, *The Twelve Months Volunteer; or, Journal of a Private, in the Tennessee Regiment of Cavalry, in the Campaign, in Mexico, 1846-7* (Cincinnati: J. A. & U. P. James, 1848), after p. 393
Courtesy of Special Collections Division, The University of Texas at Arlington Libraries, Arlington, Texas

Private Furber describes his second view from Fort Andoñega, looking east toward the mouth of the Pánuco River:

Turn completely round, with your back to the city, and the other picture is before you.... In the fort, on the right, and front, you observe the stone platforms, on which formerly stood the heavy pieces of artillery, which bore down upon the river. On the left, is a building, now decaying, with the tiles nearly gone from its roof; it was used for the barracks of the garrison, and when our naval forces first took the city, in November last, it was occupied by marines from the ships of war....

Over the broken wall in front, you observe a hill covered with bushes: — that hill is the final resting place of many soldiers of our own, and of the other regiments of our brigade.... From the front of the picture round to the right, you perceive the smooth plain spread out, not so wide as above; — on it, in the distance, is the wagon train of the brigade; — beyond this, is the river — a schooner is going out, and a steamer is towing up a brig.

MOUTH OF PANUCO RIVER, FROM FORT ANDONEGA.

35. Mouth of Panuco River, from Fort Andonega

Down the river you see another small schooner, going out; — beyond her, you perceive the mouth, the old forts, and the pilot houses; — these are about four miles distant. You observe two large ships lying off; several more are out there, but not in the view: — they draw too much water to come over the bar. — Still beyond them, are the waters of the Gulf.[1]

1. Furber, *Twelve Months Volunteer*, pp. 400-1.

Buena Vista

36.   See Plate 8
Frances Flora Bond (Fanny) Palmer after
Joseph Horace Eaton
BATTLE OF BUENA VISTA. VIEW OF THE
BATTLE-GROUND OF "THE ANGOSTURA"
FOUGHT NEAR BUENA VISTA, MEXICO
FEBRUARY 23RD. 1847. (LOOKING S.
WEST.)
Toned lithograph (hand colored), 1847
19-1/4 x 29-1/2 in. (48.9 x 74.9 cm.)
l.l. on stone: "F Palmer"
l.l.: "From a Sketch Taken on the Spot by
Major Eaton, Aid de Camp to Genl. Taylor."
l.r.: "Lith. Pub. & Printed in Colors by H. R.
Robinson, 142 Nassau St. N. York."
l.c. below title: "Entered according to Act of
Congress in the Year 1847, by H. R. Robinson, in the Clerk's Office of the District Court
of the Southern Dist of N. York."
ACM 48.71

Most of his veteran U. S. Army regulars having been drawn off for the Veracruz campaign, Taylor was left to hold northern Mexico with a force of about 6,000 men, consisting mostly of volunteers. Marching north from San Luis Potosí, Santa Anna, with an army three times that size, struck Taylor's army on February 22, 1847, at a pass known as La Angostura near the hacienda of San Juan de la Buena Vista, about seven miles south of Saltillo.[1]

By far one of the most important Mexican War prints is this grand view of the battle of Buena Vista by Major Joseph Horace Eaton, who served as General Taylor's aide-de-camp throughout the war.[2] Eaton was already a brevet major for "gallant and meritorious action at the Battle of Monterey," and he was further breveted a lieutenant colonel for his conduct at Buena Vista, which General Taylor

complimented in his official report of the latter action.[3] In his capacity as an aide-de-camp and in his spare time after the battle, Eaton apparently took notes, sketched troop dispositions, recorded the topography of the battlefield, and conversed with other participants in order to prepare his final sketch. This original view soon made its way to New York, where it was copied on stone by English-born artist Fanny Palmer for lithographer and publisher Henry R. Robinson.[4] The print was accompanied by a detailed descriptive key on a separate sheet.

On September 15, 1847, the *Daily National Intelligencer* announced that the print had just issued from the press and that copies were "ready for delivery to subscribers and others by Brook, Shillington & Co." The print won praise from this and other newspapers for its pictorial beauty and exhaustive accuracy. The *Literary World* commented:

The large size of the picture (32 by 24 inches), by allowing a minute representation of the physiognomy, so to speak, of the whole battle-ground, conveys a more vivid and distinct impression to the mind of the beholder, than could be given in any verbal description. The position of our gallant little army—the charge of the Mexican forces—the peculiar character of the ground, broken up by deep, rocky ravines—and towering over all, the grouped summits of the majestic cordilleras, with a glimpse of the grand valley opening beyond—are represented with a force and faithfulness which those who were present can best appreciate, as the certificates of many, appended to the work, testify.

The *National Intelligencer* also published a letter to Henry R. Robinson from Senator Henry Clay of Kentucky, who had lost a son in the battle, thanking the lithograph's publisher for his "patriotic work": "Although it will constantly remind me of a sad loss which I sustained on that occasion, I share, in common with the rest of our countrymen, in the glory which was won by our gallant commander and his brave army."[5]

The view contains certain inconsistencies that are common to most artistic renderings of battle scenes. Among these are the reduction of troop numbers and oversimplification of movement. A body of troops intended to represent a regiment looks more like a platoon; individual figures are always in step like toy soldiers. Somewhat unusually in Eaton's print, no dead or wounded litter the ground. Buena Vista was a complicated two-day battle; no one eyewitness could absorb all of the details of any particular scene, and even if Eaton talked to a number of other eyewitnesses, he must have heard conflicting stories. Despite these problems, a close examination of the view together with its descriptive key may prove useful to historians.[6]

The depiction of the topography is reasonably accurate. It generally agrees, for example, with the plan of the battle drawn by Brevet Captain Lorenzo Sitgreaves of the Topographical Corps, although either Eaton or Fanny Palmer condensed the scene and exaggerated the size of the mountains.[7] The buildings of the hacienda of Buena Vista were just east of the road and are not visible in the print (they would be behind and to the left of the viewer). The road from Saltillo south toward San Luis Potosí appears in the foreground and winds and stretches across the right portion of the print, disappearing just around the base of the large mountain that casts its shadow in the valley. Along the western side of the road ran a creek, seen in the right of the print, that formed a complicated network of deep, almost impassable gullies. West of and parallel to this creek was a ridge (out of the picture, to the right), so that the battle site was actually a rather broad pass. To the left of the road is the plateau, divided by smaller dry ravines into three "high tongues of land," on which most of the engagement was fought. Beyond the plateau rise the mountains, whose foothills Mexican troops successfully occupied on February 22 in preparation for a grand maneuver to turn the American left flank.

Eaton depicted the scene as it appeared on the second day of battle (February 23) at what might be considered the climax, some time just before four o'clock in the afternoon. The original American line had been almost perpendicular to the one in the picture, running from the deep network of gullies on the right across the first high tongue of land to the spur of the mountain in the center of the picture. The Mexican right worked actively during both days of the battle to turn the American left; being heavily reinforced, they succeeded in throwing back several regiments. Eaton's view shows the Mexican infantry at their furthest point of penetration along the base of the mountain, at the far left of the print.

The keystone of the American position throughout the battle was Major John M. Washington's battery of artillery, which may be seen blocking the road just to the left of the intricate maze of gullies in the right portion of the print, in the middle distance. Washington's battery checked the Mexican advance along the road on the twenty-second and repelled an assault on the twenty-third by a large column under General Santiago Blanco.[8] According to the descriptive key, Major Washington and one of his subalterns, "Brint" (Lieutenant Thomas L. Brent of the Fourth Artillery), are the officers on horseback in front of the battery's teams of horses. To the right of the battery a ditch and breastwork stretches to the gullies. It was completed by nightfall of the twenty-second and was manned the next day by two companies of the First Regiment of Illinois Volunteers under Lieutenant Colonel Weatherford. The two "baggage wagons" along the road in the foreground may actually be the two wagons mentioned by Carleton that were loaded with stone to close up the space between the breastwork and the spur in case the Mexicans attacked in that quarter.[9]

On the ridges just to the left of and supporting Washington's battery is the main body of the First Illinois, commanded by Colonel J. J. Hardin. In the dry ravine to their left are their tents, separated from the original base of the Mexican positions (seen in the far right distance) by several dry ravines that open up along the road. Lines and masses of Mexican infantry and cavalry can be made out in the far right distance, labeled in the key "Enemys Columns found hard to Attack," together with two puffs of smoke from a Mexican battery. It is from this direction that Santa Anna's vast army first appeared on the morning of the twenty-second.

On the first tongue or plateau above and to the left of the tents are "Gen. Taylor & Staff." In the grouping of six horsemen nearest the viewer on this plateau, General Taylor is on the white horse, third from the right. He had returned to Saltillo on the night of the twenty-second, arriving back on the battlefield the next day just when the situation was most critical for the Americans. All but one of the six horsemen in this grouping are facing left, probably indicating their concern for the American left flank. Just below Taylor is an isolated figure on a galloping horse. The key labels him "Crittenden," probably Thomas L. Crittenden, a civilian aide to General Taylor and one of the messengers who carried the first news of Taylor's victory back to the United States.[10]

Just beyond Taylor on the first plateau is the line of the Second Regiment of Kentucky Volunteer Infantry; immediately to their left and right are their commanders, Colonels Henry Clay, Jr. (son of the senator) and William R. McKee. Just beyond them is another line of infantry, which Eaton's key identifies as Colonel William H. Bissell's Second Illinois Regiment, shown firing a volley at the Mexican columns passing the base of the mountain beyond them. On the Second Illinois's left is Captain John P. O'Brien's smoking battery. In the early morning of the twenty-third O'Brien had commanded three guns, but one had been captured when the crumbling American left wing left him stranded on the plateau farther toward the base of the mountain. On the Second Illinois's right is another battery, unlabeled by Eaton, composed of one gun belonging to Captain Thomas W. Sherman and another belonging to Captain Braxton Bragg.[11] Farther to this battery's right, a thin line of infantry face a ravine; these may represent American skirmishers. The key notes that the two horsemen galloping just on the right of the Second Illinois are General Wool and Inspector General Churchill. In the far distance near the base of the mountain, lines of Mexican cavalry and infantry move off to the left, under the cover of a

supporting battery indicated by a cloud of smoke seen just beyond the American skirmishers.

In the center foreground of the picture, a section of Bragg's battery moves off the road toward the second tongue of land. Captain Enoch Steen gallops by just beyond them along with his dragoons. Beyond them and to the left are Colonel Albert Pike and the Arkansas cavalry, and, just above Pike, Colonel Yell, also of Arkansas, who was lanced to death shortly after this.[12] The isolated figure between the cavalry and the line of American infantry with smoking artillery batteries on its flanks is the wounded Brigadier General Joseph Lane, who had been in charge of the American left when it crumbled. The line of American infantry is labeled simply "Troops Opposing the Enemy." Apparently this was a mixed body of troops, remnants of several units that had fallen back during the collapse of the left flank. General Lane attempted to rally them without much success, but Major Dix, the army paymaster, succeeded. Dix is on the horse just to the right of the line of infantry.

On the third plateau at the far left, the key indicates part of Captain Sherman's battery in the foreground and just beyond them, to the left, the "1st Ky Dragoons"—actually a combined cavalry force of First Dragoons under Brevet Lieutenant Colonel May and Kentucky Cavalry under Colonel Humphrey Marshall.[13] They are rushing from the American rear to the center of this plateau in anticipation of an attack from the "Enemys Cavalry about to Charge," which the descriptive key indicates in the left distance. Just beyond the American cavalry, another piece of artillery is being rushed to the front. The dashing horseman at far left is Colonel Jefferson Davis,

who had come up with his men and General Taylor from the hacienda to find the American left in shambles. Davis and his Mississippians, together with what remnants they could rally of the Second Indiana, had just beaten off the advance column of Mexican light troops under General Pedro Ampudia; in this scene Davis's line of the First Mississippi, now joined with the Third Indiana, have formed a V in anticipation of the Mexican cavalry charge. Colonel Lane, commander of the Third Indiana, is the figure on horseback inside the V. At the left part of the V, a single gun of Sherman's battery fires a round in support.[14]

Because of its comprehensive detail Eaton's view also serves as a key to later events of the battle. Just after the moment fixed by Eaton, the Mississippi and Indiana V held firmly against the Mexicans, inflicting great losses on their cavalry. The Mexican advance stalled, then reeled. All of the American cavalry and artillery on the left came into play at the front, advancing to push the Mexican right against the mountain. Nine pieces of American light artillery began to wear them down, but as the Americans ceased firing momentarily to investigate a white flag, the Mexican right wing escaped and the battle resumed with greater fury.[15]

Taylor ordered the two Illinois regiments under Colonels Bissell and Hardin and the Second Kentucky under Colonels McKee and Clay to attack the retreating Mexican line at their front (at the base of the mountains in the center of the print). Unknown to them at the time, Santa Anna was assembling his reserves under General Pérez in a broad ravine (seen in the middle right of the print, running between the two Mexican batteries) for an all-out attack. When Pérez's troops emerged from the ravine, the attacking

Kentucky and Illinois troops, now greatly outnumbered, sought shelter in one of the ravines that led to the road. The Mexicans pursued them there, firing down upon them from three sides, and a body of Mexican lancers briefly blocked the end of the ravine at the road until they were driven away by Washington's battery. A small remnant of the Kentucky and Illinois troops made their escape, but among those killed were Colonels Hardin, McKee, and Clay.[16]

1. One of the best eyewitness accounts of the battle is James H. Carleton's *Battle of Buena Vista*. A captain in the First Dragoons, Carleton credits General Wool, Taylor's second-in-command, with selecting the battle site (pp. 5, 178-86). See also Smith, *War with Mexico*, 1:385-400 and notes; Smith gives a voluminous bibliography of eyewitness accounts (1:556-57 n. 8, 560-61 n. 19).

2. Eaton (1815-96), a native of Salem, Massachusetts, graduated in 1835 from West Point and later was an assistant instructor of infantry tactics there (1839-43). Before the Mexican War he also served on frontier duty at Jefferson Barracks, Missouri, and Fort Jessup, Louisiana (1843-45); earlier he had helped map the Sabine River when this formed the border between the United States and the Republic of Texas. Besides his view of the battle of Buena Vista, he is known to have made a profile sketch of General Taylor from which a lithographic portrait was made (cat. no. 42). During most of 1852-56 Eaton was stationed in New Mexico, where he studied the Zuni and Navajo Indians; he wrote an article on them for Henry Rowe Schoolcraft's *History of the Indian Tribes of North America*, which also contained prints copied from some of his sketches. Engravings from some of his sketches also appeared in W. W. H. Davis's *El Gringo; or, New Mexico and Her People* (New York: Harper & Brothers, 1857). (See Groce and Wallace, *Dictionary of Artists in America*, p. 204; Mugridge, *Album of American Battle Art*, p. 131; Thomas H. S. Hammersly, *Complete Regular Army Register of the United States: For One Hundred Years, (1815 to 1879)* [Washington, D. C.: the author, 1880], p. 421; and Cullum, *Biographical Register*, 1:619-20.)

3. Report of General Zachary Taylor, March 6, 1847, Senate Ex. Doc. 8, 30th Congress, 1st Session, vol. 2, p. 140.

4. Fanny Palmer (1812-76) emigrated to America in 1844 with her husband, Edmund Seymour Palmer, their two children, her sister, and her brother. In 1846-47 she and her husband worked together in their own New York City lithography firm of F. & S. Palmer. Deteriorating finances forced her to work elsewhere. By 1849 she was working full-time as an artist and copyist for Nathaniel Currier and later became one of the most prolific artists with Currier & Ives. See Mary Bartlett Cowdrey, "Fanny Palmer, An American Lithographer," in Carl Zigrosser, ed., *Prints: Thirteen Illustrated Essays on the Art of the Print, Selected for the Print Council of America* (Chicago: Holt, Rinehart and Winston, 1962), pp. 217-34, and Charlotte Streifer Rubenstein, "The Early Career of Frances Flora Bond Palmer (1812-1876)," *American Journal of Art* 17 (Autumn 1985):71-88.

The first American lithographer and publisher to specialize in caricatures, Henry R. Robinson produced several Texas-related prints drawn by Edward W. Clay; his caricatures were pro-Whig and anti-Democratic. Robinson first appears in the New York City Directory for 1832-33 as a broker. The following year he is listed as a carver and gilder, and then between 1836 and 1843 as a caricaturist. (See Nancy R. Davison, "E.W. Clay and the American Political Caricature Business," in Tatham, *Prints and Printmakers of New York State*, pp. 91-110; Nancy R. Davison, "Henry R. Robinson," paper presented at the North American Print Conference, New York, 1986; Groce and Wallace, *Dictionary of Artists in America*, p. 542; New York Public Library, Department of Prints and Photographs, Printmakers File.)

5. *Daily National Intelligencer*, Dec. 31, 1847, p. 3; *Literary World* no. 53 (Feb. 1848): 12-13; *Daily National Intelligencer*, Jan. 28, 1848, p. 3. Clay's letter is dated Ashland, Dec. 24, 1847.

6. One of the surviving descriptive keys is in the Texas State Archives in Austin.

7. A copy of Sitgreaves's map is published in Carleton, *Battle of Buena Vista*, opp. pp. 1. I am grateful to Thomas Kailbourn for sharing photographs of the battle site taken by C. L. Hilsabeck.

8. Alcaraz, *The Other Side*, p. 124, briefly describes this attack. Major Washington of the artillery is represented by several daguerreotypes taken soon before or after the battle (see cat. nos. 58, 59).

9. Smith, *War with Mexico*, 1:386, 555 n. 4; Carleton, *Battle of Buena Vista*, pp. 67-68.

10. Giddings, *Sketches of the Campaign in Northern Mexico*, p. 297; Ezra Warner, *Generals in Blue* (Baton Rouge: Louisiana State University Press, 1964), p. 100.

11. Smith, *War with Mexico*, 1:392.

12. One of the most interesting illustrated journals of the Mexican War was kept by Samuel E. Chamberlain, a young cavalryman in Captain Steen's First Dragoons. According to his account of the battle (*My Confession*, pp. 114-28), Steen had already been "struck in the thigh by a canister shot and disabled," so Eaton's depiction of him may be inaccurate. Albert Pike of the Arkansas cavalry wrote a poem on the battle of Buena Vista, published in George Washington Cutter, *Buena Vista: And Other Poems* (Cincinnati: n.p., 1848).

13. May is "the gallant Captain May" of Resaca de la Palma. Marshall received considerable publicity for his action at Buena Vista: at least three different lithographs showing the *Gallant Charge of the Kentucky Cavalry under Col. Marshall at the Battle of Buena Vista* appeared in 1847, by Nathaniel Currier, Sarony & Major, and James Baillie. None was prepared from an eyewitness sketch.

14. Carleton, *Battle of Buena Vista*, pp. 72-79, 94-100.

15. Ibid., pp. 101-3; Chamberlain, *My Confession*, p. 127; Alcaraz, *The Other Side*, pp. 126-27.

16. Carleton, *Battle of Buena Vista*, pp. 106-11. There are no prints by eyewitnesses of the terrible ravine episode, but there are as many as six different contemporary popular lithographs and engravings of the death of Henry Clay, Jr. Of these, two are by Nathaniel Currier (see fig. 18), one by E.B. & E.C. Kellogg, one by R. Magee, one by Butler & Lewis, and one by Joseph Ward. Two different Currier prints depict the death of Colonel Hardin.

BATALLA DE BUENA VISTA
Mexico Febrero 23 de 1847.

BATTLE OF BUENA VISTA
Mexico February 23rd 1847.

Lit. de R.C. de Tacuba n.° 14.

Luis Meunier Almacen de la Profesa 3ª Calle de S. Fransisco. n°5.

37. Batalla de Buena Vista / Battle of Buena Vista

37.

José Severo Rocha (?) after Joseph H. Eaton
BATALLA DE BUENA VISTA MEXICO
FEBRERO 23 DE 1847. | BATTLE OF BUENA
VISTA MEXICO FEBRUARY 23RD. 1847.
Lithograph, c. 1848
9-15/16 x 14-3/4 in. (25.2 x 37.5 cm.)
l.l.: "Lit. de R. C. de Tacuba no. 14."
l.r.: "Luis Meunier Almacen de la Profesa 3a.
Calle de S. Fransisco. no. 5."
ACM 36.75

The Eaton-Robinson view of Buena Vista
was copied by other printmakers without
credit. This lithograph by José Severo
Rocha, published by Luis Meunier (both
of Mexico City), is an example.[1] The title
in both English and Spanish suggests that
the print may have been sold to American
soldiers during the occupation of Mexico
City.

1. The inscription abbreviates "Rocha, Calle de
Tacuba numero 14." (See inscription on cat. no.
124.) On Rocha, see Mathes, *Mexico on Stone*, p. 17.

38.   See Plate 9

Adolphe-Jean-Baptiste Bayot after Carl Nebel
BATTLE OF BUENA VISTA
Toned lithograph (hand colored), 1851
10-7/8 x 16-3/4 in. (27.6 x 42.6 cm.)
l.l.: "C. Nebel fecit."
l.r.: "Bayot lith."
From George Wilkins Kendall, *The War
Between the United States and Mexico Illustrated* (New York: D. Appleton & Company,
1851), plate 3
ACM 186.72/3

George Wilkins Kendall was not present
at the battle and never visited the battlefield of Buena Vista, in a remote part of
northern Mexico. There is no evidence
that Nebel visited the area either; that his
rendering is so convincing is due to his
artistic and research skills. In the final
paragraph of the text accompanying this
print, Kendall acknowledged his and
Nebel's particular debt to the account of
the battle by Captain James H. Carleton
of the First Dragoons. The moment Nebel
chose to depict was one that Carleton saw
as particularly momentous, "the point
when O'Brien was so gallantly striving to
hold the Mexicans in check during their
last attack upon the great plateau. In
painting a battle scene some particular
feature of the conflict must be taken up
as the subject for the pencil, and the
obstinate holding out of O'Brien was
deemed the most important of all the varied struggles which made up the battle of
Buena Vista."[1]

This incident was one of the final
acts of the battle; it occurred while the
Illinois and Kentucky infantry were meeting with disaster in the ravine (delineated
by a thin strip of smoke in the middle
right distance of Nebel's print; the road
is at the far right). A large mass of
attacking Mexican infantry (seen in the
center distance) threatens General Taylor

and his staff (in the center foreground).
Nothing stands between them except a
battery of three guns under Captain John
P. O'Brien (in the center). Another gun,
commanded by Captain Bragg, has just
arrived in the right foreground, while at
the far left Colonel Jefferson Davis's First
Mississippi Infantry and General Joseph
Lane with the Third Indiana and remnants
of the Second Indiana rush to the weak
point. The artillerists, wrote Carleton,

knew our troops were hurrying up
from the rear, and that, if they could
retard the enemy's course but a few
minutes longer, the battle, now setting so heavily against us, might once
more turn in our favor. Sherman and
Bragg were urging their batteries
with whip, spur, and even with
drawn sabres; the dragoons were
coming on with them; while to the
left, Davis and Lane, with their riflemen and infantry,—the men with
trailed arms,—were advancing, at a
run, over the ridges and ravines; the
awful fire of musketry on the plateau, and down around that dismal
gorge, proclaiming with fearful elo-
quence the necessity of their speed.
Closer and closer pressed the Mexicans. O'Brien saw, that, if he lim-
bered up in time to save his guns, the
enemy would carry the plateau before
our other light artillery could get to
it; but that, if he stood his ground
and fought them until they were lost,
there was still a chance remaining to
retrieve the fortunes of the day. It
was a most critical moment, and his
a most perilous situation. On his
choice there rested infinite responsi-
bility. His decision, under the circumstances, was stamped with more
heroism, than any other one act of

the war. HE ELECTED TO LOSE HIS GUNS.[2]

By the time O'Brien's guns finally were captured, nearly all of his battery had been killed or wounded. But they hung on just long enough: Bragg, Davis, and Lane and their troops arrived to repel this last Mexican assault.[3] During the night, the Mexican army retreated back down the valley to the south. Taylor reported 272 killed and 387 wounded, while Mexican losses were believed to be about twice that amount. Both sides claimed victory, but the battle left the Americans in control of northeastern Mexico.

Although Kendall does not mention Eaton's view of the battle, this was undoubtedly an important source for Nebel, whose own view was taken at the first plateau seen in the center of Eaton's view. Nebel could have known the view from the lithographed versions by Henry R. Robinson or Severo Rocha. Nebel's superior artistic training, of course, distinguishes his work from Eaton's. Nebel wisely focused his print on a particular action rather than attempting to render the entire battlefield. The almost anecdotal foreground details of military action are a particular strength of Nebel's work. Having read Carleton's account and studied maps, Nebel was careful to show greater distance between the foreground and the mountains (though he still compresses the scene and exaggerates somewhat the size of the mountains). Nebel's sense of atmospheric perspective is entirely unmatched by the lithographs of Eaton's view, though in fairness to Eaton one should mention that he did not have the benefit of the fine skills of the Parisian lithographer Bayot.

Nebel's view probably served as a model for similar depictions of the battle. One of these is an oil painting in the Carl S. Dentzel collection; another is a steel engraving by James Duthie after a drawing by Hammatt Billings.[4]

1. Kendall, *War Between the United States and Mexico Illustrated*, p. 16, citing Carleton's *Battle of Buena Vista.*

2. Kendall, *War Between the United States and Mexico Illustrated*, p. 16; Carleton, *Battle of Buena Vista*, pp. 112-13.

3. According to American popular tradition, this was the point at which Taylor uttered the famous command to give the Mexicans "A little more grape [grapeshot], Captain Bragg." Contemporary prints (Nathaniel Currier, the Kelloggs, and R. Magee each issued at least one version of this incident), sheet music covers, glass bottles, and other items bear this phrase, which Bragg later stated Taylor never said (see cat. no. 44). In light of so many eyewitnesses' testimony to the heroism of O'Brien, it is curious that the Captain Bragg incident was so celebrated. Nebel more correctly chose to focus on O'Brien.

4. The oil painting is reproduced in Nevin, *Mexican War*, p. 81. The engraving after Billings is one of a series of book illustrations, published by S. Walker, in which Billings depicted Mexican War battles. (Loose, undated impressions are in the Prints and Photographs Division of the Library of Congress.) Billings (1818-74), an architect and book illustrator, apparently never went to Mexico. That he probably drew inspiration from Nebel is supported by the fact that Billings owned a copy of Kendall's *War Between the United States and Mexico Illustrated.* See James F. O'Gorman, "War, Slavery, and Intemperance in the Book Illustrations of Hammatt Billings," *Imprint* 10, no. 1 (Spring 1985): 2-10.

39.
After Thomas Mason
BATTLE OF BUENA VISTA
Lithograph, c.1847
7-3/4 x 12-13/16 in. (19.7 x 32.5 cm.)
l.c.: "Sketched by Lieut. Thomas Mason of Southwark Phila."
ACM 16.76

This curious print of the battle was made from a sketch taken from Camp Buena Vista several months after the battle, by a soldier who did not participate in it. Thomas S. Mason of Philadelphia, serving with the First Regiment of Virginia Volunteer Infantry, arrived in northern Mexico too late for the battle of Buena Vista, but his company was encamped on the battlefield for several months in 1847 as part of General Wool's army of occupation.[1]

The lithograph, similar in style to numerous contemporary popular prints of the Mexican War based upon little factual research, appears to be the work of a New York firm such as Nathaniel Currier's or James Baillie's. The print is difficult to decipher for factual detail, and it may be that Mason's original sketch was crudely drawn. The view up toward the pass of La Angostura resembles a more reliable engraving after a sketch by Lieutenant Gray of the Third Ohio Volunteer Infantry Regiment, which appeared in George C. Furber's *Twelve Months Volunteer*.[2] The hacienda of Buena Vista is visible in Mason's view at right, just beyond the camp. The smoking action at the right of the pass is inaccurate, there being no such large-scale penetration of the American right flank.

1. Mason (c. 1829-1892) served in Captain Smith P. Bankhead's Company C of the First Regiment of Virginia Volunteers, enrolling as a sergeant on September 28, 1846, at Bowling Green, Kentucky. Captain Bankhead had been unable to raise enough volunteers within the state of Virginia and had recruited fifty men in Philadelphia. Mason was promoted to second lieutenant on August 25, 1847, and was discharged at Buena Vista on December 31 of that year. After the war he worked in Philadelphia as a carpenter; he served briefly in the Civil War, contracting "sciatic rheumatism" that later left him incapacitated. (See Mason's Civil War Invalid's Pension file, application no. 432630, certificate no. 24642, RG 15, National Archives, Washington, D.C. Also see Wallace, "First Regiment of Virginia Volunteers," pp. 51-52, and *McElroy's Philadelphia Directory* for 1850, p. 280, and for 1851, p. 286.)

2. Furber, *Twelve Months Volunteer*, opp. p. 460. A similar engraving, signed "W. Roberts," appeared in Mayer, *Mexico, Aztec, Spanish and Republican* (1850), 1: opp. p. 359.

BATTLE OF BUENA VISTA

SKETCHED BY LIEUT THOMAS MASON OF SOUTHWARK PHILA

39. BATTLE OF BUENA VISTA

40.

Emil Klauprecht?
EVER MEMORABLE BATTLE OF BUENA VISTA. FOUGHT ON 22D. & 23D. FEBRUARY 1847. BETWEEN GENERAL TAYLOR & SANTA ANNA.
Lithograph, 1847
16-1/4 x 24 in. (41.2 x 60.8 cm.)
l.r. on stone: "Klauprecht"
l.r.: "Klauprecht & Menzel's Lith. Co. of Vine & 5th St. Cinci."
l.l. below title, first column: "1. Genl. Taylor & Staff / 2. Genl. Wool & do. / 3. Light Battery comnd. by Washington 4th. / 4. 1st. Company 2nd. Illinois. / 5. 2d. Illinois comnd. by Col. Bissle." second column: "6. 3d. Indiana comnd. by Col. Lane. / 7. 2d.

do. comnd. by Col. Bowels. / 8. Light Battery comnd. by Lieut. O'Brien. / 9. 1st Mississippi Rifles, comnd. by Col. Davis. / 10. 2d. Kentuckians, comnd. by Col. McKee & Clay."
l.r. below title, first column: "11. 1st. Illinois comnd. by Col. Hardin / The Kentuckians and 1st. Illinois both forming / for the last Charge / 12. Light Battery comnd. by Capt. Bragg. / U.S. Dragoons comnd. by Lieut. Col. May." second column: "14. Kentucky Cavalry comnd. by H. Marshall. / 15. Arkansas cavalry comnd. by Col. Yell. / 16. Buena Vista Ranchero & Baggage Train. / American Force 4425, Mexican Force 20,000"
l.l. to l.r. below key: "American Loss: Killed 267, wounded 456. Mexican Loss killed 2000 wounded unknown / Approved of by Genl. Wool, Assist. Adj. Genl. Mc.Dowel, Major Webster Capt. Sibley Quarter Master, Capt. Donelson, Quarter Master Capt. Brant Quarter Master. / The above Officers were engaged in the Fight / Entered according to Act of Congress in the year 1847 by Hiram Fraser & Wm. Hammer in the Clerk's Office of the District Court of the State of Ohio."
Courtesy of Prints and Photographs Division, Library of Congress, Washington, D. C.

This ambitious print's detailed inscriptions seem to suggest that it is based on an eyewitness view. The German immigrant lithographers Klauprecht & Menzel of Cincinnati had earlier made a scoop in the print business by publishing what may have been the only eyewitness views of the battles of Palo Alto and Resaca de la Palma (see cat. no. 4).[1] They evidently intended to continue capitalizing on the public's demand for prints of the war, but with their location and the increasing competition of other firms, they may have found the acquisition of eyewitness drawings from the front a bit more difficult.

Emil Klauprecht, who appears to have been the more active member of the

EVER MEMORABLE BATTLE OF BUENA VISTA.

FOUGHT ON 22ᵈ & 23ᵈ FEBRUARY 1847.

BETWEEN GENERAL TAYLOR & SANTA ANNA.

Klauprech & Menzel's Lith. Co. of Vine & 5ᵗʰ St. Cinci.

1   Genᶜˡ Taylor & Staff
2   Genᶜˡ Wool &   dᵒ
3   Light Battery comᵈᵈ by Washington 4ᵗʰ
4   1ˢᵗ Company 2ⁿᵈ Illinois
5   2ⁿᵈ Illinois comᵈᵈ by Col. Bissle.

6   3ᵈ Indiana comᵈᵈ by Col. Lane.
7   2ⁿᵈ   dᵒ   comᵈᵈ by Col. Bowels.
8   Light Battery comᵈᵈ by Lieut. O'Brien.
9   1ˢᵗ Mississippi Rifles, comᵈᵈ by Col. Davis.
10 2ᵈ Kentuckians, comᵈᵈ by Col. McKee & Clay.

11 1ˢᵗ Illinois comᵈᵈ by Col. Hardin.
      The Kentuckians and 1ˢᵗ Illinois both forming
      for the last Charge
12 Light Battery comᵈᵈ by Capt. Bragg.
13 U.S. Dragoons comᵈᵈ by Lieut Col. May.

14 Kentucky Cavalry comᵈᵈ by H. Marshall
15 Arkansas Cavalry comᵈᵈ by Col. Yell.
16 Buena Vista Ranchers & Baggage Train
      American Force 4425, Mexican Force 20.000

American Loss. Killed 267, wounded 456.

Approved of by Genᶜˡ WOOL, Assist Adj Genᶜˡ McDOWEL, Major WEBSTER.
The above Officers were engaged in the Fight.

Mexican Loss killed 2000 wounded unknown
Capt. SIBLEY Quarter Master, Capt. DONELSON, Quarter Master, Capt. BRANT Quarter Master.

Entered according to Act of Congress in the year 1847 by Bram Power & Wᵐ Zenner in the Clerks office of the District Court of the State of Ohio.

40. EVER MEMORABLE BATTLE OF BUENA VISTA

firm, was evidently a military buff who followed the events of the war with considerable enthusiasm. He has here proudly signed his name to the stone, but nowhere has he mentioned the artist of the original sketch. The artist may be Klauprecht himself, who probably would have based this view on contemporary newspaper accounts or letters from the front. Certainly he would have credited an eyewitness artist had there been one, as he did with Paldi, because this would probably have sold more prints.

Klauprecht's glorious memorial to the battle of Buena Vista contains a great amount of detail, including a list of officers and units engaged and depicted, and a putative endorsement by such notables as General Wool, Major Lucien Webster, and quartermaster Captain "Donelson" (James Lowry Donaldson).[2] The figures and horses are drawn with considerable skill, variety of poses, and imagination, unlike their more wooden counterparts in most prints by Nathaniel Currier, James Baillie, and other contemporary American popular printmakers. However, a closer comparison with known eyewitness descriptions and views disproves the historical authenticity of Klauprecht's view. According to the key, John M. Washington's artillery battery is in the left foreground next to an adobe building, when in fact Washington's battery was nowhere near any of the closest buildings — those of the hacienda of Buena Vista. There was no charge of Mexican lancers on the American right as depicted, nor does the terrain fit any of the reliable maps of the battle.[3]

1. Unlike the Paldi views, this print did not appear in Klauprecht's *Fliegende Blätter* (1846-47), as this short-lived literary journal had apparently already ceased publication.

2. For daguerreotypes of these three officers, see cat. nos. 53-57.

3. See the map by Captain Lorenzo Sitgreaves published in Carleton's *Battle of Buena Vista*, opp. p. 1.

Portraits of Zachary Taylor

41.
C. J. Pollard after "a Lieutenant of Artillery"
GENERAL ZACHARIAH TAYLOR, (OLD ROUGH AND READY.)
Lithograph, 1846
9-7/8 x 9-3/4 in. (25.0 x 24.8 cm.)
l.c.: "Entered according to Act of Congress, A. D. 1846 by C. J. Pollard, in the Clerk's Office of the District Court of N. York."
l.l. to l.c.: "As he appeared at the battle of Palo Alto: from a sketch by a lieutenant of Artillery. / Lith & Pub by T. W. Strong 98 Nassau St. N. York"
Courtesy of Missouri Historical Society, St. Louis

A study of printed portraits after sketches, paintings, and daguerreotypes taken at the front in Mexico is extremely difficult and remains to be done. Often it is impossible to tell exactly when or where a likeness was made if there is no evidence beyond the image itself. Certainly few portraits of major figures in the war were made in Mexico during the conflict—several portraits of General Zachary Taylor being the obvious exception. Taylor was the most celebrated individual of the war on either side. His long string of victories, his personality, his style of leadership, and even his distinctive physical appearance made him popular with artists, as with his troops and the American public.

A professional soldier, Taylor had served almost continuously on the frontier since the War of 1812. He was relatively unknown outside the army, even after President Polk selected him to head the "Army of Observation" in Texas in 1845. News of the victories of Palo Alto and Resaca de la Palma brought him almost

GENERAL ZACHARIAH TAYLOR, (OLD ROUGH AND READY.)
's he appeared at the battle of Palo Alto: from a sketch by a lieutenant of Artillery.
Lith & Pub by T.W. Strong 98 Nassau St. N York.

41. GENERAL ZACHARIAH TAYLOR (OLD ROUGH AND READY)

instant fame, yet, with all of the press coverage, very few Americans had any idea what he looked like. When Congress voted in the summer of 1846 to award him a gold medal bearing his profile, no model could be found; portraits of him were not available.[1] To satisfy the public's demand for likenesses, Taylor's own soldiers sketched him, and artists from as far away as Philadelphia traveled to the front to see the general. Many images purporting to depict Taylor, most of them poorly drawn or completely fictitious, were hawked by print publishers. Commenting on one of these, the editors of the New Orleans *Daily Picayune* wrote, "if Gen. Taylor had legs like those given him in the caricature, it would not surprise us that he never runs; we should wonder how he could walk."[2]

The lithograph of Taylor "as he appeared at the battle of Palo Alto: from a sketch by a lieutenant of Artillery" is not a good likeness, but it nevertheless conforms to some verbal descriptions. For example, Ulysses S. Grant later characterized Taylor's informal manner: "General Taylor never wore a uniform, but dressed himself entirely for comfort. He moved about the field in which he was operating to see through his own eyes the situation. Often he would be without staff officers, and when he was accompanied by them there was no prescribed order in which they followed. He was very much given to sit his horse side-ways — with both feet on one side — particularly on the battle-field."[3]

This last habit in particular was a hint of Taylor's courage under fire and his ability to inspire confidence in his men. Taylor was often seen astride his horse, "Old Whitey," in "the thickest of the fight, while balls were rattling around him." According to one oft-quoted anecdote, he was asked by a fellow officer if he would not like to retire out of range. Taylor's reply was "Let us ride a little nearer, the balls will fall behind us."[4]

Several lieutenants of artillery were capable artists, and many had received instruction in drawing at West Point. However, it is more likely that this lithograph was not made from a sketch from the front; it could have been drawn by the lithographer from written descriptions. Certainly had the publisher supplied the name of the unknown lieutenant, it would have added more authenticity and perhaps sold more prints.

Thomas W. Strong was active as a lithographer in New York from 1842 until 1851. The holder of the copyright, C. J. Pollard, may have worked with Strong at this time; later Pollard went to California during the gold rush and was associated with lithographer James Britton in San Francisco.[5]

1. Brainerd Dyer, *Zachary Taylor* (Baton Rouge: Louisiana State University Press, 1946), p. 185. See Linda Ayres's entry on Taylor portraits in Harold Francis Pfister, *Facing the Light: Historic American Portrait Daguerreotypes* (Washington, D.C.: Smithsonian Institution Press for the National Portrait Gallery, 1978), pp. 74-79.

2. New Orleans *Daily Picayune*, July 16, 1847, p. 2.

3. Grant, *Personal Memoirs*, pp. 84-85. Comparing Scott and Taylor, Grant wrote: "Both were pleasant to serve under — Taylor was pleasant to serve with."

4. Holman Hamilton, *Zachary Taylor*, 2 vols. (Indianapolis: Bobbs-Merrill, 1941), 1:189, quoting Henry, *Campaign Sketches*, p. 100.

5. Mugridge, *Album of American Battle Art*, p. 132.

MAJOR GENERAL ZACHARY TAYLOR

By **A.Hoffy**, under the immediate superintendence & directions of the undersigned Officers, from an **original Sketch**, taken from life at Camargo by **Captain Eaton, A.D.C.**

We the undersigned consider the above a good likeness:

Pub. by **HOFFY**, Sept. 1847, at N. 20, South 3.^d St Philadelphia.

42. MAJOR GENERAL ZACHARY TAYLOR

42.
Alfred Hoffy after Joseph Horace Eaton
MAJOR GENERAL ZACHARY TAYLOR
Lithograph, 1847
10-5/8 x 11-3/16 in. (27.0 x 28.4 cm.)
l.c.: "By A. Hoffy, under the immediate superintendence & directions of the undersigned
Officers, / from an original Sketch, taken from
life at Camargo by Captain Eaton, A.D.C. /
We the undersigned consider the above a good
likeness:"/ [pen inscriptions on stone signed
by D. Conner, U S Navy; Gio. A. McCall,
A.A.G.; Geo. Meade, Lt Topographical Engineer; Dan Ingersoll, U.S. Navy; R.P. Marley,
8 Rgt U S Infy; E.W. Moore, Com. late Texas
Navy; Robt E Haskell; Tho L Caldwell, M.D.
lately Surgeon in the Army of Occupation,
Mexico]
l.c. below pen inscriptions: "Pubd. by Hoffy,
Septr. 1847, at No. 20, South 3d. St. Philadelphia. / Entered according to act of Congress in the year 1847, by Hoffy, in the Clerk's
office of the district Court of the Eastern district of Penna."
Courtesy of Lilly Library, Indiana University,
Bloomington, Indiana

One of the most widely copied portraits
of Taylor was made from a sketch taken
in Camargo in August 1846 by Taylor's
aide-de-camp, Captain Joseph Horace
Eaton. An engraving or mezzotint by
Samuel Sartain, used as a magazine illustration, records this date and location in
its inscription.[1] Another print after this
portrait sketch, a lithograph by Alfred
Hoffy, was announced by the Daily
National Intelligencer on June 3, 1847:

Portrait of General Taylor. — We
were presented yesterday by the agent
with a lithographed portrait of the
heroic veteran, General Taylor, which
is certified by a number of the officers
of his army to be a good likeness,
and is besides, one of the most beau-

tifully executed lithographs we have
ever seen. It is copied from an original sketch, taken by Captain Eaton,
Aide-de camp, while Gen. T. was at
Camargo, and we can add the testimony of our own recollection to the
fidelity of the likeness. It is published
by A. Hoffy, of Philadelphia, in a
style worthy of the distinguished
subject, and at a price which places
it in the power of almost every body
to possess a copy.[2]

Except for the date, the description
matches the lithograph illustrated here,
which is undoubtedly a later edition of the
same portrait. Another known impression, with different signatures at the bottom, faces left,[3] as does the Sartain print.
The variations suggest the popular
demand for this image and the rareness
of Taylor portraits at the beginning of
the war.

1. Briggs collection, A71499, National Portrait
Gallery, Washington, D.C.
2. Washington, D.C., Daily National Intelligencer,
June 3, 1847, p. 3. Alfred Hoffy (c.1790-after 1860),
a native of England, worked with John T. Bowen in
New York and later in Philadelphia. He drew some
of the plates for Thomas L. McKenney and James
T. Hall's History of the Indian Tribes of North
America (1837-44). From 1839 until 1841 Hoffy
was chief artist for Huddy & Duval, producing
numerous illustrations for their U.S. Military Magazine. In 1845 he drew on stone a scene depicting
maneuvers of the artillery of the Philadelphia Greys
commanded by Captain George Cadwalader, and
in 1847 a portrait of General Winfield Scott after a
cutting by William H. Brown, printed by Wagner
& McGuigan of Philadelphia in 1847. (See Groce
and Wallace, Dictionary of Artists in America, pp.
321-22; Wainwright, Philadelphia in the Romantic
Age of Lithography, pp. 38, 42, 50, 78, 81, 101,
153, 201, 208, 215, 229, 239, 243.)
3. Illustrated in William J. Burger Historical Americana, catalogue 4 (July 1, 1986), no. 160.

43.
Albert Newsam after Jesse Atwood
MAJR. GENERAL ZACHARY TAYLOR
Lithograph, 1847
11-1/16 x 10-1/4 in. (28.1 x 26.0 cm.)
l.l.: "Painted by J. Atwood, Monterey Mexico
May 15th 1847."
l.c.: "P. S. Duval, Lith. Philadelphia."
l.r.: "On Stone by Albert Newsam."
l.c. below title, handwritten: "Head Qrs, Army
of Occupation / Camp near Monterey Mexico
May 31st, 1847 / Mr J Atwood, / Dear Sir, /
Before leaving here on your return home, I
must / tender you my sincere thanks, for I
fear the undeserved compliment / you have
paid me, in the danger, fatigue, labor and
trouble you have un- / dergone & encountered, in traveling from the City of Philadelphia to this place, / for the purpose of painting
my portrait; & and having completed the
same, / (the first ever taken of me by any artis,
& being about to leave us on your / return, I
take this opportunity of wishing you a safe,
speedy & pleasant trip / to the bosom of your
family & friends, as well as a happy meeting
with / them—and wishing you continued
health & prosperity I remain with con- /
siderations of high respect & esteem / Your
Obt. Servt., / Z. Taylor."
l.c. below handwritten text: "Published by J.
Atwood, Philadelphia."
ACM 36.78

Itinerant portraitist Jesse Atwood traveled
from Philadelphia to Monterrey, Mexico,
where he painted two portraits of General
Zachary Taylor on May 13 and 15, 1847,
less than three months after his victory at
Buena Vista.[1] On May 31, 1847, the
newspaper American Pioneer at Monterrey published an acknowledgment of
Atwood's portraits: "The concurrent testimony of all who have seen them, pronounce them excellent likenesses. The
execution is beyond praise. One of these
pictures represents Gen. Taylor in full

MAJ^R GENERAL ZACHARY TAYLOR.

Head Qrs. Army of occupation
Camp near Monterey Mexico May 31st 1847

Mr J Atwood,
Dear Sir

Before leaving here on your return home, I must tender you my sincere thanks & (for) fear the undeserved compliment you have paid me in the danger, fatigue, labor & trouble you have un= deryone & encountered in traveling from the city of Philadelphia to this place for the purpose of painting my portrait; & having completed the Same, & the first ever taken of me by any artist, & being about to leave us on your return, I take this opportunity of wishing you a safe, speedy & pleasant trip to the boom of your family & friends, as well as a happy meeting with them – and wishing you continued health & prosperity I remain with con= siderations of high respect & esteem
Your obt Servt,
Z Taylor

43. MAJR. GENERAL ZACHARY TAYLOR

uniform; the other as Rough and Ready; and any one who has ever seen the General would recognize not only the truthful expression of countenance [illegible] his brown coat and check shirt.... We believe it is Mr. Atwood's intention to copy from these pictures a full length portrait, representing General Taylor mounted upon his favorite 'old whitehorse.' "[2]

Atwood returned to the States by way of New Orleans, where the *Picayune* announced his arrival with the two portraits on June 18, 1847.[3] Soon back in Philadelphia, he called at the lithography shop of P. S. Duval, where Albert Newsam, the famous deaf-mute crayon artist employed by Duval, copied one of Atwood's portraits of Taylor on stone.[4]

Reproduced below the print is a letter of thanks from General Taylor to Atwood, dated Camp near Monterey, Mexico, May 31, 1847, in which he mentions that the portrait is "the first ever taken of me by any artis[t]." If the letter is authentic, Taylor probably meant that Atwood's was the first portrait that he had ever sat for, or the first he had approved, or the first completed, painted portrait ever taken of him. In addition to Pollard's and Hoffy's lithographic portraits (cat. nos. 41, 42), a French artist from New Orleans, Joseph Auguste de Chatillon, had evidently sketched Taylor earlier on the Rio Grande. Chatillon's lithographed portrait of Taylor "taken from nature ... at the camp near Matamoras, for the picture representing the battle of Resaca de la Palma," was published as early as May 4, 1847. A profile portrait, the lithography work is attributed to Xavier Magny, also of New Orleans.[5] Another lithographed portrait of Taylor, "Drawn the 2d Day After the Battle of Buena Vista by an Officer of U.S. Army," was published by George Hood of Philadelphia. It is a fair likeness, but is poorly drawn.[6]

Soon after Taylor sat for Atwood, sometime before June 6, the general posed again, this time for William Garl Brown, Jr., a portrait painter from Richmond, Virginia, who portrayed Taylor and his staff at their camp headquarters near Monterrey.[7] Concerning the two artists' efforts, Taylor wrote: "Without being decided fine, I imagine the likenesses painted of me by Mr. Atwood are tolerable; the one which has just been finished by a Mr. Brown from Richmond is said by those who understand or are judges of such matters to be a much better painting; Mr. B. has nearly completed a group of officers, myself & staff in addition to several others, which I imagine will be considered a good painting by connoisseurs; he is now engaged in making a painting describing the battle ground of Buena Vista."[8]

1. Jesse Atwood was born in New Hampshire about 1802 and had moved to Pennsylvania by about 1830. He is known to have worked at Deerfield, Massachusetts, in 1832; Richmond, Virginia, in 1841; and at Philadelphia in 1841 and 1843, and from 1849 to 1854. He is listed in the Philadelphia city directory as late as 1870. (See Groce and Wallace, *Dictionary of Artists in America*, pp. 14-15; *McElroy's Philadelphia City Directory for 1862* [Philadelphia: E. C. & J. C. Biddle & Co., 1862], p. 19, and for 1863, p. 51; *Gopsill's Philadelphia City Directory for 1870* [Philadelphia: James Gopsill, 1870], p. 165. A George Atwood, artist, and John M. Atwood, merchant or engraver, are also listed in Philadelphia directories in the 1860s.)

2. Monterrey *American Pioneer*, May 31, 1847, p. 2. One of Atwood's original painted portraits of Taylor is in the Historical Society of Pennsylvania, Philadelphia (accession no. 1914.7). It is an oil on canvas, 30 x 25 in., signed l.l. spandrel: "Pxt. by J. Atwood, Monteray, Mexico May 13, 1847."

3. New Orleans *Daily Picayune*, June 18, 1847, p. 2.

4. Newsam (1809-64), born in Steubenville, Ohio, went to Philadelphia at age eleven and was soon under the care of an institution. In 1827 he was apprenticed to the engraver Cephas G. Childs. When French lithographer P. S. Duval immigrated to the United States in 1831 and joined Childs & Inman, Newsam was their principal artist; according to Duval, he was exceptional at portraits and animals, and his principal talent was copying. He continued in lithography until 1859 when his eyesight began to fail and he had a paralytic stroke. (See Wendy Wick Reaves, "Portraits for Every Parlor: Albert Newsam and American Portrait Lithography," in Wendy Wick Reaves, ed., *American Portrait Prints: Proceedings of the Tenth Annual American Print Conference* [Charlottesville: University Press of Virginia, 1984], pp. 83-134; Peters, *America on Stone*, pp. 296-300; Wainwright, *Philadelphia in the Romantic Age of Lithography*, pp. 13-81 passim. For Atwood's print, also see New York *Times*, Aug. 3, 1913, p. 14.)

5. On Chatillon (1808-91) and Louis Xavier Magny (c. 1805-1855), see John Mahé II and Roseann McCaffrey, eds., *Encyclopaedia of New Orleans Artists, 1718-1918* (New Orleans: The Historic New Orleans Collection, 1987), pp. 101, 250. The National Portrait Gallery, Washington, D.C., has an impression of what is probably this portrait, but there is no inscription denoting Xavier Magny as the lithographer. Chatillon and Louis D. G. Develle, a New Orleans scene painter, incorporated their travel sketches into a grand history painting (twelve by twenty-nine feet) titled *Battle of Resaca de la Palma*, which they exhibited in New Orleans in October 1847. Taylor attended the formal public presentation of the painting on December 29. According to New Orleans newspapers Chatillon sold the painting, and apparently a portrait of Taylor, to the U. S. Congress. At one point the painting of Resaca de la Palma was reported to be hanging in the White House, but this painting and the Taylor portrait are now both missing. (J. John Perret, Department of Foreign Languages, University of New Orleans, to Amon Carter Museum, Aug. 29, 1986, Amon Carter Museum files; Matamoras *American Flag*, Aug. 14, 1846, p. 1; Mahé and McCaffrey, *Encyclopaedia of New Orleans Artists*, p. 101.)

6. Impressions are located at the Prints and Photographs Division of the Library of Congress, at the National Portrait Gallery, and at the American Antiquarian Society, Worcester, Massachusetts.

7. Letter from James E. Durivage, Monterrey, Mexico, dated June 6, 1847, published in New Orleans *Daily Picayune*, June 24, 1847, p. 2; also July 6, 1847, p. 2; Aug. 3, 1847, p. 2; Sept. 7, 1847, p. 2. The painting is in the National Portrait Gallery, Washington, D.C. For a biography of Brown (1823-94), see Groce and Wallace, *Dictionary of Artists in America*, p. 89.

8. Taylor to Dr. Robert C. Wood, July 13, 1847, quoted in Hamilton, *Zachary Taylor*, 1:246. I am unaware of any prints after Brown's paintings.

44.
After a daguerreotype by J. H. Wm. Smith
ROUGH AND READY AS HE IS.
Lithograph, 1847
15-1/2 x 10-7/8 in. (39.5 x 27.5 cm.) (comp.)
u.c.: "A Little More Grape Cap. Bragg!!"
l.c. in image: "Entered according to the act of congres, in the U.S. District Court Clerk's office / in the year 1847."
l.l. to l.r. below title: "Fac simile of Gl. Zach. Taylor from a Daguerreotype full lenght likness taken at Buena Vista, / by J. H. Wm. Smith."
Courtesy of Special Collections Division, The University of Texas at Arlington Libraries, Arlington, Texas

Perhaps the most intriguing of all wartime images of Taylor is this full-length lithographic portrait from a daguerreotype "taken at Buena Vista by J. H. Wm. Smith." Neither the lithographer nor the publisher is named on the print, but Smith may be the elusive daguerreotypist who worked in Saltillo in 1847-48 photographing American officers and military scenes. He may also be the Philadelphia publisher of an 1848 mezzotint portrait of Taylor by engraver John Sartain after another daguerreotype.[1]

The exact date when Taylor posed for Smith at Buena Vista is difficult to determine, since the inscription gives no further clues. Taylor was in the vicinity of the camp at Buena Vista before and after the battle (February 22-23, 1847), but by summer he had moved his headquarters back to Monterrey, where it remained until he departed for the States on November 8.[2]

Taylor's outfit in this portrait conforms to written descriptions of him. Captain Fletcher Archer of the Virginia Volunteers wrote that Taylor's dress "is that of a plain country farmer" and "he never wears a uniform; the neckkerchief he has had on every time I have seen him has been of checked or striped cotton, and I believe unhemmed." Captain T. B. Kinder wrote: "He looks more like an old farmer going to market with eggs to sell than anything I can ... think of; jovial and good-natured."[3] The panama straw hat was an accessory adopted by many American troops in the hot sun of Mexico. So plain was Taylor's dress that he was often not recognized by his own troops.[4]

The words "A Little More Grape, Captain Bragg" at the top of the lithograph are based on a popular anecdote about the battle of Buena Vista. According to this story, when hard pressed by the enemy, Taylor ordered Captain Braxton Bragg to use more grapeshot in his guns, saying "Give them a little more grape, Captain Bragg." The newspapers, printmakers, and hack writers picked up on the story, and it became a slogan during the 1848 presidential campaign. Bragg later claimed that Taylor never said those words to him, and that he first heard of them in the newspapers.[5]

1. On the possible identity of the daguerreotypist(s) working in Saltillo, see Martha A. Sandweiss's essay; for the daguerreotypes, see cat. nos. 45-89. An impression of Sartain's mezzotint is in the Amon Carter Museum (8.82).

2. Hamilton, *Zachary Taylor*, 1:228-48; Dyer, *Zachary Taylor*, pp. 226-49.

3. Both quotations are from Hamilton, *Zachary Taylor*, 1:20.

4. Dyer, *Zachary Taylor*, p. 185. Another fine lithographed image of Taylor, a portrait "drawn from nature" by Charles Risso, depicts "Rough & Ready. in his Battle Dress." Risso (active 1832-50) also apparently drew the image on stone, but it was printed by the lithography firm of B. F. Butler in New York in 1848. The portrait was probably taken in New Orleans, where Risso was active as a lithographer and publisher from 1837 to 1847. Taylor could have sat for Risso sometime after the former's return to New Orleans in early December 1847. (See Mahé and McCaffrey, *Encyclopaedia of New Orleans Artists*, pp. 326-27; Hamilton, *Zachary Taylor*, p. 250.)

5. New Orleans *Picayune*, Jan. 23, 1849 (evening edition), p. 1. See Dyer, *Zachary Taylor*, p. 238.

A LITTLE MORE GRAPE CAP. BRAGG!!

ROUGH AND READY AS HE IS.

Fac simile of G.ᶜ ZACH TAYLOR from a Daguerreotype full lenght likness taken at Buena Vista by A. H. Wᵐ Smith.

44. ROUGH AND READY AS HE IS

Part Two:

Daguerreotypes Taken During the Mexican War

While many photographic portraits of Mexican War-era soldiers survive, most were made in daguerreotype studios in the United States. Despite the documented activity of a number of photographers operating in Mexico during the war, only two significant collections of war-related daguerreotypes made in that country are known to survive. These daguerreotypes, described and illustrated here, are now in the possession of the Beinecke Rare Book and Manuscript Library at Yale University and the Amon Carter Museum. The twelve Yale daguerreotypes are mounted together in an elaborate wooden frame; the Amon Carter images are all uncased.

Internal evidence suggests that most of the daguerreotypes were probably made in or around Saltillo between the time of the battle of Buena Vista in February 1847 and the end of the American occupation in June 1848. While the identity of the photographer or photographers is not known, the coincidence of subject matter between the two groups of daguerreotypes suggests the possibility that the same person may have been responsible for images in both collections. The poor quality of some of the images, the varied brands of daguerreotype plates used, and the inconsistent styles of plate preparation all suggest the difficulties of working as a photographer in wartime Mexico, where supplies were hard to obtain.

Both the Yale and Amon Carter daguerreotype collections, whose histories are discussed in Martha A. Sandweiss's essay, contain American images with apparent connections to the pictures made in Mexico. These images are presented along with unidentified portraits at the conclusion of this section.

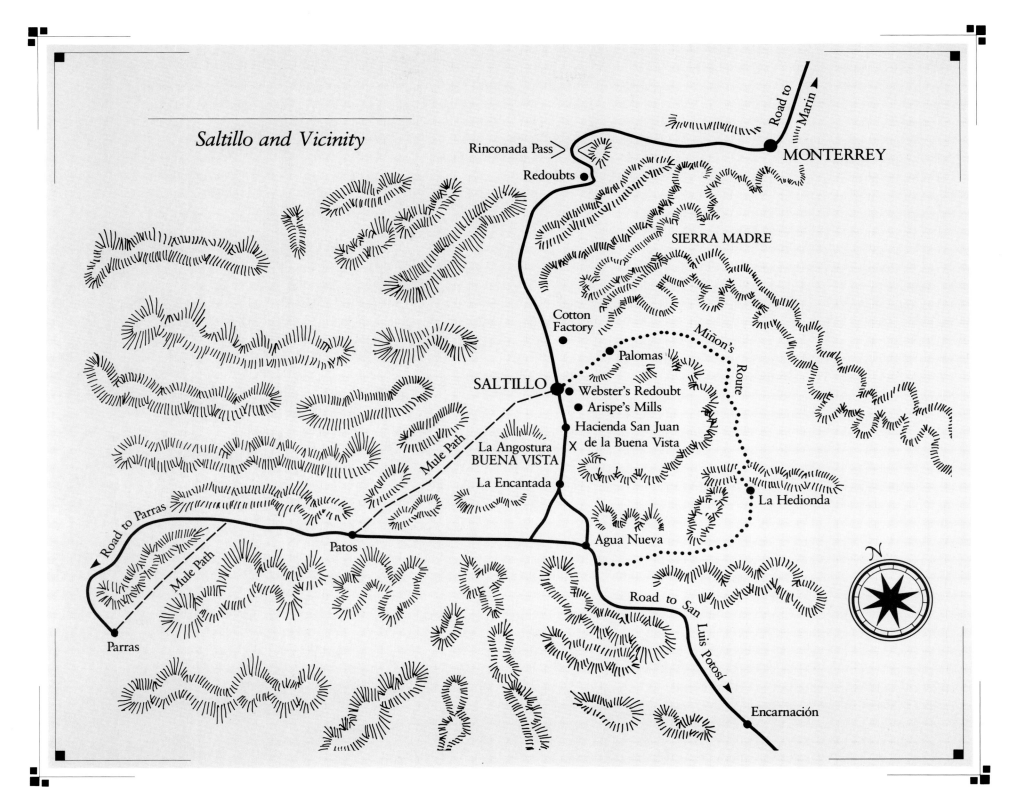

Saltillo and Vicinity

Road to Marin

MONTERREY

Rinconada Pass

Redoubts

SIERRA MADRE

Cotton
Factory

Miñon's

Route

Palomas

SALTILLO

Webster's Redoubt

Arispe's Mills

Hacienda San Juan
de la Buena Vista

La Angostura
BUENA VISTA

La Encantada

La Hedionda

Mule Path

Road to Parras

Patos

Agua Nueva

Road to San Luis Potosí

Mule Path

Parras

Encarnación

N

45. Bird's-Eye View of Saltillo, Mexico

45.

[BIRD'S-EYE VIEW OF SALTILLO, MEXICO]
Daguerreotype, sixth-plate, c. 1847
2-3/4 x 3-1/4 in. (7.0 x 8.3 cm.)
Copper-backed plate, no apparent maker's
mark; 4 corners clipped at 45° angle, long
edges turned down, u.l., u.r., and l.l. corners
turned down, l.r. corner turned up slightly;
plate holder crimp mark, l.r. corner
ACM 81.65/27

46.

[BIRD'S-EYE VIEW OF SALTILLO, MEXICO]
Daguerreotype, sixth-plate, c. 1847
2-3/4 x 3-1/4 in. (7.0 x 8.3 cm.)
Stamped u.l. corner: "Scovills"
Plated plate; 4 corners clipped at 45° angle,
u.l., u.r., and l.l. corners turned down, l.r.
corner turned up, top and right edges turned
down; plate holder crimp mark, l.r. corner
ACM 81.65/29

47.

VIEW OF SALTILLO
Daguerreotype, sixth-plate, c. 1847
Plate verso: "VIII"
Possible original paper seal
Graphite inscription on wood frame:
"3//10//[illeg.]"
Courtesy of Yale Collection of Western Amer-
icana, Beinecke Rare Book and Manuscript
Library

Visible in these three views of Saltillo is
the "Parroquia de Santiago," now Santiago Cathedral.[1] The daguerreotypist
apparently took the views from an American artillery redoubt on the bluffs south
of town.[2] Cat. nos. 45 and 46 are
reversed; no. 47 was corrected to show
the town in its proper orientation.

At the time of the Mexican War, Saltillo, the capital of the state of Coahuila,
had a population of about 18,000. Only

about sixty-eight miles from Monterrey,
it guarded the chief pass through the
Sierra Madre and dominated a prosperous
farming region from which supplies could
be drawn. Its elevation, even higher than
that of Monterrey, gave it an agreeable
climate.[3] On November 17, 1846, General
Worth's division of about 1,000 troops,
most of them regulars, became the first
American force to enter Saltillo. The only
overt Mexican opposition was a formal
protest from the newly elected governor
of Coahuila, José María de Aguirre, who
fled west to the town of Parras. On
December 21 General Wool's Centre
Division, consisting mostly of volunteers,
entered the vicinity just south of Saltillo.
On January 9, 1847, General Worth and
his division left the city to join Scott's
Veracruz campaign, while Wool's troops
remained behind as the bulk of Taylor's
occupation force in northern Mexico.

During the battle of Buena Vista
(which was fought some seven miles to
the south on February 22 and 23), a small
garrison of Americans under Major
W. B. Warren remained in the town. The
Americans barricaded the streets and
manned the redoubt they had constructed
on the heights south of town. Harvey
Neville, a first lieutenant in the Second
Illinois Regiment and a participant in the
battle, described the city as it appeared
from these bluffs in a diary entry written
around February 3, 1847: "[Saltillo] looks
very little like a city; the streets are narrow and too crooked to be traced. The
house tops are flat and grown over with
grass, and save the several steeples peeping
above the common level, there is very little
the appearance of a city till you enter the
streets."[4]

The American forces continued their
occupation of Saltillo and the nearby
camp at Buena Vista for the rest of the

war. No major battles were fought in
northern Mexico after Buena Vista, and
the occupation force saw little action
except for pursuing and defending against
Mexican guerrillas, who boldly attacked
American supply trains, harassed communications, and killed soldiers who ven-
tured out alone or in small groups. After
June 1847, most of the occupying troops
in and around Saltillo were from three
volunteer infantry regiments: the First
Virginia, the First North Carolina, and
the Second Mississippi, all of whom
arrived in Mexico after the battle of
Buena Vista.

1. Compare the photograph in Alessio Robles, Saltillo, betw. pp. 128 and 129.
2. Thomas Kailbourn to Marni Sandweiss, Oct. 16,
1988, Amon Carter Museum files. Compare the
map in Alessio Robles, Saltillo, frontispiece. The
redoubt held a battery of artillery commanded by
Brevet Major Lucien B. Webster during the battle
of Buena Vista. (See cat. nos. 55 and 56.) By coincidence, a similar view of the city appeared in an
engraving titled Saltillo, Looking North-West, published in the New York Weekly Herald, Aug. 14,
1847, p. 1, and the Herald, Aug. 15, 1847, p. 1.
The city now extends into the heights.
3. Smith, War with Mexico, 1:264-66, 508 n. 10.
4. Harvey Neville, Mexican War diary, undated
entry (c. Feb. 3, 1847); manuscript in the Chicago
Historical Society.

46. Bird's-Eye View of Saltillo, Mexico

47. View of Saltillo

48. Parroquia de Santiago, Saltillo

48.
[PARROQUIA DE SANTIAGO, SALTILLO]
Daguerreotype, quarter-plate, c. 1847
3 x 4-1/4 in. (7.6 x 10.8 cm.)
Stamped right edge: "ZOA Garant [in]" and
l.l. corner: "40"
Copper-backed plate, 4 corners clipped at 45°
angle, long edges turned down slightly; u.r.
and l.r. corners crimped
ACM 81.65/33

49.
[PARROQUIA DE SANTIAGO, SALTILLO]
Daguerreotype, quarter-plate, c. 1847
3 x 4-1/8 in. (7.6 x 10.5 cm.)
Copper-backed plate, no apparent maker's
mark (plate may have been trimmed); 4
corners clipped at 45° angle, long edges turned
down slightly; possible plate holder crimp
mark, l.r. corner
ACM 81.65/34

50.
PARROQUIAL CHURCH, E. SIDE OF PLAZA
Daguerreotype, sixth-plate, c. 1847
Plate verso: "II"
Possible original paper seal
Paper label, on cover glass: "Parroquial
Church/E. Side of Plaza"
Courtesy of Yale Western Americana Collec-
tion, Beinecke Rare Book and Manuscript
Library

These three daguerreotypes, all corrected
to show the church in its proper orientation, depict the west facade of what is
today the Cathedral of Santiago in Saltillo. The part of the building at the left,
including the completed north tower, is
the Capilla del Santo Cristo (Christ
Chapel). The larger portion at right, with
its more elaborate Churrigueresque portal
and the uncompleted south tower, is the
Parroquia or parish church. The Diocese
of Saltillo was not established until 1891,
but many of the Americans stationed at
Saltillo nevertheless referred to the Parroquia as the "Cathedral." The south tower,
completed after these daguerreotypes
were taken, made the church "one of the
highest in Mexico."[1]

There are slight differences in these
views. In the plaza in front of the church,
several young trees in planters with supports are distinctly visible in cat. nos. 49
and 50. (One of the pole supports in no.
50 appears from the other side in no. 51, a
view of the main plaza.) Pack mules or
burros appear in the foreground of no. 50.

Many American troops remarked on
the architecture of Saltillo, particularly of
the Parroquia. Captain W. S. Henry
wrote:

> Its Cathedral is a magnificent build-
> ing, a third larger than the one at
> Monterey, built of these sun-dried
> bricks, and the cement mixed with
> small stones. The interior is magnifi-
> cent — groined arches, rich and
> elaborate carvings, paneled floors,
> and ornaments of gold and silver.
> Nothing has been removed — the
> first instance, as yet; for heretofore
> every Cathedral has been stripped of
> its valuables prior to our approach.[2]

Benjamin F. Scribner, an Indiana volunteer, noted that one tower had a town
clock and the other a fine collection of
chimes.[3]

During the battle of Buena Vista, a
few American troops were posted in the
towers of the Parroquia. After the battle
the church was briefly used as a hospital
for the wounded.[4]

1. See Alessio Robles, *Saltillo*, photograph betw.
pp. 96 and 97.
2. Henry, *Campaign Sketches*, pp. 245-46.
3. Benjamin Franklin Scribner, *Camp Life of a Volunteer, or a Glimpse at Life in Camp. By "One Who
Has Seen the Elephant"* (1847; rpt., Austin, Texas:
Jenkins Publishing Co., 1975), p. 56. Scribner also
described the interior of the building.
4. Alessio Robles, *Saltillo*, p. 217; Carleton, *Battle
of Buena Vista*, p. 127; Gregg, *Diary and Letters*,
2:59.

49. Parroquia de Santiago, Saltillo

Parroquial Church
E. Side of Plaza

50. Parroquial Church, East Side of Plaza

Plaza, Saltillo, Mex.
to N.E.ᵈ

51. Plaza, Saltillo, Mexico

51.

PLAZA, SALTILLO, MEXICO, TO
NORTHEASTWARD
Daguerreotype, sixth-plate, c. 1847
Plate verso: "I"
Possible original paper seal
Paper label, on cover glass: "Plaza, Saltillo,
Mex. / to N.Ed."
Courtesy of Yale Western Americana Collec-
tion, Beinecke Rare Book and Manuscript
Library

The west facade of the Parroquia faces
the main square of Saltillo, the Plaza de
la Independencia, which is seen in this
daguerreotype. Some of the young trees
visible in views of the west facade of the
Parroquia (cat. nos. 49 and 50) are seen
here in the foreground. In the center of
the plaza is a fountain, surrounded by
several unidentifiable figures.
    Captain George W. Hughes, a topo-
graphical engineer with General Wool's
division, left a picturesque description of
the plaza, its surrounding buildings, and
the people who frequented it:

> The plaza is extensive, and the
> buildings on it generally two stories
> high, with balconies or porticoes. I
> think I can recognise in the domestic
> architecture of the cities an intimate
> blending of the Mexican, the Moor-
> ish, and the Flemish—the two last
> having been imported by the Span-
> iards, and engrafted on the original
> Aztec style. Directly fronting the
> cathedral is a beautiful and copious
> fountain, at which the female peons,
> in their picturesque costumes, may
> be seen at all hours of the day draw-
> ing water, and chatting with the
> characteristic volubility of the
> country.[1]

Indiana volunteer Benjamin F. Scribner
wrote: "The plaza, when viewed from the
church, has an imposing appearance. The
side walks around lead through arches
supported by columns. There are groves
of trees at regular distances, and fountains
in the centre."[2]

1. Hughes, *Memoir Descriptive*, p. 39.
2. Scribner, *Camp Life of a Volunteer*, p. 56.

52.

CALLE REAL & PARROQUIAL CHURCH
TO NORTHWARD
Daguerreotype, sixth-plate, c. 1847
Plate verso, in graphite: "III // &"
Possible original paper seal
Paper label, on cover glass: "Calle Real & P.
Church / to Nd."
Courtesy of Yale Western Americana Collec-
tion, Beinecke Rare Book and Manuscript
Library

This view of the Parroquia of Saltillo,
shown in its proper orientation, was
apparently taken from the roof of a
building along the Calle Real (modern-
day Calle Hidalgo) looking northward.
From this angle the elaborate south portal
and the dome are visible.

Calle Real & P. Church
to No.

52. Calle Real & Parroquial Church, Saltillo

53.

[General Wool and Staff in the Calle Real, Saltillo]

Daguerreotype, sixth-plate, c. 1847
2-3/4 x 3-1/4 in. (7.0 x 8.3 cm.)
Stamped left edge: "E. White Maker NY Finest Quality A [NY]"
Copper-backed plate; 4 corners clipped at 45° angle, all edges and corners turned down; plate holder crimp mark, l.l. corner
ACM 81.65/22

54.

General Wool and Staff, Calle Real to South

Daguerreotype, sixth-plate, c. 1847
Plate verso, scratched: "IX"
Original seal gone
Paper label, on cover glass: "Genl. Wool & Staff / Calle Real to South"
Graphite inscription on wood frame: "12"
Courtesy of Yale Western Americana Collection, Beinecke Rare Book and Manuscript Library

In these remarkable wartime daguerreotypes, Brigadier General John Ellis Wool (1784-1869), wearing a greatcoat, poses with his staff in the Calle Real in Saltillo. The two images were taken just moments apart on the same street, as is apparent from an examination of the doors and windows of the buildings facing the street. Because of the long exposure required by the daguerreotype process, the men had to halt their horses and pose in a stationary position in order to have their image recorded. Cat. no. 54 shows a corrected image; no. 53 is reversed.[1] A comparison with other portraits of Wool supports the identification provided by the label on no. 54. The identities of Wool's staff are more difficult to determine.[2] The buildings, with their drainage spouts and grated windows, are typical examples of Mexican architecture and resemble buildings recorded in cat. nos. 52, 69-72.

Wool first arrived in Saltillo on December 22 or 23, 1846. The daguerreotypes were probably made between then and the following November, when he moved his headquarters to Monterrey to succeed General Taylor as supreme commander in northern Mexico.[3] (After this time and until the end of the American occupation in June 1848, Wool may have made a few visits to the city.) Early in

March 1847 Taylor left for Monterrey, leaving Wool in charge of Coahuila and the military government of its capital, Saltillo. Wool attempted to curb violence within the district and keep supplies flowing to his army with as little inconvenience as possible to those Mexicans who did not resist the invaders. However, the occupation required strict measures, and Wool's own volunteer troops were all too prone to insubordination and to committing depredations on the Mexican population and its property. Wool enforced stiff penalties for soldiers caught disobeying his policies, and he waged a ruthless campaign against Mexican guerrillas and their suspected sympathizers. Yet he tried to follow a conciliatory policy when possible and in February 1848 declared amnesty for all who had up to that time been in arms against the United States. Wool took his duty as a soldier very seriously and had no delusions about American invincibility. Regarding Mexico, he once wrote, "Had the nation been united we could not have gained a single victory."[4]

Characteristically Wool appears in these daguerreotypes with a large escort. He was always a stickler for strong vigilance in an enemy's country, and he constantly warned volunteers against "the indulgence of any fancied security."[5] Wool's reputation as a martinet evidently caused him to fear even his own troops. In his diary entry for March 11, 1847, Josiah Gregg, in Saltillo as a translator with the Arkansas Volunteer Cavalry, apparently mistook Wool's caution for pomposity:

> About this time Gen. Wool paid a visit to the city; and one could not but note the parade and pomposity of his "suite," etc. especially when

compared with the very unostentatious style of Gen. Taylor (as also of Gen. Butler, when here). We could see Gen. Taylor riding about the city and elsewhere, frequently with no escort but his adjutant, and an aide perhaps, while Gen. Wool was not only everywhere followed by a portion of his staff, but a guard of some 20 dragoons, with drawn sabres! In this style he not only entered the city, but his guard, with sabres drawn, thus followed him from house to house, and from hospital to hospital, in his visits through the city![6]

1. Cat. no. 54 probably shows the scene in its correct orientation since the visible swords appear on the bearers' left sides. The coat button and lapel arrangements, which would help decide this issue, are harder to read.

2. See the lithographed portrait of Wool in Francis Baylies, *A Narrative of Major General Wool's Campaign in Mexico, in the Years 1846, 1847 & 1848* (Albany: Little & Company, 1851), frontispiece. It is likely that Wool's aide-de-camp, Brevet Captain Irvin McDowell (1818-85), is in the pictures, and perhaps also Inspector General Sylvester Churchill, Captain William W. Chapman, an extra aide to Wool, and David Hunter (1802-86), who may be the man on the left in no. 54 in light trousers. A comparison with later photographs suggests that McDowell may be the short, bearded fellow at right in no. 53.

3. For information on Wool see the excellent biography by Harwood Perry Hinton, "The Military Career of John Ellis Wool, 1812-1863," Ph.D. diss., University of Wisconsin, 1960. Pages 172-282 deal with Wool's activities in the Mexican War. A veteran of the War of 1812 and inspector general of the army from 1816 to 1841, Wool had been in charge of organizing, training, and equipping thousands of raw American volunteers at the beginning of the war. See also cat. nos. 18-20 and 36 for Wool's role in the war.

4. Wool in a letter to Major Dix, Dec. 30, 1847, quoted in Hinton, "John Ellis Wool," p. 224.

5. Hinton, "John Ellis Wool," p. 201, quoting Wool.

6. Gregg, *Diary and Letters*, 1:62.

53. GENERAL WOOL AND STAFF IN THE CALLE REAL, SALTILLO

54. GENERAL WOOL AND STAFF, CALLE REAL TO SOUTH

Virgª Regᵗ Calle Real to 18ᵈ

55. Webster's Battery, Miñon's Pass

56. Major Lucien Webster's Battery

55.

WEBSTER'S BATTERY, MIÑON'S PASS —
MOUNTAINS JUST NORTH OF BUENA
VISTA TO EASTWARD
Daguerreotype, sixth-plate, c. 1847
Plate verso: "IV"
Paper label, on cover glass: "Virga. Regt. Calle
Real / to Sd."
Graphite inscription on wood frame: "9"
Courtesy of Yale Western Americana Collection, Beinecke Rare Book and Manuscript
Library

56.

[MAJOR LUCIEN WEBSTER'S BATTERY —
MOUNTAINS JUST NORTH OF BUENA
VISTA]
Daguerreotype, sixth-plate, c. 1847
2-3/4 x 3-3/16 in. (7.0 x 8.1 cm.)
Stamped left edge: "[E.] White Maker N.Y.
Finest Quality A"
Copper-backed plate; 4 corners clipped at 45°
angle, 4 corners and long edges turned down;
plate holder crimp marks, u.r. and l.r. corners
ACM 81.65/42

The labels on two of the daguerreotypes in the Yale collection were evidently switched at some point, for the inscription "Virga. Regt. Calle Real / to Sd." actually fits cat. no. 69, a view of American infantrymen lined up in a Saltillo street. Conversely the inscription now attached to no. 69, "Webster's Batty, Minon's / Pass — Mts. just N. of / Buena Vista to Ed.", seems to describe the view in cat. no. 55. Brevet Major Lucien B. Webster commanded a battery of two twenty-four-pounder howitzers in the redoubt south of Saltillo from which the views in cat. nos. 45-47 were taken. During the battle of Buena Vista, 1,200 Mexican lancers under General José Vicente Miñon appeared around noon on February 23 in the valley southeast of Saltillo at Palomas Pass (presumably the "Miñon's Pass" of the inscription) and moved to cut General Taylor's communications with the town. From his redoubt, Webster sent Brevet Captain James L. Donaldson with one of the twenty-four-pounders to help drive Miñon's lancers away. To make the views, the daguerreotypist stood immediately to the south of Webster's redoubt, looking southeast across the plain over which Miñon had advanced and retreated. The mountains in the distance are the Sierra de Zapaliname, about three miles away.[1]

Webster's unit had reached Saltillo in December 1846 and was there until May or June 1848.[2] In the far right of cat. no. 56 a tent is visible, probably from the same encampment that is visible behind the artillery train in no. 55. In both views, two artillery pieces are visible (possibly the two twenty-four-pounder howitzers that Webster commanded on February 23) along with their crews and support equipment. At left in both views, four horses pull a limber (the two-wheel vehicle on which part of the crew sits) to which a gun carriage is attached. In line to the right of the gun carriage is another team of horses drawing a limber and caisson. Beyond this line is another line consisting of team, limber, and gun carriage, and team, limber, and caisson.

American horse teams and artillery crews trained rigorously in order to execute rapid and intricate maneuvers on the battlefield under fire.[3] After the victory at Buena Vista General Wool commented that "the artillery ... succeeded in the victory. But for this arm of service we should have been easily defeated."[4]

1. Thomas Kailbourn to Marni Sandweiss, October 16, 1988, Amon Carter Museum files. Mr. Kailbourn corresponded with Sr. D. Carlos Guajardo Elizondo of Monclova, Coahuila, Mexico, who was most helpful in providing him with photographs of the site as it exists today.
2. Returns of the First Artillery Regiment, April 1846-July 1848, RG 94, M727, roll 3, National Archives, Washington, D.C.
3. *The Artillery Corps of Philadelphia Greys,* sketched and drawn on stone by Alfred Hoffy and printed by P.S. Duval in 1845, depicts such "flying" units maneuvering in a field. An impression is located in the Library of Congress, Prints and Photographs Division.
4. Wool to Major Dix, March 2, 1847, quoted in Hinton, "John Ellis Wool." See also Lester R. Dillon, Jr., *American Artillery in the Mexican War 1846-1847* (Austin, Texas: Presidial Press, 1975).

57. Lieut. Dolholson [Captain James Lowry Donaldson]

57.

LIEUT. DOLHOLSON, REGULAR ARMY
[CAPTAIN JAMES LOWRY DONALDSON]
Daguerreotype, sixth-plate, c. 1847
3-1/4 x 2-3/4 in. (8.3 x 7.0 cm.)
Stamped l.l. corner: "Scovills"
Copper-backed plate; 4 corners clipped at 45°
angle, 4 corners turned down; no apparent
plate holder crimp mark
Paper label on plate verso, in ink: "Lieut
Dolholson [sic] / Reg. Army / promoted for
bravery / at Battle of Monterrey / to Brevet
Major / comander of a Battery / at Buena
Vista under / Taylor"
ACM 81.65/6

The sitter in this daguerreotype is Captain
James Lowry Donaldson (1814-85), his
name being misspelled and his rank confused in the inscription on the paper label
on the back of the plate.[1] Donaldson was
in the vicinity of Saltillo, under the command of Lucien Webster, from December
1846 until at least the end of April 1848,
during which time he must have sat for
this daguerreotype. The uniform supports
the identification of the sitter. The officer
wears the single-breasted frock coat used
for campaign wear, with buttons with
clear-cut rings around them indicating a
general staff officer (or quartermaster in
this case) and two bars on the shoulder
strap to indicate the rank of captain.[2] The
cap is somewhat obscured.

A native of Baltimore, Donaldson
graduated from West Point in 1836. At
the beginning of the Mexican War he was
acting assistant quartermaster attached
to then-Captain Webster's Company C,
First Artillery Regiment, part of Taylor's
Army of Occupation. For his "gallant and
meritorious conduct in the several conflicts at Monterey," Donaldson was breveted captain. During the battle of Buena
Vista he remained behind with Webster's
battery at Saltillo, helping to drive away

General Miñon's lancers when they
approached the town (see cat. nos.
55-56). Donaldson was promoted to the
rank of captain on March 3, 1847, also
receiving the brevet rank of major for his
conduct at Buena Vista. He served on
staff as assistant quartermaster, and from
January 17, 1847, until April 30, 1848,
he was Collector of Customs for the State
of Coahuila with the American Army of
Occupation under General Wool.[3] Donaldson led a distinguished and important
career in the quartermaster service of the
Union army during the Civil War, serving
first in New Mexico and then back east
and rising to the rank of brevet major
general. According to one biographical
sketch, he was sometimes referred to
among his fellow officers as "Truthful
James" and "Innocence Abroad" on
account of his fine moral character and
trusting nature.[4]

1. Heitman, *Historical Register*, lists no regular
army soldiers by the name "Dolholson."
2. Jacobsen, *Uniform of the Army, 1847*, n.p.
3. For biographical information I rely on Cullum,
Biographical Register, 1:637-41, except where
noted. Also see "Donaldson, J. L." in James Grant
Wilson and John Fiske, eds., *Appleton's Cyclopaedia
of American Biography*, 6 vols. (New York: D.
Appleton & Company, 1888-89), 2:198, which
gives his birth date. For Donaldson's activities during
the Mexican War see Returns of the First Artillery
Regiment, April 1846-Dec. 1847, RG 94, M727,
roll 3, National Archives, Washington, D.C.; Baylies, *Narrative of Wool's Campaign*, pp. 37-38;
Carleton, *Battle of Buena Vista*, pp. 119-23; and
General Wool's official report on Buena Vista, published in New Orleans *Picayune*, June 1, 1847, p. 1.
4. Cullum, *Biographical Register*, 1:641.

58.

MAJ. WASHINGTON, CHIEF OF
ARTILLERY
Daguerreotype, quarter-plate, c. 1847
4-1/4 x 3-1/4 in. (10.8 x 8.3 cm.)
Stamped l.l. corner: "Scovills"
Copper-backed plate; 4 corners clipped at 45°
angle, corners and long edges bent down; plate
holder crimp mark, l.l. corner
Paper label on plate verso, in ink: "Maj Wash-
ington / chief of artillery in / Gen Taylor's
Division / and Gov. of Saltillo / Grand
nephew of Gen / Washington / lost with his
Reg / in steamer San / Francisco en route /
for California"
ACM 81.65/4

58. Maj. Washington, Chief of Artillery

59. Major John Macrae Washington

59.

[Major John Macrae Washington]
Daguerreotype with applied coloring, sixth-plate, c. 1847
3-1/4 x 2-3/4 in. (8.3 x 7.0 cm.)
Copper-backed plate, no apparent maker's mark; corners clipped at 45° angle; corners and long edges turned down
ACM 81.65/10

The unusually detailed label on cat. no. 58 identifies the subject as Major John Macrae Washington (1797-1853), an identification supported by a portrait of Washington as a younger man.[1] The biographical data on the label is correct, and the uniform supports the sitter's identification as a high-ranking artillery officer.

Washington arrived in the vicinity of Saltillo with General Wool's Centre Division in December 1846 and remained until July 28, 1848. These daguerreotypes and a third, acquired from the same source, which is now in the collection of the Photo Archives of the Palace of the Governors, Museum of New Mexico, were probably taken during the same sitting. In all three, Washington wears his dress uniform, distinguished in part by epaulettes instead of shoulder straps. His double-breasted coat apparently conforms to regulations for uniforms of field-grade officers, except that the slashed flap on each sleeve with three loops and buttons is that of a captain (a major should have had four loops and buttons). Note the hook-and-eye fasteners for the collar. His sword is probably a mounted artillery officer's saber, but because of the angle only the pommel is visible, with its Phrygian helmet pattern and four-sided knuckle-bow.[2]

John M. Washington was a native of Virginia and graduated from West Point in 1817.[3] He had a long career in the corps of artillery before the Mexican War, par-ticipating in operations against the Creeks and Seminoles and in the removal of the Cherokees to Indian Territory. In 1846, as a captain, he commanded a light battery of eight guns with Wool's division on its long march from San Antonio to Saltillo, from September to December. On February 16, 1847, Washington was promoted to major of the Third Artillery.

At the battle of Buena Vista, less than a week later, Washington and his men played a key role. Guarding the road through the pass of La Angostura, Washington's battery repelled a Mexican attack on the twenty-second and covered the retreat of the Illinois and Kentucky infantry on the twenty-third (see cat. nos. 36, 38). That day Washington was made a brevet lieutenant colonel; on March 12 he was named Chief of Artillery of Wool's division (restyled the Chief of Artillery of the Army of Occupation on December 9). From June 24 until December 14, 1847, he was acting governor of Saltillo. On July 28, 1848, Washington left Saltillo in command of an expedition to Santa Fe, New Mexico.[4]

On a voyage to California on board the steamer *San Francisco*, on December 24, 1853, Washington, four officers, and 180 soldiers of the Third Artillery were swept overboard during a violent storm and drowned in the north Atlantic.[5]

1. See the photograph (neg. no. 13116) of a painting of John M. Washington, in the Museum of New Mexico, Santa Fe. The location of the painting is unknown.
2. See Jacobsen, *Uniform of the Army, 1847*, n.p. I am grateful to Michael McAfee, United States Military Academy, and Donald Kloster, Curator of Military History, National Museum of American History, for their comments on the uniform. Compare the saber with photographs in Peterson, *American Sword*, pp. 42, 43-44, 116, 118-19, cat. nos. 41, 108.
3. For biographical information on Washington, I rely on Wilson and Fiske, eds., *Appleton's Cyclopaedia*, 6:385, and Cullum, *Biographical Register*, 1:179-80, except where noted.
4. Gregg, *Diary and Letters*, p. 220.
5. An account of this disaster is reproduced in Albert G. Brackett, *General Lane's Brigade in Central Mexico* (Cincinnati: H. W. Derby & Co., 1854), pp. 296ff.

60. Burial Place of Son of Henry Clay in Mexico

61. Burial Site of Lieutenant Colonel Henry Clay, Jr.

60.

BURIAL PLACE OF SON OF HENRY CLAY
IN MEXICO
Daguerreotype, sixth-plate, 1847
2-3/4 x 3-1/4 in. (7.0 x 8.3 cm.)
Stamped l.r. corner: "Scovills"
Copper-backed plate; 4 corners clipped at 45°
angle, corners turned down, long edges turned
down slightly; plate holder crimp mark, l.r.
corner
Blue-ruled paper label on plate verso, in ink:
"Burial Place of son of / Henry Clay in Mexico"
ACM 81.65/40

61.

[BURIAL SITE OF LIEUTENANT COLONEL
HENRY CLAY, JR.]
Daguerreotype with applied coloring, sixth-
plate, 1847
2-3/4 x 3-1/4 in. (7.0 x 8.3 cm.)
Stamped l.r. corner: "Scovills"
Copper-backed plate; 4 corners clipped at 45°
angle, u.r. and l.r. corners turned down, u.l.
and l.l. corners turned up, bottom edge turned
down; plate holder crimp mark, u.l. and l.l.
corners
ACM 81.65/41

These daguerreotypes record the burial
site of Lieutenant Colonel Henry Clay, Jr.,
the son of statesman Henry Clay of Kentucky, who died in the closing hours of
the battle of Buena Vista (see cat. no. 36).[1]
Clay was buried near the site of Major
Webster's redoubt (see cat. nos. 45-47 and
55-56). The daguerreotypes were taken a
few feet apart and at slightly different
times of day, as evidenced by the changing
shadows. The whitish adobe structure
was a vault built to protect a wooden
coffin from wolves and grave robbers.

Visual images documenting grave
sites were not uncommon during the
Mexican War era. In his book "Our
Army" on the Rio Grande (1846), T. B.

Thorpe includes seven woodcut illustrations of grave sites of American officers
who were killed in the early stages of the
war. An engraving of the cemetery of the
Third Infantry at Monterrey after a sketch
by Lieutenant Alfred Sully appears in
W. S. Henry's book Campaign Sketches
of the War with Mexico (1847).[2]

A lieutenant in the First Illinois Regiment wrote: "During the day [February
24, the day after the battle of Buena
Vista], we collected and buried our dead,
amounting to two hundred and seventy.
The remains of Colonels Hardin, McKee,
and Clay were taken to Saltillo and there
interred." Josiah Gregg wrote the
Arkansas Intelligencer on March 22,
1847, from Saltillo, concerning the burial
of his friend Colonel Yell. Gregg's
description also suggests the location for
Clay's grave:

I informed you in my other letter of
the death of Colonel Yell. Supposing
his family might hereafter wish to
remove his remains, we had a tin
coffin prepared, which was placed
in a strong wooden one. The burial I
superintended myself. I had him
interred above the southern border
of the city, at the foot of the hill,
under Captain Webster's fort, so that
his grave remains protected; otherwise, there would have been much
danger that Mexican rogues might
have disinterred him for his burial
clothes. I set a cross at his head with
his name cut upon it, so that his
friends may know his grave. By him,
I had buried John Pelman, with his
grave marked in the same way. Near
by were also buried Col. Hardin,
Captain Lincoln, Captain Porter, and
others.[3]

Clay's body was later disinterred to
be transported for burial in the United
States. Perhaps the body had already been
removed when the daguerreotypes were
made. Jefferson Davis, a West Point friend
of Clay, brought the body back with him
on the First Mississippi Regiment's return
to the States; they left Brazos Santiago on
May 29, 1847.[4]

1. Henry Clay, Jr. (1811-47) graduated from Tran-
sylvania University in 1828 and the United States
Military Academy in 1832, became a lawyer and
served in the Kentucky legislature from 1835 to
1837. See Wilton and Fiske, eds., Appleton's Cyclopaedia, 1:644-45.
2. Thorpe, "Our Army" on the Rio Grande, title
page, pp. 49, 97, 100, 103, 117, 195; Henry, Campaign Sketches, p. 251.
3. Lieut. W. H. L. Wallace to George Green, March
1, 1847, in Isabel Wallace, Life and Letters of General W. H. L. Wallace (Chicago: R. R. Donnelly
and Sons, Co., 1909), p. 52; Gregg, Diary and Letters, 2:65.
4. Judy Honeycutt, "Mississippi in the Mexican
War," master's thesis, University of Southern Mississippi, 1970, p. 55.

62.

CONVENT CHURCH, SALTILLO, TO
EASTWARD
Daguerreotype, sixth-plate, c. 1847
Plate verso: "VII"
Original seal
Paper label, on cover glass: "Convent Church/
Saltillo to Ed."
Graphite inscription on wood frame: "7"
Courtesy of Yale Western Americana Collection, Beinecke Rare Book and Manuscript
Library

The Church of San Francisco de Asis,
shown here in its proper orientation,[1]
served as barracks for the Fifth Infantry
during General Worth's occupation of the
city in December 1846.[2] After the battle
of Buena Vista it served as barracks and
arsenal of Company E of the First Artillery.[3] A cemetery for Americans who died
in Saltillo hospitals was located not far
from this church.

1. Compare with a photograph, plate 92 in Atlee
Bernard Ayres, *Mexican Architecture Domestic,
Civil and Ecclesiastical* (New York: William Helburn, 1926). The decorative wall next to the horse
and rider in the daguerreotype does not appear in
the later photograph.
2. Plan of the City of Saltillo drawn by Lieut. John
J. Peck for Capt. John Sanderson, Engineer of Brig.
Genl. Worth's Division, Dec. 22, 1846, Drawer
112, Sheet 40, National Archives, Washington, D.C.
3. Abner Doubleday, unfinished military autobiography, manuscript in the New-York Historical
Society.

63.

[LIEUTENANT ABNER DOUBLEDAY WITH
UNIDENTIFIED MEXICANS]
Daguerreotype, sixth-plate, c. 1847
Plate verso, scratched: "V"
Original seal gone
Courtesy of Yale Western Americana Collection, Beinecke Rare Book and Manuscript
Library

When Robert Taft documented this
daguerreotype in his 1938 book *Photography and the American Scene*, he noted
a handwritten label identifying the picture
as "group of Mexicans — Lt. Doubleday."[1] The label apparently became
separated from the image, as the
daguerreotype now bears no identification. The central figure's appearance and
uniform, however, support his identification as Abner Doubleday (1819-93), a
tall, young first lieutenant stationed in
northern Mexico at this time and better
known as the legendary inventor of baseball.[3] In this daguerreotype Doubleday
wears a forage cap with a badge featuring
the crossed cannon indicating artillery.
Upon his unbuttoned single-breasted
jacket are shoulder straps with apparently
one bar at the ends, indicating the rank
of first lieutenant.[3]

Doubleday, attached to Company E
of the First Regiment of Artillery, first
arrived in the vicinity of Saltillo, where
this picture may have been taken, after an
exhausting forced march from Monterrey
in February 1847.[4] Hearing reports of
the battle of Buena Vista along the way,
he and his battery finally arrived at the
battlefield at dawn on the twenty-fourth,
just as the Americans learned that Santa
Anna had retreated. Doubleday remained
in Saltillo on garrison duty probably until
May 1848 or the end of the American
occupation there, except for a week's
leave in Monterrey and a trip to Parras in

March 1848.

It is not surprising to see Doubleday
here surrounded by Mexican citizens. A
student of Spanish literature in his youth,
Doubleday made acquaintances and
friends among the population at most of
the towns he visited and showed sympathy
to children caught up by the war.

1. Robert Taft, *Photography and the American Scene*
(1938; rpt., New York: Dover Publications, 1964),
pp. 484-85 n. 246a.
2. The Photo Collection, National Baseball Hall of
Fame and Museum, Cooperstown, New York, has
an engraving by J. C. Buttre after a photo by
Mathew Brady of Doubleday during the Civil War,
along with another photographic portrait. Although
these portraits were taken much later than the
daguerreotype, the similarities are striking.
    A native of Ballston Spa, New York, Doubleday
is said to have created the game of baseball while a
student in Cooperstown. He graduated from West
Point in 1842. During the Mexican War he fought
with Taylor's army in the battle of Monterrey before
coming to Saltillo. He saw considerable action in
the Union army during the Civil War, attaining the
rank of major general of volunteers. (See Thomas
M. Spaulding, "Doubleday, Abner," in *DAB*,
3:391-92.)
3. Jacobsen, *Uniform of the Army, 1847*, n.p.
4. For information on Doubleday's activities during
the Mexican War, I have relied on his unfinished
military autobiography (manuscript in the New-
York Historical Society). Thanks to Thomas Kailbourn for furnishing notes on this manuscript.

Convent Church
Saltillo to E.^d

62. CONVENT CHURCH, SALTILLO

63. Lieutenant Abner Doubleday with Unidentified Mexicans

64. MEXICAN LADY

64.
MEXICAN LADY
Daguerreotype with applied coloring,
quarter-plate, c. 1847
4-1/4 x 3-1/4 in. (10.8 x 8.3 cm.)
Copper-backed plate, no apparent maker's
mark; 4 corners clipped at 45° angle, corners
and edges turned down; plate holder crimp
mark, l.l. corner
Paper label on plate verso, in ink: "Mexican
Lady $10"
ACM 81.65/5

65.
MEXICAN FAMILY
Daguerreotype, quarter-plate, c. 1847
3-1/4 x 4-1/4 in. (8.3 x 10.8 cm.)
Stamped right edge: "[Z]OA Garantin" and
l.l. corner: "40"
Copper-backed plate; 4 corners clipped at 45°
angle, corners and long edges turned down;
plate holder crimp mark, l.l. corner
Blue-ruled paper label on plate verso, in ink:
"Mexican Family"
ACM 81.65/18

It is unclear what the ten dollar price on
the label of cat. no. 64 refers to, though
it suggests that the plate was marketed to
American soldiers as a typical Mexican
portrait. This same Mexican woman
appears in no. 65, seated third from right
on the back row.

65. Mexican Family

66.

RANCHEROS, — GREGG'S 'COMMERCE OF PRAIRIES' [POBLANAS BY CARL NEBEL]
Daguerreotype with applied coloring, sixth-plate, c. 1847
Backing verso in graphite: "VI"
Possible original paper seal
Paper label, on cover glass: "Rancheros,— Gregg's/ 'Commerce of Prairies' "
Courtesy of Yale Western Americana Collection, Beinecke Rare Book and Manuscript Library

Despite the label on the daguerreotype, Josiah Gregg's popular account of the Santa Fe Trail, *Commerce of the Prairies*, contains no such illustration. The image instead is identical to a lithograph entitled "Poblanas" in Carl Nebel's *Voyage pittoresque et archéologique dans la partie la plus intéressante du Mexique* (Paris, 1836). It is impossible to tell if the picture in the daguerreotype is a lithograph or Nebel's original painting, but the latter seems unlikely, especially since the person who labeled the daguerreotype thought it came from a book. Like Gregg's work, Nebel's book was a classic. It was published in both French and Spanish editions, and several of the fifty illustrations, many of them of the *costumbrista* or costume-picture genre, were widely copied. The image of the *Poblana* was especially popular.[1] Although not clear in the daguerreotype, the two women in the doorway are smoking cigarettes; the one at left holds the ranchero's spurs in her right hand. The daguerreotype has been hand-colored in blue, red, yellow, and white.

The dress and smoking habits of some Mexican women brought forth comments from American soldiers. H. Judge Moore wrote: "*Puros* (cigars) and *cigarritos*, are in universal use among men, women and children; but the former are composed of a very inferior article of tobacco; and the *cigarritos*, which are used mostly by the ladies, are made of a better article of tobacco than the *puros*, which is cut almost as fine as snuff, and confined in paper wrappers; the latter kind are also generally preferred by the gentlemen."[2]

1. One edition of Nebel's book has lithographic plates redrawn by Pierre-Frédéric Lehnert of Paris and was printed by Julio Michaud y Thomas in Mexico City (Amon Carter Museum 56.81). The right side of the plate entitled *Las Poblanas. Vista General de Puebla* is similar to the picture in the daguerreotype but excludes the woman's arm at far right. George Wilkins Kendall's *Narrative of the Texan Santa Fe Expedition* (2 vols.; New York: Harper & Bros., 1844), 2:324, has an engraving by A. Halbert "Adapted from Nebel" that shows two Mexican girls smoking in a doorway (see fig. 29).

2. Moore, *Scott's Campaign in Mexico*, p. 113.

66. RANCHEROS — GREGG'S COMMERCE OF PRAIRIES [POBLANAS BY CARL NEBEL]

67.

[POST-MORTEM]

Daguerreotype with applied coloring, sixth-plate, c. 1847

3-1/8 x 2-1/4 in. (7.9 x 5.7 cm.)

Stamped bottom edge: "E. White Maker Finest Quality"

Copper-backed plate; u.l., u.r. and l.r. corners clipped at 45° angle, corners and long edges turned down; plate holder crimp mark, l.l. corner

ACM 81.65/45

This view shows a body stretched out on a bed, its feet emerging from the covers at right. Although they are obscured, the unusual decorations in the scene appear to be Catholic religious symbols, suggesting that the daguerreotype might document a Mexican wake or death. Many Americans were fascinated by the customs of the local population; W. S. Henry's *Campaign Sketches* contains a description of a Mexican tomb and an engraving after a sketch by Lieutenant Alfred Sully of a Mexican funeral.[1]

1. Henry, *Campaign Sketches*, pp. 288, 289. S. Compton Smith described the customs surrounding the funeral and burial of a Mexican child in *Chile con Carne; or, The Camp and the Field* (New York: Miller and Curtis; Milwaukee: Ford and Fairbanks, 1857), pp. 78-79.

68.

COL. HAMTRAMCK, VIRGINIA VOL.

Daguerreotype with applied coloring, quarter-plate, c. 1847

4-1/4 x 3-1/4 in. (10.8 x 8.4 cm.)

Stamped top edge: "Scovills no. 2"

Copper-backed plate; 4 corners clipped at 45° angle, long edges turned down; plate holder crimp mark, l.l. corner

Paper label on plate verso, in ink: "Col. Hamtrammack / Virginia Vol."

ACM 81.65/3

The stiff-looking soldier in this daguerreotype is identified by an inscription on the back of the plate as Colonel John Francis Hamtramck (1798-1858) of the First Regiment of Virginia Volunteers.[1] His uniform and sword support this identification. In the one shoulder strap that is clearly visible, an eagle's wing appears in the center, confirming that he is a colonel. On his forage cap is the looped horn indicating infantry as the branch of service. A single digit or letter appears inside the loop, probably a Roman numeral "I" for the First Virginia Volunteers or a letter "I" for Infantry. Instead of the double-breasted coat for field-grade officers, however, he wears a single-breasted frock coat. One hand grips a sword or saber with a rather elaborate hilt that includes an eagle head pommel, an ornamented knuckle-bow of the reverse P pattern, and an ornamented counterguard. A sword or saber of this kind could easily have been worn by a high-ranking or well-to-do officer of volunteers.[2]

Colonel Hamtramck, with several companies of the First Virginia Volunteers, arrived at General Wool's camp at Buena Vista near Saltillo in the summer of 1847. Already at the camp were the Second Mississippi and the First North Carolina Volunteers. Hamtramck and his troops made a favorable impression on

Private Samuel E. Chamberlain of the First Dragoons, one of the few regular army units in the vicinity: "New regiments continued to arrive at Saltillo, generally composed of the roughs of the South, without drill or discipline. The 1st Virginia Regiment, Colonel Hamtranck [*sic*] commanding, proved a noble exception to this; both officers and men were distinguished for their high-toned, gentlemanly bearing, while the regiment bore a most deserved character for efficiency." A correspondent for the New Orleans *Picayune* conveyed a similiar impression: "The advantage of volunteer regiments having field officers who understand the profession of arms is clearly exemplified by the conduct of the Virginia regiment, who are certainly as quiet and orderly a set of volunteers as ever have been up here, and as well acquainted with the duties of soldiers."[3]

On August 21, 1847, Colonel Hamtramck took command of a brigade consisting of his regiment and the Second Mississippi. On October 22 he was appointed division commander after Wool replaced Taylor as commander of the Army of Occupation. In addition to these responsibilities, Hamtramck was appointed military governor and commandant of Saltillo on March 7, 1848, and two days later moved his headquarters to the city. He remained there until the end of the war, leaving on June 14, 1848.

The theater of operations in northern Mexico after the battle of Buena Vista was relatively inactive. As the boredom of occupation set in, discipline became a major problem. Some of the Virginia Volunteers were involved in the mutiny against Colonel Robert Treat Paine of the North Carolina regiment (see cat. no. 73). Hamtramck vigorously supported

67. Post-Mortem

Paine after this disturbance. In order to combat the excesses of the volunteers and to prevent the Americans from falling into the hands of guerrillas and bandits, Hamtramck, like Wool, emphasized discipline. This did not help his popularity. For example, Josiah Gregg wrote in his diary: "Speaking of this 'noble' colonel, I might add, for pomposity, vanity and parade, he was not even excelled by Gen. Wool. He was in almost daily habit of riding about town, in full uniform, with a long tail of a guard in his wake, putting on airs which Gen. Taylor never thought of."[4]

In the closing months of the war Hamtramck was apparently in a great hurry to leave Mexico, and in his haste he did not conduct a very thorough and proper evacuation. Gregg complained that Hamtramck took the head of the evacuation column and left the most undisciplined troops—the Mississippians and Texans—to bring up the rear, and that these troops committed atrocities upon the Mexican population.[5] One of Hamtramck's subordinates, Major Jubal A. Early, tried to prefer charges against him for several actions, including neglect of duty for abandoning his troops before they were properly conducted back to Virginia.[6]

1. Cullum, *Biographical Register*, 1: 232-33. Hamtramck was the son of Colonel John Francis Hamtramck, who distinguished himself in the battle on the Miami in 1794. The younger Hamtramck served under Major Zachary Taylor in the War of 1812 and attended West Point from 1815 to 1819. He left the army in 1822, became a planter in Missouri, served as an Indian agent from 1826 to 1831, and moved to Virginia in 1832. (For information on Hamtramck and the Virginia Volunteers, see Wallace, "First Regiment of Virginia Volunteers.")
2. Jacobsen, *Uniform of the Army, 1847*, n.p.; compare the sword with several examples in Peterson, *American Sword*.
3. Chamberlain, *My Confession*, p. 144; J. E. Durivage, letter from Monterrey of June 13, 1847, published in the New Orleans *Daily Picayune*, July 2, 1847, p. 2.
4. Gregg, *Diary and Letters*, 2:214. Gregg, an excellent traveler but a poor judge of military matters, has little good to say of anyone in his diary and letters. He despised anything that smacked of aristocracy, and the noble bearing of officers like Wool and Hamtramck brought forth Gregg's ire. One must remember that Gregg was associated with the Arkansas volunteers, whose actions in the battle of Buena Vista showed their lack of training and discipline.
5. Ibid., pp. 215, 218, 233, 234.
6. Bauer, *Mexican War*, p. 231 n. 62.

68. COL. HAMTRAMCK, VIRGINIA VOL.

69.
VIRGINIA REGIMENT, CALLE REAL, TO SOUTHWARD
Daguerreotype, sixth-plate, c. 1847
Plate verso: "X"
Possible original paper seal
Paper label, on cover glass: "Webster's Batty, Minon's/Pass — Mts. just N. of / Buena Vista to Ed."
Graphite inscription on wood frame: "Vir-Reg"
Courtesy of Yale Western Americana Collection, Beinecke Rare Book and Manuscript Library

The label for this daguerreotype has been switched with that of cat. no. 55, a view of Major Lucien Webster's artillery train. According to its proper inscription ("Virga. Regt. Calle Real/ to Sd."), no. 69 shows troops of the First Virginia volunteer infantry regiment lined up along the Calle Real in Saltillo. Recent investigations have suggested that the view was actually taken from a building on the street one block to the west, the Calle Allende. The domed building in the right background is probably the church of San Juan Nepomuceno.[1] Interesting details include the familiar roof drainage spouts common to Mexican architecture. The presence of a street lamp in the foreground just to the right of center is noteworthy, since only three or four Saltillo streets had public street lamps in 1847.[2]

The Virginia troops that garrisoned Saltillo served primarily as police and on at least one occasion were formed in several ranks spanning the width of the street to disperse some volunteers of another regiment who had gotten into a drunken brawl.

Webster's Bat?.? Miñon's Pass—M?. just N. of Buena Vista to E?.

69. VIRGINIA REGIMENT, CALLE REAL, TO SOUTHWARD

1. Thomas Kailbourn to Martha Sandweiss, Oct. 16, 1988, Amon Carter Museum files. Compare the plan of Saltillo by Lieutenant Peck cited in cat. no. 62, note 2. The Calle Real turns into the road to San Luis Potosí, along which the battle of Buena Vista was fought.

2. Vito Alessio Robles, *Coahuila y Texas, desde la consumación de la independencia hasta el tratado de paz de Guadalupe Hidalgo*, 2 vols. (Mexico City: n. p., 1945-46), 2:178-80, details the installation of these lights in 1836 by D. Antonio Bosque y Vargas, whom Josiah Gregg later befriended.

70.
[AMERICAN VOLUNTEER INFANTRY IN A STREET IN SALTILLO]
Daguerreotype, sixth-plate, c. 1847
2-3/4 x 3-3/16 in. (7.0 x 8.1 cm.)
Stamped u.r. corner: "30"
Copper-backed plate; 4 corners clipped at 45° angle, edges turned down; plate holder crimp mark, l.l. corner
ACM 81.65/21

In this view, American troops are lined up, approximately fifteen abreast, in about ten ranks, in the same street in Saltillo as in cat. no. 69. Two mounted American officers and about thirteen members of what is probably a regimental band appear in the foreground. (The bass drummer is visible in the center foreground). The same buildings, including the church of San Juan Nepomuceno, appear in both daguerreotypes; no. 70 is reversed. The lamp also appears in this view, at left above the two mounted officers. If not the Virginia regiment, cat. no. 70 may show the Second Mississippi or the First North Carolina Volunteers, who were also in Saltillo at about this time.

71.
[AMERICAN VOLUNTEER INFANTRY STANDING ALONG A STREET IN SALTILLO]
Daguerreotype, quarter-plate, c. 1847
3-1/4 x 4-1/4 in. (8.3 x 10.8 cm.)
Stamped right edge: "E. White Maker N.Y. Finest Quality"
Copper-backed plate; 4 corners clipped at 45° angle, edges turned down, no apparent plate holder crimp mark
Blue-ruled paper label on plate verso, in ink: "Mexican Soldiers"
ACM 81.65/25

Possibly the only existing daguerreotype that clearly illustrates the common soldier of the Mexican War, this view shows American volunteer infantry standing along the same street in Saltillo seen in the two previous views. The details of the windows and doorways are identical to those seen with clarity in cat. no. 69, and no. 71 may show the same troops belonging to the First Virginia regiment.

In this daguerreotype the men are uniformed strictly according to regulations for the U. S. regular army. They wear what is undoubtedly the federally issued sky blue woolen roundabout jackets and trousers with dark blue woolen forage caps. The belts are white buff leather. The officer leaning on his sword in the right part of the picture wears a dark blue frock coat and pants with a wide white stripe on the leg.[1]

1. See Jacobsen, *Uniform of the Army, 1847*, n.p.

70. American Volunteer Infantry in a Street in Saltillo

71. AMERICAN VOLUNTEER INFANTRY STANDING ALONG A STREET IN SALTILLO

72.
[VIEW ALONG A STREET IN SALTILLO]
Daguerreotype, quarter-plate, c. 1847
3-1/4 x 4-1/4 in. (8.3 x 10.8 cm.)
Stamped right edge: "E. White Maker N Finest
Quality A"
Copper-backed plate; 4 corners clipped at 45°
angle; no visible plate holder crimp mark
Paper label on plate verso, in ink: "View in
Parras [sic] / Mexico"
ACM 81.65/23

Although labeled "View in Parras, Mexico," this daguerreotype depicts the same Saltillo street seen in the three previous views. The vantage point is almost identical to that of cat. no. 69, and all of the same buildings appear in both views; only the figures are different. A mounted American soldier appears at the lower right, while beyond him are several men in Mexican costume and three American soldiers, one of them seated on the curb. Of the two standing Americans, one is probably an officer since he wears a dark frock coat and holds a sword. Hitched up on the opposite side of the street are a number of horses, presumably belonging to these men.

The mysterious men in Mexican costume might possibly be members of what was termed in the nineteenth century a "spy company," actually a reconnaissance unit.[1] The Texas Rangers who operated around Saltillo with Captain Benjamin McCulloch and others sometimes wore ranchero costumes while on scouting expeditions. McCulloch and his men passed through Mexican pickets without being recognized as Americans and scouted Santa Anna's camp at la Encarnación two days before the battle of Buena Vista.[2] At least two Mexican spy companies served in General Scott's campaign in central Mexico, working as scouts, guides, spies, couriers, escorts, and inter-

72. View Along a Street in Saltillo

preters. Several contemporary paintings, including *The Convent of Churubusco* by James Walker, depict members of these units dressed in *jorongos* or ponchos with broad-rimmed hats trimmed with red scarfs.[3] Otto Zirckel, a German who volunteered for service with the American army, described the uniform of the Mexican spy company: "The soldiers wore round felt hats encircled with a red scarf and grey jackets. The officers and noncoms wore the insignia of our army. Later their uniform was changed and they wore parrot green coatees with a red collar and cuffs."[4]

1. Joseph Hefter and John R. Elting, "Mexican Spy Company, 1846-1848," in John R. Elting and Michael J. McAfee, eds., *Military Uniforms in America*, 3 vols. (San Rafael, Calif.: Presidio Press, 1974-82), vol. 2, text accompanying plate 321.

2. Reid, *Scouting Expeditions*, pp. 26, 233-36.

3. Hefter and Elting, "Mexican Spy Company," cite James Walker's paintings. Walker's *The Convent at Churubusco* is in the Army Art Collection, U.S. Army Center for Military History, Alexandria, Virginia (see cat. no. 137).

4. Otto Zirckel, *Tagebuch geschrieben waehrend der nordamerikanischen-mexikanischen Campagne* (Halle, 1849), quoted in Hefter and Elting, "Mexican Spy Company," text for plate 321.

73.
COL. PAINE, N.C. REG. IN MEXICAN WAR

Daguerreotype, quarter-plate, c. 1847
4-3/16 x 3-3/16 in. (10.6 x 8.1 cm.)
Stamped l.l. corner: "Scovills"
Copper-backed plate; 4 corners clipped at 45° angle, corners and edges turned down; plate holder crimp mark, l.l. corner
Blue-ruled paper label on plate verso, in ink: "Col. Payne N.C. Reg. / in Mexican War"
ACM 81.65/17

Colonel Robert Treat Paine (1812-72) probably sat for this daguerreotype in Saltillo, where, as commander of the First Regiment of North Carolina Volunteers, he served from late May or early June 1847 until March 1848.[1] In this daguerreotype he wears the double-breasted frock coat that was worn by field-grade officers, both regular army and volunteer. The shoulder straps with an embroidered eagle in the center support his identity as a colonel. His saber has a pommel with a Phrygian helmet pattern and a heavy four-sided knuckle-bow that curves below the grips and ends in a quillon with a disc finial bearing what appears to be a rosette. One carrying ring is visible on the scabbard. Sabers of this type were made regulation for mounted officers of artillery and infantry.[2]

Controversy dogged Paine's brief military career. A Whig politician from Chowan County, North Carolina, he was appointed commander of the regiment of North Carolina Volunteers by Governor William A. Graham. The various companies of the state militia had previously elected their officers, and the appointment of Paine (who had no prior military experience) and his lieutenant colonel, John A. Fagg, was bitterly disputed. The company from pro-Democratic Mecklenburg County refused to serve under them and

73. COL. PAINE, N. C. REG. IN MEXICAN WAR

was instead recruited as part of the regular army Third Dragoons. The lead elements of Paine's unit did not arrive in northern Mexico until the spring of 1847 and were engaged in no major battles. General Taylor assigned the North Carolina regiment the arduous task of escorting supplies from the (by then quite unwholesome) town of Camargo to the front.

By June Colonel Paine and his troops were encamped at Buena Vista with part of the First Virginia and Second Mississippi. The North Carolina troops suffered heavily from sickness and developed a reputation for unruliness. Private Samuel Chamberlain of the First Dragoons, a rogue himself, wrote: "Men of the 2nd Mississippi Rifles, and the 1st North Carolina Volunteers under Colonel Payne, were especially unruly, committing many depredations and outrages on the inhabitants of the San Juan valley. Houses were robbed, women insulted and sometimes outraged."[3] To combat discipline problems, Paine resorted to some strict measures that added to his unpopularity and led to a mutiny in August 1847.[4] To enforce Paine's orders, Lieutenant Colonel Fagg ordered a wooden horse constructed with a sharp back upon which offenders were forced to sit for long hours. This unpopular measure brought ridicule from a number of the Virginia and Mississippi troops, who, with encouragement from many North Carolina enlisted men and even officers, entered the North Carolina camp on August 14 and partially destroyed the horse. The next night, the disorder escalated and many of Paine's own officers and troops refused to defend or support him when the intruders threw stones at him. The mutiny grew until Paine shot and mortally wounded one of his soldiers. Generals Wool and Caleb Cushing intervened; Paine was temporarily relieved of command and the North Carolina troops were sent to Saltillo and Arispe's Mills. A court of inquiry assembled at Saltillo on January 28, 1848, absolved and reinstated Paine.

In March 1848 the North Carolina regiment returned to the camp at Buena Vista, while Paine left Saltillo for Monterrey. The regiment left Mexico on June 28. After the war, Paine served in the U.S. Congress from 1855 to 1857 and as a commissioner for Mexican claims resulting from the Mexican War along with George Evans (cat. no. 95). He bought land in Austin County, Texas, in 1860.

1. Except where noted otherwise, for information on Paine's Mexican War service I rely on William S. Hoffmann, *North Carolina in the Mexican War, 1846-1848* (Raleigh, N. C.: State Department of Archives and History, 1969), pp. 16-21. For further biographical information see Robert Treat Paine's papers in the Southern Historical Collection, University of North Carolina at Chapel Hill.
2. Jacobsen, *Uniform of the Army, 1847*, n.p.; Peterson, *American Sword*, pp. 116, 118-19, cat. no. 108.
3. Chamberlain, *My Confession*, p. 144.
4. See Smith and Judah, *Chronicles of the Gringos*, pp. 424-31, for Paine's account of the mutiny, along with an account by an opposing officer. Also see Wallace, "First Regiment of Virginia Volunteers," pp. 66-68.

74.
MISSISSIPPI LIEUTENANT
Daguerreotype with applied coloring, quarter-plate, c. 1847
4-1/4 x 3-5/16 in. (10.8 x 8.4 cm.)
Stamped u.r. corner: "Scovills"
Copper-backed plate; 4 corners clipped at 45° angle, long edges turned down; plate holder crimp mark l.l. corner
Blue-ruled paper label on plate verso, in ink: "Mississippi/Lieutenant"
ACM 81.65/2

The face of this sitter, identified simply as a "Mississippi Lieutenant," is obscured and only a few details can be made out. The two bars on the shoulder strap of the single-breasted frock coat indicate a captain rather than a lieutenant. The knuckle-bow and pommel of the sword are consistent with the type used by infantry or artillery officers.[1] On the basis of the inscription, the sitter was probably a member of the Second Regiment, Mississippi Volunteer Riflemen. (The First Mississippi Rifles, under Colonel Jefferson Davis, distinguished themselves in the battle of Buena Vista on February 23 and soon afterward returned to the States.)

This ill-fated regiment, called up in late November 1846, was intended to have ten companies, each with one captain. Instead of a full complement of 1,000 men, however, only 850 could be raised. Dozens of them contracted smallpox while encamped in a low area near New Orleans and many died before and during their voyage to the mouth of the Rio Grande. They joined Taylor's force in northern Mexico, where they were too late to see any major action but still suffered from disease. On May 10, while encamped near Monterrey, they reported 156 dead, and by that time at least 65 had been discharged.[2]

74. Mississippi Lieutenant

By June 1 the regiment was encamped on the battlefield of Buena Vista, south of Saltillo, where they were soon joined by the North Carolina Volunteers under Colonel Paine and the Virginia Volunteers under Colonel Hamtramck. The health of the Mississippi regiment as a whole improved at Buena Vista, but their morale and discipline evidently left much to be desired. Officers were absent for sickness or on recruiting duty; the regiment developed a reputation as ruffians. Some of them were involved with the North Carolina and Virginia troops in the Paine mutiny in mid-August (see cat. no. 73), and there were reports that the Mississippians committed atrocities on the Mexican population. They left the Saltillo area in June 1848 with the end of the American occupation.[3]

1. Jacobsen, *Uniform of the Army, 1847*, n.p.; Peterson, *American Sword*, pp. 116, 118-19, cat. no. 108.

2. *Mississippi Free Trader and Natchez Gazette*, Dec. 1, 1846, p. 1; March 16, 1847, p. 2; March 18, 1847, p. 2; March 27, 1847, p. 2; March 30, 1847, p. 2; *Semi-Weekly Natchez Courier*, June 4, 1847, p. 1.

3. For the conduct of the regiment in the Saltillo area see Wallace, "First Regiment of Virginia Volunteers," pp. 64, 65-68; Chamberlain, *My Confession*, pp. 144-45; Gregg, *Diary and Letters*, 2:218-19. (It should be added that some casualties in the regiment resulted from Mexican guerrilla activity; see Gregg, *Diary and Letters*, 2:206.) The comings and goings of the officers are reported in the *Semi-Weekly Natchez Courier*, June 15, 1847, p. 1; July 30, 1847, p. 1; Aug. 17, 1847, p. 1; Dec. 28, 1847, p. 1. The date of the regiment's arrival in the Saltillo area is derived from a report in the New Orleans *Daily Picayune*, June 18, 1847, p. 2.

75. Colonel Edward George Washington Butler

75.

[COLONEL EDWARD GEORGE WASHING-
TON BUTLER]
Daguerreotype with applied coloring, sixth-
plate, c. 1847
3-1/4 x 2-3/4 in. (8.3 x 7.0 cm.)
Copper-backed plate, heavy plate, no apparent
maker's mark; 4 corners clipped at 45° angle,
long edges turned down; plate holder crimp
mark, l.l. corner
ACM 81.65/15

The shoulder straps with gilt decorations
in their centers on a frock coat of this
type suggest that this man is a colonel.
The sword is a dragoon saber, perhaps
the 1840 model, known as "Old Wrist-
breaker." The pommel has the Phrygian
helmet pattern and the guard is of the
half-basket type with a knuckle-bow and
two branches joining an oval counterguard.[1] The man sports a moustache,
which dragoons were encouraged to grow,
so this man was probably a colonel of
dragoons.[2]

   The sitter strongly resembles an oil
on canvas portrait of Edward George
Washington Butler (c.1800-1888).[3] Butler
was a colonel of the Third Dragoons in
northern Mexico and is documented as
having been in Saltillo in late May and
early June 1848. He was born in Tennessee, the son of Captain Edward Butler,
Adjutant General of Major General
Anthony Wayne's Army of the West.[4] The
younger Butler graduated from West Point
in 1820. He served as aide-de-camp to
Brevet Major General Edmund Gaines
and as Acting Assistant Adjutant General
of the Eastern and Western Departments,
resigning from the army in 1831 to
become a sugar planter in Iberville Parish,
Louisiana. From 1842 until 1847 he was
president of the Plaquemine Branch of
the Union Bank of Louisiana.
   With the opening of the Mexican

War he became a major general in the
Louisiana Militia, but on April 9, 1847,
he was reappointed in the regular army
as colonel of the Third Dragoons. From
around June until September 8, Butler was
with his unit at Matamoros.[5] He arrived
in Monterrey on September 23 and
assumed command of the District of the
Upper Rio Grande by order of General
Taylor. Butler was in Saltillo on Court of
Enquiry on May 15, 1848, according to
regimental returns, "by General Order
No. 18 from the War Department, Adjutant General's Office, dated April 11,
1848." He resumed command of his regiment on his return from Saltillo on June
11 and remained in command of the district at Mier until June 30. The Third
Dragoons left Mexico on July 7 and Butler
was mustered out on July 31, 1848, at
Jefferson Barracks, Missouri.
   Butler returned to his sugar plantation in Louisiana. During the Civil War
he served in the Confederate army. He
died in St. Louis on September 6, 1888.

1. See Jacobsen, *Uniform of the Army, 1847*, n.p.;
Peterson, *American Sword*, pp. 32, 35, cat. no. 32.
Thanks to Michael McAfee for observations about
the uniform.
2. My thanks to Donald Kloster for this observation.
3. Woodlawn Plantation, Alexandria, Virginia,
accession cat. no. 72.2.3
4. For biographical information on Butler I rely on
Cullum, *Biographical Register*, 1:251, except where
noted.
5. For Butler's whereabouts during the war I have
followed the Returns from Regular Army Cavalry
Regiments, 3rd Dragoons, May 1847-July 1848, RG
94, M744, roll 26, National Archives, Washington,
D.C.

76. Maj. Lewis Cass, Jr.

77. Maj. Lewis Cass, Jr.

76.
Maj. Lewis Cass, Jr.
Daguerreotype, quarter-plate, c. 1847
4-1/4 x 3-1/4 in. (10.8 x 8.3 cm.)
Stamped u.r. corner: "Scovills"
Copper-backed plate; 4 corners clipped at 45°
angle, corners and edges turned down; plate
holder crimp mark, l.l. corner
Paper label on plate verso, in ink: "Maj Lewis
Cass Jr"
ACM 81.65/1

77.
[Maj. Lewis Cass, Jr.]
Daguerreotype, sixth-plate, c. 1847
3-3/16 x 2-11/16 in. (8.1 x 6.9 cm.)
Stamped l.l. corner: "Scovills"
Copper-backed plate; 4 corners clipped at 45°
angle, edges turned down; plate holder crimp
mark l.l. corner
ACM 81.65/7

78.
Maj. Lewis Cass, Jr.
Daguerreotype, quarter-plate, c. 1847
4-3/16 x 3-3/16 in. (10.6 x 8.1 cm.)
Stamped u.r. corner: "Scovills"
Copper-backed plate; 4 corners clipped at 45°
angle, u.l., l.l., l.r. corners turned down, long
edges turned down; possible plate holder
crimp marks, l.l. corner
Blue-ruled paper label on plate verso, in ink:
"Maj Lewis Cass Jr"
ACM 81.65/8

Lewis Cass, Jr. (c. 1814-1878) was the
son of the soldier, diplomat, and statesman Lewis Cass.[1] During the Mexican
War, the son was first made a major of
volunteer infantry on March 3, 1847, and
a month later was assigned to the regular
army Third Dragoons. He joined them at
Camp Palo Alto, Texas, on May 16 and
spent the summer in Matamoros.[2] The

78. Maj. Lewis Cass, Jr.

regiment, commanded by Colonel Edward G. W. Butler (cat. no. 75), left its camp at Matamoros on September 8 and arrived at Mier on the eighteenth. While Butler took several companies on to Monterrey, Cass remained behind in command of a detachment at a camp near Mier until November 21. On December 9 he was appointed Acting Inspector General of the Army of Occupation. Cass was a member of a four-man court of inquiry into the mutiny against Colonel Paine at Buena Vista (see cat. no. 73). The court of inquiry was held in Saltillo beginning January 17, 1848; Cass probably sat for these daguerreotypes at that time. He was mustered out of the service on July 28, 1848.

Almost nothing about the sitter's undress uniform accords with army regulations: stiff white collar turned up with checkered cravat, nonregulation buttons, no belt, and striped pants. Yet the leaf in each of the shoulder straps of his coat confirms that he is a major or a lieutenant-colonel (silver leaves for the former, gold for the latter).[3]

1. Lewis Cass, Jr., of Michigan later became chargé d'affaires to the Papal States in 1849; promoted to minister resident in 1854, he was recalled in 1858. (See Leo Francis Stock, ed., *United States Ministers to the Papal States: Instructions and Despatches 1846-1868*, [Washington, D.C.: Catholic University Press, 1933], p. 17.) Lewis Cass, Sr. (1782-1866) had attained the rank of general in the War of 1812, had been an Ohio representative, governor of the Michigan Territory, and Secretary of War, and in 1847 was a U.S. senator from Michigan. A Democrat, in 1848 he ran for President of the United States against Zachary Taylor.

2. Heitman, *Historical Register*, 1:289. For Cass's movements during the war, see Returns from Regular Army Cavalry Regiments, 3rd Dragoons, May 1847-July 1848, RG 94, M744, roll 26, National Archives, Washington, D.C., except where noted.

3. Jacobsen, *Uniform of the Army, 1847*, n.p. I am indebted to Michael McAfee and Donald Kloster for their observations.

79.
[UNIDENTIFIED INFANTRY COLONEL]
Daguerreotype, quarter-plate, c. 1847
4-1/4 x 3-3/16 in. (10.8 x 8.1 cm.)
Stamped u.r. corner: "[Sc]ovills"
Copper-backed plate; 4 corners clipped at 45° angle, u.l., u.r., and l.r. corners turned down, long edges turned down; plate holder crimp mark, l.l. corner
ACM 81.65/9

The embroidered eagle on the shoulder straps of this American army officer's coat indicate the rank of colonel, but he wears a single-breasted frock coat instead of the double-breasted one specified for field-grade officers. His forage cap with a looped horn and the "I" on the shield of his eagle buttons indicate he is an infantry officer. The unit number in the horn appears to be a single digit, but this cannot be made out entirely. The officer's sword is not easily identifiable because of the angle at which it is held, but the four-sided knuckle-bow of the hilt and one of the carrying rings of the scabbard are clearly visible, together with what could be a pommel of Phrygian helmet pattern. If so, it could be a saber of the type worn by mounted officers of infantry.[1]

1. Jacobsen, *Uniform of the Army, 1847*, n.p.; Peterson, *American Sword*, pp. 116, 118-19, cat. no. 108. Thanks to Michael McAfee and Donald Kloster for assistance on the identification of the uniform.

79. Unidentified Infantry Colonel

80.
[Unidentified captain]
Daguerreotype with applied coloring, sixth-plate, c. 1847
3-3/16 x 2-5/8 in. (8.1 x 6.6 cm.)
Stamped top edge: "E. White Maker NY Finest Quality A NY"
Copper-backed plate; 4 corners clipped at 45° angle, l.l. corner bent up; plate holder crimp marks, l.l. and l.r. corners
ACM 81.65/14

This unidentified young American officer wears the single-breasted frock coat of the undress uniform, bearing shoulder straps with double bars indicating that he is a captain. His sword, only the hilt of which is visible, appears to be a type of saber adopted in 1840 for use by mounted officers of artillery and also infantry. Its hilt has a pommel of the Phrygian cap pattern, a four sided knuckle-bow, and a quillon with a disc finial.[1]

1. Jacobsen, *Uniform of the Army, 1847*, n.p.; Peterson, *American Sword*, pp. 116, 118-19, cat. no. 108. Compare the saber held by Robert Treat Paine in his daguerreotype portrait, cat. no. 73 above.

80. UNIDENTIFIED CAPTAIN

81.

[MAN IN MILITARY DRESS—OBSCURED VIEW]
Daguerreotype, sixth-plate, c. 1847
3-1/4 x 2-3/4 in. (8.3 x 7.0 cm.)
Copper-backed plate, no apparent maker's mark; 4 corners clipped at 45° angle, long edges turned down; no plate holder crimp mark visible
ACM 81.65/16

This portrait is so badly damaged that only small bits of uniform are visible; it is not illustrated.

82.

PARRAS, MEXICO
Daguerreotype, quarter-plate, c. 1847
3-1/16 x 4-3/16 in. (8.1 x 10.6 cm.)
Copper-backed plate, probably plated, no apparent maker's mark; 4 corners clipped at 45° angle, u.r. corner turned down, short edges turned down; plier mark at left center edge, no clear plate holder crimp mark
Blue-ruled paper label on plate verso, in ink: "Parras Mexico"
ACM 81.65/19

An obscured view, not illustrated, is identified by its label as Parras, a town of about 6,000 inhabitants at the base of the Sierra Madre, some ninety miles west of Saltillo. Wool's division reached Parras on December 5, 1846, and remained until December 17. The next year Alexander Doniphan's Missouri Volunteers occupied the town for a time, driving off a band of Comanche or Lipan Indians who were raiding the vicinity, and on March 3, 1848, a battalion of Virginia Volunteers and a company of Texas Rangers from Major William Lane's battalion reached Parras from Saltillo, remaining until late May. Wool's troops noted Parras's beauty and the friendliness of its inhabitants, but later relations were much more difficult due to the behavior of the American volunteers, especially the Texans.[1]

1. For the visit by Wool's division see Hughes, *Memoir Descriptive*, p. 33. See also Chamberlain, *My Confession*, pp. 69-85, and Jonathan W. Buhoup, *Narrative of the Central Division* (Pittsburgh: M. P. Morse, 1847), pp. 96-97; Chamberlain took special note of the beauty of the women in the vicinity and took a sketch of the interior of the church of San José. For Doniphan's occupation of the town, see the letter from L.A.M. (Lachlan Allan Maclean) dated New Orleans, June 15, 1847, published in the *Daily Picayune*, June 16, 1847, p. 2; Connelley, *Doniphan's Expedition*, pp. 475-81; Gregg, *Diary and Letters*, pp. 123-25. For that of the Virginians and Texans, see Wallace, "First Regiment of Virginia Volunteers," pp. 73-75, and Smith, *War with Mexico*, 2:212.

83. Cathedral in Durango, Mexico

83.

CATHEDRAL IN DURANGO, MEXICO
Daguerreotype, quarter-plate, c. 1847
3-1/4 x 4 in. (8.3 x 10.2 cm.)
Stamped u.l. corner: "Scovills"
Possibly plated plate; 4 corners clipped at 45°
angle, u.l. corner turned up, other 3 corners
bent down, long edges turned down slightly;
plate holder crimp mark, u.l. corner
Paper label on plate verso, in ink: "Cathedral
in / Durango Mexico / large enough to /
contain 20 churches / of ordinary dimensions"
ACM 81.65/35

As Durango was never formally occupied
by American troops, it is uncertain how
or why an American daguerreotypist
might have traveled there to obtain this
or the following view. Immediately after
the war, Durango served as an important
stop on one of the gold rush routes to
California.[1]

As the label on the verso of cat. no.
83 indicates, Durango's cathedral (constructed between 1635 and 1844) was
regarded as a site of great interest to
travelers. For example, the renowned
German traveler and naturalist Duke Paul
Wilhelm of Württemberg visited Durango on March 15 and 16, 1850, and
wrote that "Durango was the most beautiful city in Mexico that I saw....Some
of the churches and chapels were truly
magnificent buildings. This cathedral,
built in beautiful Moorish-Spanish style
with an excellently appointed interior,
was one of the most exquisite temples of
Spanish America."[2]

1. See Ferol Egan, *The El Dorado Trail* (New York:
McGraw-Hill, 1970), pp. 182-88.
2. For information on the cathedral, see Antonio
Arreola Valenzuela et al., *Summa Duranguense*
(Durango: n.p., 1979), pp. 99-100. Paul Wilhelm,
Duke of Württemberg, "Diary of a Journey from
New Orleans to Sacramento, California, via
Brownsville, Monterrey, Saltillo, Durango, Mazatlán
& by Sea to California, December 4, 1849 - August
20, 1850," manuscript typescript, pp. 75-76. My
thanks to David Miller, who is preparing this docu-
ment for publication. The translation is by Raymond
Spahn.

84.

GERMAN COTTON MANUFACTURER IN
DURANGO, MEXICO
Daguerreotype, quarter-plate, c. 1847
3-1/8 x 4-1/8 in. (8.0 x 10.5 cm.)
Copper-backed plate, thick and heavy plate,
no apparent maker's mark; 4 corners clipped
at 45° angle, corners and edges turned down;
plate holder marks u.l., l.l., and possibly u.r.
corners
Paper label on plate verso, in ink: "German
Cotton / Manufacturer / in Durango / Mexico / income $300 per diem / + tannery &
stores"
ACM 81.65/24

George F. Ruxton, an English traveler in
Mexico, mentions this cotton factory in
Durango in his diary entry for October 4,
1846: "There is also a mint, the 'adminis-
trador' of which is a German gentleman,
who has likewise established a cotton
factory near the city, which is a profitable
concern."[1]

The cotton or *manta* factory
belonged to Stahlknecht and Lehmann,
a German-owned firm in Durango.
According to Duke Paul Wilhelm of
Württemberg, Stahlknecht's "house and
manta factory lay on the Rio del Tunal.
A few hundred Mexican girls were
employed at the factory, one of the largest
in Mexico." Duke Paul noted that the
supervisors were from New England and
that just before or during his visit "they
had engaged in firing practice in case they
should be attacked by Indians, which did
then happen on the road from Parras to
Durango." He also recorded that "Mr.
Lehmann lived in the city in a large house
not far from the principal square" and
that Lehmann's wife was "a Venezuelan
Creole and close relative of Simón Bolí-
var." Mr. Stahlknecht's brother-in-law,
Don José F. Ramirez, was, according to
Duke Paul, "one of the most learned men

84. German Cotton Manufacturer in Durango, Mexico

85. Street Scene

in Mexico, ...renowned not only as a lawyer and later as Minister of Justice, but also as an historian."[2]

Another Mexican cotton factory, better known to American troops, was situated on the Monterrey-Saltillo road near the modern villa of Ramos Arizpe. Operated by an Englishman, it sat idle through most of the American occupation for want of raw cotton.[3] Perhaps the Durango factory did not have this problem, since it was far from the strife.

1. *Ruxton of the Rockies*, ed. LeRoy Hafen (Norman: University of Oklahoma Press, 1950), p. 129.
2. Paul Wilhelm, Duke of Württemberg, "Diary of a Journey," pp. 70, 77.
3. Giddings, *Campaign Sketches*, pp. 265-67.

85.
[STREET SCENE, BUILDINGS ON LEFT, MOUNTAINS IN DISTANCE]
Daguerreotype, quarter-plate, c. 1847
3-3/16 x 4-1/2 in. (8.1 x 11.4 cm.)
Copper-backed plate, probably plated, no apparent maker's mark; 4 corners clipped at 45° angle, u.l. and l.l. corners turned down; plate holder crimp mark, u.l. corner; horizontal polish indicating special preparation for landscape view
ACM 81.65/20

86.
[STREET SCENE, BUILDINGS ON LEFT, MOUNTAINS IN DISTANCE]
Daguerreotype, quarter-plate, c. 1847
3-1/4 x 4-1/4 in. (8.3 x 10.8 cm.)
Stamped left edge: "E. White Maker N.Y. Finest Quality A"
Copper-backed plate, possibly plated; 4 corners clipped at 45° angle, corners and edges turned down; plate holder crimp mark, l.r. edge
ACM 81.65/30

The Mexican town in these nearly identical views has not been identified; possibilities include Durango, Saltillo, or Parras. The flat structure in the right foreground is the azotea of the building from which the daguerreotypes were taken. The objects in the center are the rain spouts protruding from the rooftop.

86. STREET SCENE

87. View of City from Height

87.

[VIEW OF CITY FROM HEIGHT, LOW
ADOBE STRUCTURES, MOUNTAIN IN
DISTANCE]

Daguerreotype, sixth-plate, c. 1847
2-3/4 x 3-1/4 in. (7.0 x 8.3 cm.)
Stamped l.r. corner: "[S]covill"
Copper-backed plate; 4 corners clipped at 45°
angle, corners and edges turned down; plate
holder crimp mark, u.l. corner
ACM 81.65/26

88.

[HORIZONTAL VIEW OF TOWN WITH
MOUNTAIN IN DISTANCE]

Daguerreotype, sixth-plate, c. 1847
2-3/4 x 3-3/16 in. (7.0 x 8.1 cm.)
Silver-plated plate, heavy plate, no apparent
maker's mark; 4 corners clipped at 45° angle,
long edges turned down; no apparent plate
holder crimp mark
ACM 81.65/31

These two views are also unidentified.

89.

[LANDSCAPE, TREES IN FOREGROUND,
CHURCH BUILDING IN DISTANCE]

Daguerreotype, quarter-plate, c. 1847
3-1/4 x 4-1/4 in. (8.3 x 10.8 cm.)
Stamped u.l. corner: "Scovills"
Copper-backed plate; 4 corners clipped at 45°
angle, corners and edges turned down; plate
holder crimp mark, l.l. corner
ACM 81.65/39

This is probably a hacienda chapel or village church. Its location has not been
identified.

88. Horizontal View of Town

89. Landscape, Trees in Foreground, Church in Distance

90.
[Sailing ships at dock]
Daguerreotype, sixth-plate, c. 1847
2-11/16 x 3-3/16 in. (6.9 x 8.1 cm.)
Stamped right edge: "E. White Maker N.Y.
Finest Quality A. N.Y."
Copper-backed plate; 4 corners clipped at 45°
angle, u.r., l.l., and l.r. corners turned down,
u.l. corner turned up, long edges turned down
slightly; possible plate holder crimp mark, u.l.
corner
ACM 81.65/44

These unidentified schooner-rigged vessels could have operated in Mexican coastal waters, but no further clues or inscriptions indicate whether the daguerreotype was taken in Mexico or the United States.

91.
Fort Marion, St. Augustine, Florida
Daguerreotype with applied coloring, sixth-plate, c. 1847
Cardboard backing with brown paper seal
On verso in graphite: "No 11"
Paper label, on cover glass: "Fort Marion, St.
Aug-/-ustine, from Bay to S.W."
Courtesy of Yale Western Americana Collection, Beinecke Rare Book and Manuscript Library

This and the following view of St. Augustine, Florida, were probably acquired by the collector of this series of daguerreotypes as souvenirs of his wartime travels as he passed through Florida on his way to or from Mexico. St. Augustine, the oldest city in the United States founded by Europeans, was a favored tourist site in the nineteenth century (as it is still).[1] Fort Marion probably interested the photographer and collector with its grim yet picturesque visage and its colorful history as the nation's oldest standing fort.[2] Perhaps the collector was stationed at the nearby St. Francis Barracks.

1. Floyd and Marion Rinhart, *Victorian Florida* (Atlanta: Peachtree Publishers, 1986), p. 106.
2. Fort Marion was constructed from 1672 to 1756 as the Castillo de San Marcos by the Spanish with the help of Indian hostages and Negro slaves. The British gained control of the fort in 1763, holding it for twenty years under the name Fort St. Marks until the Spanish regained possession in 1783. After the United States acquired Florida, the fort was again renamed in 1825, this time for Revolutionary War general Francis Marion. During the Indian wars it served as a prison for several captured Indian chiefs, including Osceola. (*Florida: A Guide to the Southernmost State*, Federal Writers' Project American Guide Series [New York: Oxford University Press, 1939], p. 250.)

90. Sailing Ships at Dock

Fort Marion, St. Aug-
-ustine, from Bay to S.W.

91. FORT MARION, ST. AUGUSTINE, FLORIDA

92. CITY GATE, ST. AUGUSTINE, FLORIDA

92.

[CITY GATE, ST. AUGUSTINE, FLORIDA]
Daguerreotype with applied coloring, sixth-plate, c. 1847
Cardboard backing with blue paper seal
On verso in graphite: "No 12"
Graphite inscription on wood frame: "8"
Courtesy of Yale Western Americana Collection, Beinecke Rare Book and Manuscript Library

This view of St. Augustine's old city gate at the northern end of town is apparently reversed from its correct orientation.[1] The view is up St. George Street, looking south. This ornamental gate, built of coquina blocks and capped with representations of the Moorish pomegranate, was constructed in 1804 to replace an older coquina gate begun in 1745. For a number of years the gate guarded a drawbridge over a moat.[2]

1. Compare the photograph, c. 1875, in Rinhart and Rinhart, *Victorian Florida*, p. 107. The gate is still standing.
2. *Florida: A Guide*, pp. 250, 251 (map).

93.

[ST. JAMES EPISCOPAL CHURCH AND BURGWYN-WRIGHT (CORNWALLIS) HOUSE, WILMINGTON, NORTH CAROLINA]
Daguerreotype, sixth-plate, c. 1847
3-1/4 x 2-3/4 in. (8.3 x 7.0 cm.)
Copper-backed plate, heavy plate, no apparent maker's mark; 4 corners clipped at 45° angle, no corners or edges turned down; plate holder crimp mark, l.l. edge
ACM 81.65/28

The earliest known outdoor photograph taken in North Carolina,[1] this daguerreotype shows the neo-Gothic structure of St. James Episcopal Church in Wilmington, built in 1839 to the design of architect Thomas U. Walter of Philadelphia.[2]

The house just to the right of the church is the John Burgwyn-Wright House, sometimes referred to as the Cornwallis House since, tradition claims, General Cornwallis made it his headquarters when he occupied Wilmington in 1781.[3] The house behind it to the right is number eleven South Third Street, built around 1802. It was the home of Captain Richard Bradley, Sr., and his descendants. Bradley's grandson, Henry William Bradley (born in Wilmington in 1813), was working as a daguerreotypist in California by 1850. His well-known photographic publishing firm, Bradley & Rulofson, was in operation in San Francisco from 1863 to 1884.[4]

1. Houston Gwynne Jones, *North Carolina Illustrated* (Chapel Hill: University of North Carolina Press, 1983), p. 222.
2. Marcus Whiffen, *American Architecture Since 1780* (Cambridge, Massachusetts: M. I. T. Press, 1969), p. 57.
3. H. G. Jones to Martha Sandweiss, Nov. 10, 1981, Amon Carter Museum files.
4. James A. Miller, Jr., to Nancy G. Wynne, Sept. 9, 1984, Peter E. Palmquist to Marni Sandweiss, n.d., Amon Carter Museum files; Robert Bartlett Haas, "William Herman Rulofson, Pioneer Daguerreotypist and Photographic Educator," *California Historical Society Quarterly* 34 (Dec. 1955): 295.

93. St. James Episcopal Church and Burgwyn-Wright (Cornwallis) House, Wilmington, North Carolina

94.

[JAMES KNOX POLK]
Daguerreotype with applied coloring, sixth-plate, c. 1847-49
3-1/4 x 2-11/16 in. (8.3 x 6.9 cm.)
Stamped l.r. corner: "30"
Copper-backed plate; 4 corners clipped at 45° angle; plate holder crimp mark, l.l. edge
ACM 81.65/12

This daguerreotype of James Knox Polk, the President of the United States at the time of the Mexican War, is unrelated to any of his other known portraits.[1] Polk, the first President to sit for a photograph in the White House, noted several portrait sittings in his presidential diary. The last was for Mathew Brady, who came twice during February 1849, Polk's last full month in office. The Brady daguerreotype shows a long-haired, worn-looking man. In this view, however, Polk's hair is shorter and his face seems even more tense and haggard. Polk's appearance suggests that the portrait could have been made between the time he left office and his death just a few months later on June 15, 1849.

The other possibility is that this portrait was made when Polk visited Gardiner, Maine, in July 1847. On July 3 he stopped at Oaklands, the family home of John William Tudor Gardiner (cat. nos. 96-99). Though no contemporary accounts of the trip record a photography session, the possibility is suggested by the discovery of the portrait in a collection including other views of Oaklands and the town of Gardiner. One spectator who saw the President on his Maine tour described his "thin and silvery locks and a fatigued and careworn countenance, which me-thought, might turn the hearts of some of his most violent opposers"[2] — an account that fairly describes this daguerreotype portrait.

1. Compare the photographs of Polk in Harold Francis Pfister, *Facing the Light: Historic American Portrait Daguerreotypes* (Washington, D.C.: Smithsonian Institution Press for the National Portrait Gallery, 1978), pp. 71-73 (cat. nos. 20, 21; figs. 12, 13).
2. Gardiner, Maine, *Cold Water Fountain and Gardiner News-Letter*, July 30, 1847, p. 2: from a letter dated July 20, 1847, signed "L."

95.

GEORGE EVANS
Daguerreotype, sixth-plate, 1848
3-3/16 x 2-3/4 in. (8.1 x 7.0 cm.)
Stamped: "Scovills"
Copper-backed plate; 4 corners clipped at 45° angle; plate holder crimp mark, l.l. edge.
Inscribed on plate verso: "Geo. Evans / 1848"
ACM 83.9/1

The inscription on the back of this plate and a comparison with another photograph identify this sitter as George Evans (1797-1867), a statesman and prominent citizen of Gardiner, Maine.[1] Evans was a native of Hallowell, Maine, and graduated from Bowdoin College in 1815. Three years later he was admitted to the state bar and practiced law in Gardiner, where he lived most of his life. Affiliated with the National Republican and Whig parties, he served in the state legislature (1825-29), the U. S. House of Representatives (1829-41), and the U. S. Senate (1841-47). His exceptional knowledge of public finance and his powers of oratory were acknowledged and respected by his opponents.[2]

Evans was a friend of Robert Hallowell Gardiner, whose son was the probable collector of this daguerreotype. On his visit to the town of Gardiner on July 3, 1847, President Polk stopped at Evans's home as well as the Gardiner family house. Among the presidential retinue was Captain Enoch Steen, who had been wounded at the battle of Buena Vista. Steen was received by George Evans and his family with "particular cordiality and affection" because a son, George F. Evans, was at that time a lieutenant with Steen's company in Mexico.[3] R. H. Gardiner later recalled:

As the president, after visiting Portland and Augusta, was about

94. James Knox Polk

95. George Evans

embarking on board a steamer at Gardiner, Mr. Evans made a most touching and eloquent address to Mr. Polk as the president, alluding to the fact that although during their congressional career they had always been politically opposed, yet they had ever maintained a mutual respect for each other, and as the president, he extended to him a cordial welcome from Kennebec and Maine. Mr. Polk so highly appreciated the address, that he afterwards observed that in all his tour through, not only this state, but the whole country, he had never received so touching and generous an address as this.[4]

Later Evans was chosen to head the U.S. commission on Mexican claims resulting from the Mexican War, an investigative body that also included Robert Treat Paine (cat. no. 73).

1. *The Centennial of Gardiner* (Gardiner, Maine: Lakeside Press, 1903), opp. p. 46.

2. William A. Robinson, "Evans, George," in *DAB*, 3, part 2, pp. 199-200. See also *National Cyclopaedia of American Biography*, 13 vols. (New York: J. T. White & Co., 1892-1906), 6:299-300, and Henry Chase, comp. and ed., *Representative Men of Maine* (Portland, Maine: Lakeside Press, 1893), p. 250.

3. James W. North, *The History of Augusta ...* (Augusta, Maine: Clapp and North, 1870), p. 657; New York *Herald*, July 7, 1847, p. 3. George F. Evans (d. 1859) entered West Point in 1842 and was assigned to the First Dragoons in July 1846. He was breveted a first lieutenant in February 1847 for gallant and meritorious conduct in the battle of Buena Vista. (Heitman, *Historical Register*, 1:409.)

4. R. H. Gardiner, "Notice of Hon. George Evans," in *Collections of the Maine Historical Society* (Bath: Maine Historical Society, 1876), 7: 469-70. See also *North for Union: John Appleton's Journal of a Tour to New England Made by President Polk in June and July 1847*, ed. Wayne Cutler (Nashville, Tennessee: Vanderbilt University Press, 1986), pp. 73-74.

96.
[OAKLANDS, GARDINER, MAINE]
Daguerreotype, near sixth-plate, c. 1847
3 x 2-1/8 in. (7.6 x 5.3 cm.)
Copper-backed plate, no apparent maker's mark, heavy plate, cut down from larger plate; 4 corners cut at 45° angle, corners and edges not turned; no apparent plate holder crimp mark
ACM 81.65/36

97.
[OAKLANDS, GARDINER, MAINE]
Daguerreotype, sixth-plate, c. 1847
3-1/8 x 2-3/4 in. (8.0 x 7.0 cm.)
Stamped top center: "N-York"
Copper-backed plate, heavy plate; 4 corners clipped at 45° angle, right and bottom edges uneven, corners and edges not turned; no apparent plate holder crimp mark
ACM 81.65/37

96. OAKLANDS, GARDINER, MAINE

97. Oaklands, Gardiner, Maine

98.
[OAKLANDS, GARDINER, MAINE]
Daguerreotype, sixth-plate, c. 1847
2-3/4 x 2-1/4 in. (7.0 x 5.7 cm.)
Copper-backed plate, cut from larger plate,
edges irregular, heavy plate, no apparent
maker's mark; corners neither clipped nor
turned, edges not turned; no apparent plate
holder crimp mark
ACM 81.65/38

99.
[OAKLANDS, GARDINER, MAINE]
Daguerreotype, near sixth-plate, c. 1847
2-3/4 x 2-7/16 in. (7.0 x 6.2 cm.)
Copper-backed plate, no apparent maker's
mark; l.l. and l.r. corners clipped at 45° angle;
plate holder crimp mark, l.l. corner.
ACM 83.9/3

Designed by architect Richard Upjohn in 1835-36, Oaklands was the home of Robert Hallowell Gardiner, prominent citizen of Gardiner, Maine,[1] and his son John William Tudor Gardiner, whom circumstantial evidence points to as the likely collector of the Amon Carter Museum's Mexican War daguerreotype collection. President Polk stopped at this house on July 3, 1847, just after his visit to the home of George Evans. According to the New York *Herald*,

> the Executive procession, with an increased escort of mounted citizens, ascended the hill to the princely residence of Robt. H. Gardiner, Esq. Approaching the mansion (which is built of granite, in the Norman and Lombard style, resembling a country seat of a British peer of the realm), the escort of mounted citizens drew up in two lines, one each side of the road, facing the carriages, and sitting uncovered as the train passed through. The company were at once ushered into the house, where a collation of cakes, fruits, wines, ices, lemonade, cordials, &c., was spread out for them in a wing of the double parlor; on the other side, the family, comprising a number of interesting and intelligent ladies, through the old gentleman and his son were introduced to their visitors.[2]

1. Wayne Andrews, *Architecture in America* (New York: Atheneum Publishers, 1960), p. 52. The Gardiner house was Upjohn's first significant commission.
2. New York *Herald*, July 7, 1847, p. 3.

98. OAKLANDS, GARDINER, MAINE

99. Oaklands, Gardiner, Maine

100.
[STREET SCENE IN GARDINER, MAINE]
Daguerreotype, sixth-plate, c. 1847
3-1/8 x 2-3/4 in. (8.0 x 7.0 cm.)
Copper-backed plate, heavy plate, no apparent maker's mark; 4 corners clipped at 45° angle; plate holder crimp mark, l.l. corner and possibly l.r. corner
Torn paper label on recto, l.c.: "[illeg.]r. Me."
ACM 81.65/32

This street scene was taken in Gardiner, Maine, an identification made on the basis of the torn paper label and modern confirmations of the site.

101.
BATTLE OF THE NILE ON THE ENSUING MORNING
Daguerreotype, quarter-plate, c. 1847
3-3/16 x 4-15/16 in. (8.1 x 12.6 cm.)
Copper-backed plate, no apparent maker's mark; 4 corners clipped at 45° angle, u.l. and l.l. corners turned up, u.r. and l.r. corners turned down; plate holder crimp mark, l.l. corner
ACM 81.65/43

This is a daguerreotype copy of a print titled *Battle of the Nile, on the Ensuing Morning*, painted and engraved by English naval artist Robert Dodd (1748-1815).[1] It records Admiral Horatio Nelson's defeat of the French fleet off the coast of Egypt on August 1, 1798, during the Wars of the French Revolution. Again, the image seems to have some connection to the family of Robert Hallowell Gardiner. During the battle, Gardiner's first cousin, Captain Benjamin Hallowell, commanded one of Nelson's ships, the H. M. S. *Swiftsure*, a seventy-four-gun ship-of-the-line.[2]

100. STREET SCENE IN GARDINER, MAINE

101. Battle of the Nile on the Ensuing Morning

102.
[UNIDENTIFIED CIVILIAN WITH BADGE
ON LEFT LAPEL]
Daguerreotype, sixth-plate, c. 1847
3-1/4 x 2-3/4 in. (8.3 x 7.0 cm.)
Copper-backed plate, no apparent maker's
mark; 4 corners clipped at 45° angle; plate
holder crimp mark, l.l. edge
ACM 81.65/13

103.
[UNIDENTIFIED CIVILIAN]
Daguerreotype, sixth-plate, c. 1847
3-1/4 x 2-3/4 in. (8.3 x 7.0 cm.)
Copper-backed plate, no apparent maker's
mark; 4 corners clipped at 45° angle, corners
and edges turned down; plate holder crimp
mark, l.l. corner
ACM 81.65/11

1. Dodd was one of the principal recorders of the naval side of the American Revolution. See E. H. H. Archibald, *Dictionary of Sea Painters* (Woodbridge, England: Antique Collectors' Club, 1980), p. 95. An impression of the print is owned by the National Maritime Museum, Greenwich, England. The full inscription under the title is: "To The Right honourable Admiral Lord Nelson of the Nile, the several Captains, the officers, Seamen & Marines under his Command, this Plate, Engraved in Commemoration of their Glorious Victory on the 1st. of August 1798, / is, with due respect and admiration of their Intrepid Conduct on that ever. Memorable

Day, humbly Inscribed, — By their Obedient Servant, Robt. Dodd." (J. M. Dacey, Department of Pictures, National Maritime Museum, Greenwich, to Milan R. Hughston, July 1, 1983, Amon Carter Museum files.)
2. *Early Recollections of Robert Hallowell Gardiner, 1782-1864* (Hallowell, Maine: Printed for R. H. Gardiner and W. T. Gardiner by White & Horne Company, 1936), p. 8; Rev. George Burgess, "Notice of Robert Hallowell Gardiner," in *Collections of the Maine Historical Society* (Bath: Maine Historical Society, 1876): 404.

102. Unidentified Civilian

103. UNIDENTIFIED CIVILIAN

104.
[UNIDENTIFIED MASON]
Daguerreotype with applied coloring,
quarter-plate, c. 1847
4-1/4 x 3-1/4 in. (10.8 x 8.3 cm.)
Copper-backed plate, no apparent maker's
mark; u.r. and u.l. corners clipped at 45°
angle; plate holder crimp mark, l.l. corner.
ACM 83.9/2

The apron, sash, and other regalia in this
daguerreotype identify the sitter as a
member of the Masonic fraternity. The
sash is painted red, the color associated
with the Royal Arch Chapter degrees. The
design painted on the apron is the Holy
Royal Arch, with the coat of arms of the
"Ancients" faction. The apron flap is decorated with the Hexalpha, or star of
interlaced triangles known as "Solomon's
Seal" or the "Shield of David." Suspended
from the sitter's neck is a triangular
"jewel" of office.[1]

1. Thanks to John Hamilton, Museum of Our
National Heritage, Lexington, Massachusetts, for
identification of Masonic symbols (letter from Susan
Balthaser, Museum of Our National Heritage, to
Ben Huseman, Jan. 20, 1989, Amon Carter
Museum files).

105.
[UNIDENTIFIED CIVILIAN, SEATED AT
DESK, PEN IN HAND]
Daguerreotype, sixth-plate, c. 1847
3-1/4 x 2-3/4 in. (8.3 x 7.0 cm.)
4 corners clipped.
Stamped u.r. corner: "Lee & Co"
ACM 84.5

104. Unidentified Mason

105. Unidentified Civilian

106.

Joel White's Coat of Arms 1650
Daguerreotype, sixth-plate, c. 1847
3-1/4 x 2-3/4 in. (8.3 x 7.0 cm.)
No apparent maker's mark; 4 corners clipped
at 45° angle; plate holder crimp mark, l.l.
corner: Scratched on plate: "Maximum / recto
/ praeli impetum et / Sustinere / Joel White's
coat of arms 1650"
ACM 83.9/4

Nothing is known about the "Joel White"
in the inscription, and there is no known
connection between this family and the
Mexican War.[1]

1. Two other Whites are known to have used similar
coats of arms, one with the motto "Maximum proeli
impetum et sustinere" ("To fight and sustain the
greatest attack"). See Charles Knowles Bolton, *Bolton's American Armory* (Boston: F. W. Faxon,
1927), p. 178.

106. Joel White's Coat of Arms 1650

Part Three:

Prints of the War in Central and Southern Mexico

By November 1846 President Polk realized that the American seizure and occupation of California, New Mexico, and much of northern Mexico would not by itself bring the Mexican government to negotiate a peace settlement. He therefore directed Major General Winfield Scott to plan an amphibious attack on the principal Mexican port of Veracruz and then, if necessary, to strike inland to seize the capital city. Veracruz surrendered after a three-weeks' siege, but elsewhere Mexican resistance to the invasion continued. While the U. S. Navy conducted several expeditions up rivers along the Mexican Gulf coast, Scott and his men fought their way inland in a series of successful battles.

Although Scott's army entered Mexico City on September 13, 1847, a formal peace was not established until February 2 of the next year, when the warring factions agreed to the Treaty of Guadalupe Hidalgo. Its terms fixed most of the present southwestern boundary of the United States. For the acquisition of these vast territories (including the present states of California, Utah, Nevada, most of New Mexico and Arizona, and the western part of Colorado) the U. S. government agreed to pay Mexico fifteen million dollars in cash and to assume more than three million dollars in claims by American citizens against the Mexican government.

Lobos Island

107.   See Plate 10
Henry Dacre after Charles Crillon Barton
THE ISLAND OF LOBOS. RENDEZVOUS OF
THE U.S. ARMY UNDER GENERAL SCOTT,
PREVIOUS TO THE ATTACK ON VERA
CRUZ, FEBRUARY 9TH. 1847.
Lithograph (hand colored), 1847
16 x 25 in. (40.6 x 63.5 cm.) irreg.
l.l.: "On Stone by H. Dacre."
l.r.: "P. S. Duval, Lith. Philada."
l.l. to l.r.: "1. Transport with Troops.
2. Transpt. with Troops. 3. Transpt.
with Troops. 4. Transport with Troops.
5. St. Marys."
l.c. below title: "Drawn on the spot by Lieut.
C.C. Barton U.S. Navy. / Published by P.S.
Duval, No. 7 Bank Alley, Philadelphia."
l.c.: vignette map with title "Boat Book
Draft / of the / Island of Lobos / Gulf of /
Mexico." and legend "Lobos. / Is about one
mile round, and a quarter / of a mile wide.
Covered with Gum and / Lime Trees, and
hugged up on the Southern / side by pretty
creeping Vines and wild- / Gourds. —The
Reefs abound with all / sorts of beautiful Fish,
the Red Groupa, / Rock Cod and a species of
Porgee being / prominent. / C. C. Barton."
l.c. below map: "Entered according to act of
Congress in the year 1847, by P.S. Duval, in
the Clerk's Office of the District Court of the
Eastern District of Pennsylva."
ACM 62.81

The Mexican War demonstrated the
growing power and importance of the
U. S. Navy and merchant marine, which
dominated the Gulf of Mexico and the
waters off the coast of California. The
U. S. Home Squadron under Commodore
David Conner patrolled and blockaded
the Mexican Gulf Coast throughout the
war. The few ships of the Mexican navy
were either captured or scuttled early in
the war. Although boring, blockade and
patrol duty was not without its hazards,
as sudden storms wrecked ships and the
hot tropical climate facilitated the spread
of sickness and diseases.[1]

Artist Charles Crillon Barton, a
career navy man from Pennsylvania,
recorded this view while serving as a
lieutenant aboard the U. S. sloop-of-war
St. Mary's under Commander John L.
Saunders.[2] The St. Mary's, seen under sail
at right in the print, elicited the praise of
naval officer Raphael Semmes for "the
masterly and professional manner, in
which [she] was uniformly handled. She
performed more blockading service than
any other vessel on the station, and in fair
weather and in foul, amid reefs and shal-
lows, she was always found in her place;
an eye-sore to the Vera Cruzanos, and a
terror to all adventurous masters of merchant ships, who came with hopes of running the blockade."[3]

Lobos Island, seen in this print, was
the rendezvous point for General Winfield
Scott's invasion of central Mexico. It lay
just off the Mexican coast about 120 miles
northwest of Veracruz. According to the
log of the St. Mary's, which contains
signed watch reports by Barton among
others, the ship arrived off Lobos on February 8, 1847, having escorted transport
ships carrying troops south from Brazos
Santiago.[4] That day and the next (the date
of Barton's view) the crew was employed
at various tasks, including repair work
on their ship, constructing a bridge and a
wharf on the island, and making a casket
for a Louisiana volunteer who had probably died of smallpox, which had broken
out on one of the ships off Lobos.[5] The
St. Mary's cutters disembarked the
"Palmetto Regiment of Volunteers"
(South Carolina Volunteers) from the
transport ship Oregon. In between his
watches, Barton found time to sketch.

James D. Bruell, a seaman on board
the St. Mary's, recorded his impressions of
the work at Lobos Island many years later:

When we arrived at Lobos there were
two ships with troops, and another
arrived several hours later with surfboats stowed in the hold. . . . We had
to erect purchases to hoist the decks
up in sections in order to get the
boats out, which were very large,
each designed to carry a hundred
men. With these the troops were
landed on the island. Sappers and
miners were sent ahead to clear up
the ground, which was all covered
with bushes, and as they made room
the soldiers began to pitch their tents.
Our ship's company continued to
land the troops and stores until it
began to look like an army camp,
with a nice parade-ground cleared
away for drilling. Two more ships
arrived during the day, and we had
all we could do day and night to discharge them. Two ships left in the
meantime for New Orleans. Six remained and two more were expected.[6]

H. Judge Moore, a soldier in the Palmetto Regiment, described Lobos Island:

It is two miles in circumference, and
appears to be chiefly composed of a
formation of sea shells, which at first
has the appearance of coarse sand. . . .
    Its temperature is that of perpet-
ual summer, and the weather would
be excessively hot were it not moder-
ated by the refreshing breezes which
almost constantly blow from the
gulf. . . .

Here we were encamped within full view of the main land, and in less than one hundred miles of Vera Cruz, without artillery or fortifications, with forty or fifty merchant vessels, loaded with military stores, all of which were protected by one single man-of-war, and that arrived some eight or ten days after the island was occupied. I would hazard the assertion, that a frigate's crew, with a dozen gun boats well manned, could have sunk or captured every vessel in the harbor, and thus have left us in our isolated position, almost without provision, arms or ammunition....

Fresh levies of troops continued to arrive daily, until the island was almost completely covered with long extended lines of snow white tents, which reached from beach to beach, barely leaving space enough to drill the different regiments. I never was able to ascertain exactly the number of troops that were concentrated at this point, but it included almost the whole force which was destined to operate against Vera Cruz and the Castle, and must have been very little short of fourteen thousand effective men.[7]

These men General Scott grouped in three divisions for the coming campaign: two of regulars, under General Worth and Brigadier General David E. Twiggs, and a third, composed mostly of volunteers, under Major General Robert Patterson.

Perhaps one of the transport ships in Barton's picture is the *Oregon*, mentioned by Barton and another officer in their log entries. New Orleans *Picayune* reporter C. M. Haile was also on the scene and wrote that "on the northern extremity of

the island is a neat flag-staff, from which floats the star-spangled banner"; this may be the flagstaff at left in the lithograph.[8]

On March 1 the invasion force left the island, sailing to rendezvous with the Home Squadron off Veracruz. Lieutenant Barton may have had a later opportunity to finish his sketch, although it is not likely that he needed it. Lobos Island was the rendezvous point for the Tuxpan River expedition in April, and the *St. Mary's*, although not a part of this expedition, carried back trophies in the form of guns captured at the ports of Veracruz, Alvarado, and Tuxpan when it left Mexican waters for the Norfolk Navy Yard in May.[9]

The print, issued sometime in the latter part of 1847 by P.S. Duval in Philadelphia and drawn on stone by Henry Dacre, may have been sold separately or with another print by Barton, Dacre, and Duval of the landing near Veracruz (cat. no. 110).[10] The whereabouts of Barton's original sketches is not known, so it is difficult to determine how faithfully Dacre reproduced them. Barton was an adequate artist, as may be seen by some small watercolor illustrations that he made in a two-volume log and journal that he kept from 1827 to 1831 (see note 2). It is likely that Barton's sketches reached Duval's studio in the summer of 1847; Barton was discharged on July 1 and probably brought the sketches with him when he returned to his home in Philadelphia. One impression of the print, in the possession of the New-York Historical Society, has a pencil inscription reading: "From Lieutenant Barton to the Chief of Provisions." One wonders if the favor was reciprocated.

1. See Bauer, *Surfboats and Horse Marines*.

2. Barton was born about 1783 and entered the navy as a midshipman on December 1, 1824. During the years 1827-31, while serving on the U.S.S. *Hornet*, *Vandalia*, and *Hudson* on voyages to the West Indies and Brazil, he kept a two-volume log and journal, now located at the Historical Society of Pennsylvania in Philadelphia (MS 60-1244), that contains watercolor sketches of ships and signal flags, the earliest known evidence of his interest in sketching. As a passed midshipman, he served on the frigate *Constitution* on voyages to France and the Mediterranean in the years 1835-36. According to shipmate Charles Steedman, Barton was severely wounded in a duel during this cruise; he spent a long period of convalescence at the naval hospital in Philadelphia in 1837-38. He was promoted to lieutenant on February 25, 1841, serving on the *Cyane* in the Pacific in 1842 and the *Marion* in the Brazil Squadron in 1844 before coming to the *St. Mary's*. In addition to his Mexican War views of Lobos Island and the landing at Veracruz (cat. no. 110), he also produced a sketch (probably drawn in New York harbor in 1846 or 1847) of the ship-of-the-line *Pennsylvania*, the largest sailing ship ever built for the U. S. Navy. Like the other two sketches, it is known to us only through lithographs printed by P. S. Duval's establishment in Philadelphia. (An impression is in the Historical Society of Pennsylvania, Philadelphia.) Barton was discharged from the navy on July 1, 1847, and died at Philadelphia on August 28, 1851. He was probably related to William Paul Crillon Barton (1786-1856), first chief of the U.S. Navy's Bureau of Medicine and Surgery and a member of a distinguished Philadelphia scientific and professional family. (See Mugridge, *Album of American Battle Art*, pp. 133-35; *Memoir and Correspondence of Charles Steedman...*, ed. Amos Lawrence Mason [Cambridge, Mass.: The Riverside Press, 1912], pp. 66, 75-76; *Register of the Commissioned and Warrant Officers of the Navy of the United States; Including Officers of the Marine Corps, & c. for the Year 1832* [Washington, D.C., 1832], pp. 42-43; for 1840, p. 33; for 1842, p. 20; for 1843, p. 20; for 1844, p. 20; for 1845, p. 18; for 1846, pp. 22-23; and Mexican War Widow's Service Pension, application no. 4004, certificate no. 2245, filed July 5, 1887, by his second wife, Christiana Barton, RG 15, National Archives, Washington, D.C.)

3. Semmes, *Service Afloat and Ashore*, p. 124. Bauer lists the following statistics of this ship: "First-class sloop of war. 958 tons, 150′ x 37′ 4″ x 17′ 3″, 4 8-inch shell guns, 18 32-pdrs., 210 men, ship rig, 10.5 kts. Built by Philadelphia Navy Yard, 1836. Sold at New York, 1908." (*Surfboats and Horse Marines*, p. 257.)

4. Logbook, U. S. Sloop of War *St. Mary's*, Feb. 8 and 9, 1847, RG 45, National Archives, Washington, D.C.

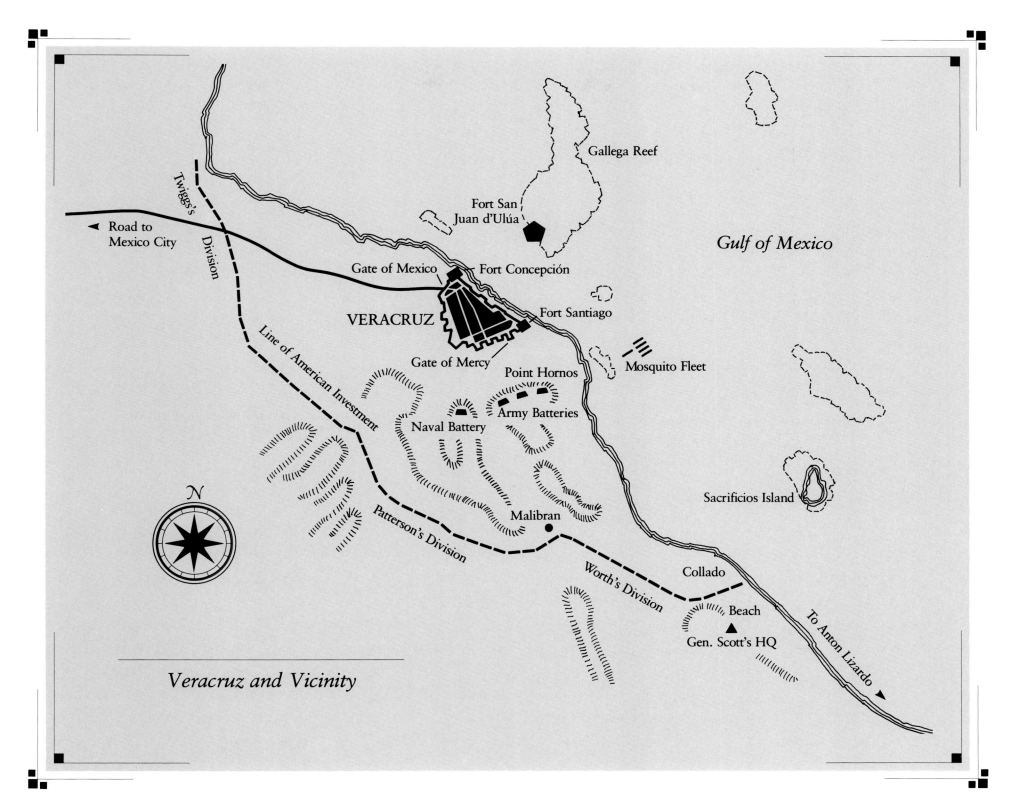

Gallega Reef

Fort San
Juan d'Ulúa

Gulf of Mexico

Twiggs's Division

◄ Road to
Mexico City

Gate of Mexico

Fort Concepción

VERACRUZ

Fort Santiago

Line of American Investment

Gate of Mercy

Point Hornos

Mosquito Fleet

Naval Battery

Army Batteries

Sacrificios Island

Malibran

Patterson's Division

Worth's Division

Collado

Beach

To Anton Lizardo

Gen. Scott's HQ

N

Veracruz and Vicinity

108. Vera Cruz

5. Bauer, *Surfboats and Horse Marines*, pp. 72-73, 75.

6. James D. Bruell, *Sea Memories; or, Personal Experiences in the U.S. Navy in Peace and War* (Biddeford Pool, Maine: the author, 1886), pp. 45-46.

7. Moore, *Scott's Campaign in Mexico*, pp. 1-4. Other accounts by soldiers stationed on Lobos include G. W. Hartman, *A Private's Own Journal* (Greencastle, Pa.: printed by E. Robinson, 1849), and Oswandel, *Notes of the Mexican War*.

8. C. M. Haile in the New Orleans *Daily Picayune*, March 26, 1847 (extra), p. 1.

9. Bauer, *Surfboats and Horse Marines*, pp. 103, 105.

10. Dacre was born in England about 1820 and is known to have worked for Duval in Philadelphia from 1847 to 1850. (See Wainwright, *Philadelphia in the Romantic Age of Lithography*, p. 226; Groce and Wallace, *Dictionary of Artists in America*, p. 162.)

Veracruz

108.
Alfred Rider after John Phillips
VERA CRUZ
Toned lithograph (hand colored), 1848
9-1/2 x 15-3/8 in. (24.1 x 39.1 cm.)
l.l.: "Alfred Rider."
l.r.: "Day & Son Lithrs. to the Queen."
From John Phillips and Alfred Rider, *Mexico Illustrated in Twenty-six Views* (London: E. Atchley, Library of Fine Arts, 1848), plate 3
ACM 10.79/3

This 1848 lithograph after a sketch by Englishman John Phillips is one of a number of published views by Europeans of Mexico's principal port of Veracruz, but it is perhaps the only one that is roughly contemporary to the American invasion. Although the exact date is not known, Phillips may have made his original sketch sometime just prior to or during the American occupation. His description accompanying the lithograph also provides a good introduction to the city:

> The town is enclosed by walls and defended by strong batteries. The streets are wide, and the public edifices and the houses generally, spacious and strongly built; but without any pretensions to architectural display. It has, however, an appearance of melancholy; and this is heightened by the numerous black vultures called "Sopilotes," observable in all directions; but which are protected by the law, owing to their usefulness as scavengers. The neighbourhood, for several miles around, presents few traces of vegetation, the surface of the ground being for the most part covered with sand. The sickly season prevails from June to October, when the winds called "Nortes" blow with great violence, and clear away the malaria.

> Immediately opposite the town, and within half a mile from it, stands the celebrated castle San Juan de Ulloa [Ulúa], on a coral reef. Merchant vessels of moderate tonnage anchor under the walls of the castle; but men-of-war and other vessels find better anchorage off the Island of Sacrificios, from which point the present view is taken.[1]

In his memoirs General Winfield Scott also noted that "the walls and forts of Vera Cruz, in 1847, were in good condition. Subsequent to its capture by the French under Admiral Baudin and Prince de Joinville, in 1838, the castle had been greatly extended — almost rebuilt, and its armament doubled.... When we approached, in 1847, the castle had the capacity to sink the entire American navy." Santa Anna had left strong garrisons in the city and castle, expecting them "to hold out till the vomito (yellow fever) became rife" while he gathered troops to repel an American invasion "at the first formidable pass in the interior."[2] Scott's own plan called for an amphibious landing and an artillery siege of the city from the land, bypassing San Juan de Ulúa and avoiding a costly infantry attack on the city.[3]

The previous French attack and occupation had already stimulated the production of prints depicting Veracruz and the castle of San Juan. The French images informed the American public as to the general appearance of the city and castle. A print by artist Eugène-Napoléon Flandin, showing French troops landing at the city's sea gate, has been confused with the American invasion.[4] A similar plate titled *Départ des Embarcations* appeared in a narrative account of the French expedition.[5] Engraver Samuel Putnam Avery copied one of these views for a cut titled *The Fortress of San Juan d'Ulloa: The American Fleet in the Offing*, which appeared in the New York *Herald* on May 8 and June 25, 1846.[6] On August 1, 1846, and on April 13, 1847, the *Herald* also published other cuts of the castle by Avery. The first was captioned "Probably to be Bombarded by the American Fleet" and the second "Before the Capitulation."[7] Another view like these, probably derived from a European print, was issued as a lithograph by the Kelloggs of Hartford, Connecticut.[8]

1. Phillips, *Mexico Illustrated*, text accompanying plate 3.

2. Winfield Scott, *Memoirs of Lieut.-General Scott, LL.D.*, 2 vols. (New York: Sheldon & Company, 1864), 1:421-23. Parker, *Recollections*, pp. 79-80, notes that Farragut witnessed Admiral Baudin's bombardment of the castle and said that the castle was quite vulnerable.

3. Scott, *Memoirs*, 1:421-23; see Smith, *War with Mexico*, 2:19-23, 332-37, for a more lengthy discussion of Scott's options, a description of the city and its defenses, and a considerable bibliography.

4. Lithographed by François-Jules Collignon and printed by Villain of Paris, the print was probably issued in 1838. An impression is in the collection of the Amon Carter Museum (51.74). Someone, perhaps a modern print dealer, either out of ignorance or in order to sell the print in America, hand colored the uniforms and flag in this impression to denote American rather than French troops.

5. M. P. Blanchard, A. Dauzats, and E. Maissin, *San Juan de Ulúa ou Relation de l'expédition française au Mexique, sous les ordres de M. le contre-admiral Baudin* (Paris: Gide, 1839), p. 367.

6. New York *Herald*, June 25, 1846, p. 2; *Weekly Herald*, May 8, 1846, p. 2.

7. *Weekly Herald*, Aug. 1, 1846, p. 1; *Herald*, April 13, 1847, p. 1.

8. An impression of *Castle of San Juan d'Ulloa, at Vera Cruz* is in the Connecticut Historical Society in Hartford.

109.

After James M. Ladd

THE UNITED STATES ARMY LEAVING THE GULF SQUADRON — 9TH. MARCH 1847.
Lithograph (hand colored), 1847
8-1/4 x 13 in. (21.1 x 33.0 cm.) comp.
l.l.: "Drawn by J. M. Ladd Esq. U.S. Navy."
l.c.: "Entered according to Act of Congress in the year 1847 by N. Currier, in the Clerk's office of the District Court of the Southern District of N. Y."
l.r.: "Lith. & Pub. by N. Currier, 152 Nassau St. Cor. of Spruce N.Y."
l.l. to l.r. below title: "The City of Vera Cruz — Castle of San Juan de Ulua and Mt. Orizaba in the distance. — The Army of 12,100 men Commanded by Genl. Winfield Scott. The Squadron Commanded by Commodore David Conner. — The management of the Surf Boats was placed into the hands of Lieut. R. Semmes U.S. Navy. / 473."
Courtesy of Beverley R. Robinson Collection, United States Naval Academy Museum, Annapolis, Maryland

The landing near Veracruz was the American military's first great amphibious invasion.[1] The landing site was at Collado Beach, which lay behind Sacrificios Island, two and one-half miles southeast of Veracruz. Near Sacrificios, the troops were transferred to sixty-five specially designed surfboats for the landing. Among the thousands of American servicemen who witnessed this scene was Midshipman James M. Ladd, serving aboard the steam gunboat *Spitfire*, who furnished the sketch for this lithograph by Nathaniel Currier.[2]

In the left foreground and middle distance are the surfboats, which naval officer W. H. Parker wrote "were built at or near Philadelphia, and were admirably adapted to the purpose. They were sharp at both ends, with flat floors and drew very little water. They carried one hundred soldiers with their arms and accoutrements, and were manned by one naval officer and eight or ten sailors. In landing in the surf our practice was to let go a kedge which we carried at the stern just before entering the breakers."[3] The surfboat crews in the print have just let go of their tow ropes and are rowing away from the warships, depicted at right. These large warships probably include, from far right, the stern of a frigate, a sloop-of-war, and another frigate. Beyond the surfboats at left are small, light-draft sailing vessels, the so-called Mosquito Fleet, which covered the landing from close in to shore. Most of these are two-masted gunboats, but one of them also has side paddle wheels and a smokestack. This is either the artist's ship *Spitfire* or the U.S.S. *Vixen*.[4] Beyond the Mosquito Fleet are more surfboats heading toward the landing zone at Collado Beach, and in the far distance is Mount Orizaba.[5] In the distant right may be seen the walls, parapets, towers, and turrets of the fortified city of Veracruz and the castle of San Juan de Ulúa.

Midshipman Ladd could easily have drawn this scene from memory rather than on location. The mobility of ships allows an artist considerable freedom to record their appearance, and Ladd could have sketched these on a number of occasions. The ships, the city of Veracruz, and the castle of San Juan de Ulúa are somewhat generalized. Even if Ladd's original drawing had been rendered faithfully from nature, the mass production methods of Nathaniel Currier's studio did not encourage fidelity to an artist's original sketch.

Nonetheless the print harmonizes with the mood of several eyewitness accounts of the event. For example, J. B. Robertson of the First Tennessee Regi-

THE UNITED STATES ARMY LEAVING THE GULF SQUADRON – 9TH MARCH 1847.

The City of Vera Cruz. – Castle of San Juan de Ulua and Mt. Orizaba in the distance. – The Army of 12,100 men Commanded by Gen.l Winfield Scott. The Squadron Commanded by Commodore David Conner. – The management of the Surf Boats was placed into the hands of Lieut.t R. Semmes U. S. Navy.

109. UNITED STATES ARMY LEAVING THE GULF SQUADRON

ment, on board one of the vessels, wrote:

The surf boats, with flags flying, loosed their cables, and, wheeling into line abreast by regular regiments and brigades, struck out for the shore, a mile distant. Surely a more magnificent sight could not be imagined than this scene presented.... The sky was clear and serene — not a breath of air was stirring — the surf, with slow and measured swell, was sweeping lazily upon the shore — the sinking sun, tipping the far-off peak of Orizaba, flashed with golden light on the burnished arms and white trappings of the troops, who, in their broad line of boats, were striving with emulous excitement to be first on shore. From the decks of the vessels, the remaining troops watched the scene with intense anxiety and painful suspense, their eyes glancing alternately from the boats to the shore, from whence they expected each moment to see the flash of arms.[6]

Another soldier, Private George Ballentine, an Englishman serving in the U.S. Army, recorded: "The scene was certainly exciting and imposing; the military bands from different regiments stationed on the decks of the steamers, transports, and men-of-war played the national airs of 'Yankee Doodle,' 'Hail Columbia,' and the 'Star Spangled Banner.' Ten thousand of our own troops were anxious and eager spectators, while the English, French, and Spanish fleets had each of their representatives scanning our operations with critical eye, and all looking with curiosity to see the spectacle of our invasion."[7]

1. For details of this operation see Bauer, *Surfboats and Horse Marines*, pp. 75-82; also Oswandel, *Notes of the Mexican War*, pp. 62-67.

2. A native of Maine, Ladd entered the navy in March 1839; after serving in the South Atlantic and Mediterranean, he attended the Naval School at Philadelphia, graduating as a passed midshipman in 1845. At the outbreak of the Mexican War he was assigned to the *Spitfire*, commanded by Josiah Tatnall and Lieutenant John J. Glasson. After the capture of Veracruz the *Spitfire* took part in the expedition against the river port of Tuxpan (see cat. no. 118). Mugridge speculates: "Ladd may have received a wound or fallen victim to the prevalent fevers.... He returned to the United States and died in the Naval Hospital at Norfolk, Virginia, on November 26, 1847." (*Album of American Battle Art*, p. 137; see also cat. no. 118, note 4.) For documentation of Ladd's naval career, see *Register of the Commissioned and Warrant Officers of the Navy of the United States; Including Officers of the Marine Corps, &c. for the Year 1842* (Washington, D.C., 1842), pp. 43, 64; for 1843, pp. 43, 65; for 1844, pp. 44, 66; for 1845, pp. 44-45; for 1846, pp. 50-51; for 1847, pp. 68-69, 117.

3. Parker, *Recollections*, p. 84. According to Bauer, *Surfboats and Horse Marines*, p. 66, the largest size surfboat could carry "45 or more men."

4. Two frigates were involved in the landing, the *Raritan* and the *Potomac*; the sloop-of-war could be either the *St. Mary's* or the *Albany*. (Bauer, *Surfboats and Horse Marines*, p. 264.) The logbook of the *Spitfire* notes that the ship carried three companies of Worth's Eighth Infantry that day (RG 45, National Archives, Washington, D.C.).

5. Mount Orizaba (Citlaltépetl), over 18,000 feet high, is the tallest mountain in Mexico and is about seventy-five miles from the coast. Ladd may have compressed the field of vision to include it. (See Moore, *Scott's Campaign in Mexico*, p. 7.)

6. John Blount Robertson, *Reminiscences of a Campaign in Mexico; by a Member of "the Bloody First"* (Nashville: John York & Co., 1849), pp. 218-19. Raphael Semmes, the officer in charge of the surfboats, also described the scene in *Service Afloat and Ashore*, pp. 126-28, as did Commodore David Conner in his official report, dated March 10, 1847 (published in "Reports and Despatches Exhibiting the Operations of the United States Naval Forces, During the War With Mexico," *Message from the President of the United States to the Two Houses of Congress*, House Ex. Doc. 1, 30th Congress, 2d Session [Washington, D.C.: Wendell and Van Benthuysen, 1848]). For good secondary accounts that use eyewitness source material, see Bauer, *Surfboats and Horse Marines*, pp. 75-82, and Smith, *War with Mexico*, 2:17-26, 333-37.

7. Ballentine, *Autobiography*, pp. 119-27.

110.
Henry Dacre after Charles Crillon Barton
LANDING OF THE U.S. ARMY UNDER GENERAL SCOTT, ON THE BEACH NEAR VERA CRUZ MARCH 9TH. 1847.
Lithograph, 1847
13-1/2 x 24 in. (34.3 x 60.8 cm.)
l.l.: "On Stone by H. Dacre."
l.r.: "P. S. Duval Lith. Philada."
l.c. below title: "Drawn on the Spot by Lieutenant Charles C. Barton, U.S. Navy. / Published by P. S. Duval, No.7 Bank Alley, Philadelphia / Entered according to act of Congress in the year 1847 by P. S. Duval in the Clerk's Office of the District Court of the Eastern Dist. of Pa."
Courtesy of Prints and Photographs Division, Library of Congress, Washington, D.C.

Another eyewitness to sketch the landing operations was Lieutenant Charles Barton of the sloop-of-war *St. Mary's*. In this view the ships of the Home Squadron are seen in the middle and right distance, at anchor between Sacrificios and the landing site at Collado Beach. The big steamer to the right of center with the pennant flying at its main mast may represent the *Princeton*. The frigate *Raritan*, Commodore Conner's flagship, may be the ship in the center with the pennant at the top of its main mast. General Scott's flagship, the army steamer *Massachusetts*, may be the little side-wheeler just to the right of center, nearest the shore; it carries a small pennant at its stern. The other ships of the landing squadron are harder to identify.[1] In the left distance are two of the schooner-gunboats of the light-draft Mosquito Fleet, along with one of the small steamers.

At 4:00 P.M. the *St. Mary's* surfboat detail of seventy men (Barton no doubt among them) began picking up the men of General Worth's division, who were nearby in the *Princeton*, the *Raritan*, and

LANDING OF THE U.S. ARMY UNDER GENERAL SCOTT, ON THE BEACH NEAR VERA CRUZ MARCH 9TH 1847.

Drawn on the Spot by Lieutenant Charles C. Barton, U.S. Navy.

Published by P.S Duval. No 7 Bank Alley Philadelphia

110. LANDING OF THE U.S. ARMY ON THE BEACH NEAR VERA CRUZ

the army transport *Edith*.[2] The surfboats (in the left distance and foreground) formed in line and raced for the shore. (The waving sailor at the helm of the nearest surfboat at far left may represent a friend of Barton's or the artist himself.) Within the hour General Worth and his entire division had landed and formed their lines, deployed to the right and left, and were advancing up the sand hills, having met, almost incredibly, no opposition from the Mexicans. Later that evening the surfboats landed Patterson's and Twiggs's divisions; by midnight more than 8,600 men had been put ashore without any accident or loss of life. The next morning more troops and supplies were landed, four surfboats from the *St. Mary's* carrying the field officers' horses and horse equipage.[3] Sometime during or soon after all of this activity, the sixty-three-year-old Lieutenant Barton took time to catch his breath and sketch.[4]

1. It is unfortunate that Barton did not give us a descriptive key for the print. The *Princeton* — a 672-ton screw-driven steamship, mounting one eight-inch shell gun, twelve forty-two-pounder carronades, and carrying 166 men — had a folding smokestack that might not be visible in the picture. Thus the steamer might be confused with any one of the larger sailing frigates, such as the *Raritan*. The latter displaced 1,708 tons and carried eight eight-inch shell guns, forty-six thirty-two-pounders, and 480 men. (Bauer, *Surfboats and Horse Marines*, pp. 254, 257.) The little steamer in the center might also be the *Petrita*. The three-masted ship at the far left of the landing squadron (just above the American flag on the beach) also appears to have a smokestack. This could be the big transport steamer *New Orleans*.

2. Bauer, *Surfboats and Horse Marines*, p. 78, identifies the ships in which Worth's division was transported. Information on the activities of Barton and the *St. Mary's* is drawn from the ship's logbook, March 9, 1847, RG 45, National Archives, Washington, D.C.

3. Eyewitness accounts of the landing include Moore, *Scott's Campaign in Mexico*, p. 6; Parker, *Recollections*, p. 84; and Bruell, *Sea Memories*, pp. 50-51. Historian K. Jack Bauer comments on the absence of casualties in the operation: "Even in the second half of the twentieth century, with all its technical advances in amphibious warfare, that would be a considerable achievement; in 1847, it was a tremendous accomplishment." (*Surfboats and Horse Marines*, p. 82.)

4. Compare this print with a watercolor sketch of the *Investment of Vera Cruz, March 10, 1847* by Lieutenant (later General) Alfred Sully of the Second Infantry, reproduced in The Chapellier Galleries, New York, auction catalogue, *American Art Selections*, vol. 6, no. 40. It is also reproduced in *American Heritage* 16 (Dec. 1964): 54.

111. See Plate 11
Artist unknown
LANDING OF THE TROOPS AT VERA CRUZ
Chromolithograph, 1848
12-1/2 x 18-7/16 in. (31.8 x 46.8 cm.)
From John Frost, *Pictorial History of Mexico and the Mexican War* (Philadelphia: Thomas, Cowperthwait and Co., 1848), frontispiece
ACM 14.80

This print is chiefly important as an early example of American chromolithography. It was produced as the frontispiece for John Frost's *Pictorial History of Mexico and the Mexican War* (1848), lithographed by the Philadelphia firms of Wagner & McGuigan and P. S. Duval. (See the discussion of chromolithography and Frost's book in Rick Stewart's essay.) The two firms' versions differ slightly, but both contain a number of glaring inaccuracies. In the version illustrated here, lithographed by P. S. Duval, flames engulf the castle of San Juan de Ulúa and the entire city of Veracruz, an exaggeration that provides more color to emphasize the new technology of chromolithography. The landmarks are oriented to suggest that the view was taken from the north, when in fact the landing was made southeast of the city. If the lithographers worked from an eyewitness sketch, they failed to reverse the image on stone so that it would print in its proper orientation. The Wagner & McGuigan version (fig. 22) also mistakes the soldiers' headgear, giving them shakos instead of forage caps.

Like this chromolithograph, popular prints of the bombardment and landing at Veracruz were often inaccurate. Naval veteran W. H. Parker tried to set the record straight when he wrote many years later: "It is generally thought that Vera Cruz and the Castle of San Juan were bombarded by the [entire] fleet. I have seen this stated in more than one 'history,' and recollect going to see a panorama in Boston shortly after the war which represented the fleet bombarding the castle while the troops were being landed on the *north* side of Vera Cruz."[1]

Philadelphia educator John Frost wrote two other popular histories of the Mexican War, *The Mexican War & Its Warriors* (New Haven and Philadelphia, 1848) and *Life of Major General Zachary Taylor with Notices of the War in New Mexico, California, and in Southern Mexico...* (New York: D. Appleton & Co., 1847). In all three books the illustrations were generally not based on eyewitness materials, though some of the portraits credit daguerreotype sources.

1. Parker, *Recollections*, p. 92.

112.   See Plate 12
After Henry Walke
THE U.S. STEAM FRIGATE MISSISSIPPI, COMRE. M. C. PERRY.
Toned lithograph (hand colored), 1847
15-7/16 x 22-1/2 in. (39.2 x 57.2 cm.)
u.c.: "Naval Portfolio No. 1. / Naval Scenes in the Mexican War. By H. Walke Lieut. U.S. Navy."
l.l.: "Lith of Sarony & Major"
l.c.: "Entered according to Act of Congress in the year 1847 by Sarony & Major in the Clerk office of the district Court of the Southern district of New York."
l.r.: "Executed by H. Walke Lt. U.S.N."
l.c. below title: "Going out to the relief of the American Steamer Hunter a French Bark (her prize) and an American Pilot Boat wrecked on Green Island reef near Vera Cruize March 21st. 1847. / Published by Sarony & Major 117 Fulton St. New York."
ACM 33.76/1

While the U.S. Army began to encircle Veracruz by constructing trenches and batteries on the land, the navy landed more troops and supplies and continued its blockade of the port, despite furious northers that hampered the operations. On March 20, while one of these storms threatened, the steamship *Mississippi* arrived off Sacrificios with the new commander of the Home Squadron, Commodore Matthew C. Perry.[1]

Perry was probably the navy's greatest authority on the new steam warships of his time and had been an advisor for the design and construction of the *Mississippi*.[2] Completed by the Philadelphia Navy Yard in 1841, this barque-rigged ship had two coal-burning side-lever steam engines that turned two paddle wheels, each twenty-eight feet in diameter. It carried two ten-inch and eight eight-inch shell guns of the Paixhans type and a crew of 257 men. The *Mississippi*

was a workhorse for the Home Squadron in the Gulf blockade throughout most of the war, but because of a comparatively deep draft it could not cross the bars at the mouths of the Mexican rivers.[3]

Early on the morning of March 21, as the norther gathered strength, the captain of an armed American steam schooner came on board the *Mississippi* to report that his vessel, the S.S. *Hunter*, and two others had run aground on the reef at Isla Verde ("Green Island" in the inscription of this print), a few miles offshore from Sacrificios. On board these wrecked vessels were about sixty people, including a mother and child. Commodore Perry got the *Mississippi* under way to rescue them; a few minutes later Commodore Conner, in the *Raritan*, signaled the fleet that "Commodore Perry commands the squadron," and the broad, blue pennant of the squadron commander was hoisted to the top of the mainmast on the *Mississippi* (where it appears in the print). Captain Isaac Mayo, four officers, and a number of seamen aboard the *Mississippi* volunteered to man three of the ship's cutters and a whale boat to save the passengers of the stricken vessels. By late morning all had been brought to shore and the *Mississippi*'s boats had returned safely to the ship.[4]

U.S. Navy Lieutenant Henry Walke depicted this dramatic scene, which was lithographed later that year by the firm of Sarony & Major in New York as the first print of Walke's *Naval Portfolio*.[5] The artist's ship, the *Vesuvius*, did not play a major role in the operations at Veracruz, and thus Walke may have had enough free time to sketch.[6]

Many interesting details appear in the print. The *Mississippi*'s engines strain against the rough sea; one of her boats casts off to assist the survivors of the wrecks, which may be seen just to the left of the ship. Beyond the wrecks, at right, one can just make out the walls of the castle of San Juan de Ulúa, and to the left, the walls, domes, and towers of Veracruz. At far left are the vessels at anchor in the harbor. Among these one can make out a ship-of-the-line, which, if not a foreign vessel, might be the U.S. line-of-battle ship *Ohio*, and the British steamer H.M.S. *Daring*, which was reportedly lying near the wrecks.[7] Unlike some of Walke's prints, this one probably was printed with the same left-right orientation as his original sketch; the ships at anchor off Veracruz appear to be properly located and the wind is correctly shown blowing from the north.

Nathaniel Currier distributed the *Naval Portfolio* for Sarony & Major. In a small, one-day advertisement in the New York *Herald* for April 12, 1848, Currier announced that the portfolio was just published and was for sale at his shop at 152 Nassau Street.[8] Currier also copied this Sarony & Major print and issued it in reverse in 1848 under the title *U.S. Steam Frigate Mississippi, In the Gulf of Mexico. March 1847*. The Currier view omits the background details and focuses entirely on the ships.[9]

1. Bauer, *Surfboats and Horse Marines*, pp. 85-88. Matthew C. Perry (1794-1858) was a younger brother of the hero of the battle of Lake Erie, Oliver Hazard Perry; he later commanded the expedition that opened Japan to American commerce. For an account of his career see Morison, *"Old Bruin"*.
2. Bauer, *Surfboats and Horse Marines*, p. 87.
3. Ibid., pp. 44-45, 256. The *Mississippi* became for the new steam navy what the *Constitution* had been to the old sailing navy. It served in Perry's Japan expedition and in the Civil War, before being sunk in the Mississippi River by Confederate batteries at Port Hudson, Louisiana, on March 14, 1863. In 1883, naval officer William H. Parker wrote affectionately of the "good old steamship *Mississippi*, a ship that did more hard work in her time than any

steamer in the Navy has done since" (*Recollections*, p. 73).
4. Morison, *"Old Bruin"*, p. 215; Bauer, *Surfboats and Horse Marines*, pp. 86-88; Logbook, U.S. Steamship *Mississippi*, RG 45, National Archives, Washington, D.C. Furber, *Twelve Months Volunteer*, pp. 506-7, also mentioned the wreck of the *Hunter*, but mistakenly believed it happened during a chase.
5. Walke (1808-96) was born on a plantation near Norfolk, Virginia, and raised in Virginia and Ohio; he entered the U.S. Navy as a midshipman in 1827. Some of his early watercolors are believed to date from 1836-39, when he served with the Pacific Squadron on the ship-of-the-line *North Carolina*. In February 1847 he was made first lieutenant under Commander G. A. Magruder on board the bomb brig *Vesuvius*; after the siege of Veracruz he participated in the Tuxpan River expedition in April and the Tabasco River expedition in June (see cat. nos. 118-23). Surprisingly, his numerous duties as second-in-command aboard the *Vesuvius* left him time to record several scenes of these operations in the sketches from which the lithographs of his *Naval Portfolio* were drawn. In New York during a nine-month leave in 1847-48, Walke himself drew four of the images on stone for the series.
Around 1855 Walke collaborated with expeditionary artist Wilhelm Heine on at least a couple of the Sarony & Major lithographed illustrations for Commodore Matthew C. Perry's *Narrative of the Expedition of an American Squadron to the China Seas and Japan. Performed in the Years 1852, 1853, and 1854* (Washington, D.C.: Beverly Tucker, U.S. printer, 1856). During the Civil War Walke served in the Union navy, achieving notable success in the river warfare of the Mississippi. He retired from the navy as a rear admiral in 1871. In later years he wrote and illustrated *Naval Scenes and Reminiscences of the Civil War in the United States on the Southern and Western Waters* (New York: F. R. Reed and Co., 1877), and furnished numerous sketches and illustrations for other books and articles on Civil War naval actions. (See especially Audrey Gardner Wright, "Henry Walke, 1808-1896: Romantic Painter, American Naval Hero," M.F.A. thesis, George Washington University, 1971; also Mugridge, *Album of American Battle Art*, pp. 137-38, and the exhibition checklist "The Legacy of Two Admirals: John A. Dahlgren (1809-1870), Henry Walke (1809-1896)," United States Naval Academy Museum, Annapolis, Maryland, May-August 1974.)
6. Donald Mugridge pointed this out in his catalogue *Album of American Battle Art*, p. 137.
7. Bauer, *Surfboats and Horse Marines*, p. 88.
8. New York *Herald*, April 12, 1848, p. 3.
9. An impression is in the Prints and Photographs Division of the Library of Congress.

113.
After James M. Ladd
BOMBARDMENT OF VERA CRUZ, MARCH 1847, ATTACK OF THE GUN BOATS UPON THE CITY, & CASTLE OF SAN JUAN DE ULLOA.
Lithograph (hand colored), 1847
8 x 13-1/8 in. (20.3 x 33.3 cm.)
l.l.: "Lith. & Pub. by N. Currier,"
l.c.: "Entered according to Act of Congress in the year 1847 by N. Currier, in the Clerk's office of the District Court of the Southern District of New York."
l.r.: "152 Nassau St. Cor. of Spruce N. Y."
l.l. to l.r.: "Falcon. Lt. Glasson. Reefer. Lt. Sterett. Vixen. Comd. Sands. Petrel. Lt. Shaw. Bonita. Lt. Benham. Spitfire. Comd. Tattnall. Tampico. Lt. Griffin."
l.c. below title: "Commanded by Josiah Tatnall Esq. U.S.N. / From a sketch taken on board the Steamer Spitfire, during the action, by J. M. Ladd U.S.N. / 467."
ACM 69.71

This is one of the best prints illustrating the ships of the renowned Mosquito Fleet. At the beginning of the war with Mexico, the U.S. Navy sorely lacked light-draft vessels that could operate along Mexico's shallow coastal waters and rivers. In May 1846, the Navy purchased several small ships originally intended for the Mexican navy, then under construction at the shipbuilding firm of Brown and Bell in New York. Two of these were the light-draft steamers *Spitfire* and *Vixen*, which appear second from right and fifth from right respectively. They were 118 feet long and 22-1/2 feet on beam, driven by side wheels enclosed in large paddle boxes; each carried a crew of fifty. The *Spitfire* mounted one eight-inch Paixhans shell gun and two thirty-two-pounder carronades; the *Vixen*, three thirty-two-pounder carronades. These vessels were the best of all the small steamers operating

LITH. & PUB. BY N. CURRIER.　152 NASSAU ST. COR. OF SPRUCE N.Y.

Falcon. Lt Glasson.　Reefer. Lt Sterett.　Entered according to Act of Congress in the year 1847 by N. Currier, in the Clerk's office of the District Court of the Southern District of New York.　Tampico. Lt Griffin.

Vixen. Comd. Sands.　Petrel. Lt Shaw.　Bonita. Lt Benham.　Spitfire. Comd. Tattnall.

BOMBARDMENT OF VERA CRUZ, MARCH 1847

ATTACK OF THE GUN BOATS UPON THE CITY, & CASTLE OF SAN JUAN DE ULLOA.

COMMANDED BY JOSIAH TATNALL ESQ. U. S. N.

From a sketch taken on board the Steamer Spitfire, during the action, by J. M. Ladd U. S. N.

113. Bombardment of Vera Cruz, Attack of the Gun Boats

in the Gulf, but they handled poorly in a rough sea and were subject to frequent engine troubles. Ladd's print also shows three small schooners purchased from Brown and Bell: the *Reefer* (second from left), the *Petrel* (fourth from left), and the *Bonita* (fifth from left). Each was only fifty-nine feet long, carried one thirty-two-pounder carronade, and was manned by a crew of forty. They were uniquely suited for Mexican service, and their crews developed great pride in them.

Two other schooner-gunboats of the Mosquito Fleet appear in the print, the *Falcon* (at far left) and the *Tampico* (at far right). Formerly named the *Isabel* and the *Pueblano* respectively, they were seized as prizes when the Americans captured the town of Tampico on November 14, 1846; both had similar characteristics to the *Reefer*, *Petrel*, and *Bonita*.[1]

By March 22, 1847, the army had constructed land batteries around the city of Veracruz and was in position to open the siege. To support the army, Commodore Perry dispatched the Mosquito Fleet under Commander Josiah Tatnall in the *Spitfire*. On March 22 and 23 these ships took up a position off Point Hornos on the east side of Veracruz, close in to the city and castle. Their small size gave them a precarious safety; the schooner *Petrel* was in fact badly hit in the course of the action and had to be towed out by one of the steamers. The artist of this view, Midshipman James Ladd aboard the *Spitfire*, had a particularly fine opportunity to observe the operations.[2]

Private George Furber of the First Tennessee Volunteers also watched these developments from his position on a sand hill on Collado Beach (out of the picture to the left):

In the city before us, and around the walls in the heavy forts, are nearly five thousand men, besides the inhabitants, well armed, with near two hundred cannon and mortars; and in the castle to the right are more than a thousand men; with more than two hundred heavy cannon and mortars, with plenty of water and provisions, they say.

. . . Turn around to the right; — see, gracefully approaching, five slender schooners on the water, and with them two steamers; — they take their positions. They are what is called the Mosquito Fleet, and each one carries heavy guns. . . . See the smoke rising from them; — how rapidly they fire.

Now, a grand scene is before us. — Seven large mortars and four six-inch cohorns, smaller, but destructive, from the trenches of batteries Nos. 1, 2, and 3, are at work, and seven heavy guns from the mosquito fleet; while so many are opening in reply from the castle and city, that we cannot keep the account.

. . . Observe the bright flashes there, as they for the instant light up the battlements of the castle, and render the heavy volumes of smoke above it luminous against the surrounding darkness. See the same from the vessels: one instant by the light you perceive the whole outline of the vessel, her masts, and spars, and smoke; and then all is dark, but again illumined; above the whole, describing long arcs of circles high in the air, see the bomb-shells rising over and falling, shown in their courses by the fuses, which twinkle like bright red stars.[3]

1. Information on the ships of the Mosquito Fleet is based on Bauer, *Surfboats and Horse Marines*, pp. 25, 54-57, 253-59. See also Parker, *Recollections*, p. 65.

2. For more on Ladd, see cat. no. 109, note 2. He signed many of the entries in the *Spitfire*'s logbook (RG 45, National Archives); among the items listed as received on board on August 24, 1846, are fifty quills and drawing paper. The Mosquito Fleet's operations around Veracruz are detailed in Bauer, *Surfboats and Horse Marines*, pp. 88-91; Semmes, *Service Afloat and Ashore*, pp. 130-32; and Smith and Judah, *Chronicles of the Gringos*, p. 191. The New York *Herald*, April 16, 1847, p. 1, contains a map showing the position of the Mosquito Fleet and mentions that the *Petrel* was struck and the *Spitfire* had a boat stove in by Mexican shells.

3. Furber, *Twelve Months Volunteer*, pp. 516-21. In spite of the many lithographs purporting to show the bombardment of Veracruz by the American fleet, Ladd's view is the only one found to be significantly accurate. Nathaniel Currier produced a similar but inaccurate print titled *Naval Bombardment of Vera Cruz. March 1847* (an impression is in the Chicago Historical Society). This print, possibly based on Ladd's view, depicts the steamer gunboats with three masts rather than two. (The three-masted steamer *Scorpion* had not yet arrived off Veracruz at this time.) Other popular prints were even more inaccurate. Sarony & Major published one view, *Victorious Bombardment of Vera Cruz, by the United Forces of the Army and Navy of the U. S. March 24th and 25th. 1847* (Amon Carter Museum 70.71), showing three American line-of-battle ships lobbing shells just a few yards off San Juan de Ulúa and the city. The line-of-battle ship *Ohio* was the only ship of this size in the American squadron at this time, and it never drew up close enough to shell the castle or city. Rick Stewart's essay discusses some of the more improbable of the popular prints.

114.

Gustavus Pfau after Henry Walke
THE U.S. NAVAL BATTERY DURING THE
BOMBARDMENT OF VERA CRUZ ON THE
24 AND 25 OF MARCH 1847.
Toned lithograph (hand colored), 1848
15-1/8 x 22-9/16 in. (38.4 x 57.3 cm.)
u.c.: "Naval Portfolio No. 8, Naval Scines in
the Mexican War by H. Walke Lieut. U.S.
Navy."
l.l.: "Painted by H. Walke Lt. U.S.N. Drawn
on Stone by Pfau."
l.c.: "Entered according to Act of Congress in
the year 1848 by Sarony & Major in the
Clerks Office of the district court of the
Southern District of N. York"
l.r.: "Lith. of Sarony & Major N. York."
l.l. to l.r., first column: "March 24th. / Capt.
J. H. Aulick. / March 25th. / Capt. J.
Mayo." second column: "Potomac, Gun 32
lbs. / Comre. A.S. Mackenzie. / ordinance
officer. / Lt. J. S. Biddle." third column:
"St. Mary's, Gun 68 lbs. / Lt. C. H. A. H.
Kennedy. / Lt. C. Steedman." fourth column:
"Albany, Gun, 68 lbs. / Lt. O. H. Perry. / Lt.
S. B. Bissell. / Mastr. Jm. Crossan." fifth col-
umn: "Mississippi, Gun, 68 lbs. / Lt. S. S.
Lee. / Lt. Jr. De Camp." sixth column:
"Potomac Gun 32 lbs. / Lt. A. S. Baldwin. /
Lt. J. M. Frailey." seventh column: "Rarritan
Gun 32 lbs. / Lt. H. Ingersoll. / Lt. R.
Semmes."
l.c. below title: "The Battery was composed of
heavy Guns. From the U.S. Squadron under
Comore. M. C. Perry, and Commanded by
the Officers in the following order opposite
their respective Guns. / Published by Sarony
& Major 117 Fulton St. New York."
ACM 33.76/8

Even with the help of the Mosquito Fleet, the army's siege guns were not adequate to reduce the city's fortifications before the onset of the *vomito* season.[1] Six heavy guns from the navy were therefore brought ashore to bombard the city. Three sixty-eight-pounders (eight-inch shell guns of the Paixhans type) and three long thirty-two-pounders were landed. Each gun was dragged with great effort a dis-tance of about three miles through loose sand and chaparral (including thorny mesquite and prickly pears) by two hundred seamen and army volunteers to a position on a hill overlooking the city, where they were manned by navy personnel.[2]

This naval battery is the subject of Navy Lieutenant Henry Walke's print. The view was taken from behind the bat-tery, probably near a trench for volunteer infantry who supported the gunners.[3] The viewer looks north toward the city of Veracruz; to the far right is the Gulf of Mexico, on the city's northeastern side.

Walke, the executive officer of the bomb-brig *Vesuvius* stationed off Vera-cruz, probably made notes or sketches on the spot while on shore leave or detached service. The *Vesuvius* apparently did not take a direct part in the bombardment of the city, so Walke perhaps had time on his hands.[4]

Fortunately, Walke's original water-color sketch (114a) for the print still exists in the U.S. Naval Academy Museum at Annapolis; a comparison of the two pic-tures demonstrates how much a print may differ from its original source. In this case the lithographer, Gustavus Pfau, working for Sarony & Major, took more than a few liberties with certain details of Walke's sketch.[5] Pfau lessened the picto-rial depth of the composition, diminishing the depression in the right foreground,

which in the original was a deep hole (the magazine, where the shot and shells were stored) and a trench (for the protection of the gun crews). Figures have been com-pletely redrawn without respect for Walke's original groupings. For example, three seamen hold the dead or wounded officer in a classical pose in the left fore-ground of the print, while in the original watercolor, four seamen, in a more natu-ral and balanced arrangement, carry the officer head first off the hill. Uniforms have been altered at random in the print (for example, some pantaloons are white in the print but dark blue in Walke's original), although they generally remain accurate.[6] In many cases the individual figures are more awkwardly rendered. Pfau omitted the wheels or blocks on the sides of the gun trucks, which are visible in the original. The city in the distance has not been greatly altered, but the per-spective of the left portion of the city wall has been distorted. Also, Mexican flags flying over various forts do not appear in the print. Exploding mortar shells can be traced in a daylight sky in the print, whereas according to Walke's original and eyewitness descriptions they could not. The transparent delicacy and vague suggestiveness inherent in the watercolor medium are lost in the transcription to stone, where all outlines are relatively crisp and clean. In general, Pfau's changes deprive the print of some accuracy and show a lack of understanding of some details of Walke's original. This distortion of the artist's intent is a common hazard in reading historical prints for historical content.

The fortifications and emplacements for this battery ("Battery Number Five") were designed by Captain Robert E. Lee of the Army Corps of Engineers.[7] Built by seamen and volunteer infantrymen, the

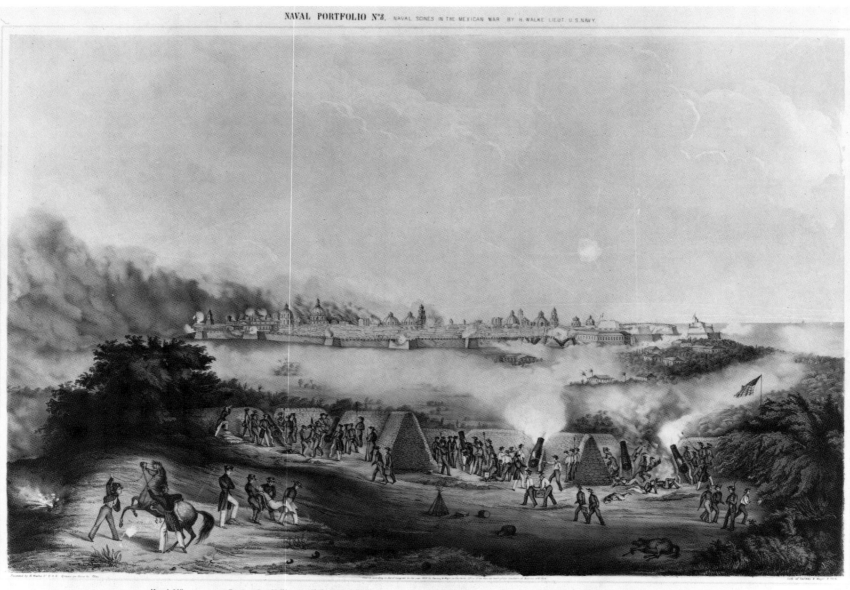

114. NAVAL BATTERY DURING THE BOMBARDMENT OF VERA CRUZ

battery had thick chaparral at its front to conceal it from the view of the Mexicans in the city for as long as possible during its construction. As depicted in the print and described in written accounts, the breastworks were built of sandbags and had six embrasures for the guns. Two traverses, also built of sandbags, divided the battery into three sections to protect the crews from exploding shells. Northers delayed the battery's completion, but finally, on March 24, all the guns were in place.

The navy personnel detached to man the guns were all volunteers, eager for a chance to fight. They were organized into shifts to alternate approximately every six hours; Captain J. H. Aulick of the *Potomac* commanded the first shift and Captain J. Mayo the second. The print's descriptive key lists each gun and the ship it belonged to, then a row of names of officers in the first shift and a row of names for the second shift. Among the officers listed are Sydney Smith Lee (Robert E. Lee's brother), Raphael Semmes, and Oliver Hazard Perry, Jr., son of the Perry of Lake Erie fame and nephew of Commodore M. C. Perry. As the inscription implies that the view is a composite of two days' action, it may be futile to try to identify particular individuals among the various crews. The Mexican shell bursting near one of the guns at right, however, may refer to a particular incident on March 24 when Lieutenant A. S. Baldwin and several men from the *Potomac* were wounded.

Private George Furber of the First Tennessee, who had helped construct the battery and drag one of the guns to it, watched the crews as they opened fire:

The chapparal in front, on the brow of the hill, was quietly cut down, and, to the astonishment of the Mexicans, so elated at the slackening fire of the mortar batteries, this opened its six pieces, with a terrific and well-directed discharge of its heavy shot; which especially the sixty-eights, made the stones and mortar fly from the buildings and walls — they crashed through blocks at a time, and a different aspect was placed upon the day. All the Mexican batteries, that could bear, immediately turned their fire upon the new and destructive work....In a short time after it opened, four sailors within it were killed, two badly wounded, and Lieut. Baldwin slightly. The dead were taken off, down to Malibran....The battery was much torn to pieces by the shot of the enemy.[8]

Each post along the city's walls had a name, and many are visible in the print. In the far right distance, on the water's edge, is Fort Santiago. Just to its left, and actually farther behind in the harbor, is a semicircle of guns along a wall, perhaps part of the sea battery of the castle of San Juan de Ulúa; many of its guns could not be brought to bear on the American positions.[9] The substantial building to its left

114A. Naval Battery During the Bombardment of Vera Cruz

and closer to the viewer is a combination barracks and prison. Just to its right was the Gate of Mercy, near which was a "very active" fort. Toward the left along the wall is a section of rubble, over which a puff of smoke may be seen — probably Fort Santa Barbara, against which the naval battery directed much of its fire. The remaining forts along the wall, continuing left, are probably San Fernando, Santa Gertrudis, San Javier and the New Gate, San Matheo, and at the end probably San Juan, with the tower of San Concepción rising above.[10]

The American eyewitnesses spoke with admiration of the gallantry of the Mexican artillerists and related that the "ground was torn, blown, and plowed up in every direction." During the few lulls and at night the batteries were repaired by the volunteers, who spoke of hearing the "continual shrieking and wailing that rose from the city." Captain Robert E. Lee stood by his brother's gun during most of the action. In a letter home he wrote: "The shells thrown from our battery were constant and regular discharges, so beautiful in their flight and so destructive in their fall. It was awful! My heart bled for the inhabitants. The soldiers I did not care so much for, but it was terrible to think of the women and children."[11]

When the Mexican gunners ceased firing on the afternoon of March 25, the American sailors in the navy battery stood on the parapet and gave three cheers. The Mexican garrison had lost an estimated eighty soldiers killed and wounded. Among the civilians, both Mexican and foreign, including women and children, one hundred had been killed and many others wounded. The streets were littered with debris and corpses. The American losses were fourteen killed and fifty-nine wounded, including seven killed and eight wounded from the navy battery.[12] On March 29 a formal surrender ceremony was held, and the Mexican troops evacuated the city and castle.

1. Apparently no print was made from an eyewitness sketch depicting the army's siege operations at Veracruz. There are, however, numerous popular prints of this subject: James Baillie published at least one version, perhaps two (see fig. 10); Nathaniel Currier, three (see figs. 8, 9). Other popular prints depict *General Scott at the Taking of Vera Cruz*; *Colonel Harney's Dragoon Fight at Medelin, near Vera Cruz*; *The Surrender and Evacuation of Vera Cruz*; and *The Grand Salute at Vera Cruz*. None of these appear to have been made from eyewitness sketches. James Walker painted at least two views of an army siege battery in action (West Point Museum, West Point, New York). These might depict siege guns during the bombardment of Chapultepec, however, and apparently these paintings were never lithographed or engraved in the nineteenth century.

2. Parker, *Recollections*, pp. 93-95.

3. Ibid., p. 95.

4. Mugridge, *Album of American Battle Art*, p. 137.

5. A native of Germany, Pfau had recently arrived in America in 1848 when this lithograph was made. He worked for lithographic firms in New York and Boston as a topographical artist. (See Groce and Wallace, *Dictionary of Artists in America*, p. 503.)

6. For information on American naval uniforms in the Mexican War see James C. Tily, *The Uniforms of the United States Navy* (New York and London: Thomas Yoseloff, 1964), pp. 89-101.

7. Information on the navy battery's bombardment of Veracruz is derived from several eyewitness sources: Captains Aulick and Mayo in "Reports and Despatches Exhibiting the Operations of the United States Naval Forces," pp. 1181-85; a map titled *Landing of the Troops on the 9th. & Bombardment of Vera Cruz on the 22d., 23d., 24th., and 25th. of March 1847*, "Copied by H. L. Edwards from a draft drawn by order of Lieut. Col. H. Wilson, military and civil governor of Vera Cruz," lithographed by P. S. Duval of Philadelphia in 1847 (an impression is in the Geography and Map Division of the Library of Congress); Furber, *Twelve Months Volunteer*, pp. 502-53; Parker, *Recollections*, pp. 91-101; Semmes, *Service Afloat and Ashore*, pp. 133-42. See also Oswandel, *Notes of the Mexican War*, pp. 84-89. Good secondary accounts include Morison, *"Old Bruin"*, pp. 215-21; Bauer, *Surfboats and Horse Marines*, pp. 92-96; Smith, *War with Mexico*, 2:17-36.

8. Furber, *Twelve Months Volunteer*, p. 526.

9. The castle may not have been quite so visible from this position, and this could be an exaggeration on the part of the artist to call attention to its general location.

10. Ibid., pp. 526-31. Furber describes each of these forts in some detail. His own engraved sketch of the bombardment, the original for which was drawn from a hill near Collado Beach, is a useful comparison for Walke's print. Also see the map published in Roswell S. Ripley, *The War with Mexico*, 2: opp. p. 31; the map published in the New York *Herald*, March 11, 1847, p. 1; and the map cited in note 7.

11. Furber, *Twelve Months Volunteer*, pp. 526, 531, 535; Robert E. Lee, quoted by Philip Van Dorn Stern, *Robert E. Lee: The Man and the Soldier, A Pictorial Biography* (New York: Bonanza Books, 1963), p. 78. At least one popular print, by the Kelloggs, depicted the scene in the city during the bombardment (fig. 21).

12. Morison, *"Old Bruin"*, pp. 219-20; see also the sources listed in note 7.

115.   See Plate 13
Adolphe-Jean-Baptiste Bayot after Carl Nebel
BOMBARDMENT OF VERA-CRUZ
Toned lithograph (hand colored), 1851
10-13/16 x 16-11/16 in. (27.5 x 42.4 cm.)
l.l.: "C. Nebel fecit."
l.r.: "Bayot lith"
From George Wilkins Kendall, *The War Between the United States and Mexico Illustrated* (New York: D. Appleton & Company, 1851), plate 4
ACM 186.72/4

Carl Nebel also chose the naval battery as his viewpoint from which to illustrate the siege of Veracruz. Kendall explains: "The reasons which induced the artist to select the navy battery as the point from which to sketch his picture were numerous — among the most important its high and commanding position, the full view of the city obtained, the importance it had in its reduction, and to pay a compliment, well-merited if poor, to the spirited officers and sailors of the American squadron."[1] Kendall should perhaps have added another reason, namely the availability of Henry Walke's 1848 print of the same subject, from which Nebel could borrow. There is no evidence that Nebel was present at the siege. Although he probably traveled through the city shortly after or during the latter part of the war, the lack of certain details in his print suggests that he did not make sketches for it while there.

A comparison of the two prints may demonstrate Nebel's reliance on Walke. The distant buildings are more generalized in the former's print, as it focuses more on the action in the foreground. Nebel's reason for this may not be aerial perspective alone; he may not have drawn a view of Veracruz from this angle himself. The palm trees in Nebel's print are artistic devices that do not appear in Walke's print. That inveterate observer of minutiae, Private George C. Furber, made no mention of palm trees in his description of the position of the naval battery but did note that "this hill, like many of the others, is covered with a species of musquit, of which the sharp thorns are several times as large as the twigs on which they grow." Furber included an engraved sketch labeled "Twig of Musquit: Species found near Vera Cruz. — Natural Size." He also observed that "thorny chapparal" covered the vicinity.[2] Clearly Walke's print approximates this description better than Nebel's.

The ellipses at the breeches of the cannons in Nebel's print are poorly drawn, that is, they do not line up along the proper axis. Walke and his lithographer, Gustavus Pfau, were more successful in their treatment of ellipses, perhaps because only Walke observed them firsthand. The gun trucks have wheels or blocks beneath them in Walke's original watercolor; these do not appear in either of the prints. Finally, the magazine in Nebel's print, in the center foreground, is a hole with a very small opening as compared with the huge crater in Walke's watercolor and the disappearance of the magazine in Pfau's print. Nebel could have seen maps or read descriptions of the battery and positioned the magazine himself.

Nebel depicted the uniforms of the naval personnel with general accuracy, perhaps in part informed by Walke's work. Some of the officers wear the dark blue, long frock coats prescribed by naval regulations for undress. Others, probably midshipmen and enlisted men, wear short blue jackets. Some of the enlisted men appear without jackets, in frocks of white cloth lined with blue cotton cloth. Some officers and men wear white pantaloons designated for tropical climates, while others wear dark blue. This seems to have varied at the discretion of the commanding officers. The variety of headgear is interesting and generally accurate. Enlisted men wear flat, black hats, while officers wear either the blue undress caps with gold bands or straw hats.[3]

1. Kendall, *War Between the United States and Mexico Illustrated*, p. 22.
2. Furber, *Twelve Months Volunteer*, p. 552.
3. Tily, *Uniforms of the United States Navy*, pp. 89-101.

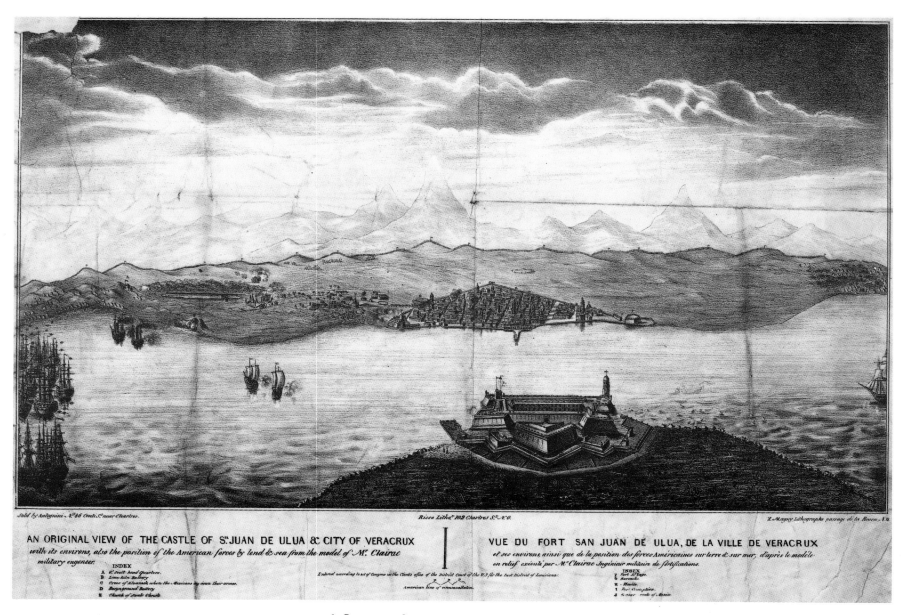

AN ORIGINAL VIEW OF THE CASTLE OF S.ᵗ JUAN DE ULUA & CITY OF VERACRUX
with its environs, also the position of the American forces by land & sea from the model of M.ʳ Clairac
military engineer.

INDEX
A   G.ˡ Scott head Quarters.
B   Lime kiln Battery
C   Grave of Alvarado where the Mexicans lay down their armes.
D   Burying ground Battery
E   Church of Santa Christi

VUE DU FORT SAN JUAN DE ULUA, DE LA VILLE DE VERACRUX
et ses environs, ainsi que de la position des forces Américaines sur terre & sur mer, d'après le modèle
en relief exécuté par M.ʳ Clairac Ingénieur militaire de fortifications.

INDEX
V   Fort S.ᵗ Jago.
Z   Barracks.
R   Moulin.
T   Port Conception.
J   Scieur made of Maria.

Entered according to act of Congress in the Clerks office of the District Court of the U.S for the East District of Louisiana.

American line of communication.

116. CASTLE OF SAN JUAN DE ULUA AND VERACRUX

116.

After a model by Clairac

AN ORIGINAL VIEW OF THE CASTLE OF
SN. JUAN DE ULUA & CITY OF VERACRUX
| VUE DU FORT SAN JUAN DE ULUA, DE
LA VILLE DE VERACRUX
Lithograph, c. 1847
14-1/4 x 25-1/8 in. (36.2 x 63.9 cm.)
l.l.: "Sold by Antognini No. 46 Conti St. near
Chartres."
l.c.: "Risso Lithor. 102 Chartres St. N.O."
l.r.: "X. Magny Lithographe passage de la
Bourse N.O."
l.l. below title: "with its environs, also the
position of the American forces by land & sea
from the model of Mr. Clairac / military
engineer. / Index / A Gl. Scott head quarters.
/ B Lime-Kiln Battery / C Cross of Alvarado,
where the Mexicans lay down their armes. /
D Burynground Battery / E Church of Santo
Christo."
l.c. below title: "Entered according to Act of
Congress in the Clerk's office of the District
Court of the U.S. for the East District of
Louisiana. / [diagram of hills with flags] /
American line of circumvallation."
l.r. below title: "et ses environs, ainsi que de
la position des forces Américaines sur terre &
sur mer; d'après le modéle / en relief exécuté
par Mr. Clairac Ingénieur militaire de fortifi-
cations. / Index / F Fort St. Yago. / G Bar-
racks. / H Moulle. / I Fort Conception. / J
Bergar route of Mexico."
Courtesy of Prints and Photographs Division,
Library of Congress, Washington, D.C.

This lithograph gives a bird's-eye view of
the city and castle from the northeast,
complete with a descriptive key.[1] It was
produced by New Orleans lithographers
Louis Xavier Magny and his brother Risso
Magny from a model exhibited in New
Orleans in "St. Charles street, opposite
the St. Charles Hotel" beginning on June
5, 1847.[2] The creator of the "modèle en
relief" was a French military fortifications

engineer named Clairac.[3] Clairac might
have served with the French forces in their
attack on Veracruz in 1838 and may have
possessed maps of the city and castle. He
could also have traveled to Veracruz in
1847 on one of the American transports
or packets out of New Orleans. Certainly
his model of the port and the disposition
of American troops indicates firsthand
knowledge.

The print is packed with detail. In
the center foreground stands the castle of
San Juan de Ulúa. At left are some of the
transports and warships of the Home
Squadron, from which small boats are
rowing toward Collado Beach. The
American line of investment extends along
the sandhills from the distant left to the
distant right. Tents mark the limits on
both ends, the tents at left occupied by
Worth's division, the tents at right by
Twiggs's. A flag on one of the hills immediately to the right of Worth's tents indicates the position of General Scott's
headquarters. Four small ships, two of
which are steamers, probably represent
the Mosquito Fleet, and the land mass
next to it is Point Hornos. Two of the
army's siege batteries are visible, with the
"lime-kiln battery" to the left of Point
Hornos, and beyond it the battery located
in one of the city cemeteries. The naval
battery, which is marked by explosions,
is in a direct line with the cemetery leading up from Point Hornos. Fort Santiago
anchors the left or southeast side of the
city wall, with Fort Concepción on the
right or north side of the city. The large
building on the southwestern side of the
city is the fortified barracks. The mole
juts out into the harbor almost from the
city's center.

1. Compare the print with the map in Ripley, *War
with Mexico*, 2: opp. p. 31.
2. *Daily Picayune*, June 5, 1847, p. 2. Louis Xavier
Magny (c. 1805-55) was born in Avignon and Risso
Magny (1798-1850) in Thore, France. Both
brothers were active in New Orleans from 1847
until their deaths, Louis Xavier being the more
prominent. (Mahé and McCaffrey, *Encyclopaedia
of New Orleans Artists*, p. 250.)
3. This man may have been related to "Hte. Clairac,"
a tailor with the New Orleans firm of Faibvre &
Clairac. (New Orleans City Directory for 1849, pp.
38, 66.)

117.

Artist unknown

CITY OF VERA CRUZ. FROM THE ROAD TO MEXICO. | VISTA DE VERA CRUZ. POR EL CAMINO DE MEXICO.

Lithograph (hand colored), 1847

9-1/4 x 12-3/8 in. (23.4 x 31.5 cm.) comp.

l.l.: "Lith. & Pub. by N. Currier,"

l.c.: "Entered according to Act of Congress in the year 1847 by N. Currier, in the Clerk's office of the District Court of the Southern District of N. Y."

l.r.: "152 Nassau St. Cor. of Spruce N. Y."

l.l. to l.r.: "San Juan de Ulúa. Conbento de San Francisco. Puerte de Mexico. Parroquia Santo Domingo. La Merced. / Farol. Cabildo. Baluarte de Conception. San Juan de Dios. Palacio Capilla Sr. del buen biaje."

Courtesy of Prints and Photographs Division, Library of Congress, Washington, D.C.

Currier's 1847 lithograph of the northwestern side of Veracruz was actually copied from a French print published sometime before the war, a lithograph by A. Saint-Aulaire after a sketch by S. Sarokins, printed by Thiery Brothers, Paris. Sarokins's sketch may date from the French occupation of the city in 1838.[1] Currier's key shows some of the forts and buildings bombarded by General Twiggs's division as it besieged this side of the city. After Veracruz surrendered, the Americans passed along the National Road, seen in the foreground, on their drive to Mexico City.[2]

1. The print is reproduced in The Old Print Shop *Portfolio*, 32:7 (1973), p. 148. "A. Saint-Aulaire" is probably Félix Achille Saint-Aulaire, born 1801. D. T. Egerton drew and published a similar but not identical view from the same side of the city in 1840.

2. Raphael Semmes left a description of this road in *Service Afloat and Ashore*, pp. 161-62.

117. VERA CRUZ FROM THE ROAD TO MEXICO

River Expeditions

118.

Joseph Vollmering after Henry Walke
THE U.S. NAVAL EXPEDITION UNDER
COMORE. M. C. PERRY, ASCENDING THE
TUSPAN RIVER...
Toned lithograph (hand colored), 1848
15-3/16 x 22-3/8 in. (38.6 x 56.8 cm.)
u.c.: "Naval Portfolio No. 2. Naval Scenes, in
the Mexican War by H. Walke, Lt. U.S. Navy."
l.l.: "Painted by H. Walke L. U.S.N. Drawn
on stone by J. Vollmering"
l.c.: "Entered according to Act of Congress in
the year 1848 by Sarony & Major in the
Clerks Office of the district Court of the
Southern district of N. York."
l.r.: "Lith of Sarony & Major."
l.c. continuation of title: "destroying the Forts,
and taking possession of the Port of Tuspan,
with the following Vessels and their Comers.
Steamer Spitfire, Comre. J. Tattnall. Steamer
Vixen Comre. J. R. Sands. / Steamer Scourge
Lt. Coming. S. Lockwood. Schooner Reefer.
Lt. Coming. T. Turner. Schooner Bonita. Lt.
Coming. T. G. Benham. Schooner Tampico.
Lt. Coming. Wm. P. Griffin. Schooner Petrel
Lt. Coming. T. D. Shaw. / with a detachment
of Officers and men in 35 barges, from the
U.S. Steamer Mississippi Comer. A. S.
Mackenzie, and Lt. J. De Camp. Ohio 74
Comer. L. M. Goldsborough. Potomac Lt. E.
R. Tompson. Raritan Capt. F. Forrest.
Albany. / Capt. S. L. Breeze. Germantown
Comer. F. Buchanan. John Adams Comer.
Wm. J. M. Cluney. Decatur Comer. R. S.
Pinckney. Bomb Brig Vesuvius Comer. G. A.
Magruder. Bomb Brig Etna Comer. G. J. Van
Brunt. B. Brig Hecla Lt. Comg. A. B. Fairfax.
/ April 19th 1847. / New York Pulished
by Sarony & Major 117 Fulton St."
ACM 33.76/2

This print and the five succeeding prints from Lieutenant Henry Walke's *Naval Portfolio* depict scenes from the U. S. Navy's expeditions up two Mexican rivers. Walke's views are perhaps the only surviving visual documentation of these operations, which, compared to the army's conquests, had very little impact on the outcome of the war and received very little attention from the American press and the publishers of popular lithographs.

Walke recorded the capture of the Mexican port town of Tuxpan while serving as executive officer of the bomb brig *Vesuvius*. His sketch was copied on stone by Joseph Vollmering and printed and published in 1848 by Sarony & Major of New York as number two in the series; Walke probably delivered his sketch to the lithographers in person sometime after the *Vesuvius* returned to Norfolk in the summer of 1848.[1] The print telescopes the action and the distances and exaggerates the height of some of the hills around the city. Nevertheless, as historian Samuel Eliot Morison has demonstrated in his masterful biography of Commodore Perry, the print records valuable historical detail.[2]

After the fall of Veracruz, Commodore Perry commanded the largest squadron of American ships ever assembled. To pursue aggressive attacks up the Mexican rivers, Perry organized and drilled an infantry brigade made up of volunteers from the ships' crews. Also available to him were small contingents of U. S. Marines. Tuxpan, one of his objectives, was the last important Mexican town on or near the Gulf not under American control. Located on a river by the same name, halfway between Veracruz and Tampico, it was fortified with guns captured from the U.S. brig-of-war *Truxton* and was

garrisoned by several hundred men under General Martín Perfecto de Cos, Santa Anna's brother-in-law.[3]

On April 18 the Mosquito Fleet (the steamers *Spitfire, Vixen*, and *Scourge* and schooner-gunboats *Bonita*, *Petrel*, and *Reefer*) entered the river; the *Spitfire* and *Vixen* had their masts removed to lighten their drafts in crossing the bar.[4] The steamers towed not only the schooners upriver, but also barges with a landing party from several other ships anchored outside the shallow bar, including the artist's ship *Vesuvius*. Naval officer Raphael Semmes was with the flotilla as it approached the town of Tuxpan:

> The river is a narrow stream, not averaging more than from two to three hundred yards in width, and is bordered by extensive marshes and lagunes for some distance up; which give place, a mile or two before reaching the town, to firm and thickly wooded banks; the tangled undergrowth running occasionally into the water. The town is situated on the left bank, and its preparations for defense were extensive and most judicious. In the lower end of the town, and immediately on the river bank, was an eminence of some eighty or one hundred feet in height, called Cerro del Hospital, on the summit of which was placed a thirty-two pounder carronade, mounted on a pivot, so as to command the river to the extent of its range, and surrounded by a ditch. At the base of this hill, and a little higher up the river, at the levee or landing-place of the town, was placed a nine-pounder carriage gun, for the protection of this point. On the opposite bank of the river were

THE U. S. NAVAL EXPEDITION UNDER COMᵒᴰᴿ M. C. PERRY.

118. NAVAL EXPEDITION ASCENDING THE TUSPAN RIVER

two forts, *La Peña*, or the Cliff, situated on a bluff sixty feet in height, about a mile and a half below the town, and the *Palma Sola* — so called from a solitary palm-tree, which grew within it — higher up, and at the junction of a small tributary with the Tuxpan.[5]

The steamers in Walke's print are, from left to right, *Vixen, Spitfire,* and *Scourge*; the schooner-gunboats are more difficult to identify. Tuxpan is in the center distance. Cerro del Hospital (Hospital Hill) is at right, La Peña at far left. La Palma Sola is apparently the smoking battery between two of the palm trees in the center of the print. The tributary joins with the Tuxpan River just beyond the steamer *Spitfire* in the center.[6]

When they came within range of the Mexican guns, the ships and boats under tow were cast off, to be powered during the engagement by sail and oar. Supported by a bombardment from the steamers and schooners, the boats' crews soon stormed La Peña, then Cerro del Hospital and Palma Sola, and carried the town. Tuxpan was occupied for four days while the forts were dismantled. On April 22 Perry evacuated the town, leaving two ships to watch the river mouth.[7]

1. Vollmering was born in Anhalt, Germany, in 1810 and worked in New York from 1847 until his death in 1887. He exhibited at the National Academy of Design, of which he was an associate member, and the American Art-Union. (Groce and Wallace, *Dictionary of Artists in America*, p. 651.) Bauer mentions Perry's order for the *Vesuvius* to leave for Norfolk around July 7, 1848 (*Surfboats and Horse Marines*, p. 131). Since some of the prints for the *Naval Portfolio* were drawn on stone by Walke himself, he probably delivered the sketches in person.

2. Morison, *"Old Bruin"*, pp. 224-27.

3. The *Truxton* had been run aground near the mouth of the Tuxpan river by a captured Mexican pilot who bravely deceived the ship's American captain. The Mexicans captured most of the crew and salvaged the guns. (Ibid., p. 224; Bauer, *Surfboats and Horse Marines*, pp. 37-40; Smith, *War with Mexico*, 2:202.) General Cos had commanded Mexican troops at San Antonio during the Texas War for Independence.

4. Semmes, *Service Afloat and Ashore*, pp. 150-51. The *Scourge*, built by Betts, Harlan and Hollingsworth of Wilmington, Delaware, in 1844, displaced 230 tons and was driven by horizontal engines that turned two screws (hence it lacked the paddle boxes seen on most Mexican War steamers). It had an iron hull, carried sixty-one men, and mounted one thirty-two-pounder and two twenty-four-pounder carronades. (See Bauer, *Surfboats and Horse Marines*, p. 258.) For the other ships of the Mosquito Fleet see cat. no. 113.

Since artist-midshipman James M. Ladd served on the *Spitfire*, it is somewhat surprising that we have no rendering by him of this action. However, since he died at the Norfolk Naval Hospital on November 26, 1847, and his name does not appear on the list of wounded for this action or the second Tabasco expedition, he may have taken yellow fever at this time, as did many sailors and marines.

5. Semmes, *Service Afloat and Ashore*, p. 151.

6. See ibid., pp. 150-57. Samuel Eliot Morison visited the site in 1965 and commented on Walke's picture in *"Old Bruin"*, p. 227. According to Morison, the town is "correctly placed, but the Puy-de-Dome-like mountain behind does not exist"; Cerro del Hospital is shown too close to the other hill at left and is "blown up to at least thrice its height." Morison (p. 226) includes a photograph of La Peña taken in 1965 that is quite similar to Walke's rendering, but he notes that La Peña and Hospital Hill are around a bend and invisible from each other.

7. Semmes, *Service Afloat and Ashore*, pp. 153-56. On pp. 156-57 Semmes publishes Perry's official report. For other reports see "Reports and Despatches Exhibiting the Operations of the United States Naval Forces," pp. 1192-97.

119.   See Plate 14
Henry Walke
THE U. STATES STEAMERS, SCORPION, SPITFIRE, VIXEN AND SCOURGE; WITH 40 BARGES IN TOW, CROSSING THE BAR AT THE MOUTH OF TOBASCO RIVER, (MEXICO.)
Toned lithograph (hand colored), 1848
15-5/16 x 22-1/16 in. (38.9 x 56.0 cm.)
u.c.: "Naval Portfolio. / Naval Scenes in the Mexican War. By H. Walke Lieut. U.S. Navy. / No. 3."
l.l.: "Lith of Sarony & Major."
l.c.: "Entered according to Act of Congress in the year 1848 by Sarony & Major in the Clerks office of the district Court of the Southern district of N. York."
l.r.: "Designed and Drawn on Stone by H. Walke Lt. U.S.N."
l.l. to l.r. below title: "Comore. M. C. Perry in Command, Supported by the Commands, of Captains. J. Mayo, S. L. Breeze, F. Forrest. Commanders Wm. J. Mc.Cluney, A. Bigelow, F. Buchanan, H. A. Adams, A. S. Mackenzie, G. A. Magruder, G. J. Van Brunt. Lieuts. Commanding S. S. Lee, S. Lockwood and J. M. Berrien. June 14th. 1847. / Published by Sarony & Major. 117 Fulton St. New York."
ACM 33.76/3

Commodore Perry conducted two separate expeditions against the Mexican state of Tabasco, located between the Isthmus of Tehuantepec and the Yucatán peninsula, north of the state of Chiapas. The symbolic significance of Tabasco — the first spot where Cortes put foot on Mexican soil — was not lost on Americans at this time.[1] American naval commanders wanted a spectacular victory that would bring their branch of service to the attention of the American public. Lieutenant Walke evidently understood this need for publicity, and among his splendid series of eight lithographs entitled *Naval Portfolio*, no less than five pertain to the second Tabasco expedition.

Both operations involved crossing the bar at the mouth of the Grijalva River below the port town of Frontera. Around seventy miles upriver from Frontera is the provincial capital, La Villahermosa de San Juan Bautista.[2] A small town with a few thousand inhabitants, it had an important trade at the beginning of the war. In Perry's first expedition, in October 1846, he had ascended as far as Villahermosa and captured several Mexican ships but withdrew because he lacked sufficient strength to take and hold the town. When he returned, in June 1847, the Mexicans had prepared better defenses upriver. W. H. Parker, one of the participants, recalled that "we expected a serious resistance. Great care was taken in organizing the attacking force. It consisted of the light vessels and cutters.... The force was divided into two grand divisions; and we had a thousand sailors and marines, and ten pieces of light artillery ready to land. The guns were the Army six-pounders and were drawn by hand."[3]

The lithographs of Walke's *Naval Portfolio* are among the few Mexican War prints to receive serious attention from modern historians. Samuel Eliot Morison utilized Walke's views of the second Tabasco expedition in his excellent reconstruction of the event for his biography of Commodore Perry; he comments on this view:

First, in the early morning of 14 June 1847, steamers *Scourge, Scorpion, Spitfire,* and *Vixen* towed two bomb brigs and two schooners up to Frontera, then returned to pick up the ships' boats and surfboats, crammed with men, and towed them across the bar.... Walke used an artist's license in depicting the scenes of this second Tabasco expedition, but his conception of the waves at the bar is not exaggerated. They became such a menace to ships entering this vital river artery that the Mexican government later dug a canal from bay to river, about three miles south of the bar....*Scorpion* (Commander Tattnall), flying the blue pennant of Commodore Perry, who may be seen conning his temporary flagship from atop the port paddlewheel box, is followed by three steamers, each towing a string of boats whose passengers are obviously in for a lively tossing. The bar was passed without incident; nobody capsized or touched bottom.[4]

Lieutenant Walke copied his own sketch for this print on stone, probably soon after he returned to the States with the *Vesuvius* in the summer of 1848. The print reverses the design of the original watercolor (119a).[5] Perhaps Walke was not worried about this change, since this view does not concern itself with specific topographical details and the ships themselves were basically symmetrical in appearance. From right to left in the print are the three-masted steamer *Scorpion,* the two-masted steamer *Spitfire,* the *Scourge,* and the *Vixen,* each towing several small boats.[6] It seems reasonable to conclude that although Walke was a participant in the expedition, he probably did not sketch this exactly "on the spot" — while waiting at the bar.

119A. U. States Steamers Crossing the Bar at Tobasco River

1. Many Americans at the time were familiar with William H. Prescott's now-classic three-volume *History of the Conquest of Mexico* (New York: Harper and Brothers, 1843). In volume 1, p. 276, Prescott retold Bernal Diaz's account: "[Cortes] . . . soon after reached the mouth of the Rio de Tabasco, or Grijalva, in which that navigator [Cordova] had carried on so lucrative a traffic. Though mindful of the great object of his voyage, — the visit to the Aztec territories, — he was desirous of acquainting himself with the resources of this country, and determined to ascend the river and visit the great town on its borders.

"The water was so shallow, from the accumulation of sand at the mouth of the stream, that the general was obliged to leave the ships at anchor, and to embark in the boats with a part only of his forces."

2. Americans at the time generally referred to the Grijalva as the "Tobasco River"; the town of Villahermosa was "Tobasco" and sometimes "San Juan Bautista."

3. Parker, *Recollections*, pp. 107-8. Parker describes the first Tabasco expedition on pp. 72-74.

4. Morison, *"Old Bruin"*, pp. 231-32. Morison's is the only account I have found that states that the steamers made two trips across the bar, but I have not examined all of the primary sources. According to an account by "one of our gallant tars" appearing in *Niles' National Register*, July 24, 1847, p. 322, "On the 12th the squadron anchored off the river Tabasco and on the 14th, all things being ready, we made sail. The steamer Scorpion, bearing the commodore's broad pennant, having in tow the Washington and Vesuvius, followed by the steamers Spitfire, Vixen, and Scourge, towing the Etna, Stromboli, Bonita, and Captain Taylor's little vessel, the Spitfire, with the patent India rubber camels, for lifting our vessels over the shoals and obstructions thrown across the river — the boats of the squadron, about fifty in number, towing astern of all, presented a beautiful sight."

5. The original watercolor sketch is in the U.S. Naval Academy Museum, Annapolis, Maryland.

6. The *Scorpion*, formerly the *Aurora*, was a 339-ton steamer built in New York in 1846 and purchased for the Navy on January 4, 1847. Powered by a coal-burning engine driving two side wheels, it carried two eight-inch shell guns, two eighteen-pounder carronades, and a crew of sixty-one. (Bauer, *Surfboats and Horse Marines*, p. 258.) The *Scourge* is easily identifiable because as a screw-driven steamer it lacked paddle boxes. See the description in cat. no. 118, note 4. For descriptions of the *Spitfire* and *Vixen* see cat. no. 113.

120.
Henry Walke
THE ATTACK OF THE MEXICANS FROM THE CHAPPERAL, ON THE FIRST DIVISION OF THE NAVAL EXPEDITION TO TABASCO (MEXICO.)
Toned lithograph (hand colored), 1848
14-15/16 x 22-1/16 in. (37.9 x 56.0 cm.)
u.c.: "Naval Portfolio. Naval Scenes in the Mexican War. By H. Walke Lieut. U.S. Navy. (No. 4)"
l.l.: "Lith. of Sarony & Major"
l.c.: "Entered according to Act of Congress in the year 1848 by Sarony & Major in the Clerks office of the district Court of the Southern district of New York."
l.r.: "Designed & Drawn on Stone by H. Walke Lt. U.S.N."
l.l. to l.r. below title: "Consisting of the U.S. Steamer Scorpion Comore. Perry, Capt. Breese, and Comaer. Bigelo. Bomb Brig Vesuvius. Comaer. Magruder. Brig Washington, Lieut. Comaer. S. S. Lee. With a Detachment of Seamen and Marines in Barges from the Steam Frigate Mississippi, under, Comaer. Mackenzie and H. A. Adams, Marines Comanded by Capt. Edson. / Published by Sarony & Major 117 Fulton St. N. Y."
ACM 33.76/4

Lieutenant Walke's next print, number four of the series, was copied on stone by the artist himself from his own sketch. The print depicts a Mexican ambush along the Grijalva River during the second Tabasco expedition. The print is apparently not reversed, since the point of attack seems to correspond with that shown on a contemporary map.[1] Of the three larger vessels in the picture, the steamer *Scorpion* is in the center, easily identifiable by the smokestack, paddle boxes, and Commodore Perry's broad pennant at the top of one of her masts. The brig *Washington* is probably at left and the *Vesuvius* to the right. If so, the

Vesuvius's big columbiad siege gun is being fired point blank at the Mexicans on shore.[2] Smoke in the tops of the three vessels indicates that the sharpshooters are busy. Sailors and marines on every vessel fire their small arms while the marines on board the two closest launches bring their six-pounder field guns to bear on the hidden enemy in the jungle at right. An officer, apparently on board the *Vesuvius* and perhaps Walke himself, described the action in a letter to the New Orleans *Delta*, which was republished in the Washington *Daily National Intelligencer*:

About sundown we left Frontera, and with an occasional interruption from overhanging branches sweeping our men overboard, we passed on very gently until three o'clock next day, when we captured a canoe with two Indians, from whom we learned that Bruno [the Mexican commander] lay in ambush, with a large force, at two favorable positions, at points fifteen and twenty miles further up. The tops were at once filled with sharpshooters, and officers were kept aloft on the look-out. The place designated as the first point of attack being passed without interruption, we were beginning to feel secure, when a heavy volley opened on us from the banks. In an instant the fire was returned from the heavy guns of the Scorpion, Washington, and Vesuvius, and from the small arms on deck and aloft. . . .

The awning of the Scorpion I was told was cut up pretty badly. The Vesuvius's sides were pretty well peppered; but for the foresight of the Commodore in stationing sharpshooters aloft we must have suffered

120. ATTACK OF THE MEXICANS FROM THE CHAPPERAL

severely; but they had heard of our being armed with revolving rifles, and had a most awful horror of exposing themselves to their effects. They were afraid of raising their heads to take aim for fear of showing themselves to the men aloft and being shot. This little brush was monopolized by the three vessels named, all the rest being some miles astern.[3]

1. See map "Sketch of the River Tabasco, From Devil's Bend to St. Juan Battista. Shewing the Landing and March of Commre. Perry's forces, June 16th. 1847" in "Reports and Despatches Exhibiting the Operations of the United States Naval Forces," betw. pp. 1088 and 1089.
2. The *Vesuvius* and the other bomb brigs were apparently hermaphrodite brigs (square-rigged forward and schooner-rigged aft). See the illustration of the bomb brig *Etna* in Bauer, *Surfboats and Horse Marines*, p. 67. The bomb brig *Vesuvius* had a displacement of 240 tons, was armed with one ten-inch columbiad (a large, smooth-bore siege gun) mounted amidship, and carried a crew of forty-seven. The *Washington* was a ninety-one-foot Coast Survey brig built in Baltimore in 1837; it carried one forty-two-pounder. (Ibid., pp. 66-67, 258, 259.) For a description of the *Scorpion*, see cat. no. 119, note 6.
3. *Daily National Intelligencer*, July 21, 1847, p. 2; compare also Parker, *Recollections*, p. 108. Morison, *"Old Bruin"*, p. 233, mentions this section of the river as being near a hamlet called Santa Teresa.

121.
Henry Walke
THE NAVAL EXPEDITION UNDER COMRE. PERRY, ASCENDING THE TABASCO RIVER AT THE DEVILS BEND JUNE, 15TH. 1847.
Toned lithograph (hand colored), 1848
15-3/16 x 21-3/4 in. (38.6 x 55.3 cm.)
u.c.: "Naval Portfolio. Naval Scenes in the Mexican War. By H. Walke Lieut. U.S. Navy (No. 5)"
l.l.: "Lith. of Sarony & Major."
l.c.: "Entered according to Act of Congress in the year 1848 by Sarony & Major, in the Clerks office of the district Court of the southern district of N. York."
l.r.: "Designed & Drawn on Stone by H. Walke Lieut. of U.S.N."
l.c. below title: "Published by Sarony & Major 117 Fulton St. N. Y."
ACM 33.76/5

This view shows one of the prominent topographical features along the Grijalva River, El Torno del Diablo (Devil's Bend), an S-turn several miles below the city of Villahermosa. Walke's view is somewhat fanciful, since he could not have observed at such a convenient range Mexican troops lying in ambush for American ships. Details were important for him, nevertheless, and several of the ships are accurately enough rendered that they may be distinguished by comparing other images and contemporary written descriptions. Beginning at far left, the three-masted side-wheel steamer *Scorpion*, bearing Commodore Perry's broad pennant, leads the flotilla; next probably comes the brig *Washington*, and behind it the bomb brig *Vesuvius* (Walke's ship), followed by several smaller launches; in the center, the paddle boxes and double masts of what is most likely the *Spitfire* can be made out, in front and to the side of which is one of the bomb brigs, *Etna* or *Stromboli*. Another vessel, not much

of which is visible, may be drawn up on the other side of *Spitfire*; this might be the schooner-gunboat *Bonita*. Farther around the bend comes another two-masted paddle wheel steamer, most likely the *Vixen*, with its tow alongside, another bomb brig (either *Etna* or *Stromboli*). Bringing up the rear is the screw-driven steamer *Scourge* towing what may be Captain George W. Taylor's merchant schooner *Spitfire*.[1]

Lieutenant Walke's original sketch (121a) for this print survives in the U. S. Naval Academy Museum. A comparison with the print shows that Walke considerably altered his own composition when he drew it on stone. The original sketch is undoubtedly less contrived. Walke depicted the leading ships in the original sketch in more of a three-quarter view. The changes in the topography are extensive: originally the river bent back around in the foreground; in the print he substituted a standing pool of water. According to contemporary maps, such pools as well as the cultivated fields seen in both versions were present in the area.[2] The fortified city in the distance at right may represent Villahermosa; if so, it seems particularly out of position in the print, when one compares it with a map. In the original watercolor Walke has prickly pear growing along the bank in the right foreground; these have been removed in the print and replaced with exotic palms. The trees at left have been enlarged in the print; below them the two Mexican officers, originally on horseback, have dismounted.

The rounding of Devil's Bend is related by the same "Navy officer" quoted in the preceding entry: "At this place we expected a most formidable opposition. Here is a long reach of a mile and a quarter in length; the river narrows, and

THE NAVAL EXPEDITION UNDER COMM.ᴿ PERRY, ASCENDING THE TABASCO RIVER AT THE DEVILS BEND. JUNE 15ᵀᴴ 1847.

Published by Sarony & Major 117 Fulton St N Y

121. Naval Expedition Ascending the Tabasco River at Devils Bend

121A. Naval Expedition Ascending the Tabasco River at Devils Bend

an obstruction thrown across the bar, with a strong breastwork commanding it. As the shades of evening stole upon us we were fired upon again from the bushes, the discharge breaking a man's leg on board of the Vesuvius. We opened the big guns on them again, cleared the woods of the musquitoes, and went to bed."[3]

1. The order of the ships is based on a description by a naval officer in a letter to the New Orleans *Delta*, published in the *Daily National Intelligencer*, July 21, 1847, p. 2. See also Morison, *"Old Bruin"*, pp. 195, 233; Bauer, *Surfboats and Horse Marines*, pp. 114-15. For the merchant schooner *Spitfire*, see cat. no. 119, note 4.

2. See the map in Morison, *"Old Bruin"*, p. 234, which is based on the map cited in cat. no. 120, note 1. Morison includes a photograph of Devil's Bend in 1965 (p. 232). No mountains or hills are visible in the distance as they are in Walke's watercolor and print.

3. *Daily National Intelligencer*, July 21, 1847, p. 2. Also see Parker, *Recollections*, pp. 108-9.

122.   See Plate 15.
J. Vollmering and Francis D'Avignon after Henry Walke
THE LANDING, OF THE NAVAL EXPEDITION, AGAINST TABASCO. (MEXICO.) COMORE. M. C. PERRY IN COMMAND.
Toned lithograph (hand colored), 1848
15-1/4 x 22-1/4 in. (38.7 x 56.5 cm.)
u.c.: "Naval Portfolio. Naval Scenes in the Mexican War by H. Walke Lieut. U.S. Navy. (No. 6.)"
l.l.: "Painted by H. Walke Lt. U.S.N. Drawn on Stone by Volmering & Davignon"
l.c. "Entered according to act of Congress in the year 1848 by Sarony & Major in the Clerks Office of the district Court of the Southern district of N. York."
l.r.: "Lith. by Sarony & Major."
l.l. to l.r. below title: "With Detachments of Officers, Seamen, and Marines, from the U.S. Steamer Frigate Mississippi, Capt. Mayo, Comers. Mackenzie, and Adams, U.S. Ship, Albany, Capt. Breese. Frigate Raritan, Capt. Forrest. U.S. Ship, John Adams, Comare. Wm. J. Mc.Cluney. U.S. Ship Germantown, Comanre. Buchanan. U.S. Ship Decater, / Comaer. Pearson. Bomb Brig, Stromboli, Comare. Walker. Bomb Brig, Vesuvius, Comare. Magruder. Bomb Brig, Etna. Comare. Van Brunt. Marines Comre. by Capt. Edson. / The landing was effected in 5 minutes, after the Comre. gave the order, (in the face of the enemy, intrenched,) by about 1000, American Seamen and Marines, armed with muskets, and 10 Brass field pieces which were served upon the enemy, after they had been driven from their works / by the heavy guns of the Steamer Scorpion Comer. Bigelow. Steamer Spitfire Lieut. Comaer. S. S. Lee. Steamer Vixen Liet. Comaer. Smith. Steamer Scourge Lieut. Comaer. S. Lockwood; and the Schooner Bonita Lieut. Comaer. Birrien; which Covered the landing. / Published by Sarony & Major 117 Fulton Street N.Y."
ACM 33.76/6

An early view of an American amphibious assault, this print by Lieutenant Walke depicts the landing of Commodore Perry's sailors and marines on the banks of the Grijalva River between the Devil's Bend and their objective, the city of Villahermosa de San Juan Bautista, during the second Tabasco expedition. According to historian Samuel Eliot Morison, who visited the site in 1965, "Walke recorded this scene with substantial accuracy." The six palm trees at the right of the print roughly correspond with the name given by the Americans to the landing site, "Seven Palms." This spot, according to Morison, "by a curious coincidence seems to be identical with the Punta de Palmares where Cortes on 13 March 1519 landed Alonzo de Avila with one hundred men to march on the town by land, while he and the boats proceeded by water. The very tactics that Perry followed!"[1]

At left in the print, one of the steamers, either *Spitfire* or *Vixen*, may be discerned by its paddle boxes and double masts. Just to its right near the shore is a small schooner-rigged vessel, probably the gunboat *Bonita*. The small cutters and surfboats (the latter with pointed sterns) of the landing party leave the ships and head toward shore, where some troops have already disembarked. The marines in the center distance, wearing forage caps, ascend the river bank and plant the Stars and Stripes. To their right, lines of sailors, wearing their characteristic blue jackets and circular-brimmed hats, hoist up with ropes the small sixpounder field guns detailed for the land operation. At the top of the hill Commodore Perry directs the action; just to his left an orderly bears the Commodore's broad pennant.

The officer from the *Vesuvius* described the landing for the New Orleans *Delta*:

The order was then given for the forces to embark in the boats and form into line, three deep, in the middle of the river. This was done with great dispatch and in beautiful order.... In advance of all was the Commodore, sitting quietly in his barge, with his broad pennant flying, forming the most conspicuous mark for Mexican shot, and his mouth puckering out as if he did not care for all the Mexican bullets in Tabasco. While forming into line a heavy cannonading was kept up from the vessels. At a signal given from the Commodore the steamers ceased firing, the men gave an awful shout, seven hundred oars dipped their blades into the water, and a thousand Yankee tars stood on the banks of the Tabasco.[2]

U. S. Navy Lieutenant W. H. Parker, who served in the advance party, later recalled: "It was hard work scrambling up the bank, which was steep, and how the guns were hauled up I never knew; but it was done, and a pretty sight it was as seen from the vessels."[3]

1. Morison, *"Old Bruin"*, pp. 235, 233. On p. 236 Morison includes a photograph of the site that he took in 1965. Cortes's landing at Tabasco is described in Prescott, *History of the Conquest of Mexico*, 1:276-79.
2. Published in the Washington *Daily National Intelligencer*, July 30, 1847, p. 2. According to Wright, "Henry Walke," p. 140, the original watercolor for this print was in a private collection in North Carolina in 1971.
3. Parker, *Recollections*, pp. 109-10.

123.
Henry Walke
THE CAPTURE OF THE CITY OF TABASCO, BY THE U.S. NAVAL EXPEDITION, AFLOAT AND ON SHORE, UNDER COMORE. M. C. PERRY.
Toned lithograph (hand colored), 1848
15-3/8 x 21-7/8 in. (39.1 x 55.6 cm.)
u.c.: "Naval Portfolio Naval Scenes in the Mexican War by H. Walke Lieut U.S. Navy (No. 7.)"
l.l.: "Lith. of Sarony & Major."
l.c.: "Entered according to Act Congress in the year 1848 by Sarony & Major in the Clerks Office of the district Court of the southern district of N. York."
l.r.: "Designed and Drawn on Stone by H. Walke, Lieut. of U.S.N. New York."
l.c. below title: "and the destruction of the Fort, Mounting three long 26 pounders, with other heavy guns, by the U.S. Steamers Scorpion, Comer. Bigelow, / Steamer Spitfire, Lieut. Coming. S. S. Lee, and Schooner Bonita, Liut. Coming. Berrian. June 15th. 1847. / Published by Sarony & Major 117 Fulton St. N. York."
ACM 33.76/7

In this lithograph, the three-masted steamer *Scorpion*, leaving a considerable wake, leads the two-masted steamer *Spitfire* towing the schooner-gunboat *Bonita* in a dramatic dash past Fort Iturbide toward the city of Villahermosa. This concluding print in Walke's series was drawn on stone by the artist himself.

Walke apparently rendered this scene with considerable fidelity to the actual event. The ships are easily identifiable and certain details are confirmed by written descriptions. The *Bonita*'s crew prepares to fire its thirty-two-pounder carronade and the *Spitfire* sports a canvas awning. Contemporary maps support topographical details such as the position of the mouth of a creek just to the left of the fort.

and the destruction of the Fort, Mounting three long 26 pounders, with other heavy guns, by the U S Steamers Scorpion Com.ᵈʳ Bigelow
Steamer Spitfire Lieut Com.ᵈᵍ SS Lee and Schooner Bonita Lieut Com.ᵈᵍ Berrian June 15ᵗʰ 1847

123. Capture of the City of Tabasco

123A. Capture of the City of Tabasco

This creek is crossed by a bridge that may be seen just to the right of center, in the distance.[1] The tower beyond it may belong to the cathedral, which dates from 1614.[2]

Some inaccuracies are to be expected. The event took place on June 16, 1847, rather than June 15 as the inscription states. Distances, of course, may be compressed for pictorial reasons; the billowing smoke from the two steamers' stacks, the smoke from their guns, the fluttering pennants and flags, and the watery splashes caused by near misses from the Mexican guns may be slightly exaggerated to reinforce the drama of the event.

One eyewitness described the action thus:

> Towards evening the advance guard came in sight of the fort commanding the approach to the city by land and water. I have never seen a more commanding position — constructed on a bluff, taking in a line of the river one mile and a half long, exposing our vessels to a raking fire the whole distance. In the fort they mounted three long 32s, three heavy field-pieces, and a 24-pounder carronade, and as the Scorpion and Spitfire came around the bend of the river, they opened on them from the fort with grape and round shot. The two little steamers came steadily along, paying more attention to steering clear of the shoals than of the shot. The Scorpion coming up first opened her fire as she got abreast, the Spitfire joining in; the grape fairly rained, and soon drove the enemy from their guns, their fire slackening, and Capt. Bigelow, thinking the fort silenced, put on steam and passed up to the city, when the fire re-opened from the fort, which the Spitfire returned most gallantly, again driving them from their guns.[3]

As the print's title implies but the print itself does not show, Commodore Perry's land force, pressing forward on a bad road past several Mexican breastworks, reached the fort and city just behind the ships. The Mexican defenders, about nine hundred men in all under the governor and captain general of Tabasco, Don Domingo Echagaray, put up a meager resistance in the face of such a superior force, then withdrew upriver; the city was surrendered by its prefect and was occupied by the Americans until July 22.[4]

The U. S. Naval Academy Museum preserves an original watercolor sketch (123a) by Walke that relates to this print. Essentially the artist did not change the topography in the lithograph, except for cropping some of the right bank of the river and including more of the left bank. The main difference is the moment of action shown in the two versions. The lithograph shows the three ships running past the guns of the fort, a scene far more interesting in terms of pictorial drama. The watercolor sketch, on the other hand, shows the fort already flying the American flag, with the *Spitfire* and *Bonita* drawn alongside it at right. In the original the *Scorpion* is in the left distance, having drawn up to the city, while along the river bank at right and along the bridge in the center distance, tiny figures representing Perry's land force march toward the city. For the lithograph Walke must have drawn his original image backward on stone, since the printed image has not been reversed from nature. Most likely he received some instruction for this from the lithographers at the Sarony & Major firm. At any rate, this is pretty impressive work for an amateur artist, and no doubt Walke, who went on to retire from the Navy as a rear admiral, could have pursued a quite different career.

1. Compare the map in Morison, *"Old Bruin"*, p. 234.
2. T. Philip Terry, *Terry's Guide to Mexico* (Boston: Houghton Mifflin, 1935), p. 561.
3. Letter of a Navy officer to the New Orleans *Delta*, published in the *Daily National Intelligencer*, July 21, 1847, p. 2.
4. See Morison, *"Old Bruin"*, pp. 230-38; Bauer, *Surfboats and Horse Marines*, pp. 111-22. Other eyewitness accounts of the second Tabasco expedition include "An officer on board the United States steamer Spitfire at Tabasco" to the *Daily National Intelligencer*, July 30, 1847, p. 2; Aug. 21, 1847, p. 2.

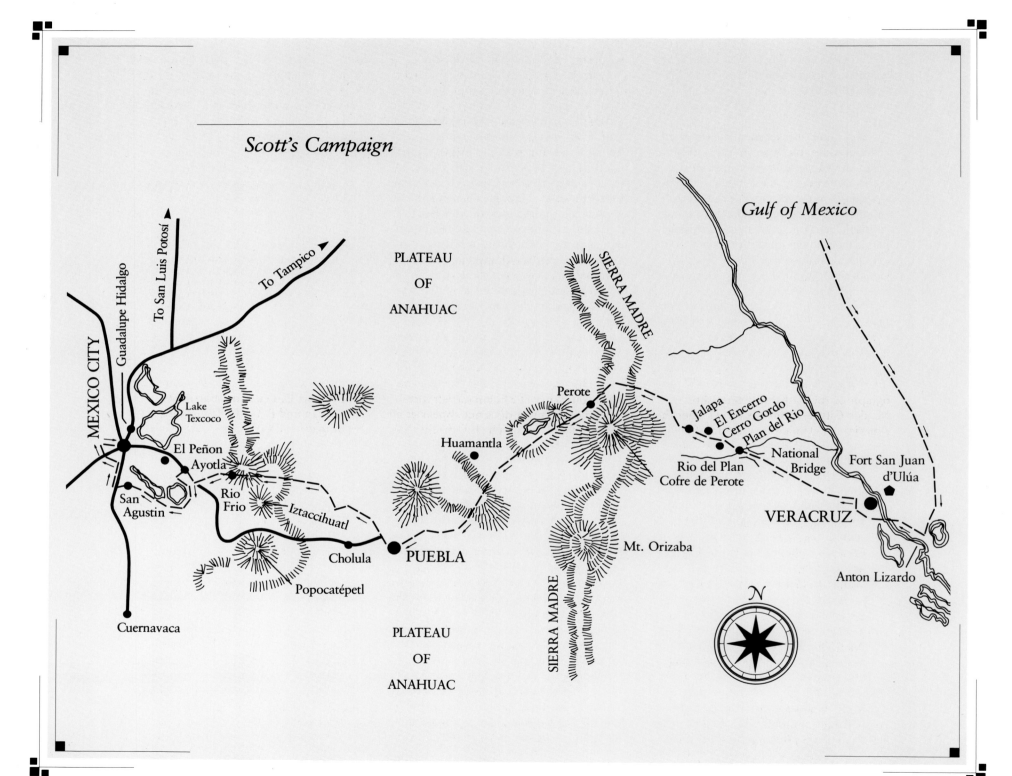

Scott's Campaign

Gulf of Mexico

To San Luis Potosí

To Tampico

PLATEAU OF ANAHUAC

Guadalupe Hidalgo

MEXICO CITY

Lake Texcoco

El Peñon
Ayotla

San Agustin

Rio Frio

Iztaccihuatl

Cholula

PUEBLA

Popocatépetl

Cuernavaca

PLATEAU OF ANAHUAC

Huamantla

SIERRA MADRE

Perote

Mt. Orizaba

SIERRA MADRE

Jalapa
El Encerro
Cerro Gordo
Plan del Rio

Rio del Plan
Cofre de Perote

National Bridge

Fort San Juan d'Ulúa

VERACRUZ

Anton Lizardo

N

Cerro Gordo

124.
H. Mendez after an unknown artist
VIEW OF CERRO GORDO WITH GENL.
TWIGGS' DIVISION STORMING THE MAIN
HEIGHTS 18TH. APRIL 1847.
Lithograph (hand colored), 1847
14-11/16 x 21-7/8 in. (37.3 x 55.6 cm.)
l.l.: "Lit. de Rocha C. de Tacuba no. 14. H.
Mendez. Lith."
l.c.: "Frente de la Profesa no. 7."
l.r.: "Propiedad de G. G. Davis."
ACM 119.72

Perhaps none of the several known prints of Cerro Gordo — the next major action of General Scott's campaign — were made from sketches drawn by eyewitnesses to the battle.[1] Curiously, however, this lithograph of the battle was published in Mexico City less than six weeks after the Americans occupied that capital. On November 25, 1847, one of the American soldiers' newspapers in the city, the *Daily American Star*, carried the following announcement of the print:

> "View of Cerro Gordo, with Gen. Twiggs' Division Storming the Main Heights, 18th April." — We received yesterday from Mr. G. G. Davis, a well executed lithographic view of Cerro Gordo; and also a "Topographical Survey of Plan del Rio and Cerro Gordo," as made by Capt. McClellan, U. S. Engineer — for both of which Mr. Davis will accept our thanks.[2]

Little is known about George G. Davis, other than that he was an American civilian who followed the army to Mexico City.[3] The inscription "Propiedad de G. G. Davis" (Property of G. G. Davis) suggests that he was the publisher. The Mexican artist who signed the stone, H. Mendez, may also have invented the design. Mendez was apparently employed by the Mexican lithographer José Severo Rocha, whose firm printed the lithograph. Mendez may have had access to an American sketch (whether by Davis or someone else) or he may have utilized eyewitness descriptions of the battle to create the scene. Whatever the case, the lithograph is rendered more naturalistically than the popular prints of the battle turned out by several American printmakers.[4]

Yet this naturalism is deceptive, for, when compared with George McClellan's map, the locations of several topographical features in the print are questionable.[5] Scale, distance, and perspective are handled arbitrarily. The hill in the left foreground of the print does not appear at all in McClellan's map. The hills in the distance, the line of American troops entering at left, and the lines of Mexican troops in the distance are confusing. Nevertheless, the right portion of the print may be somewhat accurate, for as the Mexico City *North American* reported:

> Davis' Picture of Cerro Gordo is at length out, accompanied by a chart by Capt. M'Clelland of the engineers. The whole is very well executed, but as the view is of a fight we did not see and of a side of the cerro we did not visit, we cannot speak as to its correctness. A friend who was there says he recognizes Capt. Wall's battery and Lieut. Hayden's party of road cutters. The view is of the side attacked by Gen. Twiggs' division.[6]

On April 8, 1847, General David E. Twiggs's Second Division of regulars left Veracruz along the National Road to Mexico City with orders from Scott to occupy the city of Jalapa.[7] The higher elevation and greater availability of supplies in this city would spare the American army the worst effects of the *vomito* season along the coastal lowlands. Twiggs's division met no opposition as they passed the strong, naturally defensible positions near the National Bridge.[8] However, just beyond the town of Plan del Rio, near the hamlet of Cerro Gordo, they discovered a large force of Mexican troops with cannon, entrenched in hills commanding the road. General Robert Patterson's Third Division of volunteers joined Twiggs, followed on April 14 by Scott, who was hurrying up from Veracruz with Worth's First Division.

Scott's engineers, among them Captain Robert E. Lee and Lieutenants McClellan and P. G. T. Beauregard, began a three-day reconnaissance of the Mexican position. They found the Mexican right flank to be quite formidable: on three promontories to the left of the road (the middle distance of the print) the Mexicans had situated three fortified batteries; to the left of these, the Rio del Plan ran through a gorge five hundred feet deep.[9] But the Mexican left (the foreground of the print) was weak: La Atalaya, the hill represented in the center foreground, was not fortified and only lightly defended, and a trail could be cut around the right of El Telégrafo (the larger hill at far right) through the ravines and undergrowth, leading to the road behind the Mexican positions.[10]

On the seventeenth General Twiggs's division opened the attack on La Atalaya,[11] soon taking this hill as the Mexicans fell back to their entrenched positions

VIEW OF CERRO GORDO WITH GEN.ˡ TWIGGS DIVISION STORMING THE MAIN HEIGHTS 18.ᵗʰ APRIL 1847

124. Cerro Gordo with Genl. Twiggs' Division Storming the Main Heights

on El Telégrafo. During the night, several five-hundred-man teams pulled two twenty-four-pounder field guns and one twenty-four-pounder howitzer up Atalaya while a breastwork was erected at the summit. (Two of these guns appear at the top of Atalaya in the center of the print.) A detail of sappers or engineers cut a narrow road around El Telégrafo; these men, identified in the *North American* as Lieutenant Julius Hayden's road cutters, appear in the right foreground of the print.[12] Their officer carries what looks like a lantern, perhaps to indicate that this work was done during the night or early morning.

At 7:00 A.M. the next morning, the American battery on Atalaya signaled the opening of the grand attack. General Gideon Pillow's brigade of Patterson's volunteer division made a costly diversionary attack on the Mexican right along the three strongly defended promontories. (Pillow's troops may be incorrectly indicated in the print at far left; more properly, they should be out of the picture, farther to the left.)[13] Colonel W. S. Harney and Brevet Colonel Bennett Riley, leading the main attack on Telégrafo with the two brigades of General Twiggs's division, may be seen at far right in the print, ascending the mountain.

1. Furber, *Twelve Months Volunteer*, contains two engravings made after the author's sketches of the Cerro Gordo battleground (frontispiece and p. 581). Private Furber, with the First Regiment of Tennessee Cavalry, arrived at Cerro Gordo only one day after the battle.

2. Mexico City *Daily American Star*, Nov. 25, 1847, p. 2.

3. Mexico City *North American,* Nov. 30, 1847, p. 3. Davis may also prove to be a relative of a Second Lieutenant Thomas Davis, mortally wounded at the battle of Cerro Gordo, whose grave is marked on an original map of Plan del Rio reproduced in Nevin, *Mexican War*, p. 145.

4. Among the American popular prints of the battle of Cerro Gordo are four different lithographs by Nathaniel Currier showing American troops storming the main heights (see figs. 12, 13), one lithograph by Sarony & Major (fig. 15), and *Storming of Cerro Gordo* and *Colonel Harney's Brilliant Charge at Cerro Gordo* by R. Magee. Magee also issued a lithograph showing the *Flight of Santa Anna at the Battle of Cerro Gordo*. Similar prints were also issued by James Baillie (fig. 14) and H. R. Robinson; Robinson's print, titled *Santa Anna Declining a Hasty Plate of Soup at Cerro Gordo*, was drawn by caricaturist Edward W. Clay.

5. The map is reproduced in Nevin, *Mexican War*, p. 144. Captain McClellan, the engineer mentioned as the mapmaker, is George B. McClellan, better known as one of President Lincoln's generals during the Civil War.

6. Mexico City *North American*, Nov. 26, 1847, p. 2.

7. Good secondary accounts of the march from Veracruz and the battle of Cerro Gordo include Nevin, *Mexican War*, pp. 141-49, and Smith, *War with Mexico*, 2:37-59, 343-55. Smith's bibliography lists numerous accounts by participants and eyewitnesses describing various incidents and sectors of the battle. One of the best of these is Ballentine, *Autobiography*, pp. 173-202.

8. I am unaware of any prints produced from eyewitness views of the National Bridge (Puente Nacional) during the Mexican War. The New York *Weekly Herald*, May 22, 1847, p. 1, published an engraving of the bridge by Samuel Putnam Avery, but it was derived from an aquatint after a drawing by Mrs. H. G. Ward, published in Henry George Ward, *Mexico in 1827*, 2 vols. (London: Henry Colburn, 1828), 1: plate 4. A view of the bridge at Plan del Rio appeared in Daniel Thomas Egerton, *Egerton's Views in Mexico* (London: the author, 1840), plate 9. A sketchbook by Private James T. Shannon (see cat. no. 160, note 4) contains a drawing of Plan del Rio, taken sometime after August 6, 1847, showing the bridge after it had been blown up by Mexican guerrillas. See Oswandel, *Notes of the Mexican War*, pp. 112, 140, 239.

9. Fortunately, Furber has an engraving from a sketch he made depicting these three batteries (*Twelve Months Volunteer*, p. 581), which are not shown by cat. nos. 124 or 125. As Furber appropriately observed: "The battle-ground of Cerro Gordo is difficult to [describe], on account of its being but a vast collection of massive hills, divided by deep and precipitous ravines. — No view of the whole ground can be obtained from any one place, save the height of Cerro Gordo itself" (p. 579).

10. There was some confusion among the Americans as to which hill was which. Furber, for example, called El Telégrafo "Cerro Gordo" and La Atalaya "El Telégrafo."

11. Prior to this attack, according to Justin Smith, Lieutenant Gardner with a company from the Seventh Infantry made a reconnaissance from a neighboring hill (*War with Mexico*, 2:51). This may be the hill represented in the left foreground of the print.

12. Lieutenant Julius Hayden was attached to the Second Infantry and breveted captain on August 20, 1847, for gallant and meritorious conduct in the battles of Contreras and Churubusco (Heitman, *Historical Register*, 1:514).

13. Furber's engraved view *Battery No. 2, Charged by Second Tennessee Regiment* shows the three forts attacked by Pillow's brigade (*Twelve Months Volunteer*, p. 581).

125. See Plate 16
Adolphe-Jean-Baptiste Bayot after Carl Nebel
BATTLE OF CERRO-GORDO
Toned lithograph (hand colored), 1851
10-15/16 x 16-5/8 in. (27.8 x 42.2 cm.)
l.l.: "C. Nebel fecit."
l.r.: "Bayot lith."
From George Wilkins Kendall, *The War
Between the United States and Mexico Illus-
trated* (New York: D. Appleton & Company,
1851), plate 5
ACM 186.72/5

Carl Nebel's rendering of the battle of
Cerro Gordo for George Wilkins Kendall
shows the same side of the battlefield as
the Davis and Mendez print. La Atalaya
appears in the distant left and El Telégrafo
at right. The small foothill in the left
middle distance in the Nebel print may
be the large hill at the left in the Davis
and Mendez print. If so, the discrepancy
in scale between the two artists' renditions
is quite noticeable. Kendall was present
at the battle, and while assembling his
copious notes he probably bought one of
the Davis-Mendez prints. Nebel might
have used this print and might also have
visited the site during his last trip to
Mexico; there is no evidence that he was
himself present at the battle.

Kendall commented on the print:

In the drawing of the assault upon
Cerro Gordo the artist has chosen the
period when Harney is advancing
directly upon the works on the crest,
Riley's men being seen moving to the
right. The American guns on the
height on the left, which had been
plied with great spirit by Hagner and
Steptoe, assisted by Seymour and
Brown, have just ceased their fire,
fearing that the safety of their friends
might be endangered. At the foot of
the hills, in the foreground, may be

seen a portion of Worth's division,
in readiness to assist Harney if necessary, or hold in check any force that
might move out from the Jalapa road.
The point attacked by Shields, with
the Illinoians and New Yorkers, lies
on the right of the picture and could
not be brought in.[1]

Nebel's print shows the battle probably as Kendall viewed it, from the relative
safety of General Worth's division, which
had been held in reserve. Heavy action is
alluded to only in the distance, where
Harney and Riley lead the two brigades
of Twiggs's division in the storming of El
Telégrafo. Although Kendall mentions
these officers, neither they nor the officers
of the batteries on Atalaya can be specifically discerned in the print. The blockhouse or tower in the middle of the
Mexican breastworks on the crest of Telégrafo is visible in some impressions of
Nebel's print; in others, smoke obscures
it.[2] Nebel's view does not encompass
General Pillow's attack from the American
left or, as Kendall explains, General James
Shields's attack from the American right.
Nebel, for the sake of credibility, concen-
trates on the foreground activities of
Worth's division. These are typical
groupings of military figures, at which
the artist excelled and which he could
have observed or reconstructed at almost
any time.[3]

The struggle for the possession of
Telégrafo was fierce and bloody. Harney's
and Riley's men pushed up the hill despite
losses, converging on the breastworks and
fort at the crest. There, Mexican General
Ciriaco Vásquez fell during a sharp
engagement, and the Americans soon
turned the guns they captured on the
Mexicans fleeing down the hill toward
their central camp.

Just at this moment, General Shields's
brigade, having followed a circuitous
route along the engineers' road around
the base of the hill, emerged from the
chaparral not far from the Jalapa road in
the rear of the Mexican lines. Although
Shields was severely wounded, the movement took the Mexicans completely by
surprise and a general panic ensued. Santa
Anna fled on horseback along with a large
portion of the army, while many of the
troops on the Mexican right surrendered
unconditionally. Among the estimated
3,000 Mexican prisoners was General
Rómulo Díaz de la Vega, released after
his previous capture at Resaca de la
Palma. The Americans reported around
1,000 to 1,200 Mexicans killed or
wounded, while American losses for the
two days were listed as 30 officers and
387 men, of whom 64 were killed.[4]

1. Kendall, *War Between the United States and
Mexico Illustrated*, p. 25.
2. Thomas Swift Dickey, a collector and student of
Mexican War prints, visited the Cerro Gordo battlefield sometime before 1985 and photographed the
ruins of the blockhouse on El Telégrafo. In a letter
to Ron Tyler, Jan. 22, 1985 (Amon Carter Museum
files), Mr. Dickey wrote: "I've searched and studied
this battlefield for years and am amazed at the
accuracy of Nebel's rendition of what went on there."
3. Tyler also notes that the print is shaded correctly
to indicate a morning attack (*Mexican War: A Lithographic Record*, p. 37).
4. Smith, *War with Mexico*, 2:37-59.

126.
Fd. Bastin after an unknown artist
DEFENSA DE CERRO GORDO CONTRA EL
EJERCITO NORTE AMERICANO, EL 18
ABRIL 1847.
Lithograph (hand colored), c. 1850
7-7/8 x 12-1/4 in. (20.0 x 31.1 cm.)
l.c. on stone: "Fd Bastin"
l.l.: "Julio Michaud y Thomas. Mexico."
From *Album Pintoresco de la República Méx-
icana* (Mexico City: Estamperia de Julio
Michaud y Thomas, c. 1850)
ACM 8.78

Although probably not an eyewitness
view, this lithograph, from an album that
included a number of Mexican War battle scenes, needs further study. The
topography, though generalized, conforms
basically to eyewitness accounts, and the
uniforms appear reasonably accurate. The
building on the hill at right may represent
the blockhouse on Telégrafo.

The Road to Mexico City

127.
After John Phillips
JALAPA
Toned lithograph (hand colored), 1848
10-1/2 x 15-3/8 in. (26.7 x 39.1 cm.)
l.r.: "Day & Son, Lithrs. to the Queen"
From John Phillips and Alfred Rider, *Mexico
Illustrated in Twenty-six Views* (London: E.
Atchley, Library of Fine Arts, 1848), plate 4
ACM 10.79/4

John Phillips probably painted the sketch
for this lithograph of the town of Jalapa
before the war, but it nevertheless conveys
some idea of what the town must have
looked like to the American troops as they
advanced along the National Road after
the battle of Cerro Gordo.[1] Private
George Ballentine, marching with General
Twiggs's division, wrote:

> The appearance of the country as we
> approached within a few miles of
> Jalapa, seemed one continuous gar-
> den, teeming with the richest luxu-
> riance of tropical vegetation. The
> mountain of Orizaba, with its daz-
> zling white and clear, cold summit
> piercing the cerulean blue sky,
> seemed within a few miles of us
> though in reality we were about
> twenty-five miles distant. This effect
> was produced by the remarkable
> purity and clearness of the atmos-
> phere, and the sun shining upon the
> snow which always covered it. The
> town of Jalapa is four thousand feet
> above the level of the sea, and is sit-
> uated on the side of a hill. It is
> embraced by an amphitheatre of
> wooded mountains, which rise

DEFENSA DE CERRO GORDO CONTRA EL EJERCITO NORTE AMERICANO

El 18 Abril 1847.

126. DEFENSA DE CERRO GORDO

127. JALAPA

Since the Americans often wrote of the beauty of Jalapa, it is somewhat surprising that American printmakers did not publish prints after eyewitness views of the town. An exception may be an engraving by Samuel Putnam Avery that appeared in the New York *Weekly Herald*, January 22, 1848, depicting a "View of the West Side of Jalapa with the Mountain Perote."[5] The artist of the view is not credited. Other printmakers copied Carl Nebel's lithographed view of the town that first appeared in his 1836 album, *Voyage pittoresque et archéologique.*[6]

1. Richard F. Pourade claims that Phillips's "sketches were of scenes of Mexico before the war" but unfortunately offers little proof for this (*Sign of the Eagle*, p. 166). Until more is known about Phillips, there remains a slight possibility that some of the sketches might have been done during the American occupation.

2. Ballentine, *Autobiography*, p. 216.

3. Phillips, *Mexico Illustrated*, text accompanying plate 4.

4. Smith, *War with Mexico*, 2:59-65, 74, 223-25, 230-31, 358, 361-62, 458. For a short time during Scott's occupation, the Americans published a newspaper in Jalapa, the *American Star*.

5. New York *Weekly Herald*, Jan. 22, 1848, p. 1. Descriptions of Jalapa by American troops include Oswandel, *Notes of the Mexican War*, p. 140; Semmes, *Service Afloat and Ashore*, p. 186; and Lieutenant John James Peck in a letter printed in Pourade, *Sign of the Eagle*, p. 94.

6. Otto Onken of Cincinnati lithographed a view of Jalapa that appears in Semmes, *Service Afloat and Ashore*, betw. pp. 184 and 185. It was copied from Nebel's print. The same view appeared in Oswandel, *Notes of the Mexican War*, p. 141.

immediately behind it to the height of several thousand feet; but in front, looking towards Vera Cruz, there is an open view of the seacoast, and in fine, clear weather the ships may be seen in the harbour at Vera Cruz with an ordinary spyglass.[2]

Phillips himself wrote that "the scenery is remarkably beautiful, and glows with a peculiar richness of verdure, while mountain rises above mountain, clothed with extensive forests almost to their summits. In the background of the picture, the mountain called the Coffer of Perote is seen, elevated 13,414 feet above the level of the sea."[3]

The Americans first reached Jalapa on April 19, 1847, and General Scott remained there until May 22 as he supervised the advance of his troops along the National Road. He left behind a small garrison, later withdrawn as he concentrated his forces for the attack on Mexico City. After this time, heavily guarded American supply trains and reinforcements passed through the town. Toward the end of the war, Colonel George Wurtz Hughes served as military governor. The first American troops in Jalapa found the population well disposed toward them, and the Americans apparently reciprocated with their best behavior. Later volunteer troops, however, left a different impression. Partly as a result, Governor Hughes punished American offenders with severity.[4]

128.
After John Phillips
PLAIN OF PEROTE
Toned lithograph (hand colored), 1848
10-3/8 x 15-3/8 in. (26.4 x 39.1 cm.)
l.r.: "Day & Son, lithrs. to the Queen."
From John Phillips and Alfred Rider, *Mexico Illustrated in Twenty-six Views* (London: E. Atchley, Library of Fine Arts, 1848), plate 6
ACM 10.79/6

About twenty-four miles west of Jalapa on the National Road lies the Castle of San Carlos de Perote, an eighteenth-century fort that chiefly served as a prison. The castle guarded a broad high plain, seen in this lithograph after a sketch by John Phillips. The first Americans

reached the fort in late April 1847; they found it abandoned and filled with Mexican munitions. The American army maintained a garrison there until the end of the war, using the fort as a base for anti-guerrilla patrols.[1]

John Phillips's text describes how the National Road after Perote

enters upon a level tract of country of vast extent, forming the plains of Perote; a large portion of which, called the Mal Pais, is a bleak and arid desert, composed of lava from the neighbouring volcanoes. The water from the wells is very brackish and unpalatable. Vegetation is

scarce and stunted. Rude crosses mark the spots where murders have been committed. Orizaba, towering high above the black mountains which surround it, looks cold and frowning; and, although admiring the grandeur of the scenery, the traveller is glad to pursue his journey, and to find some leagues onward that the barren lava has given place to extensive plantations of aloes and fertile fields of corn.[2]

1. Smith, *War with Mexico*, 2:61, 65, 74, 176, 361-62, 425; see also Moore, *Scott's Campaign in Mexico*, pp. 77-84. Oswandel, *Notes of the Mexican War*, p. 179, contains an engraving of the castle of Perote after a sketch by James T. Shannon, who did garrison duty there in 1847 with the First Pennsylvania Volunteers. (Shannon's original sketch is in his sketchbook, now in the Special Collections Division of The University of Texas at Arlington Libraries.) The castle of Perote held gloomy associations for the Americans, since Texans captured in the Mier and Santa Fe expeditions and in other incidents during the Texas War for Independence were held there as prisoners.

2. Phillips, *Mexico Illustrated*, text accompanying plate 6.

128. PLAIN OF PEROTE

129.
Abraham López (?)
ENTRADA DE LOS YANQUES EN PUEBLA
Lithograph, c. 1848
l.l.: [Lit.] "de A. Lopez C. de Donceles no. 18"
Courtesy of Museo de Historia, Chapultepec,
Mexico

This rare Mexican lithograph probably depicts the entrance of General Worth's division into the city of Puebla on May 12, 1847.[1] The lithographer was possibly Abraham López, who operated a shop in the Calle de Donceles number 18 in Mexico City, probably near that of J. S. Rocha in the Calle de Tacuba. López was also a printer and publisher, so his exact role in the production of this print is not certain. The view is reasonably accurate and probably based on firsthand knowledge.[2]

The American troops, including musicians, mounted officers, and several ranks of infantry, march along the present Calle 5 de Mayo past the west facade of the cathedral.[3] In the middle of the print may be seen the Plaza de la Constitución, surrounded by arcades. A resident of Puebla described the occasion:

129. ENTRADA DE LOS YANQUES EN PUEBLA

The town people seemed undisturbed. The whole city, with the exception of the dry goods shops, which remained closed, presented its ordinary aspect, and no one would have supposed that a hostile army was expected. About half past 10 o'clock a party of 100 cavalry separated from the division, and entered by the streets of Alguacil Mayor, San Cristobal, &c., &c., to the square, from which they withdrew by way of Santo Domingo to the barrack of San Jose. Curiosity to see the Yankees overcame the alarm so natural at the moment. The people crowded the streets, and nearly all the balconies in the line were filled with spectators. You will excuse this curiosity when you reflect that it was excited by the men of Vera Cruz and Cerro Gordo, who in the mouths of the vulgar passed for diabolical prodigies, and in mustachoed lips for at least human prodigies. I myself yielded to the impulse, and breaking a vow of seclusion, sallied forth to become acquainted with our future masters. Imagine my surprise, and that of all the world, when, instead of the Centaurs we expected, I saw a hundred gallows-faced men, uniformed (if the dress which most of them wore could be called such) with poverty and bad taste, many of them in their shirt sleeves, armed with sword, carbine, and pistols of a common kind, their horses large indeed, but heavy, and devoid of grace, like all their race, and with no other ornament than a plain saddle and bridle....

The uniform of all that have entered consists of a jacket and pantaloons of common light blue cloth, precisely the same as the recluses of San Roque, and with no ornament but the military insignia. All, even the dragoons, wear flat cloth caps, though several have adopted the palmy hats of the country, and we saw some enter with *tompeates* on their heads.[4]

1. Smith, *War with Mexico*, 2:70-74.

2. Compare the photograph of the cathedral in *Artes de México* 13, no. 81/82 (1966): 94.

3. The church, the second largest in Mexico, was constructed between 1562 and 1649. The west facade was completed in 1664; one of the towers dates from 1678, the other from c. 1760s. See T. Philip Terry, *Terry's Guide to Mexico* (Boston: Houghton Mifflin, 1935), pp. 509-15, including map; also *Baedecker's Mexico* (Englewood Cliffs, N.J.: Prentice-Hall, 1985), pp. 218-20.

4. New Orleans *Daily Picayune*, Aug. 11, 1847, pp. 1, 2, from the London *Times*, quoting a letter by a resident of Puebla, dated Puebla, May 16, 1847. See also Moore, *Scott's Campaign in Mexico*, pp. 96-98 (reprinted in Smith and Judah, *Chronicles of the Gringos*, pp. 227-29) for an American account of the entry.

130.
After John Phillips
PUEBLA
Toned lithograph (hand colored), 1848
10-1/4 x 15-1/2 in. (26.0 x 39.4 cm.)
l.r.: "Day & Son Lithrs. to the Queen"
From John Phillips and Alfred Rider, *Mexico Illustrated in Twenty-six Views* (London: E. Atchley, Library of Fine Arts, 1848), plate 7
ACM 10.79/7

Puebla, Mexico's second largest city, was an impressive sight for most of the American soldiers.[1] Private George Ballentine, arriving with Twiggs's division, wrote:

As we approached within five or six miles of the city we enjoyed one of the finest views of a city at a distance that I have ever seen. The lofty snow mountains of Popocatepetl and Iztaccihuatl, with their broad and heavy-looking dark bases, and their dazzlingly bright pyramidal summits, rose in the background. In front, on the side of a gently rising and delightfully wooded hill, sat Puebla; every outline of its numerous spires and churches could be seen through the highly rarefied atmosphere as distinctly as the lines of a highly finished engraving.[2]

Although this view by English artist John Phillips is probably not contemporary with the American occupation, it may give a rough idea of what the city looked like at the time. The view is taken from the eastern district of the city and approximates what Ballentine and others described. In the distance, between the snow-covered mountains of Popocatépetl and Iztaccíhuatl, is the cathedral. Several other churches are visible (the city is famous for its large number of churches). The abandoned buildings and ruins in the foreground give evidence of the decline the city had suffered after the wars for independence from Spain. Phillips may have copied Carl Nebel's view of Puebla in the latter's *Voyage pittoresque et archéologique* of 1836. Except for changes in the foreground figures, the compositions are virtually identical. Nebel's original view was taken between 1829 and 1834.[3]

General Scott stayed in Puebla more than two months, concentrating his forces for the coming attack on Mexico City. On August 7 the army began to leave on their march to the Valley of Mexico,

130. PUEBLA

leaving a garrison in Puebla with the sick. For the remainder of this campaign Scott's army was organized into four divisions, under generals Worth, Twiggs, Pillow, and Quitman, along with three dragoon regiments under Colonel W. S. Harney. In addition to the siege train, the artillery included field batteries of Duncan, Taylor, Steptoe and others, and a howitzer and rocket battery under Talcott.[4]

1. The city was known at this time as Puebla de los Angeles, but today it is called Puebla de Zaragoza in honor of the Mexican general who defeated the French there on May 5, 1862 (the celebrated "Cinco de Mayo").
2. Ballentine, *Autobiography*, p. 253. See also Moore, *Scott's Campaign in Mexico*, pp. 99-125. One of the principal attractions for American soldiers in the Puebla area was the giant pyramid at the ancient Indian city of Cholula, located about five miles west. Raphael Semmes included a lithograph by Otto Onken of Cincinnati showing American troops marching up to the top of the pyramid of Cholula in his book *Service Afloat and Ashore*, opp. p. 296. Onken's lithograph was based on a Carl Nebel view in *Voyage pittoresque et archéologique*; Onken simply added several files of American infantry and a U. S. flag. In another illustration for Semmes's book, entitled *Indians on the Plain of Puebla*, Onken copied another plate ("Indios Carboneros") from Nebel's book. U. S. Grant tells of a visit to the crater of Popocatépetl soon after the occupation of Mexico City (*Personal Memoirs*, pp. 108-11).
3. Samuel Putnam Avery copied Nebel's lithograph in an engraving that appeared in the New York *Weekly Herald*, Aug. 22, 1847, p. 1, and the *Herald*, Aug. 22, 1847, p. 1. Avery engraved another view of Puebla, taken from the southeast, for the *Weekly Herald* of Dec. 4, 1847, p. 1, but gave no credit to the original artist, who must have seen the city firsthand.
4. Smith, *War with Mexico*, 2:77-78, 93. Accompanying the American army from Puebla as an interpreter on the staff of General Worth was artist James Walker, who had lived and worked in Mexico several years before the war. Walker recorded a scene somewhere between Puebla and Mexico City in a small oil painting entitled *March from Puebla in the Order They Were Upon the Road* (Army Art Collection, U.S. Army Center for Military History, Alexandria, Virginia). To my knowledge, no contemporary print was made from this picture.

131.
After John Phillips
Rio Frio
Toned lithograph (hand colored), 1848
10-5/16 x 15-7/16 in. (26.2 x 39.2 cm.)
l.r.: "Day & Son, Lithrs. to the Queen."
From John Phillips and Alfred Rider, *Mexico Illustrated in Twenty-six Views* (London: E. Atchley, Library of Fine Arts, 1848), plate 8
ACM 10.79/8

About thirty-six miles up the National Road between Puebla and Mexico City is the town of Rio Frio, located near the pass leading down into the great Valley of Mexico. In this print, after a John Phillips original that was probably executed before the war, Mexican infantry are seen on the march with an artillery unit crossing the stream at Rio Frio. According to Phillips, Rio Frio "derives its name from a small stream which flows through a beautiful valley, affording pasturage for hundreds of cattle and sheep, and surrounded by pine-clad mountains. Rio Frio is situated on the high road from Puebla to Mexico. It contains a few Indian huts and a comfortable roadside inn. It is a strong military position, being at the entrance to a wild pass called El Pinal."[1]

An American with Scott's army described Rio Frio as he saw it on August 9:

The third day we were to encounter the much vaunted pass of "Rio Frio," and also the passage of the mountain which was to lead us to the El Dorado of our hopes, the great plain of Mexico. Our march was to be long and difficult, and 3 o'clock saw us under way with heart and hopes full of the prospect before us. The much-dreaded pass is reached and passed. The mountains which skirt the road on the left, here close upon it for about a mile, overhanging and enfi-

lading it completely, and affording with their crests most excellent coverings for an enemy's marksmen. The newly cut trees and long range of breastworks thrown up on the crest, showed us that preparations had been made, while numerous parapets with embrasures in the logs taught us what might have been done. But no men were there — the muskets and cannon were gone....Rio Frio was found to be a little stream pouring down from the snow mountain, of icy coldness and crystal purity. After a slight pause for refreshment, we commenced our ascent of the ridge which separates the plains of Puebla and Mexico, the former of which it had hitherto skirted.[2]

When the Americans reached the top of the pass just beyond Rio Frio, they had their first view of the Valley of Mexico.

1. Phillips, *Mexico Illustrated*, text accompanying plate 8. Although Phillips's picture has the spontaneity of an eyewitness wartime view, it would have been highly difficult for him to make such sketches during wartime. As an Englishman sketching Mexican troop movements in a war zone, he might have been treated as a spy. Such a danger is underscored by Jonathan W. Buhoup, a volunteer with Wool's division at Parras, who wrote that on December 12, 1846, "a Mexican was taken, who had been engaged in taking a draft of our encampment. He was adjudged to have been a spy, and the whole army were expecting to be marched out to witness the execution, but after investigating his case, he proved to be a Mexican artist. Liking the form of our encampment, he had taken the draft of it, for the purpose of displaying his genius. He was of course acquitted." (Buhoup, *Narrative of the Central Division*, p. 95.)
2. New Orleans *Daily Picayune*, Oct. 21, 1847, p. 2, quoting New York *Courier and Enquirer*. See also Ballentine, *Autobiography*, p. 260, and Grant, *Personal Memoirs*, 1:85-86. Many soldiers recorded their impressions of Rio Frio and the pass into the Valley of Mexico, but unfortunately there do not seem to be any prints derived from eyewitness sketches.

131. Rio Frio

132.

After John Phillips
SAN AGUSTIN
Toned lithograph (hand colored), 1848
10-3/16 x 15-1/4 in. (25.9 x 38.7 cm.)
l.r.: "Day & Son, Lithrs. to the Queen"
From John Phillips and Alfred Rider, *Mexico
Illustrated in Twenty-six Views* (London: E.
Atchley, Library of Fine Arts, 1848), plate 18
ACM 10.79/18

The shortest route from Puebla to Mexico
City, approaching the latter from the east,
ran directly past a heavily fortified position known as El Peñón.[1] Scott decided
to avoid this by taking an indirect
approach to the city from the southwest,
making a detour around Lakes Chalco
and Xochimilco.[2] This involved cutting a
road for artillery from Chalco to San
Agustín, a village seen in this lithograph
after John Phillips. The artist's original
sketch was probably taken shortly before
the war.[3] According to Phillips's accompanying description:

> The village of San Agustin de las
> Cuevas is about four leagues from
> the city of Mexico, charmingly situ-
> ated in the midst of handsome villas
> and orchards. It is celebrated for the
> great fête which is held annually at
> Whitsuntide and attended by every
> body in Mexico who can by any
> means provide for the occasion. Most
> fertile and beautiful as the country is
> about San Agustin, there lies imme-
> diately beyond it a tract of black lava
> and scoriae destitute of vegetation,
> called the Pedregal, extending to the
> base of the mountain Ajusco, which
> forms a part of the chain separating
> the Valley of Mexico from
> Cuernevaca.[4]

San Agustín de las Cuevas, also
known by its Indian name of Tlálpan,
was a popular gambling and recreation
center. According to the historian of the
Ninth Infantry, the town "was crowded
to excess the afternoon of the 17th of
August, many wealthy and fashionable
families from the city being of the
number. They had gone there not for recreation only, but to escape from the scene
of strife; and, unfortunately, suddenly
found themselves in the midst of the
invaders." Scott's entire army passed
through the town during the next three
days; it became a depot and, temporarily,
the base of the American army. Many of
the inhabitants fled the town, which soon
had a deserted appearance. Lieutenant
Daniel Harvey Hill of the Fourth Artillery
recorded his impressions of the town on
August 19, just before the battle of Contreras: "San Augustine is a large & beautiful town & I do not think that I have
ever seen so many fruit trees as were there.
The vile Volunteers had committed the
usual excesses & the lovely town was in
good part deserted. I observed three
beautiful girls seated in a window, calmly
looking at us as we passed and the sight
gratified me no little, though I expected
so soon to be on the field of blood."[5]

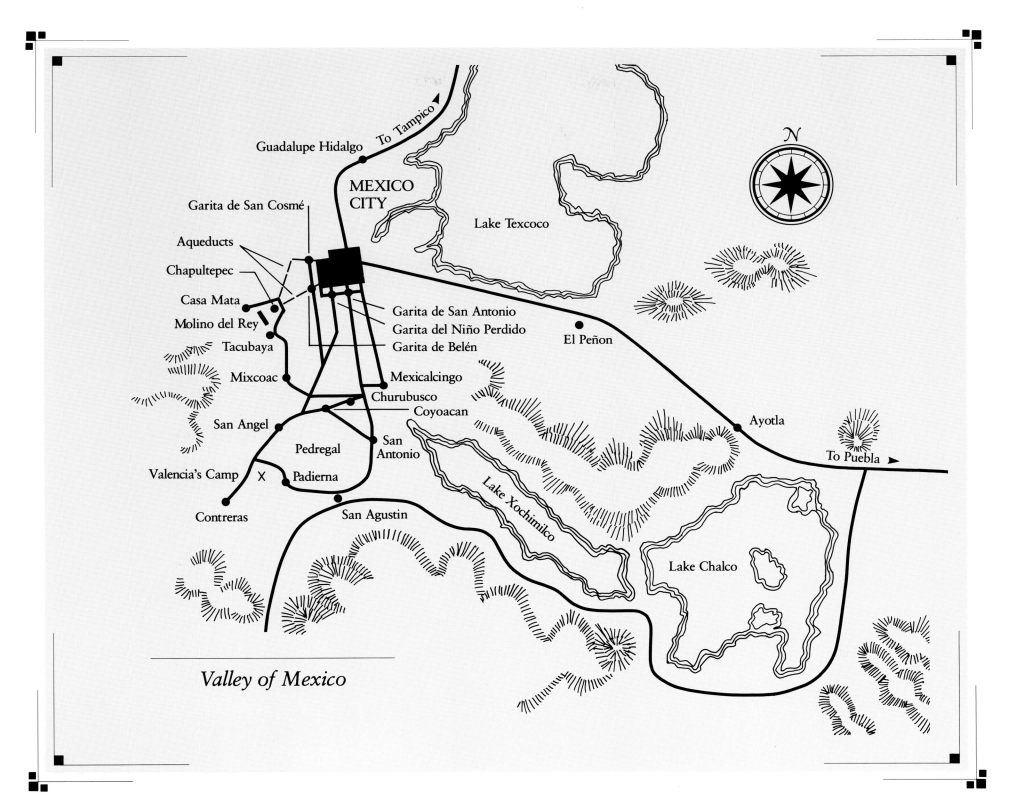

Guadalupe Hidalgo

To Tampico

MEXICO CITY

Garita de San Cosmé

Aqueducts

Chapultepec

Casa Mata

Molino del Rey

Tacubaya

Mixcoac

San Angel

Valencia's Camp

Contreras

Pedregal

Padierna

San Agustin

San Antonio

Churubusco

Coyoacan

Mexicalcingo

Garita de San Antonio

Garita del Niño Perdido

Garita de Belén

Lake Texcoco

El Peñon

Ayotla

To Puebla

Lake Xochimilco

Lake Chalco

Valley of Mexico

1. Smith, *War with Mexico*, 2:90, 92, 96-98. A lithograph of El Peñón appeared in Abraham López, *Undecimo Calendario... para el año de 1849* (Mexico City and Toluca: the author, 1848).

2. James Walker painted an oil sketch entitled *The Detour Around Lake Chalco* (Army Art Collection, U.S. Army Center for Military History, Alexandria, Virginia).

3. In the foreground of the print are two (in this impression, blue) uniformed soldiers wearing forage or barracks caps, the most common headgear worn by American soldiers in the Mexican War, suggesting a date during the American occupation. However, such caps, although relatively rare, were also not unheard of in the Mexican army; see J. Hefter, ed., *El Soldado Mexicano 1837-1847*, Documentos Historicos Militares Monografía 1 (Mexico City: Ediciones Nieto-Brown-Hefter, 1958), p. 75.

4. Phillips, *Mexico Illustrated*, text accompanying plate 18.

5. Fred R. Brown, *History of the Ninth U.S. Infantry, 1799-1909* (Chicago: R. R. Donnelley and Sons, 1909), p. 25; journal of Lieutenant Daniel Harvey Hill in Smith and Judah, *Chronicles of the Gringos*, p. 240. See also Ballentine, *Autobiography*, pp. 263-75.

Contreras and Churubusco

133.

Joaquín Heredia after an unknown artist
BATTLE OF CONTRERAS. MEXICO.
AUGUST 19 AND 20. 1847. | BATALLA DE
CONTRERAS. MEXICO AGOSTO. DIAS 19
AL 20 DE 1847
Lithograph, c. 1847-48
10-1/8 x 15 in. (25.7 x 38.1 cm.)
l.r. on stone: "J. Heredia"
l.l.: "Imp. Lit de R. C de Tacuba No. 14."
l.r.: "Luis Meunier, almacen de la Profesa 3a.
C Sn. Francisco no. 5"
ACM 31.75

Of the few existing prints of the battle of Contreras (actually fought near the hamlet of Padierna, and sometimes referred to by this name), this lithograph is one of the more intriguing. Its combined English and Spanish title suggests it was intended for sale to U. S. soldiers during the occupation. According to the inscriptions, it was drawn on stone by Mexican lithographer Joaquín Heredia and printed in Mexico City by the lithography firm of José Severo Rocha.[1] The publisher and dealer was Luis Meunier, located at the shop of the Profesa at the third Calle de San Francisco, no. 5.

Comparisons of the print with accounts of the battle, maps, and other sources reveal a number of inconsistencies. The topographical features depicted in the print are improperly placed, making orientation difficult. The artist (possibly the lithographer Heredia) incorporated details that show some knowledge of the battle, but not enough to suggest that he was present.[2]

After the Americans occupied the village of San Agustín, the engineers dis-covered that the direct route to the city from there was blocked by the heavily fortified hacienda of San Antonio, flanked on the right by impenetrable marshes and on the left by a rough, rocky lava field known as the Pedregal. San Antonio could be bypassed, however, by crossing the lava field and attacking the camp of General Gabriel Valencia and his 5,000-man Army of the North, located on a hill between the villages of San Geronimo and Contreras. Pillow's division labored to construct a road for artillery through the Pedregal, and on August 19 they broke through near Valencia's position, which appears at left in the print. Three brigades under Generals Persifor F. Smith, Bennett Riley, and George Cadwalader circled around to the right in order to try to cut off Valencia. Possibly the artist intended the troops in the right middle distance to represent Riley's brigade in an incident on August 19, when they repulsed two separate charges by Mexican lancers who bore down upon them from higher ground.[3]

The buildings in the right foreground of the print may represent the hamlet of Padierna. The hill in the foreground, swarming with American officers and dragoons, might correspond to the hill from which General Scott watched the battle. According to an officer's report published in the *Spirit of the Times*, "about half way between San Augustine and Contreras, on the right is a high hill. General Scott with his staff, took position on this hill. The dragoon reserve remained posted at the foot. The hill was covered with spectators, principally followers of the army."[4] This hill may be that seen in a much better delineated painting by artist James Walker, who no doubt observed the battle firsthand. Walker's painting, along with another he painted of Valen-

Imp. Lit de R. C de Tacuba. 1874.

Luis Meunier: almacen de la Profesa ... C S... Francisco n.º 5

BATTLE OF CONTRERAS.
Mexico. August 19 and 20. 1847.

BATALLA DE CONTRERAS.
Mexico Agosto. dias 19 al 20 de 1847

133. BATTLE OF CONTRERAS / BATALLA DE CONTRERAS

cia's camp at Contreras, suggest that distances are shortened in Heredia's print and topographical features rearranged.[5] The Valley of Mexico, for example, visible at right in the print, should be beyond the picture's margins. The print gives no hint of the ravine by which the Americans gained the rear of Valencia's position on August 20. The print may also telescope the actions of the nineteenth and twentieth, as its title implies. Thus the attack at right might be construed as a frontal assault made by Franklin Pierce's brigade on the twentieth, an attack intended as a diversion for the main American attack that day in the rear of Valencia's camp (see cat. no. 134).

1. Joaquín Heredia (active c. 1839-47) produced plates for Ignacio Cumplido as early as 1839 and was later associated with other Mexican printmakers, including Plácido Blanco, Hesiquio Iriarte, and Hipólito Salazar. (W. Michael Mathes, *Mexico on Stone: Lithography in Mexico, 1826-1900* [San Francisco: Book Club of California, 1984], pp. 19, 21, 23, 24, 51 n. 17, 52 n. 21.)

2. Compare the print with the map by P. G. T. Beauregard, reproduced in the New Orleans *Daily Picayune*, Sept. 12, 1847, p. 1. For eyewitness accounts of the battle see the New York *Herald*, Nov. 16, 1847, pp. 1-2 (official reports); New Orleans *Daily Picayune*, Sept. 8, 1847, p. 2, Sept. 9, pp. 1, 2, Sept. 30, pp. 1-2; and Ballentine, *Autobiography*, pp. 275-82. Historical accounts of the battle include Smith, *War with Mexico*, 2:95-110, and Nevin, *Mexican War*, pp. 178-89.

3. Kendall describes this in *War Between the United States and Mexico Illustrated*, p. 29. The body of Mexicans at right in the print appears to be composed entirely of cavalry, although few actions in the battle involved cavalry.

4. *Spirit of the Times*, Dec. 18, 1847, p. 508.

5. Walker's two paintings of this action — one titled either *Hill Omatuzzo* or *Coming in Sight of the Enemy*, the other *Advance to the Attack of the Camp of Valencia at Contreras* — are in the Army Art Collection, U.S. Army Center for Military History, Alexandria, Virginia.

134.   See Plate 17
Adolphe-Jean-Baptiste Bayot after Carl Nebel
ASSAULT AT CONTRERAS
Toned lithograph (hand colored), 1851
10-15/16 x 16-13/16 in. (27.8 x 42.7 cm.)
l.l.: "C. Nebel fecit."
l.r.: "Bayot lith."
From George Wilkins Kendall, *The War Between the United States and Mexico Illustrated* (New York: D. Appleton & Company, 1851), plate 6
ACM 186.72/6

Artist Carl Nebel, working in Mexico City during the American occupation, probably visited all of the nearby battlefields. One would thus expect a certain accuracy of topographical detail in his works depicting these battles, since he could probably check any details of which he was not certain.[1]

In his view of the battle of Contreras, Nebel chose a vantage point from behind Valencia's camp, looking north-northeast across the Valley of Mexico. He may have compressed certain landmarks into a more narrow field of vision; otherwise, the topography is generally accurate.[2] Unlike the equivocal print by Joaquín Heredia, Nebel's view undoubtedly represents the action on August 20.

On the previous day, the three brigades under Smith, Riley, and Cadwalader (with Smith in immediate command) had crossed, from right to left, the area beyond the hills seen in the middle distance of the print. Their probing attacks against the front of Valencia's entrenched camp had been beaten back, and the Mexican general optimistically believed he had won a great victory. In the area at far left in the print, just beyond the picture's margins, the Americans discovered another Mexican army under the personal command of Santa Anna. Had Santa Anna and Valencia coordinated their

plans, Smith's forces could have been crushed between the two. Instead, in a torrential rainstorm during the night of the nineteenth, Santa Anna withdrew his army to San Angel, giving the excuse that "it would have been equal to a defeat to have kept the troops in the open field."[3] Smith's, Riley's, and Cadwalader's brigades spent the night in the mud, however, and in the early morning darkness silently groped their way up an unprotected ravine that led to the rear of Valencia's position.

Just after dawn General Franklin Pierce's brigade made a demonstration against the front of Valencia's camp while Smith launched a bayonet assault upon the rear. Kendall commented on Nebel's print:

The time chosen by the artist, to give his drawing of the assault upon Contreras, is when Smith, Riley and Cadwalader, pouring like a torrent upon both flank and rear, have reached the intrenchments and baggage of Valencia, and are storming the mound upon which all his cannon were posted. The dip of the ground beyond, on the right of the picture and towards San Augustin, conceals the demonstration organized as a feint or false attack, and which is drawing a heavy fire from the front of the enemy's lines. In the distance, also on the right, are the lower range of mountains girding the basin of Mexico on the east. In the middle ground, and near the centre, may be seen the villages of San Angel, Coyoacan and Churubusco, with Mexicalcingo and the black mound of the Peñon beyond: in the distance are the waters of Lake Tezcoco, the same on which Cortes, three centuries before, launched his fleet of brigantines for the subjection of the great Aztec capital. Occupying the left of the picture, also in the distance, may be seen the outlines of the present city of Mexico, soon to be entered by new conquerors, the castle of Chapultepec looming up in solitary grandeur still farther to the left. The snow-clad peaks of Iztacchuatl and Popocatepetl, lying on the right and beyond San Augustin, the artist could not introduce, preferring to take his drawing from a point which would enable him to bring in the northern and more important sections of the great valley of Mexico.[4]

Lieutenant Daniel Harvey Hill, of the Fourth Artillery serving as infantry, was among Riley's brigade and left an excellent description of the attack as seen in Nebel's print:

The enemy was expecting us though he was taken somewhat by surprise as all his preparations had not still been completed. He therefore threw out an Advance corps to check us until more cannon could be brought to bear on our column. This corps poured a heavy fire into us before we had completed our deployment. Riley's brigade constituted the entire storming column and our regiment led the column.

We returned the fire of the advance Corps with deadly effect & then marched forward, the enemy falling back before us. Cannon now opened upon us, charged with grape & cannister, but owing to the fright of the gunners did us little injury.... Our advance was steady under a heavy but far from destructive fire as

the Mexicans took no aim. After fighting for half an hour we discovered that the enemy's Infantry & Cavalry were in full retreat leaving the artillerists still at their guns. We received a discharge of grape within twenty yards of the muzzles of the cannon. Capt. Drum of our Regt. captured two guns which proved to be the very guns that Lt. O'Brien of our Regt. lost at Buena Vista.[5]

Completely routed, the Mexicans fell back toward Mexico City, leaving more than a thousand prisoners, along with supplies and ordnance, in the hands of the invaders.

Ironically, American printmakers paid little attention to this overwhelming victory. Among the few popular prints is a wholly inaccurate lithograph of Contreras by E. B. & E. C. Kellogg.[6]

1. Americans stationed in and around Mexico City visited the former battle sites, just as tourists would. For example, Private G. W. Hartman of the Second Pennsylvania regiment stationed in San Angel, just outside the city, wrote in his journal entry for February 6, 1848: "Paid a visit to the battle field of Contreras." (Hartman, *Journal*, p. 22.)
2. Compare the map in Smith, *War with Mexico*, 2:80.
3. Manifesto of Antonio López de Santa Anna, dated Mexico City, Aug. 23, 1847, a translation of which appeared in the New Orleans *Daily Picayune*, Sept. 9, 1847, p. 1.
4. Kendall, *War Between the United States and Mexico Illustrated*, p. 30.
5. Lieutenant Daniel Harvey Hill, quoted in Smith and Judah, *Chronicles of the Gringos*, p. 242. Compare the account by Lieutenant William Montgomery Gardner, Second Infantry, in ibid., pp. 242-44. For the story of the capture of O'Brien's guns at Buena Vista, see cat. no. 38.
6. An impression is in the Connecticut Historical Society, Hartford.

135.
Artist unknown
ATAQUE DE CHURUBUSCO. POR LA DIVISION DEL GENERAL WORTH, EL DIA 20 DE AGOSTO, DE 1847. | ATTACH AT CHURUBUSCO. BY THE DIVISION OF GENERAL WORTH, ON THE 20TH, DAY OF AUGUST, 1847.
Toned lithograph, c. 1848
8-1/4 x 12-1/2 in. (21.0 x 31.8 cm.)
l.l.: "Litog. de Cumplido."
ACM 32.75

The sudden rout of Valencia's army at Contreras on the morning of August 20 forced Santa Anna to resort to a second line of defense. While the survivors of Valencia's army fled from Contreras toward Mexico City with General David Twiggs's division in pursuit, Santa Anna stationed forces at fortifications prepared earlier along the Churubusco River, including some in the Convent of San Pablo.[1]

From his point of view opposite the convent, General Twiggs reported a scene similar to the one depicted in this print:

Lieut. Stevens, of the engineers, was sent forward to look at the enemy's positions, supported by the company of sappers and miners. He reported a good position for Taylor's battery towards the left of the work, from which it was practicable to drive from the roof and walls of the church such of the enemy as, from their elevated position, could annoy my foot-troops destined to storm the work surrounding the church. The battery was accordingly ordered. It opened with great spirit, and remained under a most galling and destructive fire of grape, round-shot, shell and musketry, for an hour and a half; by which time, having accomplished the

ATAQUE DE CHURUBUSCO.
por la division del general WORTH, el dia 20 de Agosto, de 1847.

ATTACH AT CHURUBUSCO.
by the division of general WORTH, on the 2o.th day of August, 1847.

Litog. de Cumplido.

135. Ataque de Churubusco / Attach at Churubusco

desired object, it was withdrawn, much crippled in officers, men, and horses.[2]

The artist of this view of the American attack on the convent is unfortunately not credited. The only inscription denotes that it was lithographed by the firm of Ignacio Cumplido, a prominent Mexican printer, lithographer, and publisher. The Spanish and English titles suggest that it was produced during the American occupation and was intended to be sold to American soldiers. The format of the inscriptions is similar to that in other bilingual prints by Cumplido, which may have formed some sort of souvenir portfolio or album of Mexico and the Mexican War. Cumplido's willingness to sell prints to Americans is curious, since he served in the war as a captain in the "Victoria" batallion of the Guardia Nacional.[3]

One wonders how popular such prints were with American soldiers, many of whom were highly critical of inaccuracies. There is one curious error in the inscription of this print that American troops would have recognized immediately: while Worth's division carried the bridgehead near the convent, it was Twiggs's division that played the important part in the attack on the convent itself. The omission of Twiggs's name could have been intentional, for there was considerable posturing between the American senior officers during the occupation of Mexico City as to just exactly who had done what.

Despite these problems, many details of the print suggest a familiarity with the battle site and a certain knowledge of American uniforms. In the foreground, the officers wear forage caps and frock coats, while others wear shell jackets; several artillerymen have striped trousers.

At right, a squadron of dragoons or mounted riflemen, wearing a mixture of forage caps and straw hats, gather behind some small huts for protection from Mexican cannon and musket fire. At left, American infantry advance toward the enemy, again protected by a small building, while the foremost ranks deliver a volley. The artist rendered the vegetation with convincing accuracy, particularly the maguey, prickly pear, and palm trees, and realistically included fallen men and horses. In the middle distance, from left to right, a line of trees denotes the course of the Rio Churubusco, the banks of which served as a line of defense for the Mexican forces. Smoke billows from the bristling fortifications of the convent, accurately depicted with its bell tower, buttresses, central dome and lantern, smaller two-story outbuildings, and an outer breastworks with prepared embrasures for cannon and infantry. To the right and rear of the convent may be the *tête du pont* or fortified bridgehead that guarded the river crossing of the road from San Antonio to Mexico City. Beyond the convent and river stretches the Valley of Mexico with the buildings of Mexico City and its suburbs. Since the view shows the battle from an American perspective, it is possible that Cumplido may have utilized a sketch by an American soldier.

Cumplido (or his employees) produced strong tones to emphasize the foreground and the details of the convent, while distant and less important elements fade as the composition recedes. This creates a wonderful impression of aerial perspective, demonstrating that Cumplido's work is equal to the best single-stone lithography produced in America at this time.

1. For descriptions of the Convent of San Pablo and the battle of Churubusco see Smith, *War with Mexico*, 2:110-19; Isaac I. Stevens, *Campaigns of the Rio Grande and of Mexico* (New York: D. Appleton & Company, 1851), pp. 69-82; Moore, *Scott's Campaign in Mexico*, pp. 139-47; Kendall, *War Between the United States and Mexico Illustrated*, pp. 31-33; Semmes, *Service Afloat and Ashore*, pp. 395-411; official reports of Scott, Pillow, Worth, Twiggs, Smith, Quitman, Shields, and Harney in New York *Herald*, Nov. 16, 1847, pp. 1-2. Compare the map in Ripley, *War with Mexico*, 2: opp. p. 255.

2. Report of Brigadier General D. E. Twiggs, Commanding 2nd Division Regulars, published in the New York *Herald*, Nov.16, 1847, p. 2.

3. The other Cumplido views that may have been included in the series are cat. nos. 149, 155, and 163. Cumplido (1811-87), a native of Guadalajara, settled in Mexico City sometime in 1821 or 1822. He soon became a printer of liberal political periodicals. In 1838 he visited the United States, where he purchased a printing press and other materials that he later used to print *El Siglo XIX*, an important and long-lived daily newspaper (1841-96). In 1844 Cumplido apparently became the first to initiate the chromolithographic process in Mexico. At the end of the war with the United States, he went to Europe, later returning to Mexico with rotary and steam presses that he had purchased. In addition to his activities as one of Mexico's most prolific printers and publishers, Cumplido served as superintendent of prisons and founded a school of printing for orphans. See Ramiro Villaseñor y Villaseñor, *Ignacio Cumplido: Impresor y Editor Jalisciense del Federalismo en México* (Guadalajara: Año de la República Federal y del Senado, 1974), pp. 5-9, and Mathes, *Mexico on Stone*, pp. 17 ff.

136.   See Plate 18
Adolphe-Jean-Baptiste Bayot after Carl Nebel
BATTLE AT CHURUBUSCO
Toned lithograph (hand colored), 1851
10-13/16 x 16-15/16 in. (27.5 x 43.0 cm.)
l.l.: "C. Nebel fecit."
l.r.: "Bayot lith."
From George Wilkins Kendall, *The War
Between the United States and Mexico Illus-
trated* (New York: D. Appleton & Company,
1851), plate 7
ACM 186.72/7

At the end of his account of the battle of
Churubusco, Kendall gave a short key to
Nebel's picture:

> It being found impossible to take a
> general view of the battle of Churu-
> busco, the artist chose, as the princi-
> pal subject for his drawing, Worth's
> attack upon the tête-de-pont. In the
> centre of the picture may be seen the
> rear of the church and convent of San
> Pablo, Twiggs being at the time
> warmly engaged in front. On the
> right, beyond the taller trees, is the
> position attacked by Shields. The low
> range of mountains in the back-
> ground are those which rise to the
> southward of Contreras.[1]

After the rout at Contreras, the
infantry columns of General Worth's First
Division, seen in the fore and middle
ground of the lithograph, had pursued
the retreating Mexican garrison of San
Antonio up the road toward Mexico City
when they suddenly discovered the
strong fortification of the *tête du pont*
over the Rio Churubusco. The road enters
Nebel's picture at the left and continues
up through the middle distance until it
reaches the *tête du pont* at right. So hasty
had the Mexican retreat been that they
had had to abandon some ammunition
wagons in front of their fortifications.
Two of these are visible in the center
middle distance of Nebel's picture.

A scientifically constructed work with
embrasures, a ditch with four feet of
water, and three heavy cannon, the *tête
du pont* opened on Worth's infantrymen
with a withering hail of grapeshot and
musket fire. This was about half an hour
after General Twiggs's division (some columns of which may be seen in the left
distance) had begun its attack on the
convent. Before Worth's men, mostly
members of the Sixth Infantry, could
reach the abandoned ammunition
wagons, they moved off to the right of
the road and sought shelter in a field of
tall corn (represented in the left foreground of the print). A number of officers
and soldiers were struck down by the
heavy fire as they waited for the rest of
the division to come up. General Worth
arrived at the front and sent a battalion
of the Sixth directly up the road, but it
was repulsed a second time. Meanwhile,
Worth sent Garland's brigade and the
remainder of Clark's brigade into the
cornfields to advance along the right of
the road. From there, with the further
support of part of Pillow's division, they
successfully attacked the bridgehead;
Nebel's view shows the moment of scaling
its walls.

Throughout the engagement, George
Wilkins Kendall was with Colonel James
Duncan's battery, which was attached to
Worth's division.[2] Kendall regarded the
tête du pont as the key to the Mexican
position, and it is not surprising that he
had Nebel emphasize this part of the
action. Kendall had to choose his subjects
carefully in order not to offend the various factions among the Americans who
touted their particular claims to battle
glories. He had been a friend and aide of
General Worth; as Worth's reputation at
the end of the war had been tarnished by
these petty disputes, Kendall may have
wanted to make sure that Worth and his
men received their proper due.[3]

Compositionally, Nebel relieved the
horizontal lines of the masses of infantry
by including a silhouetted tree in the foreground. Interesting staffage, including
broken tree limbs, castaway guns and a
drum, and dead and wounded soldiers,
litter the scene and suggest the terrible
effects of combat.

1. Kendall, *War Between the United States and
Mexico Illustrated*, p. 33.
2. Copeland, *Kendall of the Picayune*, pp. 207-9.
3. For the controversy between Scott and Worth,
see Edward S. Wallace, *William Jenkins Worth:
Monterey's Forgotten Hero* (Dallas: Southern
Methodist University Press, 1953). Kendall and
Raphael Semmes criticized Scott for even fighting
the battle of Churubusco. See Semmes, *Service
Afloat and Ashore*, pp. 409-13.

CHURUBUSCO.
1847.

137. CHURUBUSCO. 1847

137.
Reinaldo after an unknown artist
CHURUBUSCO. 1847.
Lithograph, c. 1847
8-7/16 x 13-5/8 in. (21.4 x 34.6 cm.)
l.l. on stone: "Reinaldo"
l.l.: "Lit de R. C. de Tacuba no. 14."
Courtesy of Missouri Historical Society, St. Louis

This rather crudely drawn lithograph is probably the print that was announced by the *North American*, a newspaper published in Mexico City for American servicemen, on November 16, 1847: "We notice a print in the shops of calle Francisco, purporting to be designs of the battle of Churubusco. The plate may look like some part of the place we have not seen — certainly not like any portion of it we have seen."[1] The printer of the lithograph was José Severo Rocha, whose initial "R." and address at the Calle de Tacuba in Mexico City are denoted by the inscription. Little is known about the lithographer "Reinaldo" who drew the view on stone, and whether or not he invented the design is impossible to tell.

This Churubusco view is apparently based upon some accurate information. Some of the architectural features of the convent seen in the print still exist.[2] The view is faintly similar to an oil painting by eyewitness artist James Walker depicting the convent with American troops marching past immediately after the battle.[3] Also similar is the convent in Ignacio Cumplido's print of the battle (cat. no. 135). The cruder execution of Reinaldo's lithograph suggests that some of the clarity of the original drawing (if there was one) may have been lost.[4] The view is apparently taken from the southwest, and the road over which the American infantrymen are advancing is the one from the village of Coyoacán.[5] The Mexican lithographer perhaps derived some satisfaction in littering the foreground with the bodies of dead and wounded Americans, but certainly the facts of the battle support these gory details.

George Wilkins Kendall described the convent and the final assault upon it by General Twiggs's troops:

The buildings immediately belonging to the church formed a large square, the front, towards the assailants under P. F. Smith and Riley, being protected by a wall scaffolded for infantry. In the rear of this wall was a building crowded with sharpshooters; still farther in rear rose the church, its windows, roof, and even belfry...filled with men. And in addition to all, in works constructed with great science and care, were the seven pieces of artillery...so posted that they raked every approach. The garrison, under General Rincon, numbered over two thousand, the greater part of the battalion of San Patricio, composed of deserters from the American ranks, at the same time adding their effective strength. For these renegades there was no other alternative than victory or death, and they therefore held out and fought with desperation.[6]

Soon after the fall of the *tête du pont*, Twiggs's division stormed the walls of the convent. Some of the defenders surrendered, while others who were not killed, disabled, or captured fled in headlong retreat toward Mexico City. Some of Colonel W. S. Harney's dragoons pursued them up to the very gates of the city.[7] After the battle the Mexicans requested an armistice, and the war briefly paused.

1. Mexico City *North American*, Nov. 16, 1847, p. 2.
2. According to photographs taken by Ron Tyler in the 1970s (Amon Carter Museum files), a similar bell tower still exists, as do the archway and windows seen at right. The outer wall and moat are apparently gone.
3. Walker's painting is in the Army Art Collection, U. S. Army Center for Military History, Alexandria, Virginia. Views of the battle of Churubusco are less common than views of Monterrey, Buena Vista, Veracruz, and Chapultepec. One of the most intriguing may prove to be an oil painting of Churubusco by Lieutenant Albert Tracy, commissioned by General Worth, which is discussed in Rick Stewart's essay.
4. The view is stylistically similar to John Allison's view of the battle of Chapultepec (cat. no. 147), which may have been lithographed in Mexico City. Allison was probably present at the battle of Churubusco; as one of Colonel Burnett's New York Volunteers, he probably fought with General Shields's brigade at the hacienda north of the convent.
5. See the map by Sarony & Major in Ripley, *War with Mexico*, 2: opp. p. 255.
6. Kendall, *War Between the United States and Mexico Illustrated*, p. 32.
7. The pursuit of the Mexicans by Harney's dragoons and the death of Colonel Pierce M. Butler of the South Carolina Regiment in a related action behind the convent were the subjects of two popular lithographs drawn on stone by John Cameron for Nathaniel Currier (see fig. 17). Other noneyewitness prints of the battle included lithographs by James Baillie and the Kelloggs and numerous book illustrations.

138.
Pierre-Frédéric Lehnert
CHURUBUSCO 1847
Toned lithograph, c. 1850
9-9/16 x 14-3/8 in. (24.3 x 36.5 cm.)
l.r. on stone: "F. Lehnert."
u.c.: "Mexico Pintoresco"
l.l.: "Julio Michaud y Thomas Editores, Junto
al Correo Mejico"
l.r.: "Imp. Lemercier, a Paris."
From *Album Pintoresco de la República
Méxicana* (Mexico City: Estamperia de Julio
Michaud y Thomas, c. 1850)
ACM 55.81

This French-produced lithograph is
derived from the preceding print by
Reinaldo and Rocha. Lithographer
Pierre-Frédéric Lehnert redrew the figures
in Reinaldo's view completely, adding a
number of inaccuracies. It is doubtful that
American dragoons made such a ludicrous
charge against the fortifications of the San
Pablo convent (center foreground), or that
Mexican rancheros used lassoes to drag
off American infantrymen there (at left).
Lehnert had no doubt read accounts of
Mexicans' skillful use of the lasso. For
example, H. Judge Moore wrote that
"some of the Mexican Generals have
thought that the excercise of throwing
the lasso might be incorporated into the
military tactics of the republic, and be
used to advantage in breaking hollow
squares of infantry, by lassoing the men
and leading them out of lines, thus making the lasso usurp the place of the sword
in cavalry movements."[1] No accounts
confirm the use of this tactic at Churubusco, however.

1. Moore, *Scott's Campaign in Mexico*, p. 92.

138. CHURUBUSCO 1847

139.
Abraham López (?)
EL PUEBLO APEDREA LOS CARROS
Lithograph, 1847
2-5/8 x 4-7/16 in. (6.8 x 11.3 cm.)
From Abraham López, *Decimo Calendario...
para el Año bisiesto de 1848* (Mexico City
and Toluca: the author, 1847), frontispiece
Courtesy of Nettie Lee Benson Latin American
Collection, University of Texas Libraries,
Austin

This tiny Mexican print appeared in a
contemporary *calendario* (a kind of
almanac). Titled "The People Stone the
Wagons," it illustrates an incident that
occurred during the two-week armistice
after the battle of Churubusco. According
to the controversial terms of the agreement between Scott and Santa Anna, the
American army was to remain in its positions just outside the capital. A long train
of American army wagons was allowed
to pass into the city under a flag of truce
to pick up supplies purchased for the
American army. While the teamsters
waited with their wagons in the main
plaza, they were attacked by a mob of
Mexican citizens. (Apparently the teamsters had gazed at a religious procession
either indifferently or insultingly.) Six or
seven of the Americans were killed before
Commandante General J. J. Herrera with
Mexican troops could quell the riot.
Santa Anna expressed his regret for the
incident and punished some Mexican
officers. After this, greater care was taken
to conduct this business more discreetly
(in the early morning, when most of the
populace was asleep). Nevertheless, minor
riots occurred later, and the storage location of the supplies was sacked.[1]

In the print the American wagons
may be seen entering the Calle de Plateros,
on the eastern side of the main plaza or
Zócalo. At far left is one of the towers of
the Municipal Palace. At far right is the
monument at the southeastern corner of
the cathedral (at the end of the Paseo de
las Cadenas).[2]

The lithograph is important as an
example of a Mexican print based on
eyewitness knowledge. The stoning of
the American wagons is usually glossed
over in American accounts of the war
(Justin Smith confined it to a footnote),
but evidently Mexican lithographer and
publisher Abraham López saw the incident as an example of Mexican patriotism, probably not unlike the way
Americans view the Boston Tea Party. The
print did not fail to attract the attention
of the American occupation forces. The
Daily American Star, a newspaper published in Mexico City for American soldiers, announced the receipt of "The
Calendar of Lopez" on October 20, 1847.
The editor, in a racist comment not
uncommon for his time, took special
notice of the "engraving of the wagon
row, the vehicles being seen entering the
palace, with numerous *greasers*, (leperos,)
following up and stoning them."[3] López's
calendario for 1849 contains tiny lithographed views of fortifications around
Mexico City.

El Pueblo apedrea los Carros.

139. EL PUEBLO APEDREA LOS CARROS

1. Smith, *War with Mexico*, 2:395-96.
2. Compare the map of Mexico City reproduced in
Artes de Mexico 53/54, no. 11 (1964): 56-57. Also
see cat. no. 163.
3. Mexico City *Daily American Star*, Oct. 20, 1847,
p. 2.

Molino del Rey and Chapultepec

140.   See Plate 19
Adolphe-Jean-Baptiste Bayot after Carl Nebel
MOLINO DEL REY — ATTACK UPON THE
MOLINO
Toned lithograph (hand colored), 1851
10-7/8 x 16-7/8 in. (27.6 x 42.9 cm.)
l.l.: "C. Nebel fecit."
l.r.: "Bayot lith."
From George Wilkins Kendall, *The War
Between the United States and Mexico Illus-
trated* (New York: D. Appleton & Company,
1851), plate 8
ACM 186.72/8

Few prints, or images of any kind, depict
the battle of Molino del Rey, which was
fought just outside Mexico City on September 8, 1847. Although Scott originally
planned it to be little more than a raid by
Worth's division, it became one of the
bloodiest fights of the war. Many Americans wondered if it should have been
fought at all, which may explain why so
few images were made of it.[1]

However, perhaps partly because of
the controversial aspect of the battle, Carl
Nebel did two separate renderings of it,
recording different phases of the struggle.
George Wilkins Kendall was both an eyewitness and a participant; General Worth
cited Kendall and several other aides in
his official report of the battle as ones
"who came upon the field, volunteered
their acceptable services, and conducted
themselves, in the transmission of orders,
with conspicuous gallantry."[2] There is no
evidence that the artist witnessed the battle, but he probably visited the site sometime during the American occupation of
Mexico City.

On September 6, 1847, as the armistice and peace talks that had followed
the battle of Churubusco were breaking
down, the Americans observed large
numbers of Mexican troops around a
group of low, massive stone buildings
known as El Molino del Rey. These
buildings (spreading across the middle
distance of this print) were about one
thousand yards west of the castle of Chapultepec (in the distance at left), which in
turn was only about two miles from the
gates of Mexico City. A large grove of
trees and low ground separated the buildings of the molino and the castle. General
Scott received reports that the molino
housed a foundry for casting cannon, and
there were rumors that Santa Anna, in
desperate need of ordnance, was sending
out church and convent bells to have them
melted down and converted for this purpose. Scott ordered Worth to attack and
carry the molino, break up the foundry,
and destroy any munitions captured.

Nebel's first view of the battle shows
the action opposite the American center
and right. In the early morning hours of
September 8, Worth advanced from the
village of Tacubaya to within six hundred
yards of the molino. The Americans
knew little about the Mexican position;
the engineers could not get close enough
to see that the Mexicans had masked very
strong fortifications. When there was no
reply to a brief bombardment by two
American twenty-four-pounder siege
guns, Worth assumed the Mexicans had
abandoned the buildings in the center.
He sent an assault column of five hundred
picked men, led by Major George Wright,
down a gently sloping plain (in the foreground of the print) toward the molino.
These were mostly men from Worth's old
regiment, the Eighth Infantry. Behind
them he placed C. F. Smith's light battalion and George Cadwalader's brigade in
the center, and to their right Garland's
brigade and a battery under Captain S.
H. Drum. On the American left was a
battery under Colonel James Duncan and
a brigade, formerly Clark's, commanded
by Brevet Colonel J. S. McIntosh; these
men faced the Casa Mata, a stone building adjacent to the molino (out of the
picture, over the viewer's left shoulder,
and the subject of Nebel's second view of
the battle). Together, Worth's force
totaled only 2,800 men.

Thomas Mayne Reid, an army officer
who corresponded with the magazine
Spirit of the Times, described Major
Wright's assault:

> When they arrived within about half
> musket shot of the works, the enemy
> opened upon this gallant band the
> most dreadful fire.... Six pieces
> from the field battery played upon
> their ranks, while the heavy guns
> from Chapultepec, and nearly six
> thousand muskets from the enemy's
> entrenchments, mowed them down
> in hundreds. The first discharge cov-
> ered the ground with dead and dying.
> One half of the command, at least,
> fell with this terrible cataract of bul-
> lets. The others retiring for a
> moment, took shelter behind some
> maguey, or, in fact, anything that
> would lend a momentary protection.

> The Light Battalion and the 11th
> Infantry now came to the relief of
> this gallant little band, and springing
> forward amid the clouds of smoke
> and the deadly fire, the enemy's
> works were soon in our possession.
> At the same time the right and left
> wing had become hotly engaged with
> the left and right of the enemy. Gar-
> land's Brigade, with Duncan's [*sic*,
> Drum's] Battery, after driving out a

large body of Infantry, occupied the mills.[3]

In the right portion of Nebel's picture, Garland's brigade has already reached the southernmost buildings of the molino, and either Drum's battery or some captured Mexican guns now face the center of the molino. "The drawing," as Kendall states, "takes in the entire range of buildings, the roofs crowded with the enemy. Garland is just commencing the attack upon the upper point of the row, or that next Tacubaya, while the combat in front is raging with violence. On the left of the picture, above the grove of lofty trees, rises the castle of Chapultepec, the mound and growth of timber shutting out the city of Mexico from the view." The mountains in the distance are Iztaccíhuatl and Popocatépetl. In the left foreground may be seen the "intervening rows of magueys, with slight embankments thrown up in front of old ditches," that, according to Kendall, "occupied the space between the Molino and the Casa Mata."[4]

1. Artist James Walker painted an oil sketch of the battle of Molino del Rey taken from a position probably near Captain Benjamin Huger's battery (the two twenty-four pounders in the center of the American line that opened the battle). Walker's picture (in the Army Art Collection, U. S. Army Center for Military History, Alexandria, Virginia) is quite similar to Nebel's view, although they differ in certain details. Probably neither artist borrowed from the other. For accounts of the battle see Kendall, *War Between the United States and Mexico Illustrated*, pp. 35-36; Semmes, *Service Afloat and Ashore*, pp. 409-12, 431-48; and Smith, *War with Mexico*, 2:141-47.

2. Worth's official report, published in the New York *Herald*, Nov. 17, 1847, p. 1. See also Copeland, *Kendall of the Picayune*, pp. 215-17.

3. [Thomas Mayne Reid], "Sketches by a Skirmisher. Written for the Spirit of the Times by an Officer of the U.S. Army," *Spirit of the Times*, Dec. 11, 1847, p. 1.

4. Kendall, *War Between the United States and Mexico Illustrated*, pp. 36, 35.

141.   See Plate 20
Adolphe-Jean-Baptiste Bayot after Carl Nebel
MOLINO DEL REY — ATTACK UPON THE CASA-MATA
Toned lithograph (hand colored), 1851
10-7/8 x 16-3/4 in. (27.6 x 42.6 cm.)
l.l.: "C. Nebel fecit."
l.r.: "Bayot lith."
From George Wilkins Kendall, *The War Between the United States and Mexico Illustrated* (New York: D. Appleton & Company, 1851), plate 9
ACM 186.72/9

While the American right was still engaged in the attack on the molino, General Worth ordered the brigade on his left, under Colonel McIntosh, to assault the Casa Mata. This building, "instead of being an ordinary stone house, as had been supposed by the engineers, proved to be a citadel, surrounded with bastion entrenchments, and impassable ditches — an old Spanish work, recently repaired and enlarged. The reconnoissance had been as close as possible, and this mistake as to the character of the work, had been unavoidable — the work being situated in low ground, and the lower portions of it being masked by dikes and maguey plants."[1] Worse yet for the Americans, General Francisco Pérez and a fresh force of Mexican regulars lay completely hidden behind the banks of the ditch in front of the building and within its ramparts. In reserve was a large body of Mexican cavalry under General Juan Álvarez, across a large ravine on McIntosh's left.

McIntosh's fatal assault is the subject of this print. Kendall described the approach to the Casa Mata:

The ground, while it was destitute of shelter or cover of any kind, was at the same time descending, thus rendering every shot the enemy might fire effective; for the bullets which went over the front ranks of the assailants must inevitably find victims in the rear. A short distance on the right of McIntosh, and within plain sight, the contest [for the molino] still raged with fury, causing so great a desire among his men to hasten to the relief of their friends that they moved down the slope almost at a run. Not an enemy was to be seen in front of the Casa Mata, or behind its ramparts, so well were they still concealed.... Within two hundred yards of the intrenchments not a musket had been emptied on either side. But on reaching a point one hundred yards distant a wide sheet of smoke suddenly poured forth from the entire face of the work, a crashing flight of bullets beating upon the front of the assailants with frightful execution.... McIntosh, the only officer mounted and offering a fair mark, was soon struck down desperately wounded, and while lying upon the ground was hit by another bullet.[2]

Nebel undoubtedly intended the figure on horseback in the center middle distance to represent Colonel McIntosh as he was first struck. (Before the fight was over his second in command was also dead, and the third was severely wounded.) In the foreground is Duncan's artillery, which is masked at this point by the assaulting infantry. Besides the main Mexican force, Duncan had to help hold off Álvarez's cavalry, which lies out of the picture to the left. At far left, in the middle distance, a body of dragoons under Major E. V. Sumner moves past the Casa Mata toward Álvarez's position. A number of horses and men may be seen

to have fallen; Kendall reported that Sumner "was compelled to pass within range of a galling fire from the Casa Mata. Although he swept down the slope at a rapid pace, and was but a few minutes exposed, he lost nearly a fourth of his men and over one-third of his horses."[3] In the background of the print spreads Mexico City, with Chapultepec on the hill at right.

Although McIntosh's first assault was repulsed, the battle soon turned against the Mexicans. Duncan pushed his guns up close to the Casa Mata and began bombarding it with fearful effect. Álvarez's cavalry never crossed the ravine toward the American position.[4] The defenders, seeing that the molino had fallen, slipped out the rear of the Casa Mata and fell back toward Chapultepec.

1. Semmes, *Service Afloat and Ashore*, p. 440.
2. Kendall, *War Between the United States and Mexico Illustrated*, p. 37.
3. Ibid.
4. The Mexican reserve cavalry under Álvarez was estimated as outnumbering Worth's entire strength on the field. According to Semmes, Worth was so concerned about Álvarez that he dispatched an aide-de-camp to Duncan with the message to be "sure to hold the enemy's cavalry in check"; this aide was George Wilkins Kendall. (Semmes, *Service Afloat and Ashore*, p. 441; also see Copeland, *Kendall of the Picayune*, pp. 215-18.)

142.
H. Mendez
VISTA DE CHAPULTEPEC Y EL MOLINO DEL REY. TOMADA EN LA CASA DE MATA. VIEW OF CHAPULTEPEC AND MOLINO DEL REY. FROM CASA DE MATA.
Lithograph, c. 1847
9-1/8 x 14-1/8 in. (23.2 x 35.9 cm.)
l.r. on stone: "H. Mendez"
u.l.: "Propiedad del Edictor J. Rabouin."
u.r.: "Frente de la Profesa No. 7."
l.l.: "Lit. de R. C. de Tacuba no. 14."
ACM 34.75

Lit. de B.C. de Tacuba. n° 14.

VISTA DE CHAPULTEPEC Y EL MOLINO DEL REY.
Tomada en la Casa de Mata.
VIEW OF CHAPULTEPEC AND MOLINO DEL REY.
From Casa de Mata.

142. Vista de Chapultepec y el Molino del Rey / View of Chapultepec and Molino del Rey

143.

After H. Mendez
VIEW OF CHAPULTEPEC AND MOLINO
DEL REY, (AFTER THE BATTLE,) CITY OF
MEXICO IN THE DISTANCE.
Lithograph (hand colored), 1847
8-3/16 x 12-1/4 in. (20.8 x 31.2 cm.)
l.l.: "Lith. & Pub. by N. Currier,"
l.c.: "Entered according to Act of Congress in
the year 1847 by N. Currier, in the Clerk's
office of the District Court of the Southern
District of N. Y."
l.r.: "152 Nassau St. Cor. of Spruce N. Y."
l.l. to l.r.: "Where Worth's division of the
United States army (3,100 Strong) met and
defeated the whole Mexican army (14,000
Strong) under Genl. Santa Anna Sept. 8th.
1847. / From a Sketch taken from Casa del
Mata by H. Meendez and forwarded by Lieut.
Larkin Smith, U.S.A. / 553."
Courtesy of Prints and Photographs Division,
Library of Congress, Washington, D.C.

One officer who was severely wounded in
the attack upon the molino was Larkin
Smith of the Eighth Infantry, who sent an
image of the battle site to Nathaniel Currier in New York City.[1] Currier's resulting
view of Molino del Rey and the castle of
Chapultepec, taken from the Casa Mata
after the battle "from a sketch ...by H.
Meendez," is virtually identical to a lithograph by H. Mendez published in Mexico City. In both prints the Casa Mata
appears at left. The Americans had found
and exploded a quantity of useless
ammunition here at the end of the battle,
blowing the building apart. Its strong
parapets and ditches are strengthened by
a tangle of prickly pear and other plants.
Part of the low walls and buildings of the
molino appear at right. The castle of
Chapultepec with its surrounding grove
of trees is in the center distance, and
beyond it, to the left, is the City of Mexico. Figures appearing in the prints

include sightseers, an artist sketching, and
a souvenir hunter digging with his dog.

The Mexican version, drawn on
stone by Mendez and printed by José
Severo Rocha, was apparently issued first.
A slightly wider view and the inclusion of
a few details distinguish it from the version lithographed and published by Currier. (The latter omits some of the figures
and the artist's materials in the foreground.) The bilingual titles of the Mexican print indicate that Rocha and the
publisher, J. Rabouin, intended it for both
American and Mexican audiences.

Although Currier's inscription credits
a "sketch" by Mendez, it is likely that
Smith actually sent Currier an impression
of Mendez's lithograph; Currier probably
did not care to advertise the work of a
competitor. It is not certain whether
Mendez actually originated the design,
since it was common practice for a
lithographer to sign his own name on
stone whether he had copied or invented
the design. In any case, no original sketch
is known to exist for this view.[2]

The Mendez and Currier prints were
widely copied. An engraved version by

143. CHAPULTEPEC AND MOLINO DEL REY (AFTER THE BATTLE)

Samuel Putnam Avery appeared in the New York *Weekly Herald* on November 27, 1847, without credit to the original artist. The *Herald* claimed that "it is impossible for the public to have an idea of the nature of the ground, and the position and apparent impregnability of the Mexican works that surmount them, without refering to this engraving, which we recommend our readers to keep for future reference. Its accuracy, like that of all previous engravings published in this journal, may be relied upon."[3]

In addition to Molino del Rey, the Mendez-Currier view shows the castle of Chapultepec, where another battle took place five days later. Though Scott had originally hoped to avoid the strongly fortified castle, he determined that it lay in the path of the best approach to Mexico City. After a heavy bombardment of the Mexican positions, on the morning of September 13 he sent Pillow's division, supported by the remains of Worth's, to attack the west side of Chapultepec from their position at the molino. They drove the Mexican defenders through the woods in the center of Mendez's print.[4] Meanwhile Quitman's division attacked the castle on its south side, moving from right to left through the plain beyond the molino at far right.[5]

1. The inscription of Currier's print gives Smith's rank as lieutenant, but he had been promoted to captain on July 21, 1846. For his gallant conduct at Churubusco, August 20, 1847 (he was one of the first Americans to enter the *tête du pont*, capturing one of the Mexican guns and turning it on the convent), he was breveted to the rank of major. (Cullum, *Biographical Register*, 1:622; Semmes, *Service Afloat and Ashore*, p. 401; and see cat. no. 136.) Smith may have been an agent for Currier, supplying him with Mexican lithographs; see note 2 and cat. no. 154. He had served as an aide to General Worth at the beginning of the war; since Worth was also keenly interested in artistic documentation, it is likely that Smith had Worth's full authorization. (See Rick Stewart's essay for Worth's commission of paintings by another officer, Lieutenant Albert Tracy.)

2. Another Currier print (cat. no. 154) was taken "From a Sketch by Gualdi, and forwarded by Lieut. Larkin Smith." Much of Pedro Gualdi's work in Mexico was available in lithographs; in this case also Smith may have sent Currier a Mexican lithograph rather than a sketch.

3. New York *Herald*, Nov. 26, 1847, p. 2; the engraving appeared on the front page of the *Weekly Herald* on Nov. 27 and of the *Herald* on Nov. 28. The composition was often repeated. John Frost's 1848 *Pictorial History of Mexico*, p. 552, contains an engraved copy made after the Mendez-Currier or Avery print. (For Frost's book, see cat. no. 111.) A James Baillie lithograph, *Battle of Molino del Rey, Fought Sept. 8th. 1847. Blowing up the Foundry by the Victorious American Army under Genl. Worth*, drawn on stone by Magee and also published in 1848, borrows from Mendez's view probably through Currier's or Avery's print. Baillie and Magee's print shows the Casa Mata blowing up while the Americans are storming the parapets. They incorrectly assumed that the foundry was inside the Casa Mata instead of the molino. The Prints and Photographs Division of the Library of Congress has an engraving after a painting by history painter Alonzo Chappel (1828-87) that depicts the battle of Molino del Rey. It is probably based on the Mendez or Currier view. Chappel's work was part of a series of Mexican War pictures he did that were published by Johnson, Fry & Co. in 1856. Chappel apparently never visited Mexico.

4. James Walker painted an oil sketch of Pillow's attack through the woods and another showing a battery under Lieutenant T. J. (later known as "Stonewall") Jackson advancing along a road leading past the north side of the castle; see cat. no. 148, note 10. In Mendez's print, this road is obscured by the Casa Mata.

5. For an overview of the attack on Chapultepec, see Smith, *War with Mexico*, 2:147-58, and Nevin, *Mexican War*, pp. 203-6, 210-15.

144.
After John Phillips
CHAPULTEPEC
Toned lithograph (hand colored), 1848
11 x 16-13/16 in. (27.9 x 42.7 cm.)
l.r.: "Day & Son lithrs. to the Queen."
From John Phillips, *Mexico Illustrated in Twenty-six Views* (London: E. Atchley, Library of Fine Arts, 1848), plate 16
ACM 10.79/16

Chapultepec Castle was really a former palace that had been converted into a military college in 1841. According to English artist John Phillips, who described and sketched it for his book *Mexico Illustrated*, the palace was

> erected by the Spanish Viceroy, Galvez, on a porphyritic hill which rises abruptly from the plain, at about 2-1/4 miles from the city of Mexico. Its situation is most commanding, and the view from it magnificent, as besides the city, the eye sweeps over an extensive plain, a considerable portion of which is cultivated.... The view represents Chapultepec on the left, and diverging from it, an aqueduct of 900 arches, which supplies the city with water. The city itself appears in the centre of the picture, and on the right are the volcanic mountains of Iztaccihuatl and Popocatepetl.[1]

Phillips's view must have been taken before the war, or at least before the Mexicans fortified the castle in anticipation of the American advance on Mexico City. Although he mentions the American attack on the building in his text, this only proves that he wrote the text during the American occupation. Details of the picture suggest that it was based on earlier observation. Noticeably absent from this

144. Chapultepec

CHAPULTEPEC
1847.

145. CHAPULTEPEC 1847

picture, when compared with wartime views, are the parapets, timber screens, and other fortifications as well as the military college's round tower, known as El Caballero Alto.[2] Contemporary maps reveal that Phillips or his lithographer took considerable artistic license with the composition by moving mountains around and compressing and distorting distances.[3]

To suggest the military character of the site, Phillips included a squadron of mounted Mexican lancers galloping by, followed by an artillery unit with two field pieces and limbers or caissons. Perhaps he included some of these details to attract subscriptions for his portfolio from American buyers whose interest in Mexico stemmed from the war.

1. Phillips, *Mexico Illustrated*, text accompanying plate 16. The site, of course, has a much longer history. Once a stronghold of the Toltecs, the Aztec rulers first turned it into a summer residence. The castle was begun in 1783 by Don Matias de Galvez, then Viceroy of New Spain, and construction was continued under his son, Bernardo de Galvez (America's ally in the Revolutionary War and the man for whom Galveston, Texas, is named). (See *Terry's Guide to Mexico*, pp. 379, 386; *Baedecker's Mexico*, p. 174.)

2. The round tower is described by Niceto de Zamacois in his text entry for the lithographic plate "El Valle de Mexico, Tomado desde las Alturas de Chapultepec," in Casimiro Castro et al., *Mexico y sus alrededores ...* (Mexico City, 1855-56; rpt., Cuernavaca: Manuel Quesada Brandi, 1967), p. 29. Daniel Thomas Egerton's view of the Valley of Mexico, published as plate 2 in his *Views of Mexico* (London: the author, 1840), omits the round tower but brings the topographical accuracy of Phillips's view into question.

3. See the maps in Ripley, *War with Mexico*, 2: opp. pp. 176, 187, 411.

145.
Reinaldo after an unknown artist
CHAPULTEPEC 1847
Lithograph, c. 1848
8-13/16 x 14-3/16 in. (22.4 x 36.0 cm.)
l.r. on stone: "Reinaldo"
l.l.: "Lito. de Rocha C. de Tacuba. no. 14."
ACM 33.75

This primitive lithograph of Chapultepec, drawn on stone by Reinaldo and printed by José Severo Rocha, gives a simplified, somewhat inaccurate view of the American attacks on the castle.[1] At left, Pillow's division and a small storming party from Worth's, having come from the molino, advance through the woods west of the castle. Quitman's division and a small contingent from Twiggs's, having advanced along the Tacubaya causeway, attack the south side of the castle, which faces the viewer. In the middle and left foreground, Shields's brigade approaches the southwestern angle of the hill, while at right the rest of Quitman's division attacks the Mexican fortifications at the base of the hill and along the causeway to Mexico City. The Tacubaya causeway should run diagonally from the viewer's position to the southeastern base of the hill at right.

Reinaldo, working in Mexico City during the American occupation, may not have needed an original sketch to produce his view. If he did not participate himself, accounts of the battle could have reached him from Mexican and American soldiers. Interestingly, however, the view is taken from the American lines, and it is possible that the print was based on an American sketch. The short title would have drawn English- or Spanish-speaking customers.

Poor handling of perspective suggests that Reinaldo lacked proper training, not unlike some of the artists working for Currier, James Baillie, and other American firms. As with some of the hastily produced American prints, accuracy does not appear to have been of paramount importance; details are omitted for generalities and distances are distorted. For example, Reinaldo does not include the Tacubaya causeway or the fortifications around the base of the hill. He had the advantage of location over his American contemporaries, however, and this shows in his emphasis on the battle site, rather than close combat, and in the relative accuracy of his depiction of American uniforms and certain architectural details.

1. Compare the maps in Smith, *War with Mexico*, 2:50, and Ripley, *War with Mexico*, 2: opp. p. 411.

146. See Plate 21

Adolphe-Jean-Baptiste Bayot after Carl Nebel
STORMING OF CHAPULTEPEC — PILLOW'S
ATTACK
Toned lithograph (hand colored), 1851
10-15/16 x 16-3/4 in. (27.8 x 42.6 cm.)
l.l.: "C. Nebel fecit."
l.r.: "Bayot lith."
From George Wilkins Kendall, *The War
Between the United States and Mexico Illus-
trated* (New York: D. Appleton & Company,
1851), plate 10
ACM 186.72/10

Carl Nebel's illustration for Kendall was apparently the first contemporary print to depict with any accuracy the attack by Major General Gideon Pillow's division on Chapultepec's western side. An engraving by James Duthie after Hammett Billings is nearly identical to Nebel's view, but Billings probably copied Nebel.[1]

Advancing from the molino, Pillow's division captured a redan at the western base of the castle hill. They could advance no farther, however, enduring a steady barrage from the castle while they waited for scaling ladders, crowbars, pickaxes, and other implements. During the pause Pillow was wounded in the ankle. At last, a storming party of 250 picked men from Worth's division, under Captain Samuel McKenzie of the Second Artillery, led the final assault. Kendall described the hazardous ascent:

> No order could be preserved on such steep, rocky and broken ground: the more strong and resolute of the different detachments forced their way to the front and poured in their fire, the enemy returning it with spirit.... Hidden behind the rocks, and by the cover which the rough ground in front of the walls afforded, were bodies of sharp-shooters, their fire at first annoying to the assailants as they mounted the height. The Mexicans could not however withstand the close and searching aim of their opponents, and were pressed back over the ditches and walls, there to continue the contest. So incessant was the fire of the enemy at this time, and so close the range, that the Americans were every moment falling....

> Bearing to the left, and towards the northwestern angle of the castle, Mackenzie led his stormers, a continuous stream of missiles pouring from the outer works, windows and azotea. For a moment his men hesitated....But the unsparing exertions of Mackenzie, and such of his officers as were still on their feet, soon restored confidence, and again the stormers moved upward, the high and wide aim of the infantry lining the walls alone seeming to save the party from utter annihilation....

The artist has chosen as the subject for his sketch the moment when Mackenzie, after bearing to the left of the crest, has reached the ditch and is applying his ladders to the walls, and when the last of the Mexican skirmishers are being driven from the cover of the rocks to the shelter of the ramparts. No drawing could picture the conflict in the dense grove at the foot of the mound, or the sharp work on the northern side. The heavy guns of the castle are playing, not upon the stormers but upon portions of the brigades of Garland and Pierce, near the northern corner of the wall below the Molino.[2]

Prominent in Nebel's picture are the screens of timber and sandbags, which Justin Smith refers to as "blindage."[3] These queer-looking structures, which appear in several of the contemporary prints of Chapultepec, protected the defenders from falling howitzer and mortar shells.

During the American occupation of Mexico City, a dispute arose among the American officers as to whose division should receive credit for taking Chapultepec. General Pillow believed he and his men had played the most important role in the battle, while the supporters of General Quitman felt otherwise. Kendall and Nebel depicted both sides of the castle, giving the two attacks equal treatment and showing their sensitivity to the problem of rivalry among the victorious generals.

Quite a different side could be related here if prints existed depicting the action from the Mexican point of view. Major General Nicolás Bravo, the commander of Chapultepec, had only 832 infantry plus some artillerymen and engineers to defend extensive works that needed at least 2,000 men. The buildings of the castle were not as strong as they looked, and the incessant American bombardment had had a serious effect on the defenders' already low morale. Santa Anna had only sent a few reinforcements, since he also had to cover the southern gates of the city. Among Bravo's defenders were a handful of cadets from the Military College. Of these, six died defending the castle and are remembered as Los Niños Heroicos in Mexican patriotic lore.[4]

1. On Billings, see cat. no. 38, note 4. An 1898 print after French portrait painter and illustrator J. André Castaigne (1860-1930) shows voltigeurs and infantry storming the castle on this side. It is based on Nebel's or Billings's view. James Walker painted at least two versions of Pillow's attack (see cat. no. 148, note 10), but I have found no prints after Walker of this subject.

2. Kendall, *War Between the United States and Mexico Illustrated*, p. 41. For more information on Pillow's attack see his official report, published in the New York *Herald*, Nov. 18, 1847, p. 1.

3. Smith, *War with Mexico*, 2:151.

4. Bauer, *Mexican War*, pp. 313-18.

147.

After John Allison

THE NEW YORK, PENNSYLVANIA, AND SOUTH CAROLINA VOLUNTEERS WITH THE BATTALION OF MARINES ADVANCING TO THE ATTACK ON THE FORTIFICATIONS OF THE CASTLE OF CHAPULTEPEC.

Lithograph, c. 1847

16 x 20-1/2 in. (40.6 x 52.1 cm.)

l.l.: "Drawn from Nature by J. Allison."

Courtesy of Bowdoin College Museum of Art, Brunswick, Maine

The artist of this lithograph of Chapultepec's south side was John Allison, a private in Company H of the First Regiment of New York Volunteers. A native of England, Allison was listed as a "painter" when he enlisted on December 4, 1846.[1] He participated in the attack on Chapultepec and probably returned to the battlefield to sketch shortly after the occupation of the capital. The lithograph's claim to be "drawn from nature" is substantiated by numerous architectural and topographical details, but the claim should not necessarily include the figures, which Allison probably drew from memory. How much the lithographer further altered these figural details is not known.

No inscriptions on the print credit the lithographer or publisher, but the style of the print suggests that a firm in Mexico City, such as Abraham López's or J. S. Rocha's, may be responsible.[2] The absence of these credits might indicate that a Mexican lithographer preferred not to be identified as one who had business dealings with the Yankee invaders.

Allison apparently took his view from somewhere near the Tacubaya causeway, at a point where General Quitman, advancing under a heavy bombardment, ordered several volunteer regiments of his division to turn left of the road and advance across a meadow that concealed a number of wet ditches. The causeway led around to the southeastern angle of the castle and should be just out of view somewhere to the right. The causeway was blocked by what the Americans called the "gateway batteries," a strongly defended series of Mexican gun emplacements (see cat. no. 148). Also near the point where the artist took his view must have been some dilapidated buildings that served as partial cover for Quitman's division.

The artist packed his view with interesting details. Generals Shields and Quitman are visible in the left foreground of the print, along with part of their staff. Shields wears the straw Panama hat and a sling around his left arm from a wound he has just received. Quitman is the gray-bearded officer to the right. At the right of the print, American artillerists load their cannon; perhaps this is one of Captain Drum's guns, which were advanced along the Tacubaya causeway to support Quitman's division. Dead and wounded American officers and enlisted men already litter the field as the volunteer brigade of Quitman's division marches forward. One of the fallen may represent Captain Abram Van O'Linden, Allison's company commander and enlistment officer.[3] The infantrymen in the foreground wear shell jackets, forage caps, haversacks, and bayonet scabbards attached to their belts. A drummer boy (drawn as a miniature man) gazes at his comrades as they receive instructions from their commander. A rare item appears near the center of this print: a regimental flag bearing a coat of arms, perhaps belonging to the artist's own New York unit. To the left of the farthest advanced American unit is a man bearing a scaling ladder; he is part of the picked storming party.

Drawn from Nature by J. Alliam.

The New York, Pennsylvania, and South Carolina Volunteers with the Battalion of Marines advancing to the attack on the fortifications of the CASTLE of CHAPULTEPEC.

147. NEW YORK, PENNSYLVANIA, AND SOUTH CAROLINA VOLUNTEERS ADVANCING ON CHAPULTEPEC

At the base of the hill stretches the fifteen-foot-high wall that constituted part of the works of Chapultepec; billows of smoke indicate the volleys from the Mexican infantrymen behind it. Near the center of this wall are two breaches made by the American artillery. At left, leading up the hill, is the ramped entry to the castle, also crowded with Mexican defenders. At the base of the ramp is a circular redoubt, its top just visible above the trees in the far left distance. Above the ramp are the western walls and timber and sandbag screens of the gun emplacements soon to be carried by Pillow's division; these are seen in Carl Nebel's view of the western side (cat. no. 146). The appearance of the buildings on the hill clearly denotes their palatial origins.

General Quitman's official report of the battle describes the action from this part of the field and the movement of the troops depicted in the print:

> The command, partially screened, advanced by a flank the storming parties in front, under a heavy fire from the fortress, the batteries, and breastworks of the enemy. The advance was here halted under the partial cover of the raise, and upon the arrival of the heads of the South Carolina and New York regiments, respectively, General Shields was directed to move them obliquely to the left, across the low ground, to the wall, at the base of the hill. Encouraged by the gallant general who had led them to victory at Churubusco, and in spite of the obstacles which they had to encounter in wading through several deep ditches, exposed to a severe and galling fire from the enemy, these tried regiments promptly executed

the movement, and effected a lodgement at the wall.[4]

1. Envelope for "John Allison, private, Companies H & F, First Regiment New York Volunteers," Compiled Service Records of Mexican War Volunteers, RG 94, National Archives, Washington, D.C. This contains listings for Allison on the muster rolls of Companies H and F for December 16, 1846, through October 1847, and the Company H Descriptive Book. (Allison transferred briefly to Company F of the same regiment.) Allison's age was given as twenty-two at the time of his enlistment. He was discharged by reason of a substitute on November 30, 1847.

2. Besides Bowdoin College's impression, the only other impression of the print that I have seen was reproduced in the article "Guerra de E. U. a México" in the *Enciclopedia de México*, ed. José Rogelio Álvarez (Mexico City: Enciclopedia de México, 1972), 6:346.

3. See Colonel Ward B. Burnett's official report for the New York regiment, published in the New York *Herald*, Nov. 21, 1847, p. 1.

4. Report of General Quitman, National Palace, Mexico, Sept. 29, 1847, published in the New York *Herald*, Nov. 18, 1847, p. 1. In 1848 James Baillie of New York published a popular lithograph showing the *Storming of Chapultepec in Mexico ... Genl. Bravo Surrendering his Sword to Lieut. Brower of the New York Regiment*. An impression is in the Prints and Photographs Division of the Library of Congress.

148.   See Plate 22
After James Walker
THE STORMING OF CHAPULTEPEC SEPT. 13TH. 1847.
Chromolithograph (hand colored), 1848
23-9/16 x 35-15/16 in. (59.9 x 91.3 cm.)
l.l.: "Drawn on Stone, Printed in Colours, and Published by Sarony & Major. 117 Fulton St. N. Y."
l.c.: "Entered according to Act of Congress in the year 1848 by Sarony & Major in the Clerks Office of the district court of the Southern District of New York."
l.r.: "From a Painting by Walker. In the Possession of Capt. Roberts U.S.A."
l.c. below title: "N. Currier, 152 Nassau St. N. York Sole Agent."
ACM 48.74

149.
After James Walker
ATAQUE DEL CASTILLO DE CHAPULTEPEC
POR LAS DIVISIONES DE LOS GENERALES
QUITMAN Y SHIELDS, EL DIA 13 DE SEP-
TIEMBRE 1847. | ATTACK ON THE CASTLE
OF CHAPULTEPEC BY GENS. QUITMAN &
SHIELDS' DIVISIONS. SEPTEMBER 13, 1847.
Toned lithograph, 1847
7-15/16 x 12-5/8 in. (20.2 x 32.1 cm.)
l.r.: "Litog. de Cumplido."
ACM 35.75

150.
After James Walker
ATAQUE DEL CASTILLO DE CHAPULTE-
PEC, POR LAS DIVISIONES DE LOS GENER-
ALES QUITMAN Y SHIELDS, EL DIA 13 DE
SEPTIEMBRE 1847. | ATTACK ON THE
CASTLE OF CHAPULTEPEC, BY GENS.
QUITMAN & SHIELDS, DIVISION'S, SEP-
TEMBER 13TH. 1847.
Lithograph (hand colored), 1848
8-1/2 x 12-1/4 in. (21.7 x 31.2 cm.) comp.
l.l.: "Lith. & Pub. by N. Currier,"
l.c.: "Entered according to Act of Congress in
the year 1848 by N. Currier, in the Clerk's
office of the District Court of the Southern
District of New York."
l.r.: "152 Nassau St. Cor. of Spruce. N. Y."
l.c. below title: "629."
Courtesy of Prints and Photographs Division,
Library of Congress, Washington, D.C.

151.
After James Walker
THE STORMING OF CHAPULTEPEC SEPR.
13TH. 1847.
Lithograph, 1847
4-1/2 x 6-3/8 in. (10.7 x 15.8 cm.) comp.
l.l.: "Lith. by W. Endicott & Co."
l.c.: "Entered according to Act of Congress in
the year 1847 by N. Currier, in the Clerk's
Office of the District Court of the Southern
District of N. Y."
l.r.: "59 Beekman St. N. Y."
Courtesy of Prints and Photographs Division,
Library of Congress, Washington, D.C.

James Walker's paintings of the attack on
Chapultepec have been reproduced more
than any other views of the subject and
are thus well known to students of the
Mexican War.[1] What may be of surprise
to many, however, is the number of var-
iants and copies of the composition
depicting General John A. Quitman's
attack on the southeastern corner of the
castle grounds. In the years after the capture of Mexico City, a number of lithographs and engravings that appeared in
the United States and Mexico bore a
striking resemblance to Walker's paintings. Among these, perhaps only one, a
large chromolithograph by the lithography firm of Sarony & Major in New York,
credits the artist. Fortunately, Walker's
efforts attracted a lot of attention from
the beginning, so that at least some of
the relationships between the paintings
and prints may be reconstructed from
several contemporary sources.

Walker may have personally overseen
the production in 1848 of the most
important of the prints when he traveled
to New York. This is the large chromolithograph by Sarony & Major (cat. no.
148). Printed in colors from several stones
with hand coloring added, it adheres
faithfully to the original painting (148a)

148A. STORMING OF CHAPULTEPEC

ATAQUE DEL CASTILLO DE CHAPULTEPEC
por las divisiones de los generales QUITMAN y SHIELDS, el dia 13 de Septiembre 1847.

ATTACK ON THE CASTLE OF CHAPULTEPEC
by gens. QUITMAN & SHIELDS' divisions. September 13, 1847.

Litog de Cumplido

149. Ataque del Castillo / Attack on the Castle of Chapultepec
by Quitman and Shields' Divisions

that Walker did for Captain Benjamin Stone Roberts in Mexico City.[2] Technically it is a masterpiece of the chromolithographic process, which was just gaining practitioners among American lithographers at the time.

The chromolithograph shows some of the volunteer troops of Quitman's division depicted in John Allison's print of the battle, as well as those who continued along the causeway and stormed the gateway batteries on the southeastern side of the castle. Articles in American newspapers published in Mexico City during the occupation describe Walker's composition; from them a detailed key can be constructed.[3] At far left in the middle

distance, where the bombardment by Captain Drum's battery has had an effect, parts of the New York, South Carolina, and Second Pennsylvania regiments pour through breaches in the trenches and low wall below the castle. Above and beyond them, some of their comrades climb their way up to the buildings of the college. The far left side of the hill is the west side, attacked by General Pillow's troops.

In the left foreground, along the causeway, gray-bearded General Quitman, on horseback, converses with General James Shields, who is on foot and rests his wounded arm in a sling. A gun to their left, commanded by Lieutenant H.J. Hunt of Lieutenant Colonel Duncan's battery,

has just been advanced up the road to support the storming party under Major Levi Twiggs of the U.S. Marine Corps. To the right of Quitman, Major Twiggs reels backward, having received a fatal musket ball in the chest. His storming party — a light battalion of marines and about 265 picked men from his brother's (General David E. Twiggs's) division — continues its advance in the center and right of the picture. Detached parties of riflemen and volunteers occupy the edge of the ditches on each side of the road; they may be distinguished from some of the other troops by their lack of bayonets. At right, Captain Roberts, at the head of the storming party, has just taken one of the gateway batteries to the left of the road.

In a letter intended for his parents, Captain Roberts wrote:

In the ... storming and carrying of Chepultepec, the strongest fortified Palace that can be conceived, storming parties were selected from every Brigade of the Army, and General Smith selected me to command the "forlorn hope" from our Brigade, 125 picked soldiers, 12 non-commissioned and six Commissioned officers. I had the storming of a 5 Gun Battery in the rear of the hill, supported by 3,000 Mexican Infty. ...I reached the work and carried at the point of the Bayonet with about 40 only of my party, the others had been killed and wounded. I escaped untouched altho' in advance up to the very ditch of the Battery.[4]

The description of Walker's painting in the Mexico City *American Star* identifies the Mexican troops in the view: "[Those] occupying the battery on the road are the battalion of San Blas; those occupying the trenches to the left, are from Oajaca, Ligero and Querétaro. Those that are firing from the top of the wall are the Grenadiers of the Guards; and those from the top of the aqueduct are San Blas. While the force placed on the road leading to San Cosme, called the Camino real de Mejico, is the battalion of Morelia, thrown there as a reserve."[5]

The *American Star*'s account concluded:

> Upon the whole, it is one of the finest productions of the kind we have most ever seen. And being taken upon the ground, and representing faithfully one of the most gallant actions of the many that has distinguished this campaign, as an historical production it is invaluable. . . .
>
> We learn [the artist] is now engaged in another view taken from the opposite side of Chapultepec showing the operations of Gen. Pillow's command, and the others engaged on the west side. The one just completed and above described has been purchased by Capt. G. T. Davis, Aid to Maj. Gen. Quitman, who, we learn takes it with him, in a day or two, to the United States.
>
> We hope the Captain will yield to the solicitation of many of his friends, and on his arrival at New Orleans allow it to be Lithographed. The historical events connected with it would make it an acceptable visitor in every family.[6]

Walker, who had served as an interpreter with Scott's army, clearly wasted no time in setting up his studio in Mexico City. The contacts he had made during his years of living in Mexico no doubt

150. ATAQUE DEL CASTILLO / ATTACK ON THE CASTLE OF CHAPULTEPEC BY QUITMAN AND SHIELDS' DIVISIONS

helped him obtain artist's materials in a time of shortages and difficult communications. Surprisingly, the newspapers refer to Captain George T. M. Davis, who served as an aide-de-camp to Generals Quitman and Shields, as the purchaser of the painting, whereas the inscription on the chromolithograph credits a painting "in the Possession of Capt. Roberts." Further, the *Star*'s lengthy description of Davis's picture, so minute in its identification of the officers depicted, does not mention Captain Roberts's appearance at the head of his storming party.

The solution to this problem is that Walker painted the subject several times. Captain Davis's painting (now unlocated)

is the first for which there is documentation. Apparently the newspaper articles attracted the notice of a number of critical eyes within the army. When Walker's efforts were brought to the attention of General Scott, he asked Captain Roberts, whose bravery in the battle had come under Scott's personal observation, to assist Walker with some of the details.[7] On October 25, the day the *American Star*'s article came out, Roberts visited Walker's studio, as he described in a diary of his activities in Mexico that he kept for his wife: "Went to the Artist's studio who is painting the storming of Chepultepec & have ordered a copy to be painted for you. The original is in the hands of the Lithographers who thinks he will have the first copies struck off so I can send one by the train, or rather by Capt. Kearny to you." On December 13 he wrote: "I am having a splendid and large painting made by an artist of great merit in this city for which I pay $250. It will be a painting of merit and one of the most spirited battle scenes ever put upon canvas. The most conspicuous in the scene is the 5 Gun Battery taken by my storming party. If I do not get to the States I shall have it well boxed and directed to you at Barhamville."[8]

These references, besides documenting Captain Roberts's painting, also prove that Captain Davis's picture was copied

on stone and lithographed in Mexico City. The resulting print is perhaps the lithograph by Ignacio Cumplido with English and Spanish titles (cat. no. 149).

Walker's rendering for Davis not only received press coverage but became a central object in a dispute among General Scott and his officers. According to Captain Davis's account in his autobiography:

There was in the city an artist of some repute, named Walker, who had upon his easel a painting which truthfully represented the storming of Chapultepec by the two divisions commanded respectively by Generals Quitman and Pillow. This artist had

outlined that engagement from a sketch that one of the engineers present had dictated; making its foreground the side of the elevation of Chapultepec on which General Quitman with his division engaged the enemy. The knowledge (as the camp gossip had it) of such a picture being in process of execution by Mr. Walker reaching General Pillow, he sent for the artist, and as I was told, denied that General Quitman was prominent in the reduction of Chapultepec, insisted that the artist's representation of the battle was wholly at fault, and that to have it accurate, the foreground should have been taken from the side occupied by his division. He offered to purchase the picture when finished, upon the artist's terms, provided it was reconstructed as General Pillow insisted would be the truth of history. Ascertaining what was going on, I took with me a Dr. Graves, formerly a resident of Mississippi, but who for a number of years past had lived in Mexico, and we together called upon Mr. Walker at his studio.... [I inquired] particularly whether General Pillow had made him the offer of a hundred dollars for his picture of the battle of Chapultepec, conditioned upon its being remodeled to meet the representations made by General Pillow as to that battle. Mr. Walker without any hesitation replied it was true. I then said to him that, regardless of the source or the sources of his information, the representations made as to General Quitman were false; that the burden of the battle of Chapultepec was borne by General Quitman's forces; and that if Mr. Walker attempted to

THE STORMING OF CHAPULTEPEC SEP.ʳ 13ᵗʰ 1847.

151. STORMING OF CHAPULTEPEC

give a truthful representation on canvas of the battle of Chapultepec, and misrepresented the position of General Quitman in winning that victory, he, Mr. Walker, would be held personally responsible. If, on the other hand, the artist intended it as a mere fancy sketch, to gratify the vanity of the highest bidder for it, then I had nothing to say in the premises.

Davis offered to buy the painting, matching Pillow's hundred dollars, if Walker would finish it according to his original plan. In his account Davis adds that he even brought the artist a map prepared by Lieutenant Tower of the Engineer Corps "which showed with mathematical accuracy the disposition of the whole of the forces in any way engaged in storming Chapultepec, or in capturing the City of Mexico." Comparing this map to his original outline, the artist agreed that "they were almost fac-similes the one of the other."[9]

Walker finished his canvas as originally planned, selling it to Davis, but then painted another version showing Pillow's attack. He also completed several small oil sketches taken from several angles of the battlefield, one of which showed *Pillow's Attack Through the Woods* and another the *South Side of the Castle of Chapultepec*.[10] These sketches may have been done, at least in part, in the field.

By November 28, 1847, the Walker painting owned by Captain Davis had arrived at Norman's Book Store in New Orleans; the *Daily Picayune* noted that "it is full of spirit, and those who were present at the affair pronounce it correct. Great crowds have visited the store within a day or two to see it, but to give it a wider circulation, we understand that Capt.

Davis, the aid of Gen. Shields, to whom the picture belongs, has consented to have an engraving made from it. We applaud this determination, and in the mean time we would advise our citizens to drop into Mr. Norman's and see the original picture."[11]

Whether the method of reproduction chosen by Davis was engraving or lithography, American printmakers soon cranked out a number of prints derived from Walker's images. Endicott & Co. of New York printed a lithograph (cat. no. 151) that may have been based on the painting owned by Captain Davis or derived thirdhand from other prints. Endicott's print is copyrighted 1847 by Nathaniel Currier. Unlike those in many of the other images, the figures in the Endicott print advance from left to right in ranks across the picture, and in the left foreground there are two cannons instead of one. The area at distant right, which in Roberts's picture and the chromolithograph shows the gateway battery, is entirely different.

To complicate things further, the next year Currier published another lithograph of the same subject (cat. no. 150), quite similar to the lithographs of Endicott and Cumplido. The identical format of bilingual inscriptions on the Currier and Cumplido prints suggests that one was copied from the other. In these prints, a large, solid mass of infantry marches from left to right across the middle ground, and the distant right portion of the composition is poorly defined. The Cumplido print is more crisply drawn than the Currier version, and some of the figures differ. Perhaps Currier received an impression of the Mexican print from Lieutenant Larkin Smith, who had sent him other Mexican images (see cat. nos. 143 and 154).

Yet another version (not illustrated here) appeared in *Album Pintoresco de la República México, published by Julio Michaud y Thomas around 1850. Lithographer Pierre-Frédéric Lehnert drew this on stone for Lemercier of Paris, probably copying the chromolithograph by Sarony & Major.

In later years Walker repeated this composition several times. In 1857 he painted a longer, horizontal version that extended the view to encompass the aqueduct leading to the Gate of Belén and some of P. F. Smith's brigade to the right of the causeway.[12] That same year, Congress commissioned Walker to paint his most famous version, a large canvas for which he was paid $6,000. It hung in the U. S. Capitol building until 1961; today it is in the United States Marine Corps Museum in Washington, D.C.[13]

1. James Walker (1818-89) was born in Northamptonshire, England, and came to America with his parents while still a child. Around 1838 he traveled to New Orleans and then to Mexico, where he taught art at the Mexican Military College of Tampico. On contracting yellow fever he was advised to go inland to Mexico City, where he remained until the American invasion of 1847. When the Mexican government ordered all American residents to evacuate, Walker instead went into hiding for about six weeks, until he could escape over the mountains to Puebla to reach the advancing American troops. Volunteering for duty without pay, Walker served as an interpreter on General Worth's staff; he was present at Contreras, Churubusco, and Chapultepec and accompanied the army in the occupation of Mexico City.

All through this period Walker was busy making sketches of the battle scenes, possibly with the aid of a camera obscura. General James T. Shields, who is depicted with his arm in a sling in several versions of Walker's painting *The Storming of Chapultepec*, later recalled: "We were taken just as we stood, by a photographer who followed the army to take sketches whenever he could. It was afterwards transferred to canvas.... The artist happened to get his camera in focus just while I was talking to Gen. Quitman, and so I apprehend it [the painting] a more correct battle-piece than the most of those that ornament our public buildings." (Interview in the Charleston *News and Courier*, July 4, 1878, files of the Office of the Architect of the Capitol, Washington, D.C.)

Walker withdrew from the capital with the American troops in 1848 and returned to New York. In subsequent years he completed numerous oil paintings of Mexican War scenes. During the Civil War he visited battlefields, made sketches, and interviewed Union soldiers, including several generals, to get details for paintings. One large canvas, depicting the battle of Lookout Mountain, was sold to General Joseph Hooker for $20,000. (For biographical information on Walker, I rely on Marian R. McNaughton, "James Walker—Combat Artist of Two American Wars," *Military Collector & Historian* 9 [Summer 1957]: 31-35, except where noted. Walker's birth is noted in Groce and Wallace, *Dictionary of Artists in America*, p. 655.)

2. Captain Roberts's painting is today in the collection of Mr. and Mrs. David Carter, San Antonio, Texas. Roberts led the assault that took the gateway batteries below the castle. He also was in the thick of the assault on the city's Belén Garita and was credited in General Quitman's report as the man who raised the American flag over the National Palace. (See Smith, *War with Mexico*, 2:54, 104, 158, 164, 410.)

3. See especially the Mexico City *American Star*, Oct. 25, 1847, pp. 1, 2. A similar account is in the Mexico City *North American*, Oct. 26, 1847, p. 3.

4. Entry labeled "For Father & Mother," written on official stationery captured at the National Palace in Mexico City, reproduced in Benjamin Stone Roberts's diary, pp. 89-90 (typescript copy in United States Military Academy Library, West Point). Compare Quitman's official report in the New York *Herald*, Nov. 18, 1847, p. 1.

5. Mexico City *American Star*, Oct. 25, 1847, p. 2.

6. Ibid.

7. McNaughton, "James Walker," p. 32, citing a "memorandum" by General B. S. Roberts, March 28, 1908, in the National Archives, Washington, D.C.

8. Roberts's diary, pp. 87, 89-90, entries for Oct. 25 and Dec. 13, 1847. In the same entry, Roberts mentions that he was also sending his wife "some of the old Idols & other Antiquities of the Aboriginese of this Country, that have been dug up in making the defences of this City."

9. George T. M. Davis, *Autobiography of the Late Col. Geo. T. M. Davis, Captain and Aid-de-Camp, Scott's Army of Invasion (Mexico), from Posthumous Papers* (New York: Jenkins and McCowan, 1891), pp. 263-65. The continuing dispute over the painting is suggested by the Mexico City *North American*'s disclaimer: "Several have complained of our notice of Mr. Walker's picture. Will these good

people understand that we described a *picture—not a battle*?" (Dec. 3, 1847, p. 1).

10. The larger painting of Pillow's attack is mentioned in the Mexico City *North American*, Nov. 30, 1847, p. 3. Twelve small oil sketches (many with confusing or variant titles) in the Army Art Collection at the U.S. Army Center for Military History, Alexandria, Virginia, may date from the occupation of Mexico City: *The Army on the Line of March* (or *March from Puebla in the Order They Were Upon the Road*), *The Detour Around Lake Chalco*, *Coming in Sight of the Enemy* (or *Hill Omatuzzo*), *Advance to the Attack of the Camp of Valencia at Contreras*, *The Convent of Churubusco*, *Molino del Rey*, *The North Side of the Castle of Chapultepec*, *The West Side of the Castle of Chapultepec* (or *Pillow's Attack Through the Woods*), *The South Side of the Castle of Chapultepec*, *Garita of Belén — North Side of the Aqueduct*, *Garita of Belén — South Side of the Aqueduct*, and *The Aqueduct of Cosmé*.

11. New Orleans *Daily Picayune*, Nov. 28, 1847, p. 2.

12. The painting was in the possession of the Kennedy Galleries, New York, in 1966. It is reproduced in *American Heritage* 17 (June 1966): 26-27.

13. Brigadier General Edwin H. Simmons, "Who Was First at Chapultepec?", *Fortitudine: Newsletter of the Marine Corps Historical Program* 11-12 (Spring-Summer 1982): 3-6.

152.   See Plate 23

Adolphe-Jean-Baptiste Bayot and Louis-Philippe-Alphonse(?) Bichebois after Carl Nebel
STORMING OF CHAPULTEPEC — QUITMAN'S ATTACK
Toned lithograph (hand colored), 1851
10-7/8 x 16-7/16 in. (27.6 x 41.8 cm.)
l.l.: "C. Nebel fecit."
l.r.: "Bayot et Bichebois lith."
From George Wilkins Kendall, *The War Between the United States and Mexico Illustrated* (New York: D. Appleton & Company, 1851), plate 11
ACM 186.72/11

In illustrating the attack of Quitman's division during the storming of Chapultepec, Carl Nebel faced a difficult problem. He must have known that his work would inevitably be compared with James Walker's, the excellence of which was already recognized. Walker approached his subjects much the way Nebel did, but Walker had been present at the battle, had made sketches on the site, and had interviewed participants while the event was still fresh in their minds. In fact, Nebel's illustration of this subject is undoubtedly informed by Walker's compositions, for it closely resembles the 1848 Sarony & Major chromolithograph after Walker. Kendall described the illustration thus:

> In the drawing which represents Quitman's attack upon Chapultepec, the artist has introduced the works for its defence constructed at the base of the mound. On the right of the picture is the battery which swept the direct road leading from Tacubaya; a little beyond may be seen some of the arches of the aqueduct carrying water into the city through the Belen garita. In the centre, amid the smoke, are the walls and lines of breastworks occupied by the Mexican

infantry; on the left the South Caro-
linians are pouring through the
breach they had effected under a
heavy fire. Above rises the castle, the
southern and eastern fronts, with the
ramp leading up to the main and
only entrance, being visible. The
western side, assailed by Pillow's
command, is concealed. The castle
was built for the residence of one of
the old Spanish viceroys, and
although irregular in its architecture,
is still an imposing pile.[1]

Nebel did introduce a number of
small changes. He created a greater sense
of depth and perspective than in Walker's
composition by moving the position of
the viewer farther back along the Tacubaya causeway. The perspective of the
castle is more convincing, although less
detailed and probably less accurate. Nebel
added some dramatic and pictorial elements of his own: a Mexican shot
explodes among a group of infantry in
the foreground, and the maguey plants
on either side of the causeway are more
prominent. The plant at right and the
small building at left help to frame the
view. Nebel added the aqueduct at distant
right to assist the viewer with orientation.
The timber and sandbag screen on the
western side of the castle is omitted
entirely from view. Although General
Shields shows up with his bandaged arm
in Nebel's print, no officer in the print
bears any resemblance to the white-
bearded General Quitman.

This is the only print in Nebel's series
that credits not only Parisian lithographer
Bayot, but also "Bichebois," perhaps
Louis-Philippe-Alphonse Bichebois
(1801-50), a Parisian lithographer and
landscape painter.[2]

1. Kendall, *War Between the United States and Mexico Illustrated*, p. 44.
2. Benézit, *Dictionnaire*, 1:651.

153.
Emil Klauprecht (?) after Fabian Brydolf
CASTLE OF CHAPULTEPEC
Lithograph, c. 1847
13-15/16 x 23-7/8 in. (35.4 x 60.6 cm.)
l.l.: "Klauprech & Menzel's Lith. Cincinnati."
l.r.: "Drawn from nature by F. Brydolf, Sergt
15 Reg Inf"
l.l. to l.r. below title: "We, the undersigned
Officers of the U.S. Army, do hereby certify,
that the drawing of the Castle of Chapultepec,
by Sergt. Fabian Brydolf, 15 Regiment of Inf.
is a true and correct delineation of the place,
which it is intended to represent / George W.
Morgan Col 15th. Inf. J Howard Lt. Col 15th.
Inf. S Woods, Major 15 Inf. L. H. McKenney,
Major 15th do J S Perry, Capt 15th Inf G W
Bowie Capt 15 Inf. Ch Peternell 1st Lieut 15
Inf. Wm. D Wilkins 1st Lieut 15 Inf / Thos B
Tillon Adjt. 15 Inf."
Courtesy of Prints and Photographs Division,
Library of Congress, Washington, D.C.

The lithography firm of Klauprecht &
Menzel in Cincinnati issued this print
sometime soon after the fall of Chapultepec. The artist, Fabian Brydolf, claimed
to have studied landscape painting in his
native Sweden before emigrating to the
United States in 1841. During the Mexican War, he served with Company K of
the Fifteenth Regiment of Infantry and
later left a narrative of his Mexican War
experiences.[1] Of the storming of Chapultepec he wrote:

> Batteries were erected to Bombard
> this Castel and heavy fiering contin-
> ued for a couple of days with little
> result. The Castle was finaly ordered
> to be taken by storm. We had to pass
> over level ground for a considerable
> distance which was done on a run,
> we drove the Mexicans before us
> scaled the walls and took the Castle,
> the dead Mexicans lay so thick

CASTLE OF CHAPULTEPEC.

We, the undersigned Officers of the U.S. Army, do hereby certify, that the drawing of the Castle of Chapultepec, by Sergt. Fabian Brydolf, 15 Regiment of Inf. is a true and correct delineation of the place, which it is intended to represent.

George W. Morgan Col. 15th Inf.   J Howard Lt Col 15th Inf.   S Woods, Major 15 Inf.   L H McKinney Major 15th do   J S Perry Capt. 15th Inf.   G W Bowie Capt 15 Inf.   Ch. Pelernell 1st Lieut 15 Inf.   Wm D Wilkins 1st Lieut 15 Inf.
Thos B Tilton Adjt 15 Inf.

153. CASTLE OF CHAPULTEPEC

around that you could have walked on their boddys without touching the ground. I with others had the pleasure of houling down the Mexican flagg and raising ours on the top of the Castel.[2]

Since the Fifteenth Infantry Regiment remained behind to guard prisoners and to garrison the castle, Brydolf probably passed many an hour within its walls and around its grounds until the regiment left the following February 1. His view was taken from the southwestern corner of the hill below the castle. In the left foreground are the curved walls of a circular redoubt where the Mexicans had posted a four-pounder cannon, a position taken by Colonel Joseph E. Johnston with four companies of voltigeurs (part of Pillow's command).[3] The road running to the right leads to the Tacubaya causeway and the gateway batteries; the wall in front of it was stormed by the volunteer troops of Quitman's division. Brydolf's regiment, part of Pillow's division, scaled the western walls of the castle at left. The ramp that led to the castle's gate, the fortified base of the castle, and the various buildings are all clearly delineated. Also visible are the timber and sandbag screens. Mexico City is in the right distance.

1. "Fabian Brydolf's Reminiscences of the Mexican War," an original manuscript in the State Historical Society of Iowa, is published in George S. May, ed., "An Iowan in the Mexican War," *Iowa Journal of History* 3, no. 2 (1955): 167-74. Other sources for Brydolf's activities during the Mexican War are *Registers of Enlistments in the United States Army, 1798-1914* (Washington, D.C.: National Archives Microfilm Publications, 1958), vols. 46-47, January 1847-June 1849, p. 29, M233, roll 21; Returns of Company K, 15th Regiment U. S. Infantry, May 1847-February 1848, RG 94, M665, roll 163, National Archives.

Fabian Brydolf (c. 1820-1897), born in Sweden, worked variously as a journeyman house and sign painter in the Midwest, a bandsman on a river steamboat, and an interpreter for fellow immigrants before settling in Burlington, Iowa, in 1846. He enlisted there on April 14, 1847. (At his enlistment his stated age was twenty-six, but George S. May gives his birthdate as 1819, citing the *Biographical Review of Des Moines County. . .* [Chicago, 1905], pp. 901-2.) Returning to Burlington after the Mexican War, Brydolf resumed work as a sign, carriage, and ornamental painter, advertising that he could imitate "wood and marble, fresco and scene painting, paper hanging, etc." (*Business Directory and Review of the Trade, Commerce, and Manufactories of the City of Burlington, Iowa, for the Year Ending May 1, 1856*, comp. and pub. by C. M. Wilcox & Co., H. H. Hartley, and L. G. Jeffers [Burlington: Printed by the Hawk-Eye Power Press, 1856], p. 27; Burlington, Iowa, City Directory for 1859, p. 21.) During the Civil War, Brydolf served in the Union army, attaining the rank of lieutenant colonel. He lost his right arm at Shiloh but after the war resumed painting with his left hand.

2. May, "An Iowan in the Mexican War, " p. 173.

3. See Smith, *War with Mexico*, 2:151, 154; map on p. 150.

154.
After Pedro Gualdi
THE MILITARY COLLEGE OF CHAPULTEPEC. THE ANCIENT SITE OF THE HALLS OF THE MONTEZUMAS.
Lithograph, 1847
9-3/16 x 12-7/16 in. (23.3 x 31.6 cm.) comp.
l.l.: "Lith. & Pub. by N. Currier,"
l.c.: "Entered according to Act of Congress in the year 1847 by N. Currier, in the Clerk's office of the District Court of the Southern District of N. Y."
l.r.: "152 Nassau St. Cor. of Spruce N. Y."
l.c. below title: "From a Sketch by Gualdi, and forwarded by Lieut. Larkin Smith, U.S.A. / 554."
Courtesy of Prints and Photographs Division, Library of Congress, Washington, D.C.

Nathaniel Currier lithographed, published, or distributed several views of Chapultepec, some based on sketches drawn from nature and others from secondary sources. This view, taken from the southeast side of the castle near the aqueduct leading to Mexico City, is supposedly taken from a "sketch" by Pedro (Pietro) Gualdi, an Italian who had lived in Mexico City for a number of years. Gualdi was already well known for his sketches of Mexican architecture, having lithographed and published them in the album *Monumentos de México Tomados del Natural*, printed by the Mexico City lithography firm of Massé y Decaen in 1841. Gualdi also issued individually printed plates, and one of these, rather than an original sketch, may have served as the model for the Currier print.[1] Brevet Major Larkin Smith, who had served as an aide-de-camp to General Worth, also supplied Currier with a "sketch" by H. Mendez showing Molino del Rey and Chapultepec from the Casa Mata (see cat. nos. 142-43).

The stone aqueduct in the foreground of the print ran on a causeway leading east to the garita of Belén, one of the entrances to Mexico City. The aqueduct, some eight feet wide and fifteen feet high, rested on heavy arches and pillars of masonry. Before the storming of Chapultepec, Scott had assigned this route to Quitman and his division, should the castle be successfully reduced, and Quitman wasted no time in moving up the causeway after the castle's surrender. The riflemen at the head of his column advanced from arch to arch along the aqueduct, meeting a heavy frontal fire from a Mexican battery farther down the causeway.[2]

Almost identical to this Gualdi-Currier print and clearly derived from it or its presumed Mexican antecedent is an image titled "Castle of Chapultepec" that Otto Onken's lithography firm in Cincinnati, Ohio, printed as an illustration for Raphael Semmes's *Service Afloat and Ashore*.[3]

1. Gualdi (1808-57) made significant contributions to the visual documentation of architecture in nineteenth-century Mexico. Born in Carpi, in the province of Modena (Emilia), Italy, he went to Milan, where he worked at La Scala, probably as a scene painter, and studied at the Academy of Arts from 1834 until 1835. Still working as a scene painter, he went to Mexico with an Italian opera company in 1838. In 1850 he taught perspective at Mexico's famed art school, the Academia de San Carlos at Mexico City. As early as December 1851 Gualdi moved to New Orleans, where he painted oil and watercolor views of that city and its buildings. He was buried there in a tomb of his own design. (See Mathes, *Mexico on Stone*, pp. 21, 52 n. 20; Manuel Toussaint, *La Litografia in Mexico en el siglo XIX*, 4th ed. [Mexico City: Manuel Quesada Brandi, 1934], pp. 27-28; Mahé and McCaffrey, *Encyclopaedia of New Orleans Artists*, pp. 167-68.)

2. Smith, *War with Mexico*, 2:158-59. James Walker painted a small oil sketch of the aqueduct, showing the riflemen advancing under cover of the arches (Army Art Collection, U.S. Army Center for Military History, Alexandria, Virginia).

3. Semmes, *Service Afloat and Ashore*, p. 450.

THE MILITARY COLLEGE OF CHAPULTEPEC.
THE ANCIENT SITE OF THE HALLS OF THE MONTEZUMAS.
From a Sketch by Gualdi, and forwarded by Lieut. Larkin Smith, U.S.A.

154. MILITARY COLLEGE OF CHAPULTEPEC

GARITA DE BELEN.
Mexico, el dia 13 de Septiembre de 1847.

GATE OF BELEN.
Mexico, The 13ᵗʰ September, 1847.

155. GARITA DE BELEN / GATE OF BELEN

Mexico City

155.
Artist unknown
Garita de Belen. Mexico, el dia 13
de Septiembre de 1847. | Gate of
Belen. Mexico, the 13th. September,
1847.
Toned lithograph, c. 1848
7-7/8 x 11-7/8 in. (20.0 x 30.2 cm.)
l.l.: "Litog. de Cumplido."
ACM 37.75

156.
Artist unknown
Garita de Belen, Mexico, el dia 13
de Septiembre de 1847. | Gate of
Belen, Mexico, the 13th. September,
1847.
Lithograph (hand colored), 1848
8-5/8 x 11-5/8 in. (22.0 x 29.5 cm.) comp.
l.l.: "Lith. & Pub. by N. Currier,"
l.c.: "Entered according to Act of Congress in
the year 1848 by N. Currier, in the Clerk's
office of the Distrit Court of the Southern
District of New York."
l.r.: "152 Nassau St. Cor. of Spruce N. Y."
l.c. below title: "630."
Courtesy of Prints and Photographs Division,
Library of Congress, Washington, D.C.

157.
Fd. Bastin after an unknown artist
Heroica Defensa de la Garita de
Belen el dia 13 de Setiembre 1847.
Toned lithograph, c. 1850
8 x 12-5/16 in. (20.3 x 31.3 cm.)
l.l. on stone: "Fd. Bastin"
l.l.: "Julio Michaud y Thomas, Mexico"
From *Album Pintoresco de la República
Méxicana* (Mexico City: Estamperia de Julio
Michaud y Thomas, c. 1850), plate 45
Courtesy of Fikes Hall of Special Collections
and the DeGolyer Library, Southern Methodist
University, Dallas

Since Mexico City was surrounded by
marshes, the American troops could only
enter by taking the causeways. These
were flanked by water-filled ditches and
led to *garitas*, or gates with sentry boxes,
that included a large paved space and
strong buildings where taxes used to be
collected on goods entering the city. The
southern causeways led to the fortifications of the garitas of San Antonio and
El Niño Perdido, while the western

156. Garita de Belen / Gate of Belen

causeways, which led to the garitas of Belén (on the southwest side of the city) and San Cosmé (on the west side of the city, north of Belén), were also guarded by Chapultepec. After the fall of Chapultepec on the morning of September 13, the fortifications of the garitas of Belén and San Cosmé and a fortified barracks known as the *ciudadela* or citadel, near the Belén garita, were essentially the only points of resistance to the American advance on the city.[1]

Few images of any kind show the war from a position behind Mexican rather than American lines; these three prints of the Mexican defense of the garita of Belén are rare examples. The earliest of the three is probably the lithograph by Ignacio Cumplido (cat. no. 155). Judging from written accounts and from a comparison with two painted views by James Walker from the American side of the action, Cumplido's print is fairly accurate.[2] In the center of the print is the terminus of the aqueduct from Chapultepec, with its masonry buttresses; the arched gateways to the causeway appear on either side of it. Baroque volutes, a cartouche, and urn-shaped finials reflect the eighteenth-century Spanish origin of the garita. At right may be the stone house originally intended for guards and customs officials. Infantry and artillerists alike suffer under the fire of the invisible American enemy, while women and children, victims of war so seldom depicted, scurry to avoid being hit by stray shots. One of these has just exploded near a wagon, upsetting its mules and killing or wounding several soldiers.

Only one officer among several in the print wears a cocked hat; he stands to the left of center. The artist may have intended him to represent General Andrés Terrés, to whom Santa Anna entrusted

HEROICA DEFENSA DE LA GARITA DE BELEN
El dia 13 de Setiembre 1847.

157. Heroica Defensa de la Garita de Belen

the defense of the garita. Terrés described the scene in his official report of the action:

Shortly after 10 A.M., the enemy, having taken possession of Chapultepec and the fortifications around it, came down in great force, with the intention of entering the city by the garita of Belén, attacking it with all the determination and fury inspired by his recent triumph. He was detained, however, by my small force [some eighty men with three four-pounders], which fought with the greatest courage and energy, causing him a very considerable loss.... The

enemy trusted the prosperous issue of his intent to a more powerful arm, and, bringing down two 24-pounders, commenced a rapid fire. The stones of the arch over our heads were broken in all directions, wounding many of my men; they, however, continued fighting with the greatest bravery, keeping the enemy at a considerable distance. At 1 o'clock P.M., the stones which fell from the arch, wounded and completely disabled all the artillerists at my cannon, who, until then, had been fighting with the greatest enthusiasm.[3]

At length Terrés was forced to withdraw, and the American force under General Quitman occupied the garita. Quitman's men were still under heavy fire from the Mexican guns at the citadel, but when the next morning came they learned to their surprise that the Mexican army had withdrawn from the city.

Nathaniel Currier's lithograph of the Belén garita (cat. no. 156) was published in 1848 and probably was taken from the Cumplido print. Like Cumplido, Currier printed the title in both English and Spanish. Around 1850 the Mexican publishing firm of Julio Michaud y Thomas issued a copy of the print (cat. no. 157) as one of the illustrations in *Album Pintoresco de la República Méxicana*. "Fd." (Ferdinand?) Bastin, who copied it on stone, probably worked in Paris; he rearranged many of the figures.

1. An American account of the storming of the Belén garita is in P. G. T. Beauregard, "Personal Reminiscences of an Engineer Officer During the Campaign in Mexico Under General Winfield Scott in 1847-8," in T. Harry Williams, ed., *With Beauregard in Mexico: The Mexican War Reminiscences of P. G. T. Beauregard* (Baton Rouge: Louisiana State University Press, 1956), pp. 84-100. Secondary sources include Nevin, *Mexican War*, pp. 203-5, 215-16, and Smith, *War with Mexico*, 2:158-60.

2. James Walker's two small oil sketches are titled *Garita of Belén—North Side of the Aqueduct* and *Garita of Belén—South Side of the Aqueduct* (Army Art Collection, U. S. Army Center for Military History, Alexandria, Virginia).

3. Official Report of General Andrés Terrés to the Minister of War, Mexico, Sept. 16, 1847, translated and published in the New York *Herald*, Nov. 15, 1847, p. 1.

158.
Artist unknown
CITY OF MEXICO. FROM THE CONVENT OF SAN COSME. | VISTA DE MEXICO. DESDE EL CONBENTO SAN COSMÉ.
Lithograph (hand colored), 1847
9-1/8 x 12-3/8 (23.1 x 31.5 cm.) comp.
l.l.: "Lith. & Pub. by N. Currier,"
l.c.: "Entered according to Act of Congress in the year 1847 by N. Currier, in the Clerk's office of the District Court of the Southern District of N. Y."
l.r.: "152 Nassau St. Cor. of Spruce N. Y."
l.l. to l.r.: "La Merced. La Concepcion. Cathedral. Santo Diego. Mineria. La Profesa. San Augustin. San José de Gracia. / La Piñon. Santo Domingo. Hospital de San Hipolito. Garita de San Cosmé. Alameda. San Francisco. Volcan de Iztaccihuatl."
l.c. below title: "555."
Courtesy of Prints and Photographs Division, Library of Congress, Washington, D.C.

While Quitman's command fought their way into Mexico City along the direct road east from Chapultepec to the garita of Belén, Worth's division, followed by Pillow's and General Scott himself, took a longer route to the north toward the garita of San Cosmé. Worth's progress was slow, and his men fought from house to house and from rooftops (like that of the convent in the foreground of this print).[1] By nightfall they took the garita, from which Worth's artillery lobbed shells toward the main plaza and other important centers of the city. Under cover of darkness, Santa Anna and his troops withdrew from the city through the northern garitas. Soon afterward a delegation of the city government came to Worth under a flag of truce and offered to surrender the city.[2]

The specific events of September 13 may have inspired Currier to issue this print. The image is probably derived from an earlier Mexican print, as the bilingual inscriptions are similar to other Currier prints copied from Mexican lithographs.[3] By coincidence, two days before American troops attacked the San Cosmé garita, the New York *Herald* published an engraving by Samuel Putnam Avery showing this same "View of the City of Mexico, taken from the Convent of St. Cosme. — View of the Aqueduct."[4] As usual, Avery did not credit his source. Raphael Semmes included a similar view in his book *Service Afloat and Ashore*, published in 1851;[5] his illustration, lithographed by Otto Onken's firm in Cincinnati, was undoubtedly copied from the Currier, the *Herald*, or the unknown Mexican print. Onken or one of his employees added a howitzer on the azotea of the convent in the foreground as well as several files of American infantrymen advancing along the causeway.[6]

1. In the course of this fight Lieutenant Ulysses S. Grant set up a howitzer in the belfry of a church that commanded the rear of the San Cosmé garita. (Grant, *Personal Memoirs*, pp. 96-97.)

2. Smith, *War with Mexico*, 2:161-62.

3. See cat. nos. 117, 142-43, 150, and 156; cf. also no. 154. Another Mexican view issued by Currier at this time depicts the Alameda, or public park, of Mexico City. (An impression is in the Prints and Photographs Division of the Library of Congress). The view was derived from prewar prints, but its subject recalled events of the war: for example, Worth's division halted briefly at the Alameda on the morning of September 14 during the drive to take the main plaza.

4. New York *Weekly Herald*, Sept. 11, 1847, p. 1.

5. Semmes, *Service Afloat and Ashore*, betw. pp. 456 and 457. See also pp. 459-60.

6. Less accurate and generalized popular prints of the battle for Mexico City include a Currier lithograph by John Cameron purporting to depict the *Attack on the Gate San Cosme* and two generalized battle scenes by E. B. & E. C. Kellogg.

LITH. & PUB. BY N. CURRIER, Entered according to Act of Congress in the year 1847 by N. Currier, in the Clerk's office of the District Court of the Southern District of N.Y. 152 NASSAU ST COR. OF SPRUCE N.Y.

La Piñon.   La Merced.   La Concepcion.   Cathedral.   Santo Diego.   Mineria.   La Profesa.   San Augustin.   San José de Gracia.
Sante Domingo.   Hospital de San Hipolito.   Garita de San Cosmé.   Alameda.   San Francisco.   Volcan de Ixtaccihuatl.

CITY OF MEXICO.

FROM THE CONVENT OF SAN COSME.

VISTA DE MEXICO.

DESDE EL CONBENTO DE SAN COSMÉ.

158. City of Mexico. From the Convent of San Cosme

159.   See Plate 24

Adolphe-Jean-Baptiste Bayot after Carl Nebel
GENL. SCOTT'S ENTRANCE INTO MEXICO
Toned lithograph (hand colored), 1851
11-1/8 x 17 in. (28.3 x 43.2 cm.)
l.l.: "C. Nebel fecit."
l.r.: "Bayot lith."
From George Wilkins Kendall, *The War
Between the United States and Mexico Illustrated* (New York: D. Appleton & Company,
1851), plate 12
ACM 186.72/12

Carl Nebel's illustration of General Winfield Scott's triumphal entry into the main
plaza of Mexico City is almost identical
to his illustration of the plaza (159a)
published fifteen years earlier in his
famous album *Voyage pittoresque et
archéologique dans la partie la plus intéressante du Mexique*. Nebel had sketched
the buildings *in situ* sometime during his
first and longest stay in Mexico, from
1829 to 1834. For this reason, G. W.
Kendall could assert that

the strict fidelity of the picture, as
regards the architecture of the palace,
cathedral and other buildings introduced, may be implicitly relied
upon....
     In the sketch of General Scott's
entrance into the city of Mexico, the
artist gives the reader a view of two
sides of the Grand Plaza. On the right
is the national palace, with the
American flag floating in triumph;
in the centre is the celebrated cathedral, a rich and costly pile; on the
left is the house immediately on the
corner of the Plateros, one of the
principal streets, a knot of armed
leperos partially concealed behind
the parapet of the azotea. In the
foreground is the commander-in-
chief, just entering with a small dra-

goon escort, while infantry and
cavalry as well as artillery are disposed at different points.[1]

The present Cathedral of Mexico
stands on the southwestern part of an old
Aztec temple precinct. It was begun in
1573 as a replacement for an earlier
Spanish building; one of the bell towers
was not completed until 1813.[2] The Palacio Nacional (at right) was the seat of the
Mexican government, and before that the
seat of the Spanish viceroys. Americans
in the 1840s referred to it as "the Halls of
the Montezumas," and indeed before
Cortez began the original Spanish struc-

ture in 1523, Moctezuma II's "new palace" had been located on the site.[3]

Nebel went to greater lengths to
describe the buildings in the text of his
earlier album, which, together with other
sources, is useful as a key to this later
print. To the right of the main facade of
the cathedral is the ornate eighteenth-
century Churrigueresque facade of the
Sagrario, or sacristy. To the left of the
cathedral is the neoclassical cathedral
library, while beyond the library are some
private houses. Behind them rise the
cupola and dome of the convent of La
Encarnación. Between the Palacio
Nacional and the Sagrario are buildings

PLAZA MAYOR DE MEXICO.

159A. PLAZA MAYOR DE MEXICO

ENTRANCE OF THE ARMY INTO THE GRAND PLAZA AT MEXICO.

159B. Scott's Entrance into Mexico

belonging to the University and the arch-bishop of Mexico, with the cupola and dome of the convent of Santa Teresa beyond them.[4] The building in the left foreground, which the artist described in his earlier album as typical of Mexican city houses, has a sign in both his prints identifying its lower story as a wine shop.

Nebel was not the first to utilize his earlier view as a backdrop for this memo-rable event. Chromolithographer Chris-tian Schuessele, working for the Philadelphia lithography firm of P. S. Duval, and an unknown artist working for another Philadelphia firm, Wagner & McGuigan, had copied the buildings in Nebel's 1836 lithograph for their own views of Scott's entrance into Mexico City (figs. 24, 23), used in John Frost's 1848 *Pictorial History of Mexico and the Mex-*

ican War. Also that year, the same scene was copied by Christian Mayr for Edward D. Mansfield's *The Mexican War: A His-tory of Its Origins* (159b).[5] In the 1848 versions, the American printmakers envi-sioned the best of Mexican society as turning out on the balconies and in the streets for a gala parade of American troops in their full-dress uniforms. In Schuessele's print, American flags are dis-played from the balconies of the building in the left foreground. The citizens appear relieved, if not delighted, to see the con-quering Yankees.

Nebel's version of Scott's entrance sticks closer to the truth and is packed with psychological drama. There is no doubt here that the war is still on. Loaded cannons are posted to sweep the streets, while a body of dragoons in the fore-

ground gathers tensely with drawn sabers near General Scott and his staff. In a par-ticularly effective narrative detail, one of the dragoon officers, on a white horse in the center foreground, glares at a lepero on the left who is preparing to throw a stone. From the street or from doorways and partially closed windows, other citi-zens watch with fear, curiosity, appre-hension, indignation, and in the case of the lepero with the stone and the armed men on the roof, open hostility, an allu-sion to the violence that broke out shortly thereafter.

Actually, Quitman and his division were the first American troops to enter the main plaza on the morning of Sep-tember 14. P. G. T. Beauregard, an engi-neer officer serving with Quitman, recalled:

After leaving a garrison at the *garita* and at the citadel, we marched towards the main plaza of the city with only about three or four regi-ments and Steptoe's battery! We arrived and formed line of battle in front of the Cathedral as its clock was striking 7 A.M. The American flag was then hoisted on the Palace of the Montezumas! but through some mistake, the flag of the Rifle Regiment was first hoisted in its place by Captain Roberts! General Quit-man and myself then went into the Palace to see what disposition could be made of it in case of a sudden attack upon our small forces — and we three, I believe, were the first American officers who entered it.

I remember that the sight we presented marching into that immense city, being nearly all of us covered with mud, and some with blood — some limping — some with arms in scarfs — and others with heads in bandages! followed by two endless lines of gaping *leperos* and rabble was anything but glorious in appearance, for it looked more like the ridiculous than the sublime — whatever history may say to the contrary notwithstanding.[6]

Quitman sent Beauregard to notify Scott and Worth, who had advanced as far as the Alameda, that the palace and grand plaza had been taken. George Wilkins Kendall was with them, but he may have been mixed up about the exact time when he wrote: "At 7 o'clock this morning Gen. Scott, with his staff, rode in and took quarters in the national palace, on the top of which the regimental flag of the gallant rifles and the stars and stripes were already flying, and an immense crowd of blanketed leperos, the scum of the capital, were congregated in the plaza as the commander-in-chief entered it."[7] According to a foreigner residing in the capital:

Gen. Scott was already in the palace, when on a sudden the people of the low classes commenced throwing stones on the Americans from the tops of the houses, and from all the streets, whilst individuals of a better standing fired from the windows and balconies on the Yankees, who were far from expecting such treatment. Gen. Scott ordered immediately pieces of artillery to be placed in all directions and soon swept the streets with grape shot, but this proved insufficient to subdue the insurrection. Gen. Scott then sent a few companies on divers points with orders to break open every house out of which they should fire, to put to

the sword those found within, and lastly, to sack the property therein contained. This order, which was executed with great moderation (thanks to the secret instructions of Gen. Scott,) but in some cases with stern energy, soon put down the insurrection.[8]

Santa Anna resigned as president of the Republic on September 16 but remained in command of the remnants of his army, withdrawing to the town of Guadalupe Hidalgo, ten miles north of Mexico City. Toward the end of September the Mexicans formed a government-in-exile at the city of Querétaro.

1. Kendall, *War Between the United States and Mexico Illustrated*, p. 46.
2. *Diccionario Porrúa de Historia, Biografia y Geografia de Mexico*, 2d ed. (Mexico City: Editorial Porrúa, 1964), pp. 317-18.
3. *Baedeker's Mexico*, pp. 162-63.
4. For the identification of the buildings, see, besides Nebel's *Voyage pittoresque et archéologique*, the descriptive key "Esplicación de la 1a. Vista del Panorama de Mexico" in Pedro Gualdi, *Monumentos arquitectonicos y perspectivas de la Ciudad de Mexico 1841* (facsimile, Mexico City: Editorial del Valle de Mexico, 1972), n. p.
5. Mayr's engraving also appeared in some of Edward D. Mansfield's various biographies of Winfield Scott, and in Oswandel, *Notes of the Mexican War*, p. 287. There were other popular prints of Scott's entry, including lithographs by James Baillie and Nathaniel Currier and an engraving and etching by W. Ridgway after Felix O. C. Darley.
6. Williams, *With Beauregard in Mexico*, pp. 100-101.
7. New Orleans *Daily Picayune*, Oct. 14, 1847, p. 3 (letter of Sept. 14, 1847).
8. A Frenchman in Mexico City to another Frenchman in Veracruz, quoted in the New Orleans *Daily Picayune*, Oct. 14, 1847, p. 2.

The Siege of Puebla

160.
After James T. Shannon
SIEGE OF PUEBLA, BEGAN SEPT. 13TH. ENDED OCT. 12TH. 1847.
Chromolithograph, 1850
13-1/8 x 20-1/2 in. (33.3 x 52.1 cm.)
l.l.: "From a Drawing on the Spot by J. T. Shannon"
l.c.: "G. Warren Smith. Direxet. / Entered according to Act of Congress in the year 1850 by J. T. Shannon in the Clerk's Office of the District Court of Western Pennsylvania."
l.r.: "Lith. & Printed in Colors by Sarony & Major N. York."
l.l. below title: "Reference. / B. Fort Loretto, commanded by Major Gwyne, U.S.A. / D. Guadaloupe Church, commanded by Capt. T. J. Morehead. / C. Cuartel, De, San Jose, the Point of attack, commanded / by Lieut Col. Samuel W. Black, 1st. Regt. Penna. Volunteers / E. Tivilo Buildings, Mexican Batteries bearing on San Jose. / F. Col. Childs Quarters. / A. San Jose Church."
l.c. below title: "Position of the American Troops, American force 384 Men, Col. Thos. Childs Military and Civil Governor. / Mexican force, 8000, Men, Commanded by Genl. Santa Anna. / Published by G. Warren Smith & Co. for J. T. Shannon."
l.r. below title: "American Troops / A. Co, 1 Regt. Penna. Vol. Capt. Denny Pittsburgh. / C. " " " " " " Small Philadelphia. / D. " " " " " " "Hill," / G. " " " " " " " Morehead "/ I. " " " " "Danna, Wilks / K. " " " " " " Herron Pittsburgh. / 1. "Artillery "Miller U.S.A. / 1. " " " " "Kendrick "/ 1. "Cavalry " " Ford. / Thos. C. Bunting Sergt. of Penna. / Battallion, Phila. / Ordinance, Lieut. Laidlay U.S.A."
ACM 91.87

SIEGE OF PUEBLA, BEGAN SEPT. 13TH ENDED OCT. 12TH 1847.

PUBLISHED BY G. WARREN SMITH & Co. FOR J.T. SHANNON

160. SIEGE OF PUEBLA

During the American conquest of the Valley of Mexico, General Scott had left a small garrison at Puebla under Colonel Thomas Childs of the Third Artillery, to retain possession of the city and to protect and care for some 1,800 sick and wounded American troops. Childs had at his command only about four hundred effective troops, consisting of six companies of the First Regiment of Pennsylvania Volunteers under Lieutenant Colonel Samuel W. Black; one company of the Third Dragoons, commanded by Captain Lemuel Ford; some artillery under Captains Miller and Henry L. Kendrick; a small spy company of Mexicans; and a few convalescents of the hospitals, commanded by Captain Rowe of the Ninth Infantry.[1]

Soon after Scott's departure in early August, guerrilla activity increased in Puebla. On September 9 Mexican cavalry seized or drove off about seven hundred mules and horses belonging to the American army. About fifty Americans, including teamsters, clerks, quartermasters, and others, gave chase but were surrounded and nearly annihilated. Colonel Childs wisely concentrated his forces in the northeastern sector of the city around the church and cuartel of San José, Fort Loreto, and the church of Guadalupe. During the night of September 13-14, Mexican guerrilla commander Brigadier General Joaquín Rea and about 4,000 men infiltrated the city, surrounding the American position.[2] They soon cut off every kind of supply and even attempted, unsuccessfully, to change the current of the stream of water that supplied the Americans. Fortunately for the Americans, two parties from the garrison managed to secure thirty cattle and four hundred sheep before the animals disappeared from the area. Thus began a siege that lasted twenty-eight days.

One of the defenders was the artist of this print, Private James T. Shannon, a member of Company A of the First Pennsylvania.[3] He drew at least two sketches, still extant, of the American position; these probably were the basis for this chromolithograph by Sarony & Major of New York.[4] If so, the lithographer or Shannon himself rearranged the composition considerably in the print. The perspective of the cuartel or barracks of San José (the low building in the center of the picture) has been compressed into a triangular shape rather than a square or rectangle in order to include all of the landmarks in one view. Distance and scale are condensed. Details, not abundant in Shannon's sketches, are generalized and in some cases misinterpreted. For example, a broken wall appearing in the upper corner of the cuartel in one of the sketches is represented in the print as some kind of embrasure or a planned space in the original structure.

In spite of this, the print is useful in conveying some visual idea of the event. According to the descriptive key, the buildings in the foreground are the Church of San José at left, the cuartel in the center, and the headquarters of Colonel Childs at right; in the distance are Fort Loreto on the hill to the left of center, Guadalupe Church on the hill to the right of center, and farther to the right the "Tivilo buildings." According to an account of the siege included in H. Judge Moore's *Scott's Campaign in Mexico* (1849), the general hospital, located in the buildings of the churches of San José and San Juan de Dios, was the principal point of attack: "The General Hospital itself contained near 800 sick, of whom about 100 were able to do light duty; and many of those who were able to handle a musket with some effect, were soon

exhausted and their physical energies prostrated by short rations, excessive fatigue, and constant and vigilant watching by night and day, which it was necessary to undergo in order to insure a successful defense." The artist or lithographer depicted what may be a doctor attending one of these sickly defenders in the left foreground. A work detail in the center foreground fills sandbags with earth for the fortifications. Moore's account mentions that Colonel Childs had ordered a battery erected "which was formed of square bales of tobacco, something smaller than ordinary cotton bags, upon which he mounted two 8-inch howitzers, by which he could completely enfilade the street." The artist may have intended the two field pieces at right to represent these howitzers, which "did great execution against the large bodies of infantry and cavalry, and the dense masses of disaffected citizens."[5]

Also in the thick of the fight was the cuartel, which constituted the "strongest and most important line of defense" and contained the "scanty stock of provisions." The presence of death is effectively portrayed by the covered body in the right foreground and by the incapacitated men who are being carried by their comrades elsewhere in the view. Moore continues: "We were eventually driven to the necessity of burying our dead in the court-yard of the building inclosure, for the enemy had erected breastworks across every street that commanded entrance to our quarters, which rendered it almost certain death to appear in the street, or to advance even beyond the inner threshold of our works."[6]

Just beyond the foreground figures, a body of infantry moves left to reinforce the point of attack. Another detachment arrives in the distance, probably having come from Fort Loreto, where Major Thomas P. Gwynne of the Sixth Infantry commanded. The crude nature of the American flag atop the building at right may derive from the story that the defenders of Fort Loreto manufactured an American flag from the red, white, and blue fabric of an old Mexican uniform they found.[7]

The Mexicans under General Rea made several attempts to storm San José but were beaten back each time, chiefly by the American artillery. On September 22 Santa Anna, having been defeated by Scott's army at Mexico City, arrived at Puebla with a considerable force, but he withdrew nine days later to intercept a relief column from Veracruz and Perote under Brigadier General Joseph Lane. The besieged Americans mounted several sorties against the Mexican siege works, until Lane arrived at last on October 12.[8] Lane's troops were "received with the thunder of artillery, the ringing of bells, and the long and loud shouts of the almost frantic garrison, who hailed them as messengers of mercy."[9] Although Childs had only suffered fifty-two casualties, the strain on his men had been severe.

James Shannon probably made his sketches soon after the siege was lifted and brought them with him when he returned to Pittsburgh with his regiment in July 1848. Perhaps soon after that he arranged for the publication of the chromolithograph in New York.

1. Smith, *War with Mexico*, 2:173-80, 423-27; Bauer, *Mexican War*, pp. 328-31. Moore, *Scott's Campaign in Mexico*, pp. 212-34, contains an eyewitness account of the siege, as well as Colonel Childs's official report.

2. Images of Mexican guerrillas include a toned lithograph by Hipólito Salazar titled *Mexican Guerrilleros in 1848* and an almost identical copy of this published by Nathaniel Currier. Henry R. Robinson printed a lithograph of guerrillas titled *Mexicans in Ambush* drawn on stone by Napoleon Sarony. Impressions of these last two prints are in the Prints and Photographs Division of the Library of Congress. The Amon Carter Museum owns an impression of the Salazar print.

3. Shannon was enrolled in Company A as a private on November 26, 1846, at age nineteen. His regiment landed with the rest of Scott's army at Veracruz and was later at the battle of Cerro Gordo on April 18. After the siege of Puebla Shannon's company was quartered at San Angel, just outside of Mexico City. Shannon himself spent the winter of 1847-48 in a hospital in Mexico City. He was promoted to corporal on June 1, 1848, and discharged at Pittsburgh on July 24.

Sources for Shannon's Mexican War activities are in *Compiled Service Records of Volunteer Soldiers Who Served During the Mexican War from Pennsylvania*, RG 94, M1028, rolls 1 and 5, National Archives, Washington, D.C. John B. Trussell, Chief, Division of History, Pennsylvania State Archives, to Ben W. Huseman, Amon Carter Museum, Oct. 15, 1987, also cites *Pennsylvania Archives*, Sixth Series, vol. 10. The 1850 census lists a James T. Shannon, painter, age twenty-one, as living in Pittsburgh; Pittsburgh city directories in the 1850s list a house and sign painter by the name. (See 1850 Census of Pittsburgh, Allegheny Co., pp. 743-48, dwelling no. 2129, family no. 21167; Pittsburgh City Directories for 1852, 1858-59. The 1852 directory listing is for a "T. J. Shannon," no doubt the same person.) He enlisted in the Union army during the Civil War and was fatally wounded at the second battle of Bull Run, August 30, 1862. (E. W. Morgan to Mrs. H. C. Patton, April 14, 1932, in Civil War Widow's pension files, RG 15, application no. 8.945, certificate no. 7.159, National Archives.)

4. Shannon's sketchbook, now in the Special Collections Division of The University of Texas at Arlington Libraries, contains sketches, some made with ink wash over graphite, of Puebla, the castle of Perote, the burial place of Captain Walker of the Texas Rangers, a view of Popocatépetl and Iztaccíhuatl, and other interesting scenes in Mexico. The sketches apparently served as models for some illustrations in Oswandel, *Notes of the Mexican War* (1885).

5. Moore, *Scott's Campaign in Mexico*, pp. 217, 223.

6. Ibid., pp. 217, 219.

7. Ibid., p. 224.

8. On the way to relieve Puebla, Lane fought an engagement at the town of Huamantla that cost the life of Captain Samuel Walker of the Mounted Riflemen. A legendary figure even at the time of his death, Samuel Walker was a former Texas Ranger and a survivor of the Texan Mier expedition. In 1847 James Baillie published a popular lithograph by Magee of the *Death of Captain Walker at the Battle of Huamantla*. However, I am aware of no eyewitness prints of this engagement.

9. Moore, *Scott's Campaign in Mexico*, p. 228.

The Occupation

161.
After Jason D. L. Polhemus
QUARTERS OF THE 1ST. REGT. MASSTS.
VOLS. AT SAN ANJEL, 8 MILES FROM THE
CITY OF MEXICO.
Lithograph, c. 1848
7-7/8 x 12 in. (20.0 x 30.5 cm.)
l.r.: "Drawn by Polhemus N. Y. V."
Courtesy of Special Collections Division, The
University of Texas at Arlington Libraries,
Arlington, Texas

One of the principal bases of the American occupation was the suburban village of San Angel, located only eight miles from Mexico City. The village was first occupied by American troops on August 20, 1847, after the battle of Contreras. Later, after the American seizure of Mexico City, buildings at San Angel served as quarters for several regiments of volunteer troops. By November 19, 1847, these included the First and Second Pennsylvania, First New York, First South Carolina, and First Massachusetts. The bulk of these units remained there until May 30, 1848.[1]

Perhaps someone in the Massachusetts Regiment commissioned Private Jason D. L. Polhemus, a former "sign and ornamental painter" and "baker" serving with the First New York, to make the original sketch for this lithograph as a souvenir.[2] The Massachusetts unit probably lined up in front of their quarters specifically for this purpose. Corporal J. Jacob Oswandel, of the First Pennsylvania Volunteers (quartered "in a large building once used as a manufacturing establishment"), records a similar experience with his own unit in a diary entry for Febru-

ary 2, 1848: "In front of our quarters our company was formed into line, when one of our members took a drawing of our company and quarters. The intention is to have it lithographed in Philadelphia, Pa." Three days later, Oswandel wrote that in the afternoon, "one of our members took another drawing of our quarters at San Angel." Once again he noted that the artist's intention was to have it lithographed in Philadelphia. Earlier, on Christmas Eve, 1847, Oswandel "paid a visit to the Second Regiment of Pennsylvania Volunteers, the New York and Massachusetts Regiments," who "have elegant quarters fronting on the plaza of San Angel."[3] Oswandel's last statement may have referred to the Massachusetts regiment only, since the Second Pennsylvania Regiment was quartered in a former Carmelite convent (dating from 1617), dedicated to San Angelo, from whom the little town took its name.

Polhemus's view probably shows San Angel's principal plaza (the Plaza de San Jacinto) looking southwest.[4] Picturesque details of Mexican architecture and life abound in this print: a crenelated tower, flat, crenelated roofs or azoteas, drainage spouts, grated windows, balconies, and columned porticoes. A Mexican muleteer or *arriero* may be seen in the foreground as well as a *diligencia* (stagecoach) and civilians who have gathered in the square. The soldiers of the Massachusetts Regiment have lined up in battle order with their frock-coated officers in front.

Detachments from the volunteer units at San Angel escorted mule trains with supplies and mail to and from the capital, as guerrilla attacks on convoys, small groups, and individuals continually plagued the Americans for the rest of the war. The occupation troops were at times guilty of outrages of their own upon the

Mexican population, for which they were sometimes punished, sometimes not. There were deaths from wounds and sickness; one of the many disease victims among the First Massachusetts Regiment was Major Edward Webster, son of Senator Daniel Webster. By contrast, some troops had time for recreation; besides Mexico City, the Americans visited the battlefields and climbed the nearby mountains.

The lithographer of Polhemus's view is not known. Since another print after Polhemus was drawn on stone by M. H. Traubel and printed by Frederick Kuhl's lithographic firm in Philadelphia (see cat. no. 164), it is possible that they were also responsible for the view of San Angel. However, the two prints are stylistically different. The lettering on the San Angel print is cruder and suggests that whoever did it was not practiced at the backward printing necessary for lithographic copy work on stone. The lack of inscriptions crediting the lithographer also suggests the work may have been done by a Mexican lithographer who was willing to accept work from an American but preferred to remain anonymous.

Drawn by Polhemus N.Y.V.

Quarters of the 1st Regt Massts Vols at San Anjel, 8 miles from the City of Mexico.

161. Quarters of Massachusetts Volunteers at San Anjel

1. Hartman, *Journal*, pp. 21-23; Claude M. Fuess, *The Life of Caleb Cushing*, 2 vols. (New York: Harcourt, Brace and Company, 1923), 2:60; Oswandel, *Notes of the Mexican War*, pp. 423-574.

2. Polhemus was born in Salem, New Jersey, c. 1819 (as implied in the muster rolls for his company, where he is recorded as twenty-eight in 1847) or 1814 (as implied in his pension claims). He was active in New Orleans in 1837 and perhaps in 1838 as a house, sign, and ornamental painter with a partner, Francis Cook. They advertised in the New Orleans *Bee* from April 24 to August 17, 1837, claiming that they could paint military standards, transparencies, and imitations of wood, marble, and other materials. They also claimed they could do glazing and steamboat painting. According to his enlistment record, Polhemus worked as a "baker" or "broker" prior to his enlistment in New York City on August 4, 1847. He was initially attached to Company D of the First Regiment, later transferring to Company A. He served for eleven months in Mexico and was honorably discharged at Fort Hamilton, New York, in July 1848, receiving a land warrant. After the Mexican War, Polhemus worked again as a sign and ornamental painter in New York City, Brooklyn, and later Philadelphia. In the Civil War he served in the Union army as a corporal and later a lieutenant; he was hospitalized for exposure in March 1863 and in later years filed for an invalid's pension. He died in the National Soldiers' Home in Elizabeth City, Virginia, in March or April 1888. (Compiled service records for Mexican War and Civil War veterans, RG 94, and invalid's pension claim for 1883 and further claims filed Feb. 4, 1887, application no. 5220, certificate no. 4844, RG 15, National Archives, Washington, D.C.; also Mahé and McCaffrey, *Encyclopaedia of New Orleans Artists*, p. 311; *Gibson's Guide and Directory of the State of Louisiana, and the Cities of New Orleans & Lafayette* [New Orleans: John Gibson, 1838], p. 167; *L'Abeille de la Nouvelle Orleans*, April 29, 1837, p. 4; New Orleans *Bee*, April 29, 1837, p. 1.)

3. Oswandel, *Notes of the Mexican War*, pp. 424, 476, 480. Smith and Judah, *Chronicles of the Gringos*, p. 470 n. 133, note that Oswandel may have based part of his account on an unpublished diary by Private John Kreitzer, a member of Oswandel's company. The diary is today in the Historical Society of Pennsylvania library. The artist of the views mentioned by Oswandel could have been James T. Shannon, also a member of the First Pennsylvania Volunteers. One of Shannon's views, for example, served as the model for the engraving on p. 425 of Oswandel's book. A sketchbook belonging to Shannon, containing one sketch of San Angel, is in the Special Collections Division of The University of Texas at Arlington Libraries (see cat. no. 160).

4. For information on the town, see José M. Gonzalez, "San Angel," in *México y sus Alrededores* (Mexico City: Decaen, 1855-56), p. 9, which also contains two lithographed views of San Angel by Casimiro Castro and J. Campillo. One of the views apparently depicts the northern and eastern sides of the square of San Jacinto, with none of the buildings seen in the Polhemus print visible. In or near this square, some members of the San Patricio battalion —American deserters who served under John Riley in the Mexican army—were tried, flogged, and branded. Forty-two or more of them were captured after the battle of Churubusco; twenty-seven were hanged. (See Oswandel, *Notes of the Mexican War*, p. 424; G. T. M. Davis, *Autobiography*, pp. 224-27.) A sketch or painting of the execution, in the West Point Museum Collections, is reproduced in Nevin, *Mexican War*, p. 209.

162.
Abraham López (?)
LOS AZOTES DADOS POR LOS AMERICANOS
Lithograph, 1848
2-7/16 x 4-1/4 in. (6.5 x 10.8 cm.)
From Abraham López, *Undecimo Calendario ... para el Año de 1849* (Mexico City and Toluca: the author, 1848)
Courtesy of Fikes Hall of Special Collections and DeGolyer Library, Southern Methodist University, Dallas

The ugly side of the American occupation is shown in this tiny lithograph from the *calendario* by Abraham López for 1849 (published in 1848). *Los Azotes dados por los Americanos* ("Lashes Given by the Americans") depicts American troops lined up in a public square as one Ameri-

Los azotes dados por los Americanos.

162. LOS AZOTES DADOS POR LOS AMERICANOS

can soldier whips a Mexican who is bound to a street lamp. The print illustrates the public punishment of Mexicans who were caught engaging in guerrilla activities. On November 3, 1847, a correspondent for the New Orleans *Picayune* gave this graphic and racist account of just such an incident in Mexico City: "This afternoon, about 5 o'clock, a greaser was whipped in the plaza. He had attempted to kill one of our soldiers, and was sentenced to receive one hundred lashes — twenty-five on every Monday for a month. Nearly ten thousand Mexicans were in the plaza, and as soon as the whipping commenced they began to throw stones. About a dozen of our dragoons, however, charged upon the mob, when they dispersed in all directions. The greaser was then whipped and taken back to the guard-house."[1]

This unforgettable image belongs to the long Hispanic tradition of depicting scenes of martyrdom and the disasters of war. Since nineteenth-century *calendarios* were almanacs which included information on Holy Days and the martyrology of the saints, patriotic Mexicans no doubt viewed the prisoner in the print as a martyr for his country and a victim of North American aggression.

1. New Orleans *Picayune*, Dec. 19, 1847, p. 1 (letter signed "C. C.," dated Nov. 3, 1847).

163.
Artist unknown
PLAZA DE LA CONSTITUCION. (MEXICO, MAYO, DE 1848.) | CONSTITUTION SQUARE. (MEXICO, MAY, 1848.)
Lithograph, c. 1848
7-7/8 x 11-1/4 in. (19.9 x 28.7 cm.)
l.l.: "Litog. de Cumplido."
Courtesy of Missouri Historical Society, St. Louis

This lithograph by Ignacio Cumplido depicts the main plaza or Zócalo of Mexico City as it appeared toward the end of the American occupation. Although similar to views drawn years earlier by Carl Nebel, Cumplido's view encompasses the entire eastern side of the plaza as well as parts of the northern and southern sides.[1] The bilingual inscriptions suggest that Cumplido may have intended the print for American soldiers. The buildings are, from left to right: the cathedral; the Sagrario; the archbishop's palace and university building; the long, low front of the National Palace, above which flies the U. S. flag; and, at far right, the Municipal Palace. Just beyond the National Palace may be seen the dome, lantern, and cross of the Convent of Santa Teresa and the triangular pediment of the Senate. The square contains mule-drawn wagons, teamsters, stagecoaches, and other vehicles and pedestrians; in the middle is the circular base of the unfinished monument to independence. A line of what may be American infantrymen stands in front of the National Palace.

Unlike Nebel's prints, the Cumplido lithograph shows a row of young trees in front of the chained stanchions before the cathedral. Contemporary daguerreotypes of Saltillo and images of plazas in other Mexican cities confirm that the planting of trees in plazas was a common practice at this time (see cat. nos. 49-51, 161).

The inclusion of this detail may help prove with further research that Cumplido's lithograph is derived from an accurate and contemporary sketch.

Captain John R. Kenly, who commanded a company of Maryland volunteers during the Mexican War, wrote that

the great centre of the city is the grand square, upon which fronts the cathedral, the President's palace, the public buildings, and the richest shops of the metropolis. It is a large open space worthy of a large city; nothing contracted about it; paved with square flag-stones, regularly and artistically disposed, and radiating from the outer limits to a circular space in the middle, where it is designed to erect a monument commemorative of the independence of the country from Spain.

Kenly also noted that during the occupation the National Palace served as the headquarters of the American army, the barracks of the main guard of the city, and the site of a court of inquiry into the differences that arose between Scott and his subordinates after the fall of the city.[2]

On May 29, 1848, after months of negotiations, the news reached Mexico City that terms of peace had been agreed upon by the American and Mexican delegations at the nearby town of Guadalupe Hidalgo. On June 12, as troops of both nations lined up in the main plaza and crowds watched from windows and rooftops, a thirty-gun salute was fired, the American flag was lowered from the National Palace, the Mexican flag was hoisted in its place, and another salute was fired. An American band played. Then, Major General W. O. Butler (who had by this time replaced Scott) and Gen-

Litog. de Cumplido.

PLAZA DE LA CONSTITUCION.
(Mexico, Mayo, de 1848.)

CONSTITUTION' SQUARE.
(Mexico, May, 1848.)

163. Plaza de la Constitucion / Constitution Square

eral Worth and his division, the rear guard of the American army, marched out of the city.[3]

1. For sources for this descriptive key see cat. no. 159, note 4. Nebel also did a view of the southern side of the square for his *Voyage pittoresque et archéologique* that depicted one tower of the cathedral at left and the shops and buildings on the western side at right. This view was copied widely by American printmakers; these copies include an engraving for the New York *Weekly Herald*, May 29, 1847, p. 1, and an engraving for Frost's *Pictorial History of Mexico and the Mexican War* (1848), p. 592.

2. John R. Kenly, *Memoirs of a Maryland Volunteer. War with Mexico, in the Years 1846-7-8* (Philadelphia: J. B. Lippincott & Co., 1873), pp. 410-14. In 1847 Manuel Murguía, a Mexico City lithographer, lithographed a bird's-eye view of the plaza after a sketch by Pedro Gualdi. The view (an impression of which is in the Amon Carter Museum, acc. no. 131.83) is similar to the Cumplido and Nebel prints, but it shows the projected monument to independence along with flanking fountains, street lamps, and a remodeled National Palace. In 1851 Otto Onken's lithography firm in Cincinnati apparently used such a view by Gualdi to reconstruct a scene of the American-occupied plaza for Raphael Semmes's *Service Afloat and Ashore*, plate 111, p. 342 (misprint for 345). For the controversy between the American generals, see Smith, *War with Mexico*, 2:185-88, and Edward S. Wallace, *General William Jenkins Worth: Monterey's Forgotten Hero* (Dallas: Southern Methodist University Press, 1953), pp. 172-84. As a result of this and other misunderstandings, President Polk recalled Scott from command of the American army in Mexico on February 14, 1848.

3. Kenly, *Memoirs of a Maryland Volunteer*, p. 468. See also Smith, *War with Mexico*, 2:127-39, 233-52. Abraham López's *Undecimo Calendario... para el Año de 1849* (Mexico City and Toluca: the author, 1848) contains a lithographed frontispiece titled *Enarbolan el Pabellon Mexicano* depicting the ceremonial hoisting of the Mexican flag over the National Palace with troops lined up in the Main Plaza. This plate was missing from at least one copy of the *Calendario* that I examined, but was in the copy in the Special Collections Division of the Library of the University of Texas at Arlington.

164.

M. H. Traubel after Jason D. L. Polhemus
THE FIRST DIVISION VOLUNTEERS ENCAMPED AT ELENCERRO, MEXICO, UNDER COMMAND OF MAJ. GEN. ROBERT PATTERSON.
Toned lithograph (hand colored), c. 1848
13-5/8 x 25-5/16 in. (34.6 x 64.3 cm.)
l.r. on stone: "Traubel F"
l.l.: "F. Kuhl's Lith. press. 49 1/2 Walnut St. Philada."
l.r.: "Drawn by Polhemus N. Y. V."
l.l. to l.r. below title: "Fig. 1, N.Y.V. Fig. 2, 1st. Penns. Fig. 3, Massts. Fig. 4, 2nd Ohio. Fig 5, S.C. Fig. 6, 2nd. Penns. Fig 7, 4th. Ohio Fig 8, Geoa. Fig. 9, Illinois, Tenne. Keny. & Inda. Fig 10, Santa Anna's Hacienda & Quarters of General Patterson & Staff / 1st. Brigade under command of Col. F. M. Wynkoop 2d. Brigade under command of Col Chas. Brough. / This Picture is Most Respectfully dedicated to Maj. Gen. Patterson by his humble servant J. D. L. Polhemus of the New York Volunteers."
ACM 49.74

This lithograph after Jason D. L. Polhemus of the New York Volunteers depicts Santa Anna's hacienda "El Encerro" (The Retreat), which became an important and popular campsite for American troops because of its strategic and healthful location. Only a few miles southeast of Jalapa on the National Road between Mexico City and Veracruz, it was directly on the American line of communication and supply and far enough above the coastal region to be spared the worst effects of the dreaded *vomito*.

El Encerro first came under American control soon after the battle of Cerro Gordo, which was fought only a few miles down the road. Private George Ballentine of the First Artillery recorded his impression of El Encerro as he marched through the vicinity with General Twiggs's division in April 1847:

> After marching a few miles we came to Encerro, the favourite residence of Santa Anna, who owns a large and fertile tract in that neighbourhood. The house in which he had formerly lived is a large, plain building on the side of a hill about a mile from the road, and on the left hand going to Jalapa. Its situation is admirable, the view of the surrounding country being of the most delightful character, wooded mountains and grassy plain stretching away as far as the eye can see. However, what seems lacking is a good supply of water; that principal element found with fine Mexican scenery.[1]

Almost a year later, Santa Anna, having been granted permission to leave the country by both the Mexican government and American authorities, held a dinner at his old hacienda for the American officers in the vicinity. The Americans issued and honored a safeguard for him and his family and attendants to pass through to the port of La Antigua, from which they sailed on or about April 1, 1848.[2]

During the final American evacuation in June 1848, El Encerro was astir with the various volunteer regiments under Major General Robert Patterson, who were awaiting the arrival of transport ships at Veracruz to take them back to the United States. Corporal J. Jacob Oswandel of the First Pennsylvania Volunteers recorded that General Patterson took quarters in Santa Anna's residence. On June 12 Oswandel paid a visit to the residence, which he described as "situated on a hill. In the rear of the building is a pond for fish and ducks. There being no

THE FIRST DIVISION VOLUNTEERS ENCAMPED AT ELENCERRO, MEXICO, UNDER COMMAND OF MAJ. GEN. ROBERT PATTERSON.

Fig 1. N.Y.V. Fig 2, 1st Penna Fig 3, Masstts Fig 4, 2nd Ohio. Fig 5, S.C. Fig 6, 2nd Penna Fig 7, 4th Ohio Fig 8, Geoa Fig 9, Illinois, Tenne Keny & Inda Fig 10, Santa Anna's Hacienda & Quarters of General Patterson & Staff

1st Brigade under command of Col. F. M. Wynkoop 2d Brigade under command of Col. Chas. Brough.

This Picture is Most Respectfully dedicated to Maj. Gen. Patterson by his humble servant J.D.L. Polhemus of the New York Volunteers.

164. VOLUNTEERS ENCAMPED AT ELENCERRO

garden nor fruit trees the whole place looks as if deserted, and it will take sometime to bring it to proper shape again." Most interesting for the documentation of Polhemus's lithograph are the next entries in Oswandel's diary:

Tuesday, June 13, 1848. — This morning Gen. Patterson ordered all the tents to be placed in regular order, as he intends to draught the whole camp, which will make a splendid picture. In the afternoon another brigade came into camp, which make it a very large encampment.... Wednesday, June 14, 1848. — This morning the whole division encamped here, were ordered on parade to have the whole camp sketched. It was drawn by one of the New York Regiment, and Gen. Patterson intends to have it lithographed at New Orleans, which will make a handsome picture.[3]

From this it would appear that General Patterson probably commissioned Private Polhemus to make a sketch or sketches of a scene that Patterson carefully staged for the artist to record. Although the original intention may have been to have the picture lithographed in New Orleans, the short time many returning troops had there may have prevented this. Perhaps General Patterson, whose home was in Philadelphia, delivered the sketch himself to lithographers M. H. Traubel and Frederick Kuhl; Patterson and some of his soldiers arrived in Philadelphia around July 24, 1848.[4]

Details in the lithograph are carefully keyed. The buildings of Santa Anna's hacienda are in the left distance. The various regiments are lined up neatly; General Patterson and his staff may be on horseback in the center of the picture, while Polhemus may have drawn himself busily sketching in the foreground.

1. Ballentine, *Autobiography*, p. 215.
2. For a memorable description of Santa Anna's safe passage through the American lines and the dinner he held at El Encerro for the American officers, see Kenly, *Memoirs of a Maryland Volunteer*, pp. 389-98.
3. Oswandel, *Notes of the Mexican War*, pp. 581, 582. See also Hartman, *Journal*, pp. 24-25.
4. Oswandel, *Notes of the Mexican War*, pp. 602, 610, 615. Traubel (1820-97) was born in Frankfurt-am-Main and trained in Germany. Sometime before 1847 he came to Philadelphia; since the lithograph of El Encerro was printed by Frederick Kuhl's lithographic press, it is possible that Traubel's first American job was with this firm. From 1853 to c. 1870 he headed the firm of M. H. Traubel & Co. in Philadelphia. (See Groce and Wallace, *Dictionary of Artists in America*, p. 635.) Frederick Kuhl was active as a lithographer in Philadelphia from 1844 until 1850; by 1856 he was in San Francisco. (Ibid., p. 378.)

Lemercier, Rose-Joseph, 36, 127, 149

Literary World, 10, 158

Lobos Island, 257-58

López, Abraham, 300, 316, 327, 353, 356 (n. 3)

López, Urbano, 127

Louisville *Daily Gazette,* 38

M

McClellan, George B., 293

McCown, J. P., 126

McCulloch, Benjamin, 124, 129, 213

McIntosh, James S., 101, 106, 317-19

McKavett, Captain, 124

McKee, William R., 160, 161, 200

McKenzie, Samuel, 326

Maclean, Lachlan Allan, 142, 149 (n. 3)

Magee, R., 42 (n. 55), 161 (n. 16), 164 (n. 3), 295 (n. 4), 322 (n. 3)

Magny, Louis Xavier, 171, 277

Magny, Risso, 277

Manigault, Arthur M., 51

Mansfield, Edward D., 346

Marshall, Humphrey, 160, 161 (n. 13)

Mason, Thomas S., 164

Massachusetts, 264

Matamoros, Mexico, 111; American occupation of, 50-51

Matamoros *American Flag,* 50-51

Matteson, Tompkins, 42 (n. 55)

May, Charles A., 20-21, 26, 61, 106, 108 (n. 8), 160

Mayer, Brantz, 111

Mayo, Isaac, 267, 273

Mayr, Christian, 346

Mejía, Francisco, 104

Mendez, H., 293, 296, 321

Menzel, Adolphus, 108

Meunier, Luis, 163, 306

Mexican War, causes of, 17, 99, 101; histories of, 5, 33, 36-39, 102, 266-67, 346; public attitudes to, 1, 7, 16-17, 22, 63, 64, 167

Mexico City, American occupation of, 34, 36, 51-53, 293, 345-47, 353-56; daguerreotypists in, 50-53; fighting around, 8, 316-43; printmakers in, 16, 163, 293, 300, 306, 314, 316, 321, 353-54

Mexico City *American Star,* 50, 53, 293, 316, 331-32

Mexico City *North American,* 293, 314

Meyers, William H., 135

Michaud y Thomas, Julio, 127, 149, 334, 343

Michelin, Francis, 104 (n. 5)

Miñon, José Vicente, 192

Mississippi, 267-68

Molino del Rey, battle of, 8, 9, 317-22

Monclova, Mexico, 134

Monterey, California, 135-37

Monterrey, Mexico, 170; described, 115, 120, 122-23; battle of, 13-14, 15, 29-30, 115-29, 194

Monterrey *American Pioneer,* 61, 170

Moore, H. Judge, 206, 257-58, 315, 349

Morison, Samuel Eliot, 281 (n. 6), 282, 288

Morse, Samuel F. B., 9

Mosquito Fleet, 262, 264, 268-70, 277, 279-91

Murguía, Manuel, 356 (n. 2)

N

National Bridge (Puente Nacional), 293

National Intelligencer, 10, 14, 158, 159, 170, 283

National Road (Camino Nacional), 278, 293, 297, 299, 302, 356

Naval actions, in Mexican War, 14, 99, 101, 135-36, 154, 236, 257-58, 262-71, 279-91

Nebel, Carl, 13, 36-38, 55, 109-10, 129, 163-64, 275, 296, 308, 312, 317-19, 326, 335-36, 345-46; biography, 110 (n. 1); *Voyage pittoresque et archeologique...,* 7, 13, 35, 55, 110 (n. 1), 127, 206, 298, 301, 302 (cat. no. 130, n. 2), 345-46, 354

Neville, Harvey, 177

New Mexico, 140-44

New Orleans, and the Mexican War, 6, 17; daguerreotypists in, 49, 50; printmakers in, 16, 171, 277, 358

New Orleans *Crescent,* 38

New Orleans *Delta,* 6, 38, 283, 288

New Orleans *Picayune,* 6, 13, 17, 18, 36, 53, 60, 122, 129, 168, 171, 207, 258, 334, 354

New Orleans *Tropic,* 11

New York, printmakers in, 16, 102, 123, 136, 158; *see also* individual printmakers by name

New York *Herald,* 5, 16-24, 26, 27, 61, 102, 104, 111, 113, 126, 136, 138, 246, 262, 268, 298, 302 (n. 3), 322, 343

New York *Sun,* 19

Newsam, Albert, 171, 172 (n. 4)

Nile, battle of the, 248

Niles' National Register, 6, 39, 101

Noessel, George, 53

O

Oaklands (Robert Hallowell Gardiner estate), 47, 241, 246

O'Brien, John P., 160, 163-64, 309

Occupation of Mexico, by American troops, 44, 50-57, 174-217, 226, 298, 299, 300, 311, 326, 332-34, 345-58

Eyewitness to War

Edited by Matthew Abbate

Designed by James A. Ledbetter

Typeset by Typography Plus, Inc.

Printed by South China Printing Company